MONITORING FOR A SUSTAINABLE TOURISM TRANSITION
The Challenge of Developing and Using Indicators

MONITORING FOR A SUSTAINABLE TOURISM TRANSITION
The Challenge of Developing and Using Indicators

Graham Miller
*University of Surrey,
Guildford, UK*

and

Louise Twining-Ward
*New York University,
New York, USA*

CABI Publishing

CABI Publishing is a division of CAB International

CABI Publishing
CAB International
Wallingford
Oxfordshire OX10 8DE
UK

CABI Publishing
875 Massachusetts Avenue
7th Floor
Cambridge, MA 02139
USA

Tel: +44 (0) 1491 832111
Fax: +44 (0) 1491 833508
E-mail: cabi@cabi.org
Website: www.cabi-publishing.org

Tel: +1 617 395 4056
Fax: +1 617 354 6875
E-mail: cabi-nao@cabi.org

A catalogue record for this book is available from the British Library, London, UK.

Library of Congress Cataloging-in-Publication Data

Miller, Graham.
    Monitoring for a sustainable tourism transition: the challenge of developing and using indicators / Graham Miller and Louise Twining-Ward.
        p.   cm.
    Includes bibliographical references (p.   ) and index.
    ISBN 0-85199-051-7 (alk. paper)
    1. Ecotourism--Management--Evaluation.   2. Sustainable development--Evaluation.   3. Economic indicators. I. Twining-Ward, Louise. II. Title.
    G156.5.E26M55 2005
    910′.68--dc22

                                                                        2004026372

ISBN 0 85199 051 7

Typeset by AMA DataSet Ltd, UK.
Printed and bound in the UK by Biddles Ltd, King's Lynn.

Contents

Contributors

Main Authors

Dr Graham Miller is a Lecturer in Management at the University of Surrey, England, where he teaches issues relating to business ethics and the tourism industry. Graham has a PhD and Masters degree in Tourism Management from the University of Surrey, UK and an undergraduate degree from the University of Salford. Beyond indicators for sustainability, Graham's main research interest is in the forces that enable and prevent the drive for a sustainable transition. This has led to examinations of the attitudes of tourism companies to corporate responsibility and of consumers to more sustainable tourism products. Related research has examined the level of ethical instruction tourism students receive, the accessibility of tourism establishments in the UK for the disabled consumer, and the role of farm diversification in rural sustainability.

School of Management, University of Surrey, Guildford, Surrey GU2 7XH, UK. E-mail: G.Miller@surrey.ac.uk

Dr Louise Twining-Ward is a Lecturer at New York University, USA, and a part-time consultant specializing in tourism planning, management and development. She has a PhD and Masters from the University of Surrey, and completed her undergraduate studies in Geography at the University of Durham and the Autonomous University of Barcelona. Her doctoral studies specialized in techniques for monitoring sustainable tourism, using the case study of Samoa, where she lived for 8 years working closely with the Samoa Tourism Authority. Her consultancy work includes tourism feasibility studies, strategic planning, impact assessment, curricula design, training workshops and seminars. Her research interests include complex adaptive systems, resilience, monitoring sustainable tourism development and stakeholder participation.

369 Sterling Place, New York, NY11238, USA. E-mail: louisetw@verizon.net

Other Contributors in Alphabetical Order

Martine Bakker. Born and raised in the Netherlands, Martine Bakker acquired a Bachelors degree in business administration at Nijenrode University and a Masters degree in communication science at the University of Amsterdam. She has worked for 5 years as an external consultant in tourism development and planning, including an extensive project in the Netherlands Antilles, Caribbean. Continuing her studies in the USA, Martine earned a Masters degree in Tourism and Travel from New York University. She is currently living in the New York metropolitan area and works as an independent market researcher. Her areas of expertise include coastal and island tourism planning and optimizing information systems for tourism planning. Martine is co-author of Chapter 8.

23 Lincoln Avenue, Old Greenwich, CT 06870, USA. E-mail: martinebakker@nyu.edu

Giulia Carbone has been Programme Officer at the United Nations Environment Programme, Division of Technology, Industry and Economics, since 1997. Her area of work is sustainable tourism, including the coordination of the Tour Operators' Initiative, whose Secretariat is hosted by UNEP-DTIE. She obtained a Master of Science in Marine Policy from the London School of Economics (1993), a Bachelor of Arts degree in Environmental Economics from the University of California (1990) and in Geography from the University of Genoa, Italy (1995). Giulia is co-author of Chapter 11.

United Nations Environment Programme, Tour Mirabeau 39–43, quai André Citroën, 75739 Paris Cedex 15, France. E-mail: giulia.carbone@unep.fr

Toni Duka is currently the part-time project manager for the TOMM on Kangaroo Island. She has a background in environmental management, and has worked in this field for 9 years, covering a range of fields from management of public lands to the implementation of management programmes for overabundant native species. Toni also has experience in community development and works part-time as a Community Development Officer on Kangaroo Island. Her current focus for the TOMM process is managing the indicator development and monitoring programmes, progressing sustainable funding options and supporting the TOMM Management Committee as Executive Officer. The current focus of the Management Committee is to ensure the ongoing evolution of TOMM. Toni has been a long-term resident of Kangaroo Island and along with her environmental background is very passionate about the success and longevity of TOMM as a management tool for Kangaroo Island. Toni is co-author of Chapter 9.

Kangaroo Island Council, PO Box 121, Kingscote, South Australia, 5223. E-mail: toni.duka@kicouncil.sa.gov.au

Prof. Bryan Farrell, Professor Emeritus, Department of Environment Studies, University of California, Santa Cruz, has a background in geography, environmental studies and tourism. He has a PhD from the University of Auckland, an MA from the University of Washington, and a BA from the University of Canterbury. He was formerly founding Head of the Department of Geography at the University of Victoria (Can.), Director of the University of California's Center for South Pacific Studies and Chair of the Department of Environmental Studies at the University of California at Santa Cruz. His major work in tourism, *Hawai'i the Legend that Sells*, resulted from a decade's study of the development of Hawaii. From the late 1980s, he has been following revised ecosystem ecology with an eye to its application to tourism. Research interests include the integration of ecosystem and complexity theory, sustainable development, culture and tourism. Bryan is co-author of Chapter 1.

27567 Sugar Pine Drive, Lake Arrowhead, Blue Jay, PO Box 3242, Blue Jay, CA 92317, USA. E-mail: bryan-farrell@earthlink.net

Xavier Font is Principal Lecturer in Tourism Management at Leeds Metropolitan University. In the last 5 years he has undertaken research and consultancy for UNEP, WTO, EC, Ford Foundation, Travel Foundation, Foreign and Commonwealth Office and WWF International, Germany and Netherlands. He is author of the TOI reporting users and corporate social responsibility manuals, and contributor to their tourism eco-labels report. Xavier is co-author of Chapter 11.

Tourism Hospitality and Events School, Leeds Metropolitan University, Leeds LS1 3HE, UK. E-mail: xfont@leedsmet.ac.uk

Elizabeth Jack is the principal of Centre of Sustainable Tourism; a specialist tourism advisory and facilitation service based in Fremantle, Western Australia. Elizabeth has a background in community-based sustainable tourism and has worked in this field for 15 years, specializing in the areas of marketing, business development, strategic planning and management, facilitation and community engagement. In 1999, her business won a national tender to project manage the Tourism optimization Management Model on Kangaroo Island in South Australia and Liz is retained as a strategic adviser to the project. She is currently a board member of Ecotourism Australia and the Forum Advocating Cultural and Ecotourism (FACET) WA and in between caring for two children under 2, undertakes a range of consulting/advisory projects. Liz is co-author of Chapter 9.

Centre of Sustainable Tourism, 1 Nannine Ave, White Gum Valley, WA 6162, USA. E-mail: liz@sustainabletourism.com.au

Richard Tapper is Director of the Environment Business & Development Group and Visiting Fellow at Leeds Metropolitan University. He is former Head of Industry Policy at WWF UK. He is an adviser on sustainable tourism issues for the TOI, having been part of the development of the reporting indicators and procedures for sustainable supply chain management. Richard is co-author of Chapter 11.

Environment Business & Development Group, 16 Glenville Road, Kingston upon Thames KT2 6DD, UK. E-mail: rtapper@dircon.co.uk

Acknowledgements

Both authors would like to recognize the support of Bryan Farrell, Mark Hampton, Andrew Holden, Regina Scheyvens, Emma Stewart, Hugh Sommerville and Pam Wight who reviewed the material for this book. We are also indebted to Martine Bakker, Giulia Carbone, Toni Duka, Xavier Font, Liz Jack and Richard Tapper for the valuable contribution their input has made to the book.

Particular thanks go to Professor Farrell, for his untiring interest, encouragement and stimulation.

The publication would not have been possible without the support of CABI Publishing and the authors are especially grateful to Rebecca Stubbs for her assistance throughout the process.

GM – To Petal and bump, for giving me something else to think about.
LTW – To Max and Cate for their patience and Tom for his support.

List of Boxes

List of Figures

List of Abbreviations

ABI	Association of British Insurers
BITC	Business in the Community
BP	British Petroleum
Calpers	California Pension Fund
CEO	Chief executive officer
CFC	Chlorofluorocarbons
CSR	Corporate social responsibility
DCMS	Department for Culture, Media and Sport
DEFRA	Department for Environment, Food and Rural Affairs
DETR	Department for Environment, Transport and the Regions
DEH	Department for Environment and Heritage
DFID	Department for International Development
DJSI	Dow Jones Sustainability Index
EC	European Commission
EIA	Environmental impact assessment
EU	European Union
FEE	Foundation for Environmental Education
FTO	Federation of Tour Operators
GDP	Gross domestic product
GIS	Geographical information system
GNP	Gross national product
GRI	Global reporting index
IGBP	International Geosphere-Biosphere Programme
IHEI	International Hotels Environment Initiative
ILO	International Labour Organization

IISD	International Institute for Sustainable Development
IUCN	World Conservation Union
LAC	Limits of acceptable change
LDC	Less-developed country
MDG	Millennium Development Goals
MEA	Millennium Ecosystem Assessment
NEF	New Economics Foundation
NGO	Non-governmental organization
NPF	Norwegian Petroleum Fund
NRC	National Research Council
ODI	Overseas Development Institute
OECD	Organization for Developed Economic Countries
PAC	Project Advisory Committee
PAVIM	Protected Areas Visitor Impact Management Planning Process
PPT	Pro-poor tourism
PRA	Participatory rural appraisal
PSR	Pressure, State, Response
SATC	South Australian Tourism Commission
SD	Sustainable development
SIDS	Small island developing states
SME	Small and medium-sized enterprise
SOPAC	South Pacific Applied Geo-science Commission
SPREP	South Pacific Regional Environment Programme
SRI	Socially responsible investment
SSTIP	Samoan Sustainable Tourism Indicator Project
STA	Samoa Tourism Authority
SVB	Samoa Visitors Bureau
SWA	Samoan Water Authority
TALC	Tourism Area Life Cycle
TCSP	Tourism Council of the South Pacific
TOMM	Tourism Optimization Management Model
TOI	Tour Operators' Initiative
UKCEED	United Kingdom Centre for Economic and Environmental Development
UN	United Nations
UNCED	United Nations Conference on Environment and Development
UNCSD	United Nations Commission for Sustainable Development
UNDP	United Nations Development Programme
UNEP	United Nations Environment Programme
UNESCO	United Nations Education and Social Cultural Organization
USAID	United States Agency for International Development

VFR	Visiting friends and relatives
VIMM	Visitor Impact Management Model
WBCSD	World Business Council for Sustainable Development
WCED	World Commission for Economic Development
WGBU	German Advisory Council on Global Change
WHO	World Health Authority
WRI	World Resources Institute
WTO	World Tourism Organization
WTTC	World Travel and Tourism Council
WWF	World Wide Fund for Nature

Foreword

In all subject areas there are times of change, some more important than others, and some moving more quickly than others. I remember clearly when the idea of sustainability was introduced on the University of Hawaii tourism bulletin board Trinet, and the initial reaction was an unequivocal scepticism of what appeared to be a faddish flash in the pan, echoed equally clearly in publications by several of tourism's leaders who saw it not too differently as old hat, something we had all been aware of for years, now presented under a new name. Now debate has not departed but subsided, and sustainability has a place in much tourism training, in leading journals and in one especially that is devoted entirely to its study. Not bad going for little more than a decade and development has by no means finished.

Change is again upon us and exciting developments, are, if not here securely, then just around the corner ready to meet the challenges. Here I have to say in all honesty that I am not writing this as an independent assessor, but at this point as an enthusiastic advocate of what is taking place elsewhere, especially where it appears clearly applicable to tourism. New approaches to sustainability are complicated and difficult to summarize. Fundamentally, they are predicated on a new world view in which the earth and its components – natural and human – all operate as a system of systems with their own modes of behaviour. One characteristic explained in the book is that rather than a world in balance we are dealing with an unpredictable and unstable world, which is always in one of several dynamic states, and true stability, if and when it occurs, never remains that way for long. In this unstable world, causes for decisions made in tourism are largely multiple and the outcomes are usually numerous, in no way proportional to the intensity of the original input, and seldom end up in the place or places originally intended. Furthermore, the total of all the effects caused to the target area and elsewhere in the system might take from days to months or even years to actually arrive. The systems there and those we make or modify are always evolving, changing and through connections affecting other components, often well away from the operating centre of tourism.

The effect, if the new concepts are applied, is that we find that tourism is not quite tourism as we know it but is now embedded in a much larger ecosystem than the industrial core usually referred to as the 'tourism system'. If we believe that detailed knowledge of the behaviour of the overall system may add considerably to our management of tourism, then in the interests of both industry and sustainability many things must be reconsidered in the light of the new contexts we find ourselves working in.

I might say that to my knowledge such a wealth of otherwise unavailable materials has never been brought together in one place before. The material reflects the existing state of the art in tourism monitoring and brings together advanced ideas regarding sustainable development not yet apparent in tourism. There are then at least two parallel threads that may be perceived in the following chapters: first, the very best in contemporary tourism study and secondly, possible ways these may be modified in the context of world changes in science. This all makes for exciting reading, but of course, the new views are unlikely to be accepted without critical evaluation. One view is not right and the other wrong. It is up to the reader to evaluate the views and to accept or reject on the basis of the arguments presented.

Sustainability or a sustainability transition both need specificity and ways to make the concepts operational. Skilful selection of indicators that point to key aspects of sustainability and just as skilful monitoring are key. Once monitored, adept assessment of what decisions to take in the interests of the destination based on past experience are essential. Ways of doing this more successfully than in the past are clearly presented along with well-chosen case studies that add to the wealth of informed opinion that can be found within the various chapters.

The authors, both young academics and doctoral graduates from the University of Surrey and both operating at the leading edge of their interests, need to be congratulated for bringing together such a fine selection of expertise and expository writing that should be of particular value to seasoned academics, students and to those in a managerial capacity. For me, it has been an honour to be asked to write a foreword to this publication.

Bryan Farrell
Lake Arrowhead
28 October 2004

Introduction

This book challenges readers to consider new ways of thinking about sustainable tourism. The book considers the process of moving towards sustainability, the changes necessary, the effects and the complexity of these changes. These new ways of thinking encourage the reader to view tourism as a complex system, intricately connected with ecological and social systems. By recognizing this complexity, the importance for sustainable tourism of monitoring, adapting and learning from our actions can be understood.

Tourism literature invariably explains the concept of sustainable development in the words of the 1987 Brundtland Report, suggesting that it is a goal that may be achieved and maintained in perpetuity by following a number of rules on resource use and doing the 'right thing'. This book shows this to be far from reality. Our knowledge today of social and ecological systems has greatly improved, but it has not kept pace with our ability to alter these systems. Hence, we need to recognize our knowledge limitations, continue in a more humble manner and seek greater understanding of the complex systems with which tourism interacts. Recognizing this complexity, sustainable development is shown throughout this book to be a dynamic process of change, rather than a static target. Given this, tourism managers must learn to take advantage of change through continual monitoring and social learning in order to make a shift towards more sustainable states. Sustainability can therefore be seen as a process of transformation, a transition that varies over time and space, and this book suggests novel ways of approaching this challenge. Yet, change is not always easy to inspire, the old is comfortable, reassuring and routine. Translating this new knowledge of complex systems into new ways of planning and managing tourism may take many years to show results. Sustainable development in its unrevised form has taken at least three decades to find its way into major institutions and there is still a long way to go.

Throughout, the authors consider the concept of monitoring sustainable tourism from a sustainable development perspective. This book does not adopt the conventional reductionist approach (seeking to simplify complex systems) that dominates much tourism literature to date. Instead, the new ways of looking at tourism and sustainable development discussed are based on advanced research in studies outside tourism, including ecology, the study of complex systems, global change and the pioneering field of sustainability science. As a consequence of this approach to sustainable tourism, the material presented in the early chapters of this book may be unfamiliar and challenging to the reader. Based on this theory, the rest of the book stresses the practical, business and technical issues involved with developing programmes to monitor sustainable tourism.

In Chapters 1 and 2, we trace the evolution of sustainable development and suggest ways in which our approach to tourism may be augmented by improved knowledge of complex systems, in particular the use of comprehensive, interdisciplinary approaches, stakeholder participation and adaptive strategies. Change is shown to be inevitable and unpredictable, surprises abound and only those who are prepared are likely to benefit from the opportunities that arise. Monitoring in the context of complex systems is shown to become central and requires strong emphasis on the development of objectives, quality control, communication with stakeholders, learning how to respond to issues at different scales, designing indicators with management goals in mind and systems that can provide feedback on management efforts.

The case for monitoring sustainable tourism is further established in Chapters 3 and 4, which set out the arguments for public and private sector stakeholders to get involved in monitoring. This is an important discussion as without a clear rationale it is less likely that monitoring programmes will be developed. While the principal reason for commercial organizations to monitor may be to prove to customers, government, suppliers and financial institutions that they are pursuing a more sustainable agenda, the intrinsic case for businesses to adopt a more responsible path is also discussed. It is easy to dismiss such an approach as idealistic, but to deny the role of principle in any argument is to surrender an important weapon in the fight for greater sustainability. Regardless of the intrinsic or instrumental approach, Chapter 3 stresses the importance of quality, credible monitoring systems that promote trust and meet the increasing need for information. Chapter 4 continues this argument, but investigates the contribution monitoring can make to governments, non-governmental organizations (NGOs) and communities in their journey towards greater sustainability. Much of the material for these chapters comes from outside the tourism industry, but is directly applicable to challenges the industry faces now and will face in the future. In order to behave in a manner befitting its size, tourism needs to learn to stand on the shoulders of its industrial peers who have a longer history.

Part III of the book focuses on monitoring concepts and techniques and comprises Chapters 5, 6 and 7. Chapter 5 provides the foundation for the section, exploring the fundamental questions to be addressed in the development of a monitoring programme and suggesting alternative approaches. Issues such as what to measure, the type of indicators, how to organize these indicators, where to measure, how much it costs and how to present the data are discussed in depth, along with background to monitoring in general. Chapter 6 then addresses the technical challenge of developing a set of sustainable tourism indicators that are comprehensive in scope, involve a high degree of stakeholder participation and are adaptive to change. Alternative approaches are discussed and different options are presented in order to provide readers with ideas for use in different environments and circumstances. The implementation and use of indicators is the subject of Chapter 7, which addresses the frequently ignored issue of how to interpret and communicate indicator results effectively. A particular focus is put on the vital issue of how to convert indicator results into tangible action to promote greater sustainability.

All the theory, concepts and techniques in the world are only of any value if they can be operationalized. To this extent, Chapters 8–11 are the acid test of the value of indicators and monitoring for a transition towards sustainability as these chapters provide examples of monitoring in practice. Despite the newness of this field, monitoring projects have been selected to give readers an understanding of the challenges, constraints and successes of monitoring at international, national, regional and sectoral scale, and for different purposes. Chapter 8 reviews the work of the World Tourism Organization, which has made a long and ongoing commitment to sustainable tourism monitoring. It highlights the evolution of approaches used over the last decade, examines their strengths and weaknesses and provides a review of lessons that can be learned from the largest tourism monitoring programme in existence. Chapter 9 provides an example of regional level monitoring from the now well-known Tourism Optimization Management Model (TOMM) established on Kangaroo Island, South Australia. Written by the original and current TOMM Project Managers, this chapter provides a clear account of the project's development and an exceptionally candid evaluation and critique of the work. In Chapter 10, a national perspective to monitoring is provided using the case of Samoa, which has been the focus of extensive research by this book's second-named author. The chapter updates previous writing on this case with detailed discussion of the development of the indicators, as well as a critical reflection on the strengths, weakness and lessons learned from the project. The final case study examines monitoring not by geographic level, but as applied to the commercial tour-operating sector. The Tourism Operators' Initiative (TOI) is a European voluntary programme that recognizes if the commercial sector is to raise itself from its sustainability slumber and instead play its role in a sustainable transition, then it must begin to monitor the effects of its actions and inactions. Established in 2000 it is still early days for the TOI, but the principles, indicators and processes are presented and discussed here in order to demonstrate the way the industry is choosing to develop, along with perspectives on its future development.

Lessons learned from the theoretical background, technical discussions and case studies are then reviewed in the concluding chapter, which recommends reconceptualizing sustainable tourism to encompass new knowledge of complex systems in an interdisciplinary, stakeholder-driven and adaptive approach. It is recommended that this involve a continual process of monitoring, adaptation, learning and fine-tuning tourism systems to work more closely with the complex system in which they operate and of which they are an inextricable part.

What becomes very clear by the end of the book is that without information and the ability to monitor progress, it will be difficult to make constructive progress towards a sustainability transition. The development and use of indicators may not be infallible; indeed there are many dangers involved, such as the replacement of ideology with managerialism, the over-reliance on targets and the difficulties of establishing cause-and-effect relationships with any certainty. There are also barriers to the development of indicators such as technical expertise, know-how, resources and short-term political, business and personal horizons. Despite these constraints, indicators have proven themselves to provide a useful and pragmatic addition to what has to date been a rather grey and fuzzy processes characterized by a lack of tools, empirical understanding and theoretical unity. Indicators can help a community, business, country or NGO establish their sustainability objectives, define what they mean by sustainability, establish what progress they are making and prioritize areas for further work. Simply the process of finding out what it is that can be measured is instructive, as are the collective gathering of information, interpretation of results and the satisfaction of seeing these converted into positive action.

Although at times this book may seem to digress from the subject of tourism, the authors posit that this is what is required if the study of tourism is to advance. Serious students will benefit from the new perspectives on sustainability that are explained and the extensive list of bibliographic resources to explore. There is practical value from the insight into why monitoring matters as well as technical assistance provided by how to develop indicators and establish monitoring systems. The case studies help to avoid the trap of developing theories and concepts in isolation from practice, or concepts that are irrelevant to tourism. The authors hope that many of the ideas introduced are unfamiliar and challenging to the reader. Much work has been committed to bringing this material to the study of tourism and it is hoped that the reader benefits from this work and is enthused to take up the challenge of monitoring for a sustainable tourism transition.

1   Introduction to Sustainability

Sustainable Development

1

Introduction

Despite more than two decades of research, there is still little consensus on the nature, objectives and applicability of sustainable tourism, and few discussions on the theoretical underpinnings of the concept. One reason for this is the reluctance of tourism researchers to do more than scratch the surface of the sustainable development literature and uncover the wealth of information and knowledge that has been generated in this area by scholars of both environment and development. It is argued here that the recent history of sustainable tourism is so brief, and its antecedents so essentially part of the chronology of sustainable development, that an understanding of the origins, philosophies, issues and contemporary explanations of sustainable development can provide vital clues to the appropriate implementation of sustainable tourism.

This chapter is primarily about sustainable development. Tourism readers may be taken outside their usual sphere of discussion in order to understand the origins and evolution of the concept of sustainability, explore some of the reasons why progress to date has been so disappointingly slow and uneven, and look at how knowledge of complex systems helps to advance contemporary understanding of sustainable development.

The chapter is divided into three parts. The first part reviews the emergence of the sustainable development debate from an historical perspective, looking at the parts played by the environmental and conservation movements. This demonstrates the changes in viewpoints over time to a point where today there is an increasing appreciation that to more fully understand sustainability and what is to be sustained, the world we live in

©G.A. Miller and L. Twining-Ward 2005. *Monitoring for a Sustainable Tourism Transition* (G.A. Miller and L. Twining-Ward)

must be conceived as a whole, as landscapes and ecosystems in which humans and nature co-evolve and are inextricably linked.

The second part of the chapter looks at how new knowledge in the fields of ecology, complex systems and global change can contribute to contemporary understandings of sustainable development and its implementation. Key issues and lessons learned include the need for a more comprehensive, systemic approach, with greater emphasis on enhancing system resilience and building the capacity to adapt to unexpected change.

The third part of the chapter presents the emerging science of sustainability, a field that acknowledges key issues identified above, is in line with new understanding of complex systems, regards sustainability as a journey rather than a destination, and insists on the integration of human and natural systems and the need for interdisciplinary rather than sector-specific approaches. In this context, the use of adaptive management, a tool that assists with organizational learning, stakeholder participation and monitoring, is highlighted for application to sustainable tourism later in this book.

Although many of the terms and phenomena described may be new to readers, a sound foundation in contemporary understandings of sustainable development requires a rudimentary knowledge of complex adaptive systems, which represent all integrated natural and social systems. Once explored, the need for a more comprehensive approach, greater monitoring and stakeholder involvement – the three central tenets of this book – becomes clear.

Historical Context

Amongst tourism scholars, apart from a useful historical account provided by Hardy *et al.* (2002), there is a widespread perception that sustainable development is largely a western invention, a product of the US conservation movement (Harrison, 1996; Hall, 1998; Hall and Lew, 1998a; Weaver and Lawton, 1999). The origins of sustainable development are in fact far from transparent or ecologically one-sided. Considerable overlap exists between the ideas and actions of pioneer thinkers in the conservation and environmental movements, developing world delegates and advocates reporting to international conferences and governmental and non-governmental organizations (NGOs). This section shows how together these voices led to the emergence of the ever-evolving paradigm of sustainable development.

Conservation and environmentalism

Almost since the earliest writings of mankind, concern has been raised over aspects of conservation and resource usage. Efforts to protect wetlands as sources of fish were reportedly taking place in China in 6 AD (Conca *et al.*, 1995). Plato, writing over 2400 years ago, commented on the over-farming in Attica (Middleton and Hawkins, 1998). The origins of the modern conservation movement appear to be more recent, stemming in part from 19th-century Europe, when traditional ideas that humans have dominion over nature were replaced by the 'preservation ethic' (Hall, 1998; Western, 2000). Subsequently, with the assistance of international organizations such as the World Conservation Union (IUCN) and the United Nations Education and Social and Cultural Organization (UNESCO) humans started to be understood as part of nature rather than separate, superior and antagonistic to it, and active steps were taken to embrace social and conservation challenges under one umbrella (Adams, 1990; Hardy *et al.*, 2002).

Similar changes were occurring in the emphasis of the nascent environmental movement in both North America and Europe during the 1960s. Through influential publications such as Carson's (1962) *Silent Spring,* Hardin's (1968) *The Tragedy of the Commons,* Meadows *et al.*'s (1972, 1992) *Limits to Growth* and Schumacher's (1973) *Small is Beautiful,* the environmental movement began to make the world aware of the disastrous environmental effects of uncontrolled human activities. The movement has been successful in instigating some enlightened legislation, but a number of their assertive spokespersons often exaggerated actual situations and well-known scientists were known to wear two hats, as scientists in the academic world and as advocates in public.

An important and more scientific approach to the debate has come from the field of ecology. The 10th Pacific Science Congress, held in Honolulu in 1961, pioneered efforts towards the integration of the human and natural world which later became mainstream through important contributions such as *Ecological Principles for Economic Development* (Dasmann *et al.*, 1973) and the *World Conservation Strategy* (IUCN, 1980). These works had important ramifications not only for ecology but also for the emerging sustainable development debate, paving the way for the integration of social and environmental concerns, crucial to contemporary understandings of sustainable development.

Development debate

During the post-Second World War period and up to the 1970s, development policies had an almost exclusively economic rather than ecological or social focus, often with disastrous consequences. As Hardy *et al.* (2002) comment, these policies were based on the idea that humans could overcome poverty and improve nature through technology, intelligence and 'neo-welfare economics'. Export-oriented growth models were pursued focusing on primary commodities, on the basis that the benefits would eventually 'trickle down' to the poorest in society (Rostow, 1960; Brohman, 1996). However, the capitalist agricultural systems, large-scale industrialization and mass tourism developments these policies imposed, were often ill-suited for the environment or culture of the countries concerned (de Kadt, 1979). Dependency theorists contend that transnational companies introduced exploitive trade relationships that left developing countries with debt and dependency, a growing gap between rich and poor, and a seriously degraded environment rather than improved quality of life (Brandt, 1980; Britton, 1982; Wall, 1997). Although such sweeping statements over-simplify the impacts of post-war development policy, the critique helped to redirect attention towards the links between maldevelopment and environmental degradation.

These linkages were further forged by UNESCO's Man and the Biosphere Programme and the 1972 UN Conference on the Human Environment in Stockholm. Representatives from developing countries made it clear that conservation would not be part of their agenda until active steps were taken to alleviate poverty and bring about greater equity in trade relations, effectively connecting issues of environmental degradation with poverty alleviation (Dasmann, 1984). The United Nations Environment Programme (UNEP) describes how resolutions were officially forged a year later in the signing of what became known as the Cocoyoc Declaration (UNEP, 1984; Farrell, 1990).

During the 1980s, three independent commissions on international development were conducted; *Common Security* (Palme Commission, 1982), *North–South: A Programme for Survival* and *Common Crisis North–South* (Brandt, 1980, 1983), inspiring a new approach to development that focused on the 'basic needs' of those living in poverty (UNEP, 1984; Haq, 1995). This philosophical shift moved development thinking away from the dogma of economic growth as espoused by Rostow and others, to an understanding of human development in terms of quality of life and enlarging people's choices. This is illustrated in wide membership of the above-mentioned commissions and the following contemporary definitions of development: 'The real aim of development is to improve the quality of human life. It is a process that enables human beings to realize their potential, build self-confidence and lead lives of dignity and fulfilment' (IUCN *et al.*, 1991, p. 130).

> The product of development is people who are healthy, well-nourished, clothed, and housed; engaged in productive work for which they are well-trained; and able to enjoy the leisure and recreation we all need.
>
> (Munro, 1995, p. 28)

The emergence of the ideas and then the term sustainable development gained currency from work of the IUCN and related agencies in the 1970s and 1980s, as well as attempts to institute eco-development and alternative technology in the developing world in the earlier decade (Sachs, 1974; Dasmann, 1984). The popularization of sustainable development, however, is attributable to the Brundtland Commission report entitled *Our Common Future* (World Commission for Economic Development (WCED), 1987). In what has become known as the Brundtland Report, public and international governmental affirmation of the need for the integration of economic and environmental issues was brought dramatically to the fore-front of the development debate unfortunately with minimal guidance for making its ideas operational. The report makes serious assertions, which warranted utmost emphasis: 'Failure to manage the environment and to sustain development threatens to overwhelm all countries. Environment and development are not separate challenges, they are linked. Development cannot subsist upon a deteriorating environmental resource base; the environment cannot be protected when growth does not account for the costs of environmental destruction' (WCED, 1987, p. 37).

It defines sustainable development as 'development that meets the needs of the present without compromising the ability of future generations to meet their own needs' (WCED, 1987, p. 43). Core values were identified as a desire to combat poverty and achieve long-term equity and ecological well-being through a global reorientation of economic growth and trade relations, and stabilization of population growth. Inevitably, the reality has fallen short of these expectations and much may be criticized in the light of today's knowledge. Despite the now apparent flaws in the approach, however, it must also be acknowledged that for an international report few can match its immediate impact then, and its enduring effects on academic research now.

From Rio to Johannesburg

Five years after the Brundtland Report, the United Nations Conference on Environment and Development (UNCED), popularly known as the 'Rio Earth Summit' marked a significant change in direction for the sustainable development debate with a much improved partnership between developed and developing nations, and wider participation of NGOs. The Rio Earth Summit succeeded in putting together five documents, one of which, Agenda 21, has proved particularly influential, outlining a basis for implementing sustainable development at the local, national and international level (UN, 1993).

Notwithstanding the apparent consensus at Rio, the United Nations Commission for Sustainable Development (UNCSD) reported to the follow-up meeting (*Earth Summit + 5*): 'we have to face up to the fact that, on the ground, progress is, in truth, limited, and on many matters, things are still going in the wrong direction' (UNCSD, 1997). The meeting called for improved international cooperation and stronger political will. This resulted in agreement 3 years later, on the Millennium Development Goals (MDGs), signed by all 191 United Nations (UN) Member States in 2000. The MDGs consisted of eight goals, shown in Box 1.1, and 18 targets all to be achieved by 2015.

The emphasis of the MDGs on poverty alleviation and human development rather than the environment is illustrative of the shift in focus of the sustainable development debate since Stockholm and Rio. The *Rio + 10*

Box 1.1.   UN Millennium Development Goals.

1.   Eradicate extreme poverty and hunger.
2.   Achieve universal primary education.
3.   Promote gender equality and empower women.
4.   Reduce child mortality.
5.   Improve maternal health.
6.   Combat HIV/AIDS, malaria and other diseases.
7.   Ensure environmental sustainability.
8.   Develop a global partnership for development.

Source: UN (2000).

Summit in Johannesburg continued this lead, building on Agenda 21 and the work of the *Millennium Declaration*. The main areas addressed in the *Rio + 10 Plan of Implementation* were poverty, production and consumption, protecting and managing the natural resource base, sustainable development in a globalizing world, health and the means and framework for implementation. Like the MDGs it was an outcome-based programme, with emphasis on establishing partnerships, networks and implementing change through clear goals, targets and indicators.

Despite progress made as a result of these international agreements, the gulf between 'developers', 'economists', 'politicians' and 'environmentalists' in their different interpretations of the concept of sustainable development creates an unfortunate barrier to its effective implementation. Whilst some groups are pushing for greater consideration of conservation of natural systems, others are emphasizing the more human aspects namely the role of economic growth, trade and technology, and the desirability of intergenerational and international equity (Pearce *et al.*, 1993).

In this way, it can be understood that the concept of sustainable development, emphasized by the Brundtland Report and continued by the MDGs and *Rio + 10* is a politically popular compromise. The unfortunate fallout from this collaboration is that sustainable development has become distanced from contemporary economic and ecological advances as explained in Box 1.2.

Sustainability Revised

It was during the late 1980s to the mid-1990s that the science community began to realize that sustainable development had been sidelined by social and political interests, as well environmental and NGO advocates, and diverted away from the solid scientific foundation laid down by documents such as Dasmann *et al.* (1973) and IUCN (1980) and especially Clark and Munn (1986). Although the Brundtland Report has been embraced in tourism, as a research contribution it was eclipsed just over a decade after its publication, by the National Research Council's, *Our Common Journey: A*

Box 1.2.   National Research Council Sustainable Development Update.

The reconciliation of society's developmental goals with the planet's environmental limits over the long term is the foundation of an idea known as sustainable development. This idea emerged in the early 1980s from scientific perspectives on the interdependence of society and environment, and has evolved since in tandem with significant advances in our understanding of this interdependence. During the concept's first decade, it garnered increasing political attention and acceptance around the world – most notably through the activities of the Brundtland Commission (1983–1987), and the UNCED held in Rio de Janeiro in 1992.

　　As the 20th century draws to a close, however, the difficulties of actually delivering on the hopes that people around the world have attached to the idea of sustainable development have become increasingly evident. In part, these difficulties reflect political problems, grounded in questions of financial resources, equity, and the competition of other issues for the attention of decision makers. In part, they reflect differing views about what should be developed, what should be sustained, and over what period. Additionally, however, the political impetus that carried the idea of sustainable development so far and so quickly in public forums has also increasingly distanced it from its scientific and technological base. As a result, even when the political will necessary for sustainable development has been present, the knowledge and know-how to make some headway often have not.

Source: NRC (1999, p. 2).

Transition to Sustainability (NRC, 1999), a thoroughly scholarly work on the subject little known by the tourism community. The central problem highlighted by the NRC authors was not the disagreements between economists and conservationists, but the much more serious issue that contemporary sustainable development work was founded on a less than sound world view, deterministic, cause and effect, linear science and orthodox 'equilibrium' based ecological theory. While conventional linear methods may provide valuable results within a short time span, in discussions of sustainability, they are inadequate. The reasons for this are explained below.

　　Equilibrium ecology has its roots in Clements's (1874–1945) theory of successional change, that suggests ecosystems move in highly ordered and sequential cycles towards a sustained climax, and that all ecosystems, if unaltered by human behaviour, will eventually reach a 'self-perpetuating climax state', a point of equilibrium (Clements, 1916). As a result, the term 'sustainability' became synonymous with the notion of balance and was adopted by the international organizations envisaging that a steady succession of doing 'the right thing', would lead to a sustained plateau that, with wise management, could be maintained in perpetuity.

　　Although credible at the time, new ecosystem findings have allowed these notions to be effectively bypassed. During three decades of careful scientific observations, researchers, led by ecologist C.S. Holling, found that equilibrium ecology produced a number of anomalies: estimates of fish or wildlife population or sustainable yields seldom conformed to real-life observed fluctuations, weather predictions were consistently different from actual weather experienced and ecosystems seemed to regenerate in unexpected ways after a disturbance rather than returning to the previous stable state (Gunderson *et al.*, 1995a). With contemporaneous new knowledge emerging from work in areas ranging from particle physics and ecological economics to thermodynamics and global change science, Holling and co-workers in ecosystem theory consolidated their growing understanding that orthodox approaches to the biosphere, which reduce complex natural and social systems to their constituent parts and interpret sustainability as the achievement of a steady-state equilibrium, consistently fail to explain the unpredictability of real-life situations (Gell-Mann, 1994; Gunderson *et al.*, 1995a; Holland, 1995; Westley, 1995). The group found that concepts of climax, equilibrium and optimality are not wrong but only a partial explanation of the behaviour of complex systems, where periods of stability are interspersed by sudden, chance, dynamic perturbation events, called 'surprises' (Holling, 1978, 1986; Gleick, 1987).

Like all complex adaptive systems, tourism systems are frequently subject to 'surprise'. In recent history, surprises that influence change across both spatial and temporal scales have occurred with the Asian economic meltdown of the late 1990s, the September 11th attacks on the USA and the outbreak of SARS, all having a sudden and unpredictable affect on visitor flows. Consequently, although discussion of ecosystem theory may at first seem a world away from sustainable tourism monitoring, complex systems are critically relevant to our revised understanding of sustainable tourism.

Complex adaptive systems

Based on research noted above, it can now be said with a high degree of confidence that all natural and social systems, including tourism, are complex adaptive systems (Gunderson *et al.*, 1995b; NRC, 1999; IGBP, 2001). They are complex because they are more than the sum of their parts, they are structured in layers from the bottom up and have the ability to self-organize, change in form, cooperate or compete, resulting in multiple system changes of an unpredictable nature (Malanson, 1999; Marten, 2001; Gunderson *et al.*, 2002). They are adaptive because following a system change, they do not regenerate their old system but reorganize into a system that is more in tune with the new environment, constantly learning and adapting to suit their changing surroundings (Kauffmann, 1995; Odum *et al.*, 1998; Holling, 2001). All complex systems, whether biological or social, are characterized by non-linear dynamics, i.e. there is no simple, straight-line relationship between cause and effect as conventionally assumed but a complex interaction resulting in unpredictable outcomes. Holling illustrates the behaviour of complex systems, their unpredictability, their changing behaviour over time and the inevitability of surprise with the adaptive cycle, a reclining figure of eight, first published in 1986 and since then considerably refined (Gunderson *et al.*, 1995a,b; Marten, 2001; Gunderson and Holling, 2002).

A stylized representation of the adaptive cycle shown in Fig. 1.1 can be understood in terms of four ecosystem functions: exploitation, conservation, release and reorganization. The front-loop (right-hand side) moving from exploitation to conservation, equates with the increasing maturity of a tourist area well known to tourism researchers (Butler, 1980). It involves the incremental accumulation of capital, energy, materials and investment, increasing system vulnerability and decreasing resilience. Over time, however, the system inevitably becomes over connected or 'brittle'. Holling (2001, p. 394) describes this as 'an accident waiting to happen', when a surprise event such as the Bali bombings can flip the system into a state of intense oscillation or chaos, which may trigger the collapse or reorientation of the destination (Holling, 1986, 1995; Peterson *et al.*, 1998). The collapse of the system (release) and subsequent reorganization (back loop, far side) may take place over a short period of time (switch) or decades (progressive change), can be local or global, but either way it is followed by reorganization, as all players (plant, animal and other human stakeholders) jockey to see which few or combination will gain favourable positions and control the newly created system. Holling (2001, p. 398) explains this as an unpredictable process, a time of crisis and opportunity, and a highly fertile

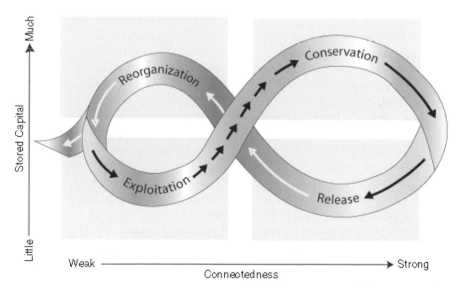

Fig. 1.1. Holling's adaptive cycle. Source: Farrell and Twining-Ward (2004, p. 281).

environment for novel entrants 'waiting in the wings' for the appropriate moment. In social and economic systems about which much less is known, the novel entrants are inventions, creative ideas and innovative people, when movers and shakers may seize the moment and create new forms of entrepreneurial activity (Russell and Faulkner, 1999, 2004; Holling, 2001). Small changes are likely to modify the ecosystem but not effect dynamics in any significant way; dramatic changes may create new systems dependent on the degree of disturbances countered by system resilience.

Although Holling emphasizes the uncertainty and unpredictability of complex systems, this does not preclude the possibility of using the cycle to better understand their behaviour. In tourism, just half the cycle has proven itself extremely helpful in the analysis of destination evolution, so by analysing the whole cycle, even more might be revealed about how to plan for change and reconsider the notion of tourism impacts in the light of non-linearity. Through close monitoring and experimentation, ways of increasing system resilience may be learned, helping to maintain the system in a productive state as long as possible and resisting the decline by adapting to changing circumstances. Furthermore, an improved appreciation of tourism time scales (rather than ecological) may emerge, roughly indicating durations tourism may take to pass through stages in a cycle.

Some system cycles in ecosystem ecology have been found that do not adhere to the behaviours suggested by the adaptive cycle model and are called maladaptive. The possibility of such cycles being found in tourism may throw new light on aspects of tourism areas that need to be addressed in efforts to move towards greater sustainability.

The adaptive cycle therefore has implications far outside its original emphasis, with the potential to change the way sustainable development and tourism is approached and managed. An important lesson at this stage is the need to adapt to change, the expected reality, rather than attempting to prevent it from occurring. Adaptability is the capacity of actors in the system to manage for resilience, technically speaking the adaptive capacity of ecosystems (Walker, 2004). Conway (1987, p. 25) explains: 'By focusing on resilience, we will better understand the extraordinary richness and diversity of behaviour of natural and human-managed systems in a changing world. In practical terms, this means placing less emphasis on trying to control systems to reduce their variability and instead placing greater faith in working with, and taking advantage of, natural capacities for resilience.' Box 1.3 explains more about resilience, which has become somewhat of a rallying call for new ecosystem ecologists.

Future management of integrated social–ecological systems, of which tourism is an example, depends on close monitoring and understanding of system behaviour, enabling managers to learn how to improve a system's resilience and take advantage of beneficially productive states, feedback loops and self-organization to improve the management of systems rather than working against forces at play (Marten, 2001).

Box 1.3. Managing for resilience of coupled human–natural systems.

Surprises in ecosystem management can come from unexpected flips that affect fish, forests, crops and people. The surprises are created in cycles of long phases of increasing growth, efficiency and predictability followed suddenly by brief phases of reorganization and surprise.

Resilience (the capacity of a system to absorb disturbance, undergo change and still retain essentially the same function, structure, identity and feedbacks) can increase or decrease as the system passes through these cycles. Variability and flexibility are needed to maintain the resilience of nature and people. Attempting to stabilize such systems in some perceived optimal state (the command-and-control approach to management), whether for conservation or production: (i) reduces resilience; and (ii) often results in the system being close to a critical threshold.

There are four crucial aspects of the resilience of a system at a particular organizational scale:

- Latitude: the maximum amount of change it can experience before losing its ability to recover (before crossing a threshold which, if breached, makes recovery difficult or impossible);
- Resistance: the ease or difficulty of changing it – how 'resistant' it is to being changed;
- Precariousness: how close it currently is to a limit or threshold;
- Panarchy: because of cross-scale interactions, the resilience of a system at a particular focal scale will depend on the influences from states and dynamics at scales above and below. For example, external oppressive politics, invasions, market shifts or global climate change can trigger local surprises and flips.

Adapted from: Walker (2004).

Global change

The ideas explained above are being expressed with increasing clarity through innovative research of the emerging field of global change science, which has considerable relevance to sustainable development. Steffen *et al.* (2004, p. 11) explain this concept: 'The term 'global change' usually refers to the broad suite of biophysical and socio-economic changes that are altering the functioning of the Earth system at the global scale. In essence, it refers to the remarkable change in the human–environment relationship that has occurred over the last few centuries.'

Concern about social–ecological change has long been the driving force behind the sustainable development debate, owing to an awareness of the shear scale of human interaction with the environment. In the 1990s, it was increasingly recognized that the earth operated as a whole system of connected parts. How these parts are connected, change and adapt has become the focus of global change theory (IGBP, 2001). The realization that environmental issues such as acid rain, emission of greenhouse gases, and disasters like Bhopal and Chernobyl, have transnational consequences, reinforced the need to better understand human–nature interactions (Kates and Clark, 1996). This has been given additional urgency with new evidence that non-linear changes in the Earth system are the norm, not the exception (Steffen *et al.*, 2004).

The German Advisory Council on Global Change (WGBU, 1996) attributes complex global and environmental degradation patterns to a discrete number of chronic syndromes, which are trans-sectoral in nature and provide a new basis for global change research. The seven syndromes that were given uppermost priority in the report include:

- Contaminated Land Syndrome;
- Dust Bowl Syndrome;
- Mass Tourism Syndrome (Box 1.4);
- Sahel Syndrome;
- Smokestack Syndrome;
- Urban Sprawl Syndrome;
- Waste Dumping Syndrome.

The high priority given to the problems caused by tourism is an indication of the relevance of global change to tourism and vice versa.

More recently, the International Geosphere-Biosphere Programme (IGBP), after 10 years of detailed studies of the Earth system, has led many authoritative researchers to conclude that the earth and human–nature relationships are entering a period of unprecedented and accelerating transformation, altering essential biogeochemical and biotic structures of the earth (NRC, 1999; IGBP, 2001). 'The changes taking place are, in fact, changes in the human–nature relationship. They are recent, they are profound, and many are accelerating. They are cascading through the Earth's environment in ways that are difficult to understand and often impossible to predict. Surprises abound' (IGBP, 2001, p. 3). The Amsterdam Declaration on Global Change combines the results of research from four international global change research programmes: IGBP, International Human Dimension Program on Global Environmental Change, World Climate Research Program, and the international biodiversity research programme, DIVERSITAS. The findings of this combined research programme are shown in Box 1.5.

The world of social systems in some ways is infinitely more complicated than natural ecosystems. It allows for a variety of adaptations, and diverse responses to the same or similar situations that are capable of wreaking the utmost damage to the biosphere as well as their own life-support systems (Holling and Sanderson, 1996). Wilson describes it this way; that while preoccupied with the great advances and changes of the 20th century '. . . humanity managed collaterally to decimate the natural environment and draw down the non-renewable resources of the planet with cheerful abandon. We thereby accelerated the erasure of entire ecosystems and the

---

Box 1.4. Mass Tourism Syndrome.

The Mass Tourism Syndrome describes the network of causes and effects generated by the steady growth of global tourism in recent decades and which leads to major environmental degradation in certain regions of the world. Typical 'hot spots' are coastal areas and mountainous regions. Winter sports and pony trekking, for example, cause destruction or impairment of plant cover and tree vegetation, leading to biodiversity loss and soil erosion when reinforced by mechanization and other types of interference with the balance of nature (levelling, modifications to terrain, snow cannons), and hence a greater danger of landslides and avalanches. Mass tourism involves, for example, the conversion of semi-natural areas through the construction of touristic infrastructure (hotels, holiday homes, transport routes) and damage to or loss of sensitive mountain and coastal ecosystems (e.g. dune landscapes, saltwater marshes). The rapid growth of long-distance air travel in recent years has caused pollution of the Earth's atmosphere. In the regions affected – especially on islands – the demand for freshwater is greatly increased (swimming pools, high levels of water consumption by tourists). Typical impacts include over-exploitation of freshwater resources, which raises the spectre of the regions' livelihood being destroyed through exhaustion of groundwater stocks, desiccation of soils and erosion. The substantial and often seasonally varying stress on tourist regions results in serious problems regarding sewage treatment and disposal, with contamination and eutrophication of surface water or coastal ecosystems the possible consequence. Waste disposal problems are also on the rise. Typical examples are the overdevelopment of previously semi-natural areas in Spain (Costa del Sol, Lanzarote), and the consequences of trekking tourism in Nepal.

Symptoms: loss of biodiversity, enhancement of the greenhouse effect by air travel, lack of freshwater supply, soil erosion, inadequate disposal of sewage and waste, fragmentation of landscapes by settlements, high consumption of resources.

Source: WGBU (1996, pp. 119–120).

---

extinction of thousands of million-year-old species. If Earth's ability to support our growth is finite – and it is – we were mostly too busy to notice' (Wilson, 2002). Fortunately, there appears to be another way. Using foresight informed by appropriate science, serious and thoughtful political discussion and reflective policy, human groups are capable of moving expeditiously towards transition to sustainability. How this might be done is explored below.

Applications for sustainable development

Underlying the progress made in ecosystem ecology and global change theory are a number of lessons for sustainable development and therefore also sustainable tourism.

Box 1.5.   Amsterdam Declaration on Global Change.

1. The Earth system behaves as a single, self-regulating [authors of this present article would use self-organizing rather than self-regulating] system comprised of physical, chemical, biological and human components.
2. Human activities are significantly influencing Earth's environment in many ways in addition to greenhouse gas emissions and climate change.
3. Global change cannot be understood in terms of a simple cause–effect paradigm. Human-driven changes cause multiple effects that cascade through the Earth system in complex ways.
4. Earth system dynamics are characterized by critical thresholds and abrupt changes. Human activities could inadvertently trigger such changes with severe consequences for Earth's environment and inhabitants.
5. In terms of some key environmental parameters, the Earth system has moved well outside the range of the natural variability exhibited over the last half million years at least. The nature of changes now occurring simultaneously in the Earth system, their magnitudes and rates of change are unprecedented.

Source: Moore *et al.* (2001).

---

*   First, sustainable development is not an ecological, economic or social problem but a combination of all three, and as a result, requires interdisciplinary and integrated modes of inquiry.
*   Secondly, complex systems such as those involved in sustainable development are inherently unpredictable and therefore require approaches based on non-linear science (Farrell and Twining-Ward, 2004).
*   Thirdly, because of the evolutionary nature of sustainable development, policies and actions need to be continually modified and adapted to evolving conditions (Holling, 1993).
*   Fourthly, in order to reduce the vulnerability of the Earth system to abrupt change, monitoring is required from local to global scales, enhancing system knowledge and extending human foresight.

Like any challenge to an established paradigm, the ideas of new ecosystem ecologists and complexity theorists have been slow to gain acceptance with mainstream sustainable development policy or sustainable tourism researchers, but there are already promising signs of change (Fraser Basin Council, 1997; Ayensu *et al.*, 1999; Russell and Faulkner 1999, 2004; World Resources Institute (WRI) *et al.*, 2000; Lowe, 2001; Folke *et al.*, 2002). In their efforts to implement Local Agenda 21, for example, Fraser Basin Council in British Columbia, Canada, have included in their principles for sustainability elements such as integration, adaptive approaches and the management of uncertainty. In 2000, a UN-led international collaboration of governments, NGOs, leading scientists and major stakeholders produced the Millennium Ecosystem Assessment (MEA). This has a focus on complex systems referred to as 'biological systems', which it monitors over a period of 4 years, hoping to disseminate worldwide, leading-edge approaches to ecosystem management, including guidelines of the handling of uncertainty (MEA, 2002, 2003).

In 2002, a group of 25 eminent scholars put the case to the World Summit in Johannesburg in a paper entitled *Resilience and Sustainable Development: Building Adaptive Capacity in a World of Transformation* (Folke *et al.*, 2002). They draw attention to what they see as the twofold fundamental error underpinning policies for natural resource management: (i) the assumption that human and natural systems are separate; and (ii) that ecosystems respond to human action in a linear fashion. They also identify the need to replace rigid management strategies with management that enhances resilience through understanding of complex systems. This work reinforces the notion that linear reductionist science, based on sequential phases of inquiry and applications of specialist knowledge on a piecemeal basis, conflicts with what is now known about the behaviour of complex systems. A fundamentally different approach to sustainability was found to be needed, to help managers at all levels cope with complex system behaviour. This is called sustainability science (NRC, 1999; Lowe, 2001).

Sustainability Science

The Folke *et al.* (2002) paper stressed the need for more scientific input to the sustainability debate, that has been ongoing since Clark and Munn's (1986) ground-breaking *Sustainable Development of the Biosphere*. Sustainability science is described as 'a new multi-disciplinary approach [authors of this chapter prefer 'interdisciplinary' to describe the wide integrated approach necessary] to science that recognizes the limitations of traditional scientific inquiry in dealing with the complex reality of social institutions interacting with natural phenomena' (Sustainability Science Forum, 2002). This is not a modified form of sustainable development or a new variant, but a step-change in the way that sustainable development, and by default its descendant sustainable tourism, is conceptualized and managed.

Sustainability science is a new field that needs to be explored by students of sustainable tourism as it provides novel approaches to understanding the character of interactions between nature, and society and the behaviour of complex systems (Kates *et al.*, 2001). Raskin *et al.* (1998, p. 4) note the challenge is to 'develop a science of sustainability that maintains a commitment to rigor, while recognizing the inherent uncertainty in complex systems and the need for advice on how to make sustainable choices'. The NRC (1999) clarifies that sustainability science involves the merging of four distinctive fields of study: biological, social, geophysical and technological systems research. This is shown graphically in Fig. 1.2.

This new approach sees sustainable development as requiring a journey or transition towards meeting human needs, preserving life-support

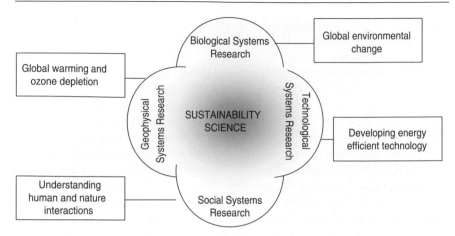

Fig. 1.2. Research components of sustainability science. The boxes show examples of areas of research that have contributed to a more scientific understanding of sustainable development. Source: adapted from NRC (1999, p. 281).

systems and reducing poverty (NRC, 1999). NRC (1999, p. 176) explains: 'any successful quest for sustainability will necessarily be a collective, uncertain and adaptive endeavour in which a society's discovering of where it wants to go and how it might try to get there will be inextricable intertwined'. The notion behind the term 'transition', used widely in sustainability science, is not whimsical or to provide an answer to sceptics who demand to be shown examples of sustainability. Transition is specific and scientifically based on system behaviour. Complex systems operate at both temporal and spatial scales. Any action, managerial or policy, is likely to have a number of outcomes, coming to fruition at different and unexpected times sometimes months even years after the initial input. Consequently, actions to create a simultaneous sustainability are likely always to fall short, understandings change and co-evolve with the place in which actions are taking place and the process is best described as an ongoing transition (Farrell and Twining-Ward, 2005).

The key research priorities of sustainability science are summarized by Kates *et al.* (2001) in Box 1.6. In this current work, the need to foster integrative science, place-based approaches and the use of monitoring to help enhance understanding of the transition towards sustainability in tourism is stressed.

The new tools and concepts that have been devised for the study of ecology, sustainability science and global change science are well matched with the way in which complex systems function and may also be of use for tourism purposes. These include adaptive management and co-management, ecosystem cycle theory, scenario planning, simulation models, adaptive/ integrated environmental assessment, integrated landscape planning, regional information systems and, recently, resilience analysis and management

Box 1.6. Core questions of sustainability science.

1. Integrative science
How can the dynamic interactions between nature and society be better incorporated into emerging models and conceptualizations that integrate the Earth system, human development and sustainability?

2. Place-based science
What determines the vulnerability or resilience of the nature–society system in particular kinds of places and for particular types of ecosystems and human livelihoods?

3. Critical loads and carrying capacities
Can scientifically meaningful 'limits' or 'boundaries' be defined that would provide effective warning of conditions beyond which the nature–society systems incur a significantly increased risk of serious degradation?

4. Focused research programmes
What systems of incentive structures – including markets, rules, norms and scientific information – can most effectively improve social capacity to guide interactions between nature and society towards more sustainable trajectories?

5. Understanding and monitoring the transitions
How can today's operational systems for monitoring and reporting on environmental and social conditions be integrated or extended to provide more useful guidance for efforts to navigate a transition towards sustainability?

6. Consumption patterns determinants and alternatives
How are long-term trends in environment and development, including consumption and population, reshaping nature–society interactions in ways relevant to sustainability?

7. Integrating global national and local institution into effective research systems
How can today's relatively independent activities of research planning, monitoring, assessment and decision support be better integrated into systems for adaptive management and societal learning?

Source: Adapted from NRC (1999) and Kates *et al.* (2001).

(Walker *et al.*, 1999; Folke *et al.*, 2002). Common to these are the principles of adaptive management, monitoring and stakeholder participation. These are discussed in the remainder of this chapter.

Adaptive management

Adaptive management is described by Clark (2002) as an idea whose time ought to have come. It is the process of building resilience and coping with the uncertainty inherent in complex systems through a continual process of experimenting, monitoring and social learning (Holling, 1978; Walters,

1986). Rather than trying to obtain and then maintain an idealized equilibrium state, adaptive management is designed progressively to accumulate knowledge and test uncertainties through social learning, preparing managers and stakeholders to experiment, probe, adapt to and benefit from small- and large-scale system change (Berkes and Folke, 1998). Further explanation is provided in Box 1.7.

Adaptive management was developed by Holling, Walters and colleagues in the late 1960s as a strategic alternative to rigid 'command-and-control' type management systems that they saw as flawed in the face of non-linear behaviour of complex systems (Walters and Hillborn, 1978; Walters, 1986). It was designed to improve management through regular assessment and monitoring of system behaviour and learning from the results of operational experience (Clark, 2002). Nyberg (1999) summarized the aims of adaptive management as follows:

- To continually find better ways of meeting goals;
- Identify key gaps in understanding;
- Improve understanding of ecosystem responses, thresholds and dynamics, in order to adapt practices to fit changing social values and ecological conditions;

Box 1.7.   Adaptive management.

Adaptive management has been defined in various ways since its development in the early 1970s. Different people and organizations continue to have somewhat differing views of the best definition for their purposes. The BC Forest Service adopts the following definition:

> Adaptive management is a systematic process for continually improving management policies and practices by learning from the outcomes of operational programs. Its most effective form – 'active' adaptive management – employs management programs that are designed to experimentally compare selected policies or practices, by evaluating alternative hypotheses about the system being managed.

Adaptive management is a social as well as scientific process concerned with the need to learn through monitoring and close observation. Consequently, it requires an open management process that seeks to include past, present and future stakeholders. It must focus on the development of new institutions and institutional strategies just as much as it must focus upon scientific hypotheses and experimental frameworks.

Actual policy implementation is a process grounded in the local. It depends upon local constraints, the present state of local institutions and the personalities of key people. Any policy exercise must seek to transfer knowledge and understanding to local individuals, but that is not all it must do. It must also develop institutional flexibility by encouraging the formation of networks of individuals that bridge institutional boundaries.

Adapted from: BC Ministry of Forests (2004a,b), Resilience Alliance (2004).

- Gain reliable feedback about effectiveness of alternative policies/practices;
- Encourage innovation and learning (social learning);
- Pass on information and knowledge gained through experience;
- Foster an organizational culture that emphasizes learning and responsiveness; and
- In some cases, adaptive management may also help detect cumulative, long-term, large-scale and emergent effect of actions.

Over the last two decades, adaptive management has generated an increasing amount of literature (Conservation Ecology, 2004). Amongst the most influential texts on adaptive management are Walters (1986), who looks at quantitative and modelling aspects, Lee (1993) discussing the social and institutional context for adaptive management and Gunderson *et al.* (1995a) who look at how social and ecosystems respond to management actions.

Adaptive management principles have been applied to a wide range of ecosystems in North America (Lee, 1993; Nyberg, 1999), are being used to manage social systems and have begun to be recognized by tourism researchers (Manning, 1998; Rollins *et al.*, 1998; Reed, 1999; Twining-Ward, 2003). Rollins *et al.* (1998) report on the use of adaptive management to assess the effectiveness of three alternative strategies for dealing with recreation conflicts in British Columbia. They explain that using adaptive management helped researchers design programmes to generate feedback and then adjust policies accordingly. Similar principles and methods were adapted for use in Samoa by Twining-Ward (2002, 2003) to develop and manage a set of sustainable tourism indicators (see Chapter 10).

Not all applications have fulfilled their promise, however, as adaptive management is not always simple to implement. Clark (2002) puts this down to the fact that most institutions are not very good at learning, especially when it involves costly revisions of operating procedures. Rollins *et al.* (1998) explain that managers are often uncomfortable with change and understandably dislike making, and admitting making, mistakes. Adaptive management offers no set procedures or prescriptive frameworks, wherein lies its flexibility for application and further evolution at a range of scales and contexts and the difficulties in its application. As explained in Box 1.6 above, stakeholder participation and monitoring are integral components of the adaptive management process and explained further below.

Stakeholder participation

Understanding that humans are part of ecosystems has led to greater efforts to incorporate stakeholders as integral rather than extra components in resource management. Like resilience, participation emerges as a common thread linking the political rhetoric of international organizations with revised ecosystem ecology, sustainability science and sustainable tourism (Wilcox, 1994; Pretty, 1995, 1998).

Article 21 of the UN Universal Declaration on Human Rights states that the will of the people shall be the basis for the authority of any government, and that any person should have the right to participate in the government of his country either directly or through an elected representative (UN, 1948). This declaration updates the work of British philosophers John Locke and Thomas Hobbes on the need for government to protect the rights of humans, and to operate for the benefit of, and in accordance with, the wishes of humans. Individually we accept the constraints imposed by government in return for control of government, who exert control over the collective, or the community. Without participation in government (at any level), we only suffer the imposition of control with none of the benefits of influencing the manner or extent of the control.

Participation was also firmly advocated in an influential report from the WCED (1987), as well as the Rio Earth Summit (UN, 1993). Chapter 23 of Agenda 21 notes the need for new forms of participation and greater role for stakeholders in decision making. Other chapters specify the need for active participation in capacity-building programmes, and the widest possible participation in the preparation and implementation of National Sustainable Development Strategies (UN, 1993), but despite the spotlight, techniques and procedures for stakeholder participation are in many areas still poorly developed.

One of the participatory tools that has been widely tried and tested is Participatory Rural Appraisal (PRA) a technique developed in Kenya in the late 1980s to encourage and assist rural communities to manage their resources sustainably (Odour-Noah *et al.*, 1992). Since then, a number of variants have evolved in different countries, contexts and organizations, including rapid rural appraisal, participatory evaluation, logical framework approach and stakeholder co-management (Borrini-Feyerabend *et al.*, 2000). In tourism, there has been an increasing attempt to undertake stakeholder analysis and collaborative tourism planning (de Araujo and Bramwell, 1999; Sautter and Leisen, 1999; Hardy and Beeton, 2001). These approaches are designed to identify, involve and empower stakeholders to solve their own problems in a bottom-up fashion, undertaking collective planning and action, and sharing and analysing knowledge.

As these techniques have become mandatory in many development projects, there has been a tendency for stakeholder participation to become an end in itself, an item to be ticked off rather than an active learning process. Adaptive management can assist in this respect by providing a framework for stakeholder participation and encouraging social learning, a dynamic process that helps people position their businesses to respond and cope with change. Social learning involves sharing both implicit/tacit knowledge (internal to the organization; gained through individual experience and organizational culture) and explicit (public) knowledge and information between stakeholders within the community or social setting, transferring knowledge from one group of stakeholders to another, and building expertise to understand and maintain human and social resources (Parson and Clark, 1995). Incorporating social learning techniques in stakeholder participation can help make stakeholder involvement become a more positive and forward-looking technique, moving on from consultation to situations of collaborative co-management. Both adaptive management and social learning and their application to monitoring sustainable tourism are explored further in Chapters 6 and 7.

Monitoring

Monitoring enables system managers to learn more about the behaviour of the system they are managing by measuring progress, defining challenges and sounding alarm bells. It also makes it possible to assess system 'health' and find out the direction elements are moving in as well as finding ways to increase system resilience and adaptive capacity. Like participation and resilience, monitoring is an old tool that has been rediscovered, reviewed and revitalized in the context of revised approaches to sustainability. Box 1.8 shows how monitoring combined with human foresight and political willingness can in some instances reduce or even eliminate the effects of abrupt system changes, a finding also noted by Holling (2001) and with parallels in the rejuvenation stage of Butler's Tourist Area Life Cycle (TALC).

Despite the positive results shown in the ozone hole example, there is no guarantee that humans will always be so successful in response to crises, as Stepp *et al.* (2003) caution. Without close monitoring of system behaviour, critical thresholds may be reached or passed before humans are aware of the need to change behaviour. For example, a lagoon on a tropical island may just be able to cope with the amount of nutrients leaking from the existing hotels' sewage systems, but with the addition of one more hotel, the balance may suddenly tip resulting in a severe algae bloom, from which the local dive operations may never recover.

Agenda 21 places considerable emphasis on the need to monitor sustainable development using indicators. Since the Rio Earth Summit, many organizations, led by those associated with the UN, have begun to develop indicators as tools for monitoring progress made towards sustainable development (UNCSD, 2001a). The International Institute for Sustainable Development (IISD, 1997) explains: '. . . concern about assessing progress towards sustainable development has fuelled a growing international interest in measurement techniques. Measurement, as an indispensable tool to make the concept of sustainable development operational, helps decision

Box 1.8.   Monitoring the ozone hole.

The most well-known abrupt change in the behaviour of the Earth system that have already occurred is the formation of the ozone hole over Antarctica. The ozone hole was the unexpected result of the release of synthetic chemicals chlorofluorocarbons (CFCs) used in aerosols and refrigerants (that were thought at the time to be environmentally harmless). Together with a number of other conditions, the provision of excess chlorine in the atmosphere from the CFCs triggered the abrupt change in the chemistry of the lower stratosphere and led to the formation of the ozone hole.

   However, had it not been for close monitoring, the situation could well have become much more serious and widespread before it was noticed. Scientists with the British Antarctic Survey had routinely and consistently monitored the column of ozone concentration over Antarctic since 1950s and thus observed the unexpected loss of the ozone in the southern high latitudes before the hole reached catastrophic proportions.

   The global response to the ozone hole via the Montreal Protocol, which banned the use of ozone deleting substances in 1987, was fast and effective. The quick response involved public perception that this environmental change was harmful to human health, scientific agreement on the agent and cause of the change and a technological solution (chemical substitutes) that did not require a change in societal behaviour. In this case, societal response was apparently sufficient to reverse the changes under way in the ozone layer. Other kinds of potential abrupt changes, however, may prove less amenable to such rapid and effective response, given the need for all three of the conditions above to be met.

Adapted from: Steffen *et al.* (2004, pp. 14, 15, 19).

makers and the public to conceptualize objectives, evaluate alternatives, make policy choices, and adjust policies as well as objectives based on actual performance.'

   Monitoring has also emerged as crucial in the context of complex systems characterized by crises and surprises (Gunderson, 2003). However, Folke *et al.* (2002) report to the World Summit in Johannesburg, that assessing and evaluating sustainability in the context of complex systems requires a significant shift in perspective. Rather than monitoring stable states, they note that system managers need to cope with multiple scales of variables, non-linear interactions and multi-stable behaviour. Busch and Trexler (2001) identify what they see as five key principles for monitoring in the context of sustainability science:

- Purpose-orientated: strong emphasis on setting and addressing objectives for monitoring;
- Information management: quality control and communication with stakeholders;

- Temporal and spatial monitoring: learning how to respond to issues at different scales;
- Action: monitoring programmes designed with management goals in mind;
- Feedback: monitoring that evaluates management efforts.

These principles are seen here as fundamental to any approach to monitoring sustainability and are returned to again later in Chapters 6 and 7.

Summary

In order to facilitate an effective transition to sustainable tourism, tourism researchers need to keep abreast of new knowledge and understanding in fields related to sustainable development. This chapter has tracked the sustainable development journey from small beginnings to mainstream international politics and contemporary advances in ecological and sustainability science. Important landmarks have been the realization that humans and nature are closely integrated as complex, adaptive social–ecological systems.

The central part of this chapter outlined the case for the reconnection of science with sustainability. It explained the changes that have taken place from the traditional established view of ecology based on balance and harmony, to the realities of non-linear dynamics and complexity theory that are markedly changing contemporary ecological thinking.

Sustainability science is highlighted in the third section of this chapter as a new and evolving field that involves adjusting sustainable development to take on board new ecological thinking. This requires a fundamental change of direction away from the dogma of economic growth and stability, and towards the much more urgent issue of how to build system resilience and adaptive capacity, using integrated and interdisciplinary research that involves trial and error, and a degree of experimental probing known as adaptive management. To facilitate this endeavour, managers need better information about the integrated social–ecological system they are managing, increasing the need for improved indicator design and monitoring. Acknowledgement of and commitment to these core principles now needs to be applied to the way in which sustainable tourism is conceptualized, planned, monitored and managed.

This chapter has aimed to inform about contemporary thinking in sustainable development. Too much sustainable tourism literature still looks back to the Brundtland Report for guidance. Readers are encouraged to break this mould and step outside what are normally considered the boundaries of sustainable tourism to understand it as a complex system. As Farrell and Twining-Ward (2004, p. 288) state, 'If sustainability is not the objective, there is no need for change, but if the transition is desired and more complete and effective tourism is to be practiced, then investigation of appropriate applications from other fields to tourism should proceed with haste'. The following chapter aims to apply what has been learned to sustainable tourism before addressing the question of sustainable tourism monitoring in more detail.

Sustainable Tourism 2

Introduction

Hunter (2002) argues that a detailed discussion of sustainable development is not easy to have. Perhaps as a consequence, the literature on sustainable tourism has tended to avoid the sustainable development material and instead concentrates on a more sectorally specific interpretation. Such an approach may have done much to simplify and enhance the appeal of the concept for the commercial industry, but the separation of tourism from a broader understanding of sustainable development processes is not only intellectually poor, but potentially damaging to the concept, however conceived. Where tourism researchers have acknowledged the link between sustainable development and sustainable tourism, there has been a tendency to retain disciplinary boundaries, with an over-emphasis on the biophysical environment. As a consequence, the sustainable tourism debate has become skewed and relatively oblivious to the valuable interdisciplinary information available. Hence, while a detailed discussion of sustainable development presents significant challenges, the value of having this discussion is a more informed understanding of the issues to be faced in the journey towards more sustainable tourism. Although the authors understand the time pressures on academics and students, the reader is strongly encouraged to review Chapter 1 first before moving on to Chapter 2, rather than attempting to read this chapter in isolation from the rest of the book.

Chapter 1 demonstrated the historical as well as newly emerging interpretations of sustainable development and argued for a shift to a comprehensive, participatory and adaptive approach to thinking about sustainable

©G.A. Miller and L. Twining-Ward 2005. *Monitoring for a Sustainable Tourism Transition* (G.A. Miller and L. Twining-Ward)

development in line with the emerging science of sustainability and complex systems. Chapter 2 continues these themes and demonstrates their applicability to the tourism industry. The chapter begins by explaining the background to the sustainable tourism debate using Jafari's (1989) framework. This reveals how the literature on sustainable tourism has become fragmented and separated from the parent concept of sustainable development resulting in the current narrow sectoral conceptualizations of sustainable tourism. While authors such as Hunter (1995, 1997, 2002) and Collins (1999) have argued for the need to conceptually reunite sustainable tourism with sustainable development, research by Miller (2001a) shows vast disagreement amongst tourism academics over interpretations of sustainable tourism. The second part of the chapter uses Farrell and Twining-Ward's (2004) framework to argue for a reconceptualization of sustainable tourism in line with complex systems and examines the implications for integrating a systemic, stakeholder-driven and adaptive approach to current sustainable tourism thinking.

Historical Context

Jafari (1989) argues that tourism literature can be divided into four main categories; advocacy, cautionary, adaptive and knowledge-based. However, to avoid confusion with the use made in this book of the word 'adaptive' to signify the response made to a complex system, Jafari's (1989) third stage (adaptive) will be referred to throughout instead as 'alternative'. Although it is possible to find examples of a type of thinking that exists out of its epoch, these groups of literature relate loosely to periods in time, and so demonstrate the evolutionary pattern of thinking in tourism.

Advocacy

During the 1950s and 1960s, the tourism industry was typically seen as being an economic panacea and one largely bereft of impact. Zierer (1952, in Cohen, 1978, p. 218) states confidently, 'a notable characteristic of the tourism industry is that it does not, or should not, lead to the destruction of natural resources'. Stankovic (1979, p. 25) is similarly effusive, 'It is a characteristic of tourism that it can, more than many other activities, use and valorise such parts and elements of nature as are of almost no value for other economic branches and activities'. The tourism industry was seen as a source of wealth for the developing 'South' and a tool for the redistribution of income from the wealthier 'North', within this period the potential for negative impact was largely unquestioned. The product was simple and highly reproducible and as a result, destinations as diverse as the Caribbean,

Senegal, Hawaii, the Gambia, the Philippines and Bali, tempted by lucrative foreign exchange earnings, tax receipts and the lure of potential tourism multipliers, provided attractive incentives for foreign investors and multinational hotels (Poon, 1993). Tourism was also vigorously encouraged by international organizations such as the UN, International Monetary Fund and the World Bank. The latter lent nearly US$500 million for tourism projects during the period 1969–1979 (Lanfant and Graburn, 1992; Burns and Holden, 1995; Brohman, 1996).

Cautionary

As the industry expanded, so disquiet surfaced, at least amongst tourism academics, and the unquestioning acceptance of tourism as a panacea was replaced in the 1970s and early 1980s by an era of great critique. The neoclassical economic theories, on which mass tourism development models were founded, were challenged and tourism was criticized as widening the gap between rich and poor, increasing crime rates and disrupting traditional life styles (Turner and Ash, 1975; Doxey, 1976; Cohen, 1978; de Kadt, 1979; Krippendorf, 1982; Smith, 1989). Dependency theorists argued that instead of benefiting tourism destinations, mass tourism developments were designed: 'to meet the economic and political requirements of the colonial powers' (Britton, 1982, p. 333). Britton's (1983) study of tourism in Fiji found that it could aggravate already serious racial and class tensions and lead to a situation of dependency on metropolitan operators. Dogan (1989, pp. 216–217) claims, 'For several months each year, the touristic centers of the Third World countries are swarmed by tourists from the industrial nations who leave behind them bewildered people, crippled institutions, and a ravaged environment'.

The cautionary stance taken by the writings of the day was typified by Plog (1974, p. 4) who famously observed, 'Destinations carry with them the potential seeds of their own destruction, as they allow themselves to become more commercialised and lose their qualities which originally attracted tourists'. Amongst the many epoch-marking works, Budowski (1976) and Cohen (1978) focused on the environmental impacts of tourism, Cohen (1972), de Kadt (1979), Doxey (1976) and MacCannell (1976) the sociocultural impacts, and Bryden (1973) questioned the economic value of tourism. These views were encapsulated in the seminal book by Mathieson and Wall (1982) and the model of the TALC by Butler (1980). A number of different explanations have been provided to explain tourism's tendency to produce negative social and environmental impacts, perhaps one of the most significant being the characteristics of 'common pool resources' and the principle of carrying capacity explained in Boxes 2.1 and 2.2.

Box 2.1.   Common pool resources and the Tragedy of the Commons.

Butler (1991) notes that many of the physical features on which the tourism industry depends can be characterized as common pool resources such as beaches,
mountains, lakes and forests. Common pool resources (alternatively referred to as
'public goods') are the property of no one in particular and so have 'open access'
and can be used by anyone to any extent. As such, they are vulnerable to over
exploitation, a notion Hardin (1968) refers to as the Tragedy of the Commons.
Hardin explains that in the short term, the individual advantage of over-using
shared resources (e.g. pumping sewage into the sea) is perceived as being greater
than the potential long-term shared losses (deterioration of bathing water) that
result from their deterioration. Hardin provides the classic example of common
land with 12 cows, one owned by each of 12 farmers. Any one of the farmers
would benefit personally from the decision to place an extra cow on the land, and
so pursue his own interests, by being able to share the costs of the extra cow (in
terms of the reduction in grass available, damage to the land, etc.) amongst the
farmer and his colleagues. Hence, benefits are concentrated, costs are shared and
so a self-interested approach is encouraged, which often means there is little
motivation to engage in re-investment or ongoing maintenance of the land.

Box 2.2.   Carrying capacity and limits to growth.

Concern over limits to growth is not new. Nineteenth-century classical economists such as Thomas Malthus (1766–1834) and David Ricardo (1772–1823) pre-
dicted that, as populations tend to increase geometrically and food supply
arithmetically, it was inevitable that in the future there would be diminishing
returns in production. Although such doomsday forecasts are now understood to
be over-simplistic, the idea of certain 'limits' to growth has remained. In 1972,
Meadows *et al.* published a ground-breaking report entitled *Limits to Growth*
that hypothesized in a world of finite resources, if current growth trends in world
population, industrialization, pollution, food production and resource deple-
tion continue unchanged, the limits to growth would be reached within 100
years. Many of these predictions have been since proven wrong but their effect
was to draw attention to the possibility of impending environmental and social
crisis.

   In the hope of addressing the issue of the scale in mass tourism, many authors
have suggested adapting the biological concept of carrying capacity to tourism,
suggesting there should be imposed limits to growth. Carrying capacity was originally used to describe how a population grows from a small number to its final
maximum number, illustrated by an S-shaped growth curve. Mathieson and Wall
(1982) explain its interpretation in a tourism sense: 'Carrying capacity is the maximum number of people who can use a site without an unacceptable alteration of
the physical environment and without an unacceptable decline in the quality of
the experience gained by visitors' (Mathieson and Wall, 1982, p. 21). Butler's
(1980) well-cited article, 'The concept of the tourist area cycle of evolution:

implications for the management of resources', suggests that after a slow initial development period, tourism may grow rapidly and ultimately exceed destination carrying capacities, resulting in the degradation of tourism resources, and a consequent reduction of the attractiveness of the destination.

Alternative

The response adopted by the protagonists of the tourism industry during the mid-1980s was described by Jafari (1989) as 'adaptive', although it was in fact dominated by the promulgation of alternative forms of tourism, which gave rise to the widespread vilification of mass tourism (Turner and Ash, 1975; Smith and Eadington, 1989; Butler, 1990; McElroy and de Albuquerque, 1996). Through the rejection of the previous approach, the most sustainable form of tourism risked being overlooked because of the ideological filters through which tourism development was viewed during this period.

Although seldom precisely defined, alternative tourism can be interpreted as an umbrella term covering a range of new forms of tourism that emerged during the 1980s and early 1990s in response to the perceived costs of mass tourism (Mowforth and Munt, 1998). Butler (1990, p. 40) explains, 'It is an alternative to the Costa Bravas, the Daytona strips, Atlantic Citys [sic] and Blackpools of the world. Alternative to large numbers, tasteless and ubiquitous development, environmental and social alienation and homogenization.' Alternative tourism has been described using varying terms including soft and educational tourism (Krippendorf, 1982), co-operative tourism (Farrell, 1986), appropriate tourism (Richter, 1987), responsible tourism (Wheeller, 1991), special-interest tourism (Hall and Weiler, 1992), the now popular term ecotourism (Boo, 1990; Ceballos-Lascurain, 1991) and the newly emerging pro-poor tourism (PPT) discussed in Box 2.3 (DFID, 1999a).

Despite differences in terminology, there appears to be many similarities in alternative forms of tourism. They tend to be predominately small scale, intended or claiming to benefit the local population, conserve the environment and treat the host culture with sensitivity, and in the case of PPT assist with poverty alleviation (Krippendorf, 1982; Wheeller, 1991; Cater, 1993; Weaver, 1998; DFID, 1999b). Weaver (1998, p. 31) explains, 'At the risk of oversimplification, a major distinction between "old" and "new" forms of tourism is the shift in focus from the well-being of the tourist industry to the well-being of the host community'. An early practical example of alternative tourism was established in Lower Casamance, Senegal, to counteract some of the negative aspects of mass tourism development that had been experienced on the coast (Saglio, 1979). Instead of large tourist enclaves, simple tourist lodgings were developed using traditional architecture and local materials, and a village cooperative managed the project.

Box 2.3. Pro-poor tourism.

Pro-poor tourism (PPT) is an attempt to make the tourism industry behave more effectively towards social issues in tourism destinations, with particular regard to the plight of those living in poverty. Advocates believe tourism has an untapped contribution to make towards poverty alleviation because of its labour-intensive low-skill requirements, the opportunities it can create in the informal sector and the fact that it is built on natural and cultural resources, which many poor people have. PPT seeks to achieve its goals not by increasing the size of the industry but redistributing benefits and creating opportunities for disadvantaged groups. Strategies for promoting PPT involve the removal of red tape and unfair advantage to foreign investors, expanding backward linkages between tourism business and the informal sector, addressing social and cultural impacts, and building a supporting tourism policy and processes that allow for the participation of the least powerful stakeholders. Examples of pro-poor strategies include:

- Increased economic benefits by boosting local employment wages, boosting local enterprise opportunities and creating collective income sources, e.g. fees, revenue shares;
- Enhanced non-financial livelihood impacts by capacity building training, mitigating environmental impacts, addressing competing uses of natural resources, increasing local access to infrastructure and services;
- Enhanced participation and partnership by creating a more supportive policy/planning framework, increasing participation decision making, building pro-poor partnerships with the private sector and increasing flows of information and communication.

Source: DFID (1999a), ODI (2003).

During the last decade, as well as receiving praise, alternative tourism has also been the subject of substantial critical debate (Pigram, 1990; Wheeller, 1992, 1994a; Wight, 1995). Wheeller, for example, stresses that alternative tourism cannot possibly replace mass tourism: 'We have, on the one hand, a problem of mass tourism growing globally, out of control, at an alarming rate. And what is our answer? Small-scale, slow, steady, controlled development. They just do not add up' (Wheeller, 1991, p. 92). Carey *et al.* (1997) point out that many mature destinations simply cannot afford to adopt small-scale tourism because of the significant economic implications of so doing, while Mowforth and Munt (1998) provide an excellent example of the economic problems Belize faced in trying to become the world's premier ecotourism destination.

Alternative tourism has also been criticized as promoting distinct class prejudice, providing tourism for the affluent, well-educated and middle class, with the implication that elite travellers are preferable to the charter crowd (Richter, 1987; Butler, 1990; Wheeller, 1994b). Furthermore, Butler (1990, 1991) suggests alternative tourism, rather than a solution to mass tourism, may just be its vanguard, opening up new and potentially more sensitive destinations to the development of mass tourism. As a result of these difficulties, although alternative tourism has provoked some useful discussion and several small-scale success stories, it has done little to address the overall 'problematique' of mass tourism.

Knowledge-based

By the end of the 1980s, Jafari (1989) believed the sustainable tourism debate entered a period typified by a need for knowledge about the different forms of tourism and their potential impacts. This position was achieved by recognizing that any type of tourism could potentially be made more sustainable, giving rise to moves to develop indicators as a way to monitor progress towards sustainability, rather than adopting a more ideological view of what forms of tourism should be introduced. Butler (1990, p. 41) comments with alacrity, 'to promote one form of tourism as a solution to the multiple problems which can be caused by extensive and long term development is somewhat akin to selling nineteenth century wonder medicines'.

International conferences are easily criticized for being opportunities to escape the office and meet up with old friends. While the authors would not dispute these social benefits, conferences have also acted as a heuristic in the development of sustainable tourism. The Globe '90 Conference in Vancouver discussed the challenge of applying the wider principles of sustainable development to the tourism sector (Tourism Canada, 1990), while the Lanzarote World Conference on Sustainable Tourism in 1995 went a step further on the basis of Agenda 21 and produced a Charter for Sustainable Tourism that has since been adopted by the UN General Assembly. The Charter identifies a number of principles and objectives for sustainable tourism including the need for integrated planning, consultation of stakeholders and improvement in the quality of life of the host population. It stresses that sustainable tourism should be based on the diversity of opportunities offered by the local economy and gives special attention to vulnerable and degraded areas, using such tools as impact assessment; feasibility studies and codes of conduct (World Conference on Sustainable Tourism, 1995). Similar principles are outlined in the Bali Declaration on Tourism adopted at the World Tourism Organization (WTO) forum in 1996, the Malé Declaration on Sustainable Tourism Development adopted at the Asia-Pacific Ministers Conference on Tourism and Environment in 1997, and the Berlin Declaration adopted at the International Conference of Environment Ministers on Biodiversity and Tourism in Berlin in 1997.

More recently, the role of the private sector is stressed in the World Travel and Tourism Council (WTTC) report Agenda 21 for the Travel and Tourism Industry: Towards Environmentally Sustainable Development (WTTC *et al.*, 1997). However, although the importance of partnerships between government, industry and NGOs is understood, the resulting partnership focuses on environmental sustainability and so cannot be said to adopt a comprehensive approach. Like the changes that were taking place in sustainable development thinking at the time, a movement can be traced from the environmental leanings of the early years to greater focus on social issues and poverty alleviation with the emergence of PPT explained in Box 2.3. Further to these contributions has been the formulation of WTO's Global Code of Ethics for Tourism, adopted by WTO members during the 1999 WTO General Assembly (Box 2.4). The code is described as 'a blueprint' for ensuring the sustainability of the tourism sector and for minimizing negative impacts. Unlike previous charters and codes of conduct, WTO intends it to be a regulatory mechanism, with a panel of experts to evaluate and settle disputes (WTO, 2001a).

The effect of these agreements and conferences has been a proliferation of sustainable tourism writing, leading Velikova (2001) to argue that the concept of sustainable tourism is today promoted in the literature as fulsomely as the tourism industry itself was 30 years ago. Initially perhaps this may have been the case, but the discussion on sustainable tourism is not presented in an uncritical manner anymore with an increasing number of more sceptical observers who question whether sustainable tourism is actually feasible in practice (Bramwell and Lane, 1993; Wheeller, 1993; Harrison, 1996; Clarke, 1997; Stabler, 1997; Butler, 1998; Sharpley, 2000).

Box 2.4.   World Tourism Organization Code of Ethics.

The World Tourism Organization (WTO, 1999, p. 1) state that, 'The Global Code of Ethics for Tourism sets a frame of reference for the responsible and sustainable development of world tourism', believing the code is necessary to '. . . help minimize the negative impacts of tourism on the environment and on cultural heritage while maximizing the benefits for residents of tourism destinations'. The code consists of ten articles, nine of which outline the 'rules of the game for destinations, governments, tour operators, developers, travel agents, workers and travellers themselves', while the final article refers to mechanisms for enforcing the code. No mention is made as to how this code should be regulated.

1. Tourism's contributions to mutual understanding and respect between peoples and societies;
2. Tourism as a vehicle for individual and collective fulfilment;
3. Tourism, a factor for sustainable development;
4. Tourism, a user of the cultural heritage of mankind and a contributor to its enhancement;
5. Tourism, a beneficial activity for host countries and communities;
6. Obligations of stakeholders in tourism development;
7. Right to tourism;
8. Liberty of tourism movements;
9. Rights of the workers and entrepreneurs in the tourism industry;
10. Implementation of the principles of the Global Code of Ethics for Tourism.

These criticisms are to be valued and form the basis of the following critique of sustainable tourism, but the authors who have written on sustainable tourism have added much to their field. By expanding the subject they have undoubtedly attracted attention to tourism from government, destinations, industry and residents. Students will have been encouraged to study tourism as a consequence of the rise of writings on sustainability and academics will have been enticed into the field also. This has improved the standard of writings and allowed specialist journals to emerge. The rise of ecotourism has done much to raise the profile of sustainability discussions, although it has also checked the drive for a comprehensive approach, necessitating the rise of PPT and other approaches to tourism representing particular elements of sustainability. The debate on sustainable tourism has come a long way and the following section describes where the authors believe the debate rests currently. This critique examines three main issues of dispute, those of sectoral scale, spatial scale and temporal scale, before explaining the approach taken throughout the rest of this book.

Current Conceptualization of Sustainable Tourism

Typical of an increasing number of authors, Garrod and Fyall (1998) express a desire to move on from the semantics to the practicalities of the concept. They note 'defining sustainable development in the context of tourism has become something of a cottage industry in the academic literature' (Garrod and Fyall, 1998, p. 199). Indeed, the spawning of sustainable tourism definitions is not something that this book wishes to add to. However, Hunter (2002) asks whether the calls for the debate to move on from conceptual wrangling to matters of implementation have not been premature. A key disagreement that remains within the literature is conceptually where the sectoral borders of sustainable tourism exist, with one view of sustainable tourism placing the tourism industry at the centre of a narrow consideration, while another view sees sustainable development as the broader goal to which tourism should aspire.

Sectoral scale

The sector-specific approach to sustainable tourism only concerns itself with issues that affect its ability to sustain itself in the future. Butler (1993a, p. 29) describes sustainable tourism in this context as 'tourism which is in a form which can maintain its viability in an area for an indefinite period of time'. The essential canon is that tourism is concerned to maintain 'its' viability over an indefinite period of time. This is clearly the inward-looking approach to sustainable tourism that has been fostered by those in the tourism industry, and not the definition that has crossed from the developmental literature. Hence it is possible for decisions promoting sustainable tourism (using this definition) to contradict the needs of sustainable development. Muller (1994) (Box 2.5) reflects this limited view of sustainable tourism and calls for balance between all the components of the tourism industry in order to result in sustainable tourism. However, any balance sought is likely to be heavily in favour of the economic over the environmental (reflecting our anthropocentrism), discount consequences for the future in favour of the present and reflect other interests and biases each of the stakeholders may have.

Hunter (2002) (Box 2.6) on the other hand reminds us that one person's balance is another's imbalance and as such, we can never hope to achieve 'balance' even if this was a desirable outcome. Further, this search for balance within the tourism industry fails to acknowledge tourism's role more broadly with other elements of the economy and society, and is at odds with

Box 2.5. Muller's Magic Pentagon.

Muller's 1994 paper produced a pentagon to explain diagrammatically what he saw as the five main components of sustainable tourism: unspoilt nature, healthy culture, a high degree of subjective well-being, optimum satisfaction of guest requirements and economic health. For Muller, the 'target situation is balanced tourism development' and '. . . establishing harmony in this magic pentagon to maximise the positive relationships between all the factors'. A consequence of following this drive for balance would be the upgrading in importance of natural and cultural considerations, while downgrading economic and financial factors in their importance. Muller talks throughout of 'achieving sustainable tourism', which implies sustainable tourism is a steady-state concept that once it can be identified can be pursued until it is realized. However, perhaps the main weakness of Muller's argument is the pursuit of balance ignores the realities in destinations, which might make the pursuit of balance counter developmental over the short to medium term.

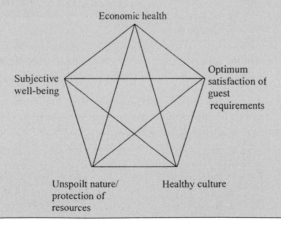

the current movement away from equilibrium-based sustainability models to focus on the management of change (see Chapter 1). If a tourism-centric approach is adopted, sustainability can indeed be seen as a threat to business success and one can understand why McKercher (1993) is able to critically ask 'can tourism survive sustainability?' A broader interpretation could ask 'should tourism survive sustainability?'

Box 2.6. Hunter's adaptive paradigm.

Two articles from within the tourism literature that have made among the most important contributions to the sustainable tourism debate were written by Colin Hunter. In 1995, Hunter argues that the 'dominant paradigm of sustainable tourism' is a tourism-centric approach where the needs of tourism development are balanced against the needs of the environment. Hunter argues that such a parochial conceptualization leads to inadequate consideration of the geographic scope and scale of resources, while it also fails to identify the inter-sectoral links between tourism and other activities. The figure below is taken from Hunter (1995) and shows how he believes the concerns of sustainable tourism are often marginal to the concerns of sustainable development (model 2). Indeed, one could perhaps go further and argue that often the concerns of those in the industry could be described as being entirely removed from the motivation of sustainable development, illustrating the distance still to be travelled before sustainable development becomes central to the concerns of sustainable tourism (model 1).

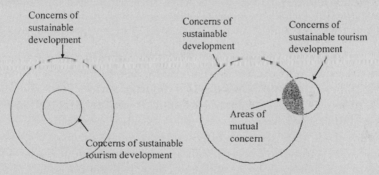

Model 1: Total Immersion   Model 2: Partial Immersion

Hunter's (1997) paper argues that sustainable tourism has come to be understood as an overly simplistic and inflexible concept, divorced from the sustainable development debate. Reuniting sustainable tourism with sustainable development, Hunter calls for sustainable tourism to be seen as an 'adaptive paradigm', one where multiple positions can be seen as promoting sustainability, but determined by the circumstances and needs of the destination.

Serious students of sustainable tourism should read these seminal articles by Hunter and understand the importance of a flexible, more sophisticated interpretation of sustainable tourism within a developmental context.

Pursuing this adaptation of McKercher's (1993) question, Butler (1993a, p. 29) expands his previous definition to describe tourism in a sustainable development context as:

> . . . tourism which is developed and maintained in an area in such a manner and at such a scale that it remains viable over an indefinite period and does not degrade or alter the environment (human and physical) in which it exists to such a degree that it prohibits the successful development and well-being of other activities and processes.

The crucial part of this approach is that tourism's place within a broader social and economic context is recognized. This approach is also supported by Godfrey (1998, p. 214) who usefully comments, 'sustainable tourism is . . . not an end in itself, nor a unique or isolated procedure, but rather an inter-dependent function of a wider and permanent socio-economic development process'. When the industry is considered in isolation, without regular monitoring, the opportunity costs of tourism on other sectors may not taken account of, with the result that tourism may be promoted, at any cost (Clarke, 1997; Blake, 2000). Urry (1990, p. 23) reminds us that 'the more exclusively an area specialises in tourism, the more depressed its general wage levels will be'. The UNEP (1995, p. 30) recognizes this risk and reports:

> . . . we want to counter the danger of one-sided economic development and over dependence on the tourist trade. We support the strengthening of agriculture and small-scale trade as well as their partnership with tourism. We strive for a qualitative improvement of jobs in tourism. We also continually explore all possibilities for the creation of new jobs outside the tourist trade.

This position reflects Hunter's (1995, 2002) hope that destinations can, where necessary, adopt a less tourism-centric, less precious approach.

Adopting this broader perspective requires a wider understanding of how tourism operates as a complex system as well as enhanced interdisciplinary cooperation. Newman *et al.* (2001, p. 30) note, 'Understanding the dynamics of the total system is often constrained by a lack of coordination among experts and the public'. Such an acknowledgement requires a concomitant acceptance that our ability to control all the potential influences on our business is reduced and we need to accept that there are issues too complex to understand or control, and too removed to predict. This will require a huge change in the way we view our world and a reduction in the arrogance of 'managerialism' that assumes all potential harmful factors in the external environment can be identified and avoided. Too often, complex problems originating outside our field of control gives rise to fatalism and resignation, as was evident during the 2001 foot-and-mouth disease in the UK (Miller and Ritchie, 2003). However, the increasing recognition of the value of building resilience (explained in Chapter 1 as the capacity of a system to cope with large- and small-scale change) through disaster and crisis management plans may illustrate human ability to accept complex situations and to plan for how to adapt to rather than control an extreme event should one occur.

Spatial scale

The Brundtland Commission (WCED, 1987) stressed the importance of working at the global scale to tackle global problems and there is at least political attraction in addressing the solution at this scale and allowing the results to filter down. However, from a pragmatist's and local community advocate's position, the smaller the identifiable region, the simpler it may be to implement sustainable tourism strategies at that level. Thus, the Rio summit gave rise to Agenda 21 and to Local Agenda 21, which stressed the 'think global, act local' mantra.

As with the problem of relating tourism with other industrial sectors, so the problem of geographical scale relates not so much to the level of consideration, but the inter-dependence of these regions. Collins (1996) refers to the 'upstream' and 'downstream' origin and manifestation of problems, reminding us 'tourism destinations do not exist in spatial isolation'. A review of the sustainability of Jersey shows unusual insight in this regard, particularly for an island state, observing, 'Sustainability is about maintaining that valued quality of life whilst at the same time having regard to our impact on the world beyond our immediate shores' (Romeril, 1997, p. 3.4). Weaver and Lawton (1999) suggest that in an ideal world the remits of planning departments would match environmental features such as rivers and mountains. However, given that the tourism industry has largely underestimated the impact of its own behaviour on itself and has been unconcerned with the risks to other industrial sectors, there is little surprise that scant regard has been paid by the industry to the damage it has caused to other industrial sectors or geographical regions. The result is that under the tourism-centric paradigm, resources are channelled into a region's tourism sector to prevent or address problems, or to expand the tourism product, but the neighbouring regions and related sectors bear at least some of the cost without any financial reparation (Hunter, 1995). Germane to this, Todd and Williams (1996) reveal the problems encountered in neighbouring regions with the expansion and development of the Aspen ski resort.

Wheeller (1992, 1993, 1994a,b) is perhaps the most famous questioner of the ramifications of aiming for sustainability at a specific geographical scale and has constantly identified the problem being one of numbers of visitors and not the manner in which they are managed or distributed. Thus, for Wheeller, until the problem is addressed at a global level, then so much of current practice looks to be peripheral. Interpreting this narrow spatial consideration a different way would see actions to promote sustainability within the area of concern as exporting unsustainability to

neighbouring regions. Sharpely (2000, p. 9) states, '. . . developing sustainable forms of tourism in some areas simply sweeps the problems of tourism
under the carpet of other destinations'.

Opposite to Wheeller, Wall (1997, p. 46) believes that given local differences and the need to ensure a fit between the problem and the response,
responses must be designed at a local level:

> While most would agree that if tourism is to contribute to sustainable
> development it must be economically viable, environmentally sensitive and
> culturally appropriate, the forms which this might take are likely to vary with
> location. This in turn means that it will be very difficult to come up with
> useful principles for tourism development which are true for all places
> and all times.

The complexity of solutions is likely to grow in proportion to the spatial
scale and also the degree of cross-sectoral application. Thus, a tourism-
centric approach at a local scale should be more readily implemented than
the global, multi-sectoral solution attempted by the Brundtland commission (WCED, 1987). However, in global terms, the value of the rewards of a
single-sector, single-scale solution is commensurately lower – a problem of
pragma versus dogma.

Yet, despite recognition over the implications for global sustainability,
there is increasing consensus in sustainable development and tourism literature recommending a 'place-based' approach to sustainable development
(Lew and Hall, 1998; Potts and Harril, 1998; Bramwell and Sharman, 1999;
NRC, 1999). The NRC report (NRC, 1999, p. 22), for example, suggests
that with the use of representative stakeholders, a particular 'place-based
interpretation' of sustainability can be created that is not possible through
the use of imported specialists, consultants or managers. Hence, local-level
efforts determine what sustainability means to that specific locality. Potts
and Harril (1998, p. 137) recommend applying the principles of 'mutuality
and locality' to a community's planning process as opposed to 'cookie-cutter'
techniques, which they say 'de-value social networks and the unique characteristics of place'. Stankey (1999, p. 180) is critical of those that seek 'simplicity
and universality' rather than adapting to site- or area-specific conditions.
He sees such 'cookbook' approaches as focusing attention on finding universal answers rather than more importantly, the solutions to specific local
problems. Hunter (1997) also notes that sustainable tourism needs to address
different goals in different situations and Laws et al. (1998, p. 9) explain:

> Each destination therefore has the challenge of identifying the factors causing
> change locally, and of understanding their dynamics in its own context.
> Consequently, a policy adopted in one particular situation must not be
> regarded as a model solution for another destination. Nor indeed would
> current policy be adequate for dealing with future problems in the same
> destination.

Hudson and Miller (2004) discuss the tension between the ski industry in Banff National Park and local residents, and ask whether the support for the National Park is not indicative of a move to a new, stronger environmental ethic being seen in richer parts of the world. In the trade-off between income generation and environmental conservation, local residents are being increasingly successful in arguing for the prevention of further expansion of ski developments, even though this could mean Banff loses its market to other skiing areas able to expand and update facilities. Such a situation is undoubtedly caused by the growing economic and political strength and confidence of the local residents, but can be seen also as a form of 'social learning' discussed in the previous chapter, based on knowledge of previous implications of the tourism industry. This stronger interpretation of sustainable tourism is, on the surface, in stark contrast to an interpretation where income is placed over the needs of the environment. However, in each instance, there is no perfect balance, but the destination is able to choose for itself what it wants the tourism industry to contribute in a place-based context. Thus, the definition of sustainable tourism has to focus on whatever is determined in the destination to contribute most to an improvement in the quality of life.

Adopting a place-based approach to sustainable tourism fits with the principle of sustainable development promoting individuals' self-determination. Yet, in combining the need for a broad, inter-disciplinary, non-linear, complex, adaptive understanding with a place-based approach, there may be a need to reconcile intellectual rigour with practical realities. By adopting a locationally specific approach, the lessons from 'local successes' can be used to cumulatively improve the pool of knowledge about tools and management practices that may be applied later at other scales. In contrast, adopting the global approach, although not impossible to implement, would involve the examination of a different and much more complex set of variables. The increased complexity of the challenge and the time it is likely to take to examine may render it vulnerable to being dismissed as unfeasible before any significant successes could be achieved. This leads us to the question of the timeframe that sustainable tourism should be considered within.

Temporal scale

A key confusion within the problem of temporal scale lies in the fact that many tourism scholars still view sustainability as a state that is achievable in a particular period of time rather than an ever evolving process or transition as explained in the previous chapter. This is discussed by Butler, in a conversation with Hall (Hall and Butler, 1995). They note that 'we [the tourism community] imply that sustainable tourism by its very nature is static tourism and that it therefore will go on forever...' (Hall and Butler, 1995, p. 102). As explained in Chapter 1, all ecological systems are now understood to be dynamic and characterized by unpredictable change. The work of the 'adaptive ecology group' in the 1970s and 1980s (as discussed in Chapter 1) challenged conventional emphases on maintaining ecosystem equilibrium and demonstrated that, rather than being stable, natural systems are complex and ever-changing and as a result, management strategies need to be adaptive. In addition, human and social systems can be seen to have dynamic goals, meaning that the quality of life aspirations of people will be constantly shifting. This work was found to have parallels with new understandings of complexity theory, which suggests all complex systems, whether biophysical or social, are unpredictable and characterized by 'non-linear dynamics', where small inputs can have multiple and unpredictable outputs.

Although the dynamic nature of tourism has been frequently referred to in tourism literature (Inskeep, 1977, 1991; Mathieson and Wall, 1982; Butler, 1990, 1995; Pearce, 1995; Hall, 2000), so far only a few scholars have recently begun to apply the knowledge of complex systems to the study of tourism (Faulkner and Russell, 1997; Hein, 1997; Greiner and Walker, 1999; Reed, 1999; Russell and Faulkner, 1999; Walker *et al.*, 1999; Abel, 2000; Farrell and Twining-Ward, 2004).

Laws *et al.* (1998, p. 6) explain how conventional tourism research methods are more attuned to the analysis of stable systems, uniformity, equilibrium and linear relationships. They explain that the problem with research based on this view of the world, is that there is no room for the unexpected events that inevitably surprise and confound researchers, forecasters and planners alike:

> The inadequacies of conventional approaches in coping with change and transition have given rise to the chaos/complexity perspective in which the predisposition to assume a linear, clockwork world is displaced by concepts which depict a confusing world of non-linearity and surprise, juxtaposed with attributes normally associated with living organisms, such as adaptation, coherence and self organization.

Similarly, McKercher (1999, p. 426) criticizes mainstream tourism research in its interpretation of systems as 'expectable, stable, orderly and conducive to linear change'. Instead he views the tourism system as complex and uncontrollable, characterized by non-linear, non-deterministic chaotic behaviour. Jennings (2001, p. 67) suggests tourism should be studied 'as a dynamic system rather than a steady state or predictable system', while Reed (1999, p. 352) emphasizes the complexity of the biophysical and socio-economic systems within which tourism planning is undertaken and recommends managers 'recognize and deal with change, complexity, uncertainty and conflict'. For tourism this means sustainable tourism is not a static goal which can be achieved in a calculable number of years, but a process or journey which involves moving towards a more desirable future, with discernible changes appearing through time, instead of by a fixed time (NRC, 1999).

Similarly, there will not be a time when it is possible to identify the achievement of sustainable development, partly because of data restrictions, but principally because the dynamic nature of the concept means that the goal posts are constantly moving. As such, sustainable development and sustainable tourism will always be open to critics who argue that the concept is weak because it is impossible to point to a destination and show 'sustainability'. However, uncertainty about the length of the process should not deter scholars and practitioners from engaging in sustainable tourism research, as only through further time and place-based investigation is the path towards sustainable development likely to become clearer. In many cases, therefore, criticisms of sustainable tourism may not be reflections of the failure of the concept itself, but the failure of those involved in tourism to take on board progressive interdisciplinary knowledge on the subject.

Reconceptualizing Sustainable Tourism

The discussion above has revealed contrasting views, conflicting approaches and a large number of unresolved issues. Tourism academics have not yet strayed far from familiar disciplinary shores, and there is clearly a need to enhance knowledge in these areas and apply what has been learned in fields such as sustainability science to tourism. Farrell and Twining-Ward (2004) carefully lay out the framework for reconceptualizing sustainable tourism by integrating knowledge of complex adaptive systems and applying non-linear science to the management of tourism. This approach calls for a comprehensive, stakeholder-driven, adaptive approach, which is explained more fully in the remainder of this chapter.

Comprehensive approach

Growing international support for sustainable development has paved the way for a more integrated and comprehensive approach to development and the environment in which programmes to address social issues are inextricably linked to conservation. It is suggested that a basic understanding of non-linear complex systems can not only greatly aid such synthesis, its application appears essential to effect a transition to sustainability. Systems thinking is not a new area of research. Systems have been studied with increasing sophistication since the time of the ancient Greeks who observed the regularities and constancy of the solar system and its relationship with the Earth. Since the 17th century, systems in various forms have become an integral part of the paradigms of scientific thought and applied to various studies of the natural world as well as to complicated human activities.

Tourism researchers have generally supported the use of systems. Hall (2000) notes that a system is a powerful analytical tool, an integrated whole

whose essential properties result from the relationships between its constituent parts. Hall goes on to explain that systems thinking is the understanding of a phenomenon within the context of a larger whole, and that
systems analysis can help explain some of the multiple and complex interactions which take place in everyday life. In a similar vein, Berkes and Folke
(1998) suggest a systems approach is replacing the view that resources can
be treated as discrete entities in isolation from the rest of the world and
can help provide a holistic view of the components and the interrelationships in the real world. There appears to be sufficient evidence from international research institutions to support this claim (WGBU, 1996; Gallopín
et al., 1998; IGBP, 2001; NRC, 2001).

As systems have no regard for disciplinary boundaries, and do not differentiate between biophysical or human components, they are particularly
compatible with a comprehensive approach. In contrast to simple systems,
which are linear and expected to function in a predictable fashion rather
like a machine, with large inputs yielding proportionally large results, complex systems function in a non-linear fashion, and even quite small inputs
can produce multiple and unpredictable outcomes. Following the arguments explained in the previous chapter, it is proffered here that both
biophysical and human systems, including tourism, should be understood
as mainly complex systems, characterized by non-linear complex system
behaviour.

The work of other researchers supports this position. Russell and Faulkner
(1999) and McKercher (1999) suggest that conventional tourism models
(e.g. Leiper, 1979, 1990; Mill and Morrison, 1985; Murphy, 1985; Gunn,
1988) are derived from the Newtonian/Cartesian paradigm, in which the
universe operates as a perfect machine and where objects and events can be
understood by disaggregating them into their simple component parts.
Although this approach can be useful for study purposes as shown by
Pearce (1995), and of course, also for teaching purposes, both McKercher
(1999) and Russell and Faulkner (1999) effectively argue that tourism is
more than a collection of its obvious manifestations and constituent parts,
and should not be separated from the wider community with which it is
interconnected. McKercher (1999) also notes that simple tourism systems
provide little assistance in understanding the dramatic chance events that
frequently affect tourism destinations. Hall (2000) points out that they
provide only a partial insight into the complexities of tourism.

Although many scholars encourage integration in tourism, and others
note the shortcomings of conventional models, the actual use of more comprehensive systemic approaches to the study of tourism is rare. In the
mid-1980s Getz (1986) surveyed over 150 models used in tourism studies,
and found very few made any attempt to take a whole-systems approach.
More recent examples of appreciating tourism as a complex system can be
found in the work of Hein (1997), Faulkner and Russell (1997), Laws *et al.*
(1998), McKercher (1999), Greiner and Walker (1999), Walker *et al.*

(1999) and Abel (2000). Hein (1997, p. 360) emphasizes that studying the interrelationships between tourism and economic, political and cultural spheres of activity can assist in 'identifying probable trajectories of change' and points out the consequences of specific development strategies on other elements of the system. Greiner and Walker (1999) and Walker *et al.* (1999, p. 60) take this idea several steps further in their modelling of tourism development in Douglas Shire, Australia, where they find that conceptualizing tourism as a whole complex system is an essential precondition for implementing sustainable tourism, observing, '. . . if we view tourism as a complex system, it seems more likely that a large range of activities and factors have to be managed simultaneously for regional tourism to be successful and sustainable in the long-term'.

Yet, apart from these few examples, invariably where the term 'tourist system' is used in the literature, it is defined in simple, linear terms and other essential elements are discarded under the heading of 'impacts' or relegated to the 'external environment' under which the 'real' tourism system operates. It is argued here that the full human and biophysical fabric of tourism is wide and deep, including such subsystems as transportation, water supply, food production, the availability of labour, community and life support systems. In this way, to study just the core tourism components and hope to comprehend sustainable tourism is at best naïve and at worst misleading. It is from understanding the whole, complex system that answers to a number of tourism's challenges are more likely to be found, and this necessitates a comprehensive approach.

Stakeholder-driven

Chapter 1 showed how public involvement and participation are vital to the whole tourism development process, helping planners to ask the right questions and providing them with a reasoned, defensible basis for their judgements. Hence, stakeholder theory has come to be used to promote collaboration among key players in the planning process (Sautter and Leisen, 1999). Bramwell and Sharman (1999) report that a stakeholder-driven approach can help to avoid conflicts, resulting in policies that are more politically legitimate and improve the coordination of policies by promoting consideration of the wide-ranging effects of tourism. Exploring the role of community involvement in creating strategies for the sustainability of farm tourism in Cumbria, Harper (1997) explains how workshops and group discussions enabled previously antagonistic groups to identify common problems and agree on joint marketing strategies. Greiner and Walker (1999, p. 6) also note the intrinsic benefits of this approach, 'In addition to effecting learning, stakeholder participation also builds ownership of the problems and the solutions and therefore the research'. Summarizing, Marien and Pizam (1997, p. 165) opine:

> Sustainable tourism cannot be successfully implemented without the direct
> support and involvement of those who are affected by it. Therefore,
> evaluating a community's sensitivity to tourism development is the first step
> in planning for sustained tourism development.

Yet, despite the many advantages of stakeholder participation in progressing the transition towards sustainability, it is not often fully incorporated
in sustainable tourism management or research. Whilst several tourism
researchers comment on attempts to undertake collaborative tourism
planning (Bramwell and Sharman, 1999; De Araujo and Bramwell, 1999;
Sautter and Leisen, 1999; Sirakaya *et al.*, 2001) and others have engaged in
stakeholder analysis (Hardy and Beeton, 2001), the authors have been able
to find very few who have engaged in participatory action research
(Wadsworth, 1998; Twining-Ward, 2003). Hardy *et al.* (2002) note tourism
researchers' tendency to lean towards economic and environmental considerations rather than recognizing community involvement and livelihood
opportunities, and concur that stakeholders have been under-represented
in the literature on the subject. Some of the reasons for this are the significant challenges of working closely with stakeholder groups and these are
explored more fully in Chapter 4.

However, as with sustainable tourism and sustainable development, the
fact that there are difficulties in operationalizing the concept, does not con-
sign the concept to the 'bad ideas' or 'too difficult' bin. Stakeholder participation is an essential part of adaptive management strategies as public
participation has been shown to help reduce uncertainty and identify
knowledge gaps ultimately improving the basis on which decisions are
made (Newman *et al.*, 2001). Put simply, for sustainable tourism to be
place-based and promote the developmental needs of the destination with
greater surety, tourism needs to be more stakeholder-driven.

Adaptive

Adaptive management, as explained in Chapter 1, is based on the fact that
knowledge of ecosystems is incomplete and the future is unpredictable, so
management of any aspect of the complex system needs to involve a comprehensive, systemic approach, which includes experimentation, adaptation, monitoring and social learning. By working closely with stakeholders
to develop and monitor experimental strategies, when events turn out to be
different from those expected, adaptation can be fast and the change can
often lead to a beneficial learning process rather than something to avoid
at all costs (Holling and Bocking, 1990; Tainter, 1996). With all the global
political and social events in recent years that have affected the tourism
industry, it seems difficult to argue that tourism would not benefit from a
wider, more flexible approach to management.

Central to adaptive management is the design of monitoring systems that can provide reliable information about management experiments and to construct management institutions and processes that are able to learn from their mistakes. Reed (1999) notes that in adaptive management, when a policy is successful, the hypothesis is validated, and when it fails, the adaptive process is designed so that learning occurs and adjustments can be made until better systems are put in place.

There are only a few documented examples of where the principles of adaptive management have been used for managing tourism. These are mostly in British Columbia, the original home base of the adaptive ecology group (Holling and Chambers, 1973; Moser and Petersen, 1981; Manning, 1998; Rollins *et al.*, 1998; Reed, 1999; S.E. Reid and J. Marion, 2004, unpublished results). Two of the most noteworthy are included in Box 2.7.

Similar results to those explained in Box 2.7 were found by Rollins *et al.* (1998) in British Columbia, the Clayoquot Sound Scientific Panel (1995) and Manning (1998) on Vancouver Island, Reed (1999) in Squamish in Canada, Walker *et al.* (1999, p. 60) in Douglas Shire, North Queensland, Australia and Twining-Ward (2003) in Samoa (see Chapter 10). These projects all show how the ability to learn and adapt is imperative for managing complex systems, and how close stakeholder involvement can assist in getting to the root of natural resource conflicts. The examples serve to demonstrate some of the practical and institutional challenges to the effective implementation of adaptive management. Adaptive management may at first seem a vague concept, but in the context of non-linear complex systems such vagueness provides flexibility and is an essential advantage. Adaptive management advises a much more proactive approach to managing change involving an ongoing process of experimentation, learning and adaptation.

Summary

The aim of this chapter has been to demonstrate how the current understanding of sustainable tourism has evolved over time and to suggest a way forward that is more in line with an understanding of complex systems. The authors feel strongly that if tourism is to deliver the social and economic benefits its promoters frequently promise, then the discourse on sustainable tourism needs to reconnect with the material drawn from the wider interdisciplinary sustainable development literature as well as many other relevant sources. The chapter has taken the reader on a journey through the historical and conceptual emergence of sustainable tourism. It has identified some of the significant milestones along the way as well as some of the less successful avenues that have been explored. Key issues raised include the spatial and temporal scale of interpretation and the

Box 2.7. Examples of adaptive management in use.

The first known exercise in using adaptive management for tourism situations recorded in the literature was the Gulf Islands Recreational Land Simulation Study in 1968, where, according to Gunderson *et al.* (1995b), participants attempted to explore ways to bridge gaps among scientific disciplines, and enhance cooperation between technical experts and policy designers. During this study, Holling, Walters and colleagues introduced the basic concepts of adaptive management and experimented with its implementation. They found that adaptive management, through its flexibility and monitoring capabilities was extremely useful for managers struggling to cope with the social ecological dynamics of ecosystems. As a result, the technique was further developed as Gunderson *et al.* (1995b, p. 490) explain, 'to deal with the unpredictable interactions between people and ecosystems as they evolve together'.

Another early example of how adaptive management principles can be applied to tourism was demonstrated in Obergürgl, a small ski village in the Austrian Alps that was facing considerable ecological and social difficulties as tourism grew rapidly during the 1960s (Farrell and Runyan, 1991). As a result of the work of plant ecologist Walter Moser, in 1971, the village was selected as part of UNESCO's Man and the Biosphere Programme. During the 4 years over which the project ran, residents worked alongside scientists systematically to identify problems and model prospects for the village using an environmental assessment and management process, adaptive management's predecessor (Moser and Petersen, 1981; Holling and Bocking, 1990). As a result of the project, alternative scenarios for the development of the village were created, and because of their participation in the project, the villagers of Obergürgl were able to make more informed decisions about their preferred future for the resort.

The work in Obergürgl was also significant in that it was a very early demonstration of how a comprehensive, interdisciplinary and participatory approach could potentially be effective in the implementation of sustainable tourism. The project resulted in considerable social learning on the part of citizens and the scientists involved as Holling and Bocking suggest (1990, p. 294), 'people themselves had become the architects of their own sustainable development'.

disharmony between tourism-centric and wider, more complete perspectives on tourism as a complex system.

The danger of a disconnect also exists between the literature and the realities of the industrial coalface. A text that calls for sustainable tourism to be regarded as a comprehensive system, stakeholder-driven and accepting the principles of adaptive management, is particularly vulnerable to criticisms from those representing the harsh realities of the commercial industry. However, the high fashion displayed on the catwalks of London, Paris and Milan bears little relation to the fashions people wear on the high street, but the value of these initial displays in changing the direction of the current fashion is not questioned. So, it should be with academic literature and the commercial industry, whereby discussions help to change the overall framework of consideration. It is entirely possible (and with good reason) that academics have never been compared to catwalk fashion before, but the separation of theory from practice is only a problem if there is no transference from one to the other; the distance is not an issue. Indeed, one can argue that there is an important role for the academic literature in maintaining a distance in order to keep challenging the commercial industry. However, such a stance also requires the commercial industry and other stakeholders to respond to the challenges laid down and engage in the sustainable tourism debate.

Unless reasons can be found and arguments developed for the key stakeholders to be involved to promote sustainability, then the detail over how monitoring is conducted, becomes redundant. The following two chapters focus on the reasons why these stakeholders should seek to get actively involved in sustainable tourism discourse and action to secure a more sustainable tourism industry.

II Motivations for Monitoring

Chapters 1 and 2 have shown how current thinking on sustainability in general and sustainable tourism specifically have developed through time. Moving beyond these conceptualizations, the authors have suggested new ways of thinking about sustainable tourism, as a comprehensive, stakeholder-driven, complex, adaptive process. However, in an increasingly individualistic society, it is essential to remind ourselves that without a meaningful rationale for sustainability, it will not be pursued. Academics and others can continue to debate what sustainability is, but the only thing this is likely to sustain is the debate itself. Difficult times and challenging decisions lie ahead and these will not be taken without a good reason to do so. The purpose of the following two chapters is therefore to examine what arguments different stakeholders find convincing in order to change current thinking and behaviour in the interests of a sustainability transition. The role of monitoring is given increasing prominence within the book from this point on. Monitoring is shown to be important because it has a central role in promoting sustainability. Hence, if a motivation can be demonstrated to pursue sustainability, then monitoring is one way to operationalize this aim. Beyond this, Chapters 3 and 4 show how monitoring can help to demonstrate reasons for various stakeholders to think more carefully about sustainability.

Chapter 3 examines the role of private sector organizations, which is taken to mean commercial companies. The motivations for companies to be more sustainable can be examined according to whether a company believes it has a responsibility to be more sustainable or not. If a company is convinced of its need to act responsibly, then monitoring is the means through which the company can makes its transition. However, the principled argument is not one that holds much ground with commercial organizations. From the time of Adam Smith through to Milton Friedman's seminal article on the social responsibility of business, actions beyond the legal minimum have been derided as economically inefficient and therefore irresponsible. Sustainability will be pursued where there is a financial reward for doing so and as such, the remainder of the chapter considers the role of the consumer, technology, public relations opportunities, pursuit of more efficient ways of working, and changes to market conditions all as potential reasons for companies to follow a sustainability transition. An area that has received little consideration within the tourism literature is the role of the financial industries such as pensions and insurance companies to influence the way their clients do business. Potentially this could have significant impacts on the tourism industry and so is introduced for further examination.

Chapter 4 considers a grouping of public sector bodies, which are government, NGOs and then local residents. In contrast to Chapter 3, the reasons why these bodies should want sustainability are more straightforward and have been heavily investigated, and so the chapter concentrates instead on how monitoring can help to facilitate the transition. Little attention has been paid to this in the tourism literature, so again examples come from outside tourism.

By the end of Chapters 3 and 4 the reader should be ready to move willingly to Chapters 5, 6 and 7, which explain the process of how indicators can be developed that will aid sustainability. If the reader is not convinced of the reasons to pursue sustainability, then the argument falters and the great sustainable tourism debate will show itself unsustainable after all.

Private Sector Drivers $\boxed{3}$

Introduction

The previous chapters have examined the context, evolution and issues related to sustainable development and sustainable tourism. Chapters 5, 6 and 7 demonstrate the significant practical and resource-based challenges to developing indicators and monitoring systems. In order to have the fortitude to face these challenges, a very strong case needs to be made for the need for sustainability and the contribution monitoring can make towards progress in this arena.

Chapters 3 and 4 should be considered collectively. They divide stakeholders, admittedly somewhat artificially, into public and private sector, with commercial industry, consumers and the finance industry described as private sector and government, residents and NGOs categorized as the public sector. The stakeholder groupings utilized are not important. What is important is the strength of the arguments, which resonate for the different stakeholder groups to promote sustainability and the role of monitoring in assisting with this process. In order to see why monitoring matters to the private sector, a key question relates to whether the reader feels businesses have any kind of moral or ethical responsibility to promote sustainability. If business does have such a responsibility, then monitoring is important to facilitate and assess progress towards sustainability. Alternatively, if the private sector cannot be held responsible, or only responds to sustainability when there is a profit motive involved, monitoring can demonstrate how issues beyond simply the economic can affect long-term business success.

The chapter begins, therefore, by asking if there is a moral responsibility for industry to be committed to greater sustainability, before moving on to examine the more instrumental, business case for why a company might promote sustainability. A key component of the business case for promoting sustainability is winning greater customer numbers and improving customer loyalty, the role of the consumer is given special attention. Finally, the example of the finance industry is used to show how the private sector can move towards greater sustainability. The financial sector is particularly reliant on information and monitoring is shown to be crucial if it is to fulfil its potential in terms of sustainability.

Consistent with the main themes of this book, the role of different private sector stakeholders is examined and an interdisciplinary approach is applied, looking at what the tourism industry can learn from efforts to apply sustainability to other areas.

Does Industry Have a Moral Responsibility to Promote Sustainability?

The Scottish philanthropist Andrew Carnegie argued that 'great power begets great responsibility' (Carnegie, 1889). Hertz (2001) uses this approach to argue that after government replaced the church as being the principle influence in people's lives, the world is now entering a third stage, whereby the corporate world has usurped the role of government and today has a greater influence on the lives of people than any other force. This 'silent takeover' is evidenced by the decline in political activism through party membership and more obviously through the declining numbers voting in national and regional elections.

In addition to falling political involvement, there has been a de-linking of organized labour and commerce, such that levels of unionism have fallen throughout the world, removing an important safety net for worker rights. Alongside this, commercial powers have grown. Stiglitz (2002) demonstrates how 51 of the largest economies in the world are corporate rather than national. Thus, Wal-Mart has a larger economy than does Pakistan, Exxon is bigger than the Czech Republic and General Motors has a larger economy than Hungary. Not only has there been a dramatic increase in the size of companies, but their reach has expanded. Yet, although companies have become more globalized, Korten (2001) calculates only 1% of the world's population can be said to have a consequential participation in corporate ownership, and as a result, global corporations have moved beyond the reach of the state, and ordinary people.

For Evan and Freeman (1993), it is not the size of the companies that provides the responsibility, but the effect business has on the lives of people. For a service industry like tourism, this aspect of the business is clear and should be well understood. Evan and Freeman (1993) follow the philosophy of Immanuel Kant to assert that business has a responsibility, otherwise it is guilty of treating humans simply as a resource and failing to recognize the human quality. Pheby (1997) goes further and argues business's responsibility comes from the opportunity it has to advance sustainability.

Whether the noted size and power of companies adds up to a moral responsibility is a question most famously addressed in the seminal article on the social responsibility of business by the Nobel Prize winning economist Milton Friedman in 1970. Friedman (1970, quoted in Hartman, 2000) explains, '. . . there is one and only one social responsibility of business – to use its resources and engage in activities designed to increase its profits so long as it stays within the rules of the game, which is to say, engages in open and free competition without deception or fraud'. Friedman's argument has two elements, first that a corporation cannot have a conscience and so cannot be held to be morally responsible. Increasingly, nations are introducing laws that embody companies with the same rights and responsibilities as individuals, and although many of these laws are proving difficult to operationalize this is the less convincing of Friedman's two arguments and is addressed in Box 3.1, while a brief excerpt from John Steinbeck's famous novel *The Grapes of Wrath* is enclosed in Box 3.2.

Friedman's second argument asserts companies should not be held responsible to society and instead business's only responsibility is to maximize the long-term profits for shareholders. These arguments have shown themselves to be so fundamental to capitalism and the topic of corporate responsibility that they will be used here as the framework for the following discussion of whether industry can be said to hold a moral responsibility to promote sustainability.

Box 3.1. Can a corporation have a conscience?

As corporations are not human, Friedman argues they can have no intentions and as such, cannot be held responsible for their actions. To bring a legal challenge under criminal law against an individual, it is necessary to show that there was a guilty intention in the party. To recreate this for an organization it has been necessary to remove the corporate veil and embody the organization, making the CEO as the brain of the organization responsible for the actions of the corporate body. It is the difficulty of establishing the intentions of the CEO that has proven to be the weakness of corporate manslaughter laws in bringing any prosecution through criminal law, although the legal cases brought against senior managers in the wake of the Enron collapse perhaps provide some evidence of progress. Friedman dismisses the argument of a corporeal corporation as irrelevant because it is still impossible to punish companies for their behaviour, instead only the people within them. Companies cannot be put in prison, have rights denied to them or even be physically hurt. The punishment that companies typically receive is financial, and this is a punishment of shareholders, employees and customers rather than the company itself.

Box 3.2. *The Grapes of Wrath.*

In John Steinbeck's novel, *The Grapes of Wrath*, the banks that foreclose on money owed by farmers are likened to machines and monsters. Explaining the position of the bank to the assembled group of Oklahoman farmers, Steinbeck writes (2000, p. 35):

> We're sorry. It's not us. It's the monster. The bank isn't like a man.

> Yes, but the bank is only made of men.

> No, you're quite wrong there – quite wrong there. The bank is something else than men. It happens that every man in a bank hates what the bank does, and yet the bank does it. The bank is something more than men. I tell you. It's the monster. Men made it, but they can't control it.

Source: Steinbeck (2000).

In response to the position explained in Box 3.1, Goodpaster and Mathews (1982) assert that companies are more than the sum of their parts, and not simply a collection of people and physical resources. If an organization were simply a collection of people and things, then it would be sufficient to appeal to the moral responsibility of individuals. However, the gap between the morals shown by people as individuals as compared to when they are being employees demonstrates the different pressures and so the effect of a corporation on the parts of an organization. This is the difference that Goodpaster and Mathews (1982, p. 40) believe is why organizations can be held responsible, stating, '. . . an organization reveals its character as surely as a person does'.

Friedman cites a number of reasons to support this thesis that business should not be held responsible to do more than maximize long-term profits for the shareholders of the business. First, Friedman argues that the business does not belong to those who are managing the business, instead they are the agents of the true owners, the shareholders. The managers hold a 'promissory arrangement', with the shareholders to maximize returns to the shareholders. Where managers do not seek to maximize profits then they are guilty of stealing the money of shareholders and of being inefficient with the resources of society, as they are not put to optimum use. Worse, where companies do exhibit social responsibility, they are threatening the competitive position of the organization, shareholder's returns, jobs of employees and contracts of suppliers.

Hence, Friedman adopts a very narrow view of to whom a company is responsible and then a narrow view of what it is that shareholders want from the companies in which they are invested. Further, Friedman ignores companies without shareholders and in so doing does not consider the case of small and medium-sized enterprise (SME) or private companies, which make up the majority of the tourism industry. By excluding SMEs from his analysis, Friedman feeds the misunderstanding that SMEs are necessarily more responsible in their behaviour than larger organizations.

Friedman's second main criticism of why business should not be held morally responsible to promote sustainability in society is that business leaders are not elected by society and so cannot be said to know what society wants. Business people do not have a democratic mandate, they cannot be voted out if their actions prove to be unpopular and it is therefore the role of politicians in government to determine social policy. With specific reference to the natural environment, Bowie (1990, p. 89) agrees with Friedman but then goes further, 'Business does not have a responsibility to protect the environment over and above what is required by law; however it does have a moral obligation to avoid intervening in the political arena in order to defeat or weaken environmental legislation'. Hence, it can be argued that if companies involve themselves in the social policy arena to secure more favourable business terms, then it is reasonable to hold business responsible for the consequences. Logically, if business genuinely feels it cannot be held responsible for promoting sustainability because it is not elected by society, then it should not seek to influence legislation.

A continuation of this argument is that business does not feel qualified to make social policy decisions. In its annual statement, British Petroleum (BP) (2004, p. 32) accepts it has, '. . . a role to play as a corporate citizen, but not necessarily the . . . expertise to act alone'. Friedman believes managers are skilled at running a business and generating profits, but are not anthropologists, environmental scientists or economists. As such, Friedman concurs with another famous economist, Adam Smith that businesses should be left to make profits and innovate, because this is what they do best and this is what their optimum role in society is. To counter this position, Andrews (1980, p. 99) opines, 'The business firm, as an organic entity intricately affected by and affecting its environment, is as appropriately adaptive . . . to demands for responsible behaviour as for economic service'. Hoffman (2002, p. 717) agrees, 'Corporations have special knowledge, expertise and resources which are invaluable in dealing with the environmental crisis'. Hence, being able to run a business is not a disqualification from being able to influence social policy. Indeed, as consumers, we continually make decisions about the nutritional quality of food, or the impact of a purchase, we are not qualified to make. Further, the belief that managers need to be qualified to make a decision does presuppose that all other management decisions are based on evidence and qualified opinions.

If business claims it is not qualified to become involved in sustainability, the assumption is that industry is not currently making decisions that affect society. Or worse, that industry can somehow choose to be apart from society and that business can opt in or opt out of ethics. De George (1978, p. 49) is passionate that a non-decision about ethics is still a decision, he declares:

> The wags who wink at immorality in business, arguing that ethics and business
> are two separate spheres and never the twain shall meet, are short-sighted and
> look only as far as the last line of their financial statements. Society is larger
> than that; business is part of society; and ethics has as much a place in
> business as in any other part of social life. When all members of society realize
> that fact and act accordingly, society will be that much better off.

Aside from any sense of moral responsibility, simply the size of industry and
its prominence in daily life, means the leadership organizations provide is
central in setting the ethical climate for society. Indeed, if organizations are
not to be held responsible, then it is difficult to resist claims that any other
organization, or member of society should be.

The last point Friedman makes strikes to the complexity of the debate
over sustainability and corporate social responsibility. Friedman argues that
companies have always looked after the interests of their suppliers, employ-
ers, customers as well as the shareholders they are mandated to consider,
because this makes good business sense. Friedman does not encourage
short-term over long-term profits, and would support a pay rise for employees if this meant an increase in employee retention, productivity and a
reduction in recruitment costs. Similarly, an expensive and ongoing campaign to clean up a beach would be supported if it generated greater
long-term benefits for the company than it cost. As such, decisions based on
the principle of promoting sustainability could produce the same response
as decisions based on the outcomes, which might decide to support sustainability because it is ultimately in the long-term shareholder interest.
Box 3.3 briefly dips into ethical theory to differentiate between principles
and outcomes-based decisions as the implications of this distinction are
important for the question of whether industry will support efforts to
develop indicators of sustainable tourism.

Updating Friedman (1970), Bowie points to a trend away from the
Kantian perspective of ethics and towards a position where ethics are considered only when they can produce greater profits (Bowie, 2002). He cites
the increase in the number of US companies calculating the benefit
accrued from their charitable donations, rather than just giving money to
charity because it is felt to be the right thing to do. Thus, ethics are seen
not to have an intrinsic value, but are attractive because of their extrinsic
worth. In a tourism context, Wheeller has argued that we support sustainable
tourism because it makes us feel better – not because of a philanthropic concern for the environment and so there is no such thing as pure altruism
(Wheeller, 1993, p. 128). In fact, he says ecotourism's impotence is its main
attraction calling it 'the perfect political fob, it soothes consciences,
demands no sacrifices and allows extended holiday choice while providing
an ideal shield, doubling as a marketing ploy, for the tourism industry'.

The business case to adopt a more sustainable agenda is discussed
below, as this is increasingly the argument that resonates with the private
sector. However, the danger in accepting entirely the business case for

> **Box 3.3.** Principles or pragmatism.
>
> Chyryssides and Kaler (1993, p. 232) state, 'What defines social responsibility is not the exclusion of profit as an outcome, but its exclusion as a motive: the fact that when an act is done simply as a means to the end of profit it is not then an act of business social responsibility'. This position adopts a deontological perspective, one typified by a sense of duty, rights and principles, influenced by the writings of the German philosopher Immanuel Kant. A deontological approach enjoys a rich historical legacy, dating back to philosophers such as Socrates. Deontology is concerned with the idea of universal truths and principles, which should be adhered to regardless of the circumstances. Kant's categorical imperative states that a person faced with a problem should be able to respond consistently and in conformity with their moral principles and also feel comfortable with the decision being made in full view of others.
>
> An alternative, teleological view can be understood as 'consequentialism' following from the philosophical work of Jeremy Bentham and John Stuart Mill on utilitarianism. Decisions are made in view of expected outcomes, which eliminate the universality of decisions and subordinates principles to context. The outcome may be the same as that taken by a deontologist, but the reasoning would not be made on the basis of principle, but because this was the most expedient decision. A common expression for the two approaches would be that deontology places the means as more important than the end, while for teleology it is the end that justifies the means.

sustainable development is that should there be a shift in economic trends, then the business case may disappear, or at least weaken, and the progress made will also disappear. The fundamental question of whether business has a moral responsibility to promote sustainability does not weaken or diminish according to the economic climate. It is easy to dismiss this theorizing as unrealistic and naïve of the business world, but if we accept that business operates within a society of people and not just for business's sake, then as De George (1978) argues, it is business who should listen to the wishes of people, rather than people accepting the position of business. The next part of this chapter explores the value of consumer involvement, while Chapter 4 discusses the value of local community involvement in sustainable tourism, enabling a business to understand what it is that society wants assistance from industry to sustain.

Is There a Business Case for Sustainability?

If businesses do not accept a moral responsibility to promote sustainability, then monitoring can assist by demonstrating reasons for businesses to be interested in sustainability. One of the most important contributors to the business case for sustainable development has been the World Business Council for Sustainable Development (WBCSD), formed by some of the largest companies in the world just prior to the Rio Earth Summit in 1992. The WBCSD are in no doubt as to the basic mechanism through which sustainable development should be promoted, the moral argument is immediately dispensed with, commercial reasons cited, and the market becomes the tool through which to promote sustainability. The business approach to promoting sustainability is to tie the commercial interests of business to the goals of society. This can be done through technological development, public relations benefits, cost savings and improving the market conditions, discussed below. However, perhaps the reason most commonly cited for business to adopt a more sustainable agenda is consumer demand, this is discussed first.

Consumers

There is a long tradition in Europe of consumers applying pressure to companies to change their practices, amongst the earliest being a consumer campaign in the UK organized by Elizabeth Hayrick in the 1790s against the 'blood-stained luxury' of sugar produced and imported using slavery. This campaign led to the East India Company supplying sugar grown in plantations without slavery, and then formed the basis of the anti-slavery movement, which ultimately led to the abolition of the slave trade within the colonies in 1807 (Hilton and Gibbons, 2002, p. 53). More recently, companies became the object of criticism, not because they were necessarily the cause of the problem, merely an example of them. South African companies have been targeted for boycott during the apartheid regime, French wine boycotted during that country's nuclear testing in the South Pacific and Burma avoided by many travellers as a result of their human rights record.

Cowe and Williams (2001) argue that the loss of trust amongst consumers in business, coupled with the rise in power of companies (as discussed earlier by Hertz, 2001) has been behind the increased attention and vigilance paid by consumers towards the behaviour of business in general and has singled out specific companies for attention.

The New Economics Foundation (NEF, 2001) has devised a shopping basket of ethical products and so tracks the growth of purchases for these products and markets in the UK. There is an enormous range in the market penetration of products, and these will of course, vary from country to country. In the UK, organic foods and fair trade products have received significant attention in the media (particularly since 'mad cow' and then foot-and-mouth disease), but still only occupy around 1% of the total food market. Specific products, such as free-range eggs, have achieved a much higher level of success, and the Freedom Food eggs have more than 20% of the market (Cowe and Williams, 2001). Other products, such as unleaded petrol and recycled paper have been able very quickly to achieve a dominant position in the market, through the assistance of tax incentives and regulation, creating a template for how to bring new fuels and products to the marketplace more quickly in the future. Tourism is identified as an industry where there is potential for significant increase in ethical consumption, although progress to date has been slow and inconsistent (NEF, 2001). One of the brightest lights of the ethical consumerism movement appears to be the expansion of ethical pension policies, mortgages, shares and other financial products, which will be discussed in the following section. Business in the Community (BITC, 2003) estimate the total value of ethical consumption in the UK in 2003 was over £19 billion and growing rapidly, the majority of which is food and financial services (Box 3.4).

The evidence presented demonstrates that consumers are beginning to provide an opportunity in the products they consume, but in terms of responsibility Bowie (2002, p. 718) argues, 'If we as consumers are willing to accept the harm done to the environment by favouring environmentally

---

Box 3.4. Who are ethical consumers?

Cowe and Williams (2001) arrange UK consumers into five groups, based on their purchasing behaviour. The study included qualitative research and a quantitative survey of 2000 people; it was conducted for the Co-operative Bank by MORI in 2000.

- 'Do what I can' (49%). This group can be described as the average citizen, they are older, less likely to live in London and do not hold ethical concerns particularly strongly. This group do not feel that they can influence business as consumers.
- 'Look after my own' (22%). A young group, urbanized, unmarried, low-income, tabloid reader. Members of this group are most likely to be unemployed and least likely to be trade union members. This group is the least concerned with ethical issues and do not feel empowered as consumers.
- 'Conscientious consumers' (18%). Car owners, share owners and home owners. Concerned about ethical issues, particularly the treatment of workers and environmental impact. Will look for information on ethical products, will recycle and buy recycled products as well as Fair Trade products. This group do not lead the ethical consumerist movement, but they are aware of it and participate in the more obvious examples.
- 'Brand generation' (6%). This group is consumerist in that it is most concerned with brand names, product quality and value for money. They exhibit little ethical concern, but do recycle and have secondary concerns about worker treatment and environmental matters.
- 'Global watchdogs' (5%). The most affluent group, middle-aged, professionals, left-wing politics. This group feels empowered as consumers, but wants more information in order to make decisions. This group is the most active in ethical consumerism and takes the lead in looking for an ethical label ahead of any purchase; the group is happy to boycott a product or company.

Source: Cowe and Williams (2001).

unfriendly products, corporations have no moral obligation to change so long as they obey environmental laws'. Adam Smith and other neo-classical economists would argue that consumers are being responsible by pursuing their own self-interests, for it is in this way that the resources of society are put to optimum use. Hardin (1968, p. 1244) disagrees that the benefits of society are best served by addressing our own individual desires, stating firmly, 'Ruin is the destination towards which all men rush, each pursuing his own best interest in a society that believes in the freedom of the commons. Freedom in a commons brings ruin to all.' If consumers act in their own self-interest, then the consumer can be seen to be behaving in the same instrumentalist manner as corporations, consuming products that meet needs to assuage guilt, or meet other social needs, rather than feeling morally compelled to purchase one product over another. In which case, the company, as a reflection of the actions and desires and ethics of consumers, is mirroring our own behaviour.

Galbraith (1972) discussing his 'accepted sequence', initially argued producers simply responded to the wishes of the consumer and so the power in the relationship rested with consumers. Klein's (1999) thesis is that consumers have been able to preserve consumer sovereignty in the face of enormous expansion in size and scope by business. Klein argues that as corporations have moved away from manufacturing and towards a more service-based business model, where corporations add value to products made by others, so these corporations have revealed their Achilles heel, the need to preserve the brand and corporate reputation. In a world with global communication, the brand has revealed itself to be far more vulnerable to attack than distant factories would be.

Crane and Matten (2004, p. 291) believe consumer sovereignty represents an opportunity for the consumer to promote sustainability, as '. . . the corporation begins to act as a conduit for the exercise of consumers' political rights as a citizen'. Hertz (2001, p. 190) continues this theme, 'Instead of showing up at the voting booth to register their demands and wants, people are turning to corporations. The most effective way to be political today is not to cast your vote at the ballot box but to do so at the supermarket or at a shareholder's meeting. Why? Because corporations respond.'

Corporations may well respond more quickly than governments, and respond in accordance with the wishes of consumers, but does this promote sustainability? Doorne (2000) questions the implications of consumer sovereignty for the self-determination of local residents and destinations in tourism in New Zealand. Indeed, even where consumers are convinced of the personal benefits of sustainability and become minded to encourage a genuinely more sustainable agenda, there is a good possibility they may be unsure of what this means or how to bring it about and may, unknowingly, worsen the situation. If, for example, tourists mistakenly see sustainability as connected with elitism and anything but mass tourism, then this may be the direction the industry is encouraged to take. The confusion amongst an academic audience as to what really is sustainability is portentous for what consumers might understand by the term. Within the tourism industry, Miller (2001b) has described this position of assumed consumer sovereignty as one where the tour operators are 'contentedly constrained', effectively absolved of responsibility and willing to be led by the wishes of the consumer, wherever they may take the industry.

Tourists' 'domain' of interest (Smith, 1990) may extend beyond matters that affect them personally, or they may rest with matters central to their holiday. Wheeller (1994b) has long extolled the anthropomorphic hypocrisies of our interests in protecting some animals, but not others, while Miller (2003) showed that consumers professed an interest in social issues ahead of environmental concerns. Yet, this is the danger of a scenario where purchases become the equivalent of votes for social policy, the equivalent of a *Big Brother/Pop Idol* culture where we vote for the 'survival' of a destination or species through its value to the market rather than its intrinsic right to exist. Totemic causes are protected, the whale saved, dolphins protected from tuna fishermen, without any understanding of the value of these species or causes, relative to other, less photogenic ones. If we accept the market as a great arbiter of understanding, a Delphic oracle of the modern day, deny thoughts about principles of right and wrong but trust instead that the market will determine what is right, then we must accept the consequences of the market, as surely as do the farmers in John Steinbeck's novel. The real danger with ethical consumerism is that it risks trivializing and cherry-picking issues of global sustainability to actions we can take whilst shopping – the contrary of a comprehensive and integrated approach, which can in turn lead to gaps and 'free riders'.

Advocates of sustainable consumption would claim this approach reinforces the message of sustainability at a time when we are shopping and so are relaxed and receptive to information. Yet, there is a lack of evidence of consumer sovereignty in the tourism industry. Smith (1990, p. 35) believes, '. . . consumers are not sovereign, but one can refer to a degree of sovereignty, enhanced by choice, information and possibly retailer assessment; but restricted by limitations on competition, actions by the state, and individual wealth'. If the tourism consumer does represent an opportunity to promote sustainability, then it is necessary for greater choice, information and disclosure about the impacts of the product and a drastically improved contribution from the retailer.

Further, the 'inseparability' of production and consumption increases the physical proximity of tourists to the consequences of their consumption decisions and should serve to reduce the difference between what tourists say they are interested in and what they take action about. Cowe and Williams (2001) describe this as the 30:3 rule, whereby 30% of consumers who state their interest in ethical consumption, will result in 3% of the market share. Tourists, choosing a hotel with poor hygiene standards or badly treated staff are more immediately and obviously affected by the impacts of their purchase decisions. This is unlike the purchase of a pair of running shoes, or a football, where the physical separation of production and consumption is greater. As such, it is perhaps reasonable to expect a higher ratio of activist consumerism in tourism than many other industries. However, Hjalager (1999, p. 16) concludes, 'Radical expressions of consumerism have not yet invaded the field of tourism. Consumerism is hampered by the lack of targeted information on both the consumer and the producer side of the market.'

This position accords with research by Miller (2003) and Tearfund (2002) showing that tourists hold industry responsible for the provision of more information. Encouragingly, the WBCSD (2002, p. 231) recognize the active role business needs to play in the provision of information, stating 'If business believes in a free market where people have choices, business should accept responsibility for informing consumers about the social and environmental effects of these choices'. Perfect information is the perfect market regulator, but any such information needs to be based on a strong monitoring programme, lest the information is discredited, trust in business further reduced and the consumer either looks elsewhere for information, or stops looking. Commensurately, information needs to be accepted fairly by stakeholder groups and not manipulated for other goals; Chapter 4 discusses the role of NGOs in empowering communities through the dissemination of accurate information.

Technological development

Innovation is central to the future of business, and as such is an appealing way for business to attempt to promote sustainability. Hence, organizations continually need to develop new, better ways to perform the tasks of old, and to bring added and desired value to the consumer. Such a situation is obvious in the search amongst many island destinations for ways to differentiate their tourism products without needing to compete exclusively on prices. If the consumer has an unmet need for products making a contribution to sustainability, then this may be one area where innovation can focus. Alternatively, reducing physical inputs into the product will reduce costs and so prices for the consumer, which will always be desired.

However, while technological development may be cited as a key way for business to promote sustainability (*The Economist*, 2002), the potential available for companies does not disguise the potential limitations of this approach at a broader level. Ekins (2002) uses the Commoner–Ehrlich equation (Box 3.5) to demonstrate the extent of any technological improvements in order to move significantly towards sustainability. This model adopts an entirely linear approach, so the impact may be much greater or much less than shown. In this respect the equation is of little value, but it does demonstrate, even by a linear estimation which ignores

---

Box 3.5. Benefits of technology.

Simplistically, if the environmental impact (*I*) created in the world is a function of the amount of people (*P*), the amount they consume (*C*) and the technology available to manage these impacts (*T*) then we can show

$$I = P \times C \times T$$

where *I* = environmental impact (e.g. tonnes of emissions); *P* = population; *C* = consumption (e.g. spending per head); *T* = technology available.

Source: Ekins (2002).

---

unexpected variations, the size of the challenge for any hoped for technological solutions.

Ekins (2002) shows that by 2050, if the population doubles and consumption quadruples (2–3% per annum), then technology must reduce impacts by a factor of 16 in order for the impact to halve, as required to make a meaningful movement towards sustainability. Within today's dominant business ethic, this will need to be accomplished through more efficient use of resources, the substitution between resources (abundant for scarce, renewable for non-renewable), a reduction of emissions or change from harmful to benign production processes and a change in the structure of production or consumption. What the current ethic does not entertain is a reduction in the amount of production or consumption. This leads Carmen and Lubelski (1997, p. 29) to comment, '. . . even if every company on the planet were to adopt the best environmental practices of the leading companies such as The Body Shop, Patagonia or 3M, the world would still be moving towards sure degradation and collapse'. More dryly Daly (1973, p. 19) observes, '. . . while technology will continue to pull rabbits out of hats, it will not pull an elephant out of a hat – much less an infinite series of ever-larger elephants!'

Beyond innovation at the product level, there is innovation at the market level that may be appealing to business. Principal amongst these developments is the nascent market for carbon emissions permits, an information intensive market, which *The Economist* (1999) predicts may become the next trillion dollar industry and Sommerville believes could form the basis of a global currency within the next 50 years (Sommerville, 2004, personal communication). Under this proposal, companies would be allowed to produce a given amount of emissions per year, and would need to secure additional permits to pollute beyond this. The hope for this scheme is that companies will be allowed to trade their emissions in the same way that other resources are traded, providing an incentive for companies to reduce their pollution and so be able to sell unused permits to those companies who are either unable or unwilling to reduce their pollution levels below those permitted. BP (2004) is a strong advocate of this approach, as are other major companies, reflecting the preference of business for the problem to be addressed through the market, rather than with legislation limiting pollution levels. However, the appeal of this approach for the markets does not necessarily reflect its efficacy in tackling sustainability. Any successful market will be dependent on effective monitoring of emissions to assess the size of the challenge in order to determine the number of permits to be issued. Monitoring emissions will thus provide a market reason for companies to pursue sustainability, and can then provide information on the areas in which companies can become more sustainable.

Public relations benefits

A frequently heard criticism of corporate responsibility by companies is that it is all just a publicity exercise with no real substance behind the message. Sternberg (1995) draws distinction between the internal actions of a company, designed to achieve improvements, and those external actions, designed to raise profile and gain customers, whereas Wilson (2000) is critical of '. . . the continuing tendency of PR to impose and promote cosmetic solutions instead of the management producing real solutions'.

The Association of British Insurers (ABI) argues that it is not the absolute level of actions taken, but the imbalance of actions and communications that risks undermining the good work more earnest companies are undertaking (ABI, 2001). Monitoring can effectively address this issue, enabling companies to determine the extent of any claims to make. A company can adopt Friedman's approach to business through profit maximization, but if they feel sustainability is not important to them, then following the ABI approach, they should not profess to support it. By contrast, a company that does make stringent efforts to promote sustainability may feel justified in highlighting its efforts. Hudson and Miller (2004a) showed the danger of this when a Canadian heli-skiing company had previously been advised to advertise its environmental credentials to a greater extent, but in doing so, had brought itself to the attention of local environmental charities, who previously had not been aware of the basic business activities of heli-skiing. Once a company has raised its head above the parapet it is not possible to retreat. Companies like Body Shop have traded on their heightened ethical stance and in so doing have made themselves a target for investigative journalists and NGOs. Christian Aid (2004) draw distinctions between the stated Corporate Social Responsibility (CSR) positions of Shell, Coca-Cola and British American Tobacco and their actual activities in the Niger Delta, India and Kenya, respectively. Rigby (2004) focuses attention on the standard practice of evading as much tax as possible, but having a CSR policy that contributes back only a fraction of the money directed away from government. The investigation of such inconsistencies between missions and behaviour is a fertile area of research for tourism academics. Box 3.6 shows the potential imbalances that can exist but is not able to hypothesize what the likely proportions of tourism organizations within each category might be.

An interesting anomaly to this model, Hartman (2002) cites the example of the US outdoor clothing company Patagonia, that refuses to trade on their strong sustainability credentials because through monitoring their own manufacturing process they acknowledge everything they make causes some pollution and so they cannot claim to be entirely sustainable. While this is a noble, modest and honest recognition of the effect of business, it does also cost sustainability an exemplar, a champion in business, who could encourage less active companies to become more so. Here, adopting a strict definition of sustainability risks removing the concept from public awareness and so destroying the reason many more instrumental companies are taking any actions at all.

Yet, earlier research by Miller (2001b) showed that it was not so much the carrot of market advantage that encouraged tourism companies to adopt a more sustainable agenda, but the stick of being exposed as a laggard in the industry to consumers and peers, which would threaten corporate reputation. Indeed, it can be argued that the drive for further professional recognition of the tourism industry has been one reason behind attempts to improve the sustainability of the industry and to 'prove' efforts made. Linked with this is the ability to rebut attempts for greater legislative involvement in an industry if it appears to be able to demonstrate it keeps its own 'house in order'.

Ecoefficiency

The fourth area where monitoring matters in convincing business that it can benefit from promoting sustainability, is in terms of cost savings. This is an area where monitoring programmes established by organizations like the International Hotels Environment Initiative (IHEI) have made significant contributions. Three issues for business to concentrate on are: first, to increase efficiencies in operations in order to reduce waste, perhaps through the use of information technology to assist with resource use. Secondly, to re-valorize by-products and move towards a zero waste target, examples of this include the selling of waste products as natural fertilizers for farmers, although attention needs to be paid to the form of inputs required for this to happen. This approach draws on the analogy of an ecosystem whereby an output from one process becomes an input to the next, and is referred to as closing production loops. The third approach is the least explored, but shifts attention from end-of-pipe, to the beginning of the production process as the aim is to innovate new products which are less consumptive of resources (WBCSD, 2001).

Frankel (2001) is critical of this cost-saving approach to sustainability, comparing such companies to Janus, the Roman God with two faces

Box 3.6. A model for responsible marketing.

		Environmental communication Measured by analysis of brochures, newsletters, websites, company reports, press releases, signs and awards	
Environmentally responsible behaviour Measured by analysing • Environmental policy • Policy on wildlife • Policy on vegetation • Waste management • Fuel management • Energy and recycling • Forest harvesting • Education and training • Community relations • Research and knowledge		*Low*	*High*
	Low	*Inactive* No support of involvement from top management Environmental management not necessary No environment reporting No employee environmental training or involvement	*Exploitive* Some involvement of top management Environmental issues dealt with only when necessary External reporting but no internal reporting Little employee training or involvement
	High	*Reactive* Some involvement of top management Environmental management is a worthwhile function Internal reporting, but no external reporting Some employee environmental training or involvement	*Proactive* Top management involved in environmental issues Environmental management is a priority issue Regular internal and external reporting, including environmental plan or report Employee environmental training or involvement encouraged

Source: Hudson and Miller (2004a).

looking in opposite directions. Frankel cites the example of Wal-Mart, which has several 'ecostores' in addition to its vast number of normal stores. Yet, he claims the new stores do not address the social damage Wal-Mart causes by apparently driving out diversity from local shops, undermining the sense of community or obliging people to drive to out-of-town developments. The pressure to keep prices lower is aided by Wal-Mart's eco-efficiency, but Frankel (2001) argues any reductions do not offset the externalities of the store on a wider basis. Although Wal-Mart's monitoring of these new stores versus its normal stores will show the environmental improvement, monitoring over an expanded range of indicators would identify the social and economic impact it can cause. If Wal-Mart is convinced of the PR benefits, cost savings, technological developments or consumer preference for adopting social and economic sustainability, then developing a monitoring programme can reveal priority areas to address. If implemented on an ongoing basis with consistent monitoring, stakeholder involvement and social learning, this process could be considered an example of corporate adaptive management, whereby a variety of ecofriendly products are piloted, monitored, and adjustments made to the way the firm operates on the basis of lessons learned. The danger comes that in the pursuit of efficiency in the detail of operation, the big issues such as treatment of employees, siting of development, or the provision and maintenance of adequate infrastructure is overlooked. Again, care needs to avoid piecemeal treatment of sustainability issues.

Improve market conditions

ABI feels that companies pursuing unsustainable practices threaten the long-term financial success of businesses and so weaken the performance of the insurance industry for its members. ABI therefore argues for improved market conditions by standing against monopolies, subsidies, corruption and for greater transparency, accountability and reliability in markets. The WBCSD (2001) state:

> Markets, like democracies, only function properly if there are governance mechanisms in place to ensure high levels of transparency. For transparency combined with timely information enforces market discipline and contributes to accountability and integrity within the market system. Transparency helps the market work for all, not just the few.

Monitoring matters to business through providing data about the performance and behaviour of companies in order for the overall market conditions to be improved.

Pedelty (2004) believes

> . . . all large UK businesses ought to be mandated to report on their ethical and environmental performance; this would significantly enhance the ability

of a wide range of stakeholders to effectively compare the performance of
business. The provision of such information would also allow capital,
consumer and labour markets to function more efficiently.

The WBCSD (2001) recognize that, '. . . before companies can make the
case that sustainable development is good for business, they must be able to
measure performance . . . this is a vital step if sustainable development
performance . . . is to become synonymous with shareholder value'. Thus,
the provision of information is a key element in the push for more sustainability through the market. Yet, beyond the need for information for
businesses to make decisions, there is the need for information at a higher
level in order to assess the contribution business is making to society. Such
information would demonstrate whether the current business ethic of promoting sustainability through the market is sufficient, or if there is a need
to move to a more stringent ethic where consumption patterns are over-
hauled rather than simply reducing inputs.

As a result of improved data, businesses are increasingly recognizing
the financial benefits to be had from adopting a more sustainable approach,
but a lot more remains to be done in this area to reveal to companies the
areas where their efforts need to be focused. Wilson (2000) concludes,
'. . . the business case is overwhelming and supplements the moral case'.
Reidenbach and Robin (1990) and Miller (2001b) suggest there is evidence
of the moral argument holding some sway in business, but this is in only the
minority of cases. As a consequence, where sustainability is pursued, it is
predominantly for business reasons. Roddick describes the tourism industry as being at least 10 years behind other industries even in this respect
(Roddick, 2004). One sector that has made promising steps towards
sustainability is the finance industry. The efforts made by financial businesses are examined here in the hope that tourism may be able to learn
from the experience and that pressure may be brought to bear on tourism
by the financial industries to encourage it to take greater and more productive steps towards sustainability.

The Role of the Finance Industry in Promoting Sustainability

Horizontal integration makes definitions difficult, but the financial industry is loosely defined as pension funds, banks and insurance companies,
and has not previously enjoyed a reputation for being the most ardent of
supporters for sustainability. Indeed, being strongly supportive of the Fried-
man-esque position on corporate responsibility, only the most instrumental
reasons would be sufficient to move the financial industries to promote
sustainability. The legal position has always encouraged pension fund managers to optimize the return, although the Cadbury Report (1992) and the
recent Terrorism Act (2000) in the UK have strengthened the transparency
requirements for reporting. The consequences of any shift in focus away

from simply profit maximization are potentially enormous, not just for the financial sector but on all other industries directly or indirectly reliant on the sector, including tourism. The Federation of Tour Operators (FTO) representing the very largest tour operators in the UK has acknowledged the need for the tourism industry to do more to promote corporate responsibility, not in response to retail consumer pressure, but the institutional consumer in the shape of the investment community.

To give some idea of the value of investment funds, the world's largest funds are the Norwegian Petroleum Fund (NPF, 2004), thought to be worth around €115 billion, the Californian pension fund for public employees (Calpers, 2004), which is worth an estimated €135 billion, and the pension fund for public sector employees in the Netherlands (ABP, 2004), worth €157 billion. These funds are amassed from either the monthly payments of workers into their pension plans, or in the case of the NPF, from the revenues collected from oil reserves and invested for the future prosperity of the country. Such an amount of money clearly gives these funds enormous influence over the companies they do or do not invest in, and the basis on which they decide to remain invested in. Crane and Matten (2004) report on the controversy caused when it was established that the NPF had been investing in a Singaporean company that developed antipersonnel mines, despite Norway being a driving force in the prohibition of landmines in 1997, even awarding a Nobel prize to one of the principals of the movement. Further investigation uncovered NPF was invested in companies engaged in child and slave labour, genetic engineering, producers of cluster and nuclear bombs, rainforest exploitation as well as companies supporting the regimes in Burma and Sudan – almost everything to which the Norwegian government was officially opposed. This led to an impassioned public discussion over whether such funds should be used to push Norway's view of the world, or instead to simply generate funds for the future of the country.

The main reason why institutional investors are increasingly seeking to be involved with promoting sustainability is the putative improved financial performance of the company. In a turbulent environment, companies that manage risk will show themselves to be more successful in the long term. The assumption is that we live in a turbulent environment and so the approach companies are taking is one of risk management. Expanding the parameters of investigation will enable companies to identify a greater range of uncertainties and so help them to prepare adequately for change and prolong productive states (see Holling's adaptive cycle in Chapter 1). Evidence abounds of companies such as Nike, Shell and Monsanto that failed to identify aspects of their business as being of major importance to consumers, with the consequent boycott of products and significant impacts on their share prices. The problem exists then in determining how far back along its supply chain a company needs to explore and to take corrective action over any problems discovered (see Chapter 11).

Knowledge of complex systems helps us to understand that such change and turbulence is inevitable, and the best that can be done is to be informed and monitor continuously so that the company is not surprised by unexpected events and is instead in a position to take advantage of post-crisis situations. Klein (1999) believes the anonymity of companies without a retail presence affords them the luxury of paying less regard to social issues. However, the insurance industry as a business-to-business sector over the 10 years prior to 2000, calculates that climate change has cost it over $400 billion (*The Economist*, 2000). Clearly, the insurance industry has ignored the effects of climate change on its business, to the ultimate detriment of its shareholders. The insurance industry is now adopting an increased presence in the study of climate change and by being more aware of the impacts of the environment on business performance, it has given added weight to the use of tools such as Environmental Impact Assessments (EIA), environmental auditing and indicator development, which seek to identify in advance potential future problems facing the companies it insures. While this can be seen as a very instrumental reason to conduct EIAs, if companies cannot achieve insurance cover without demonstrating their sustainability awareness, then sustainability will receive an enormous boost.

Faulkner (2001) identifies how, for many parts of the tourism industry, such as those operating in remote, fragile environments, the threat of disaster is much higher, so the need to manage risk and uncertainty will become more pressing. If the industry fails to monitor and manage its risks to the point that it causes the insurance industry to make significant payouts, then there will likely be significant financial pressures applied in the future.

This need to avoid disaster is consistent with the established key to investing profitably over the long term on the stock market, which is not to try to keep identifying the next Microsoft, but to keep avoiding the next Enron. As such, sustainability fits well with the aims of institutional investors, which is to secure a long-term, stable profit. Prestbo (2000) explains, 'Companies pursuing growth in the triple bottom line tend to display superior stock-market performances with favourable risk/return profiles. Thus, sustainability becomes a proxy for enlightened and disciplined management.' Such an approach cannot be infallible, but the aim is that there are fewer shocks for investors. There is a premium paid by those seeking to buy shares in companies known to be able to produce a regular and stable profit. Indeed, such companies will form the core of any share portfolio (ABI, 2001). Hence, such companies will consequently benefit from a higher demand for their shares and so a higher share price. A higher share price will not only deter rival takeover bids, but it can provide a company with greater access to capital through further share issues.

The belief that companies who address their sustainability issues outperform those companies that do not is difficult to assess because of the confounding factors present in any analysis. However, the development of investment funds concentrating on companies that meet definitions of being socially responsible does provide a measure by which the performance of companies can be assessed. Funds can be referred to as 'single-issue' funds, and have traditionally applied negative filters/screens such as no tobacco, or no apartheid, or no military arms (the so-called 'sin stocks') seeking to exclude the worst companies rather than reward the best. More recent funds have moved beyond a single issue to include a range of issues for consideration and added the application of positive criteria such as whether a company has implemented a CSR policy or whether it actively pursues sustainability. Such funds have become known as Socially Responsible Investment (SRI) funds. In the USA, $2.34 trillion was invested in SRI funds in 2001, representing $1 in every $8 invested, although the stringency of screening is open to question. In Europe, the market is smaller, with institutional shareholders holding £336 billion in SRI funds, while the retail market (open to private shareholders) is £12.2 billion (BITC, 2003). The figures show not only the importance of this market, but the extent to which institutional investors, driven by long-term shareholder value rather than moral responsibility or altruism, have committed to this market, demonstrating the business case for companies adopting a genuine sustainability agenda with monitoring at its core. Business in the Community state, '. . . the business case for this action is compelling' (BITC, 2003).

The ABI (2001) quotes a series of studies showing how portfolios of companies with superior management of sustainability challenges have outperformed other companies. The performance is improved across not just profitability, but also greater resilience to change, demonstrating that the higher returns are not the consequence of a high-risk strategy. ABI (2001) cites research by the US Environmental Capital Markets Committee, which found a moderate positive correlation between environmental and financial performance, but could not show causation. This would indicate that while the addition of environmental consideration is not enough to improve financial performance, it is indicative of a well-run company, which will deliver strong financial performance. Such a position should discourage the most cynical attempts to adopt a new greener image, as the evidence would suggest the changes need to be more fundamental to the way a company integrates its core activities with the external environment.

The expansion of interest in socially responsible investment has led to the development of the Dow Jones Sustainability Index (DJSI) and the FTSE4Good as alternative indices to the main stock market listings in New York and London (Box 3.7). Companies are reviewed using eligibility criteria, and all companies listed receive the results of the assessment in order for them to identify areas for improvement and take part in the social learning experience. Further, the information is benchmarked against other companies from the same industry to enable competitor analysis. A cynic might suggest that a way to forestall the move to greater responsibility in investment could be through calling for better data with which to make decisions. Yet, the President of the Dow Jones Indexes demonstrates the importance of sustainability data by stating, 'The financial world is learning to work with non-financial data, and that alone is important for sustainability', before continuing, '. . . but in the absence of data, and of measurement standards that produce such data, sustainability won't fully register in the financial world's evaluations' (Prestbo, 2000). Hence the challenge exists for social scientists and financial managers to develop data that can be useful to enable the financial industries to pressure companies to improve their sustainability.

Despite the opportunity the financial industry provides, there are limitations to this approach. *The Economist* (2003) is sceptical of the extent to which even the institutional shareholders pressure companies to behave in a more sustainable way. Refuting this possible conflict of interests, there has been a recent rise in US-style shareholder activism into company affairs, whereby investors are taking shares in a company in order to force it to improve its performance. This high-level consumerism challenges the argument of Friedman (1970) discussed earlier, asserting that shareholders

---

Box 3.7. The Dow Jones Sustainability Index.

The DJSI was launched in 1999 and by February 2004 had a market capitalization of $6.5 trillion. The index has slightly outperformed the main Dow Jones index over this period, despite the technology bubble bursting. Financial sustainability is a key inclusion criteria, along with environmental and social dimensions.

Each company in the main Dow Jones Index is rated according to a sustainability assessment, which includes a questionnaire to the company, company documentation, contact with the company and an analysis of information in the public domain. Although the information is checked against externally available information, the reliance on the information provided by the company can be seen as a weakness of the index. About 60% of the assessment is generic to all companies, while the remaining data comes from industry specific questions and research. The index is split into 60 industry groups to enable comparison between competitors in the same industry, who will face similar pressures and sustainability challenges.

Analysis is conducted by consultants before being independently audited. The 'best in-class' label is granted for the top scoring 10% on the sustainability assessment of each industry group to be included within the DJSI, but a formula exists to prevent poorly performing industrial sectors, or distant second place companies from being included. However, the DJSI does not exclude industrial sectors such as arms, tobacco, alcohol, etc., although specialized indexes are available which do exclude these industries. This inclusive approach believes it is better to encourage all companies to be more sustainable than punish companies for aspects of the business beyond their control. As such, the index measures process and relative progress rather than absolute levels of sustainability performance. The consequence of this is that some companies are included that have recently received significant attention for their poor ethical positions.

Sources: DJSI (2004), Crane and Matten (2004).

want profit maximization. Pratley (2004) cites the Interfaith Centre on Corporate Responsibility, which holds an investment portfolio of $110 billion, who, having taken a considerable shareholding of Coca-Cola, have encouraged the company to examine the economic impacts of HIV/AIDS in Africa, and so to provide free anti-retroviral drugs to all its employees in Africa. Relying on peer pressure, the group is now hopeful that Pepsi will follow suit. Guinness has already adopted this policy and it demonstrates the value for sustainability of working within the system as opposed to boycotting companies for bad behaviour. This approach by interest groups should also signal to the tourism industry the danger of being seen not to take issues of their impact seriously.

As the pressure for sustainability and transparency within a company develops, so the drive for more information will increase, leading to improvements in monitoring and indicators. Yet, Crane and Matten (2004) refer to the informational asymmetry between the shareholders and the managers of the company, and just as with the section on consumers, so shareholders need more information if they are to make better decisions and enforce their rights to take an active role in the management of companies.

The Turnbull Report was an attempt to redress this imbalance, calling for all companies quoted on the stock market in Britain to include a section on managing risks in its annual report. Turnbull made it clear that this section was to include environmental, ethical and social risks (ABI, 2001). Currently, the ABI is satisfied with the standard of 80% of FTSE 100 companies reporting on environmental, social and ethical matters, although this satisfaction drops for smaller companies. Clearly the request for more information is given greater strength by those institutional investors who are asking for it. In the UK at the time of writing, three companies together own almost 20% of all the shares listed on Britain's stock market, compared with the millions of retail consumers who might all separately want more information from companies. The need for information to make decisions is the same, but the concentration of power demonstrates the more efficacious route.

However, there is a danger that the drive for information gathers to a pace beyond the ability to provide that information safely and accurately. As an example, Shell is being sued by shareholders over claims that it misrepresented the amount of oil it held in its reserves and so beneficially affected the share price in its favour (Walsh and Morgan, 2004). If such a piece of evidence can be shown to be material as a reason for buying shares in Shell, then the shareholders will win their case. If sustainability does indeed prove itself to be more than a passing fad, and evidence suggests that companies who strongly support sustainability do better financially, then measuring and assessing a company's sustainability will become a key indicator of likely future financial returns. The possibility therefore arises that just as the method of measuring oil reserves for Shell has led it to court, (and this for a tangible product like oil), so too could indicators of sustainability if they appear to present an overly positive picture of the company's performance. Clearly this position is some way ahead, but it is important to note that while the financial industry presents an enormous opportunity to enhance the drive for sustainability, so to it carries important challenges to the scientists charged with developing the indicators to provide the information in a manner that does not threaten the credibility of the subject.

Summary

This chapter has presented a series of reasons why monitoring matters for business and explored the rationale for businesses to promote sustainability. The debate has journeyed outside the tourism arena, evidence of both the progress made in other industrial sectors and the lack of substantial involvement by the commercial tourism industry in the debate. The commercial industry may feel that it can quieten its sense of moral responsibility. Many companies do, but if the industry believes it does not have a responsibility beyond that to its shareholders, then it risks damaging the concept for those who do work genuinely to promote sustainability.

The business case for sustainability is often more convincing for hard-headed business people and this chapter showed five arguments to support greater efforts in this respect. For the tourism industry, the consumer has yet to reveal its potential positive effect by encouraging industry to be more sustainable. The lack of regularity to purchases, the size of the purchase, intangibility of the product at the time of purchase and so the sense of risk are all compounded by a general lack of information. It is easy for the consumer to blame industry and industry to argue it is led by the consumer, but if industry is to increase its margins and secure its future, then it needs to take the lead and provide more information for consumers to make better decisions. These 'better' decisions should not be confused with an elitist approach to tourism; mass tourism can be as sustainable as ecotourism can be unsustainable. Yet, if the information is provided and consumers of some types of holiday show themselves to be uninterested, then producers will need to work with their supply chain to build-in sustainability to the basic product, rather than making it something additional to the holiday bill or activity programme. Clearly the starting point is to develop better information about the contribution made, which means the development of indicators becomes central to the business case for sustainability.

The need to innovate is crucial to the continuance of any industry and with the arrival of the low-cost airlines, technological challenges to the package holiday, greater experience of travelling further distances and the threat of terrorism meaning the tourism industry must innovate in order to survive. The potential benefits available from cutting costs, reducing risks and creating fair market conditions means sustainable tourism represents one positive way in which the industry can face the future.

Finally, this chapter extended the instrumentalist approach to promoting sustainability and considered the role of the financial industries to pressure companies directly and indirectly into a change in their behaviour. The combination of improved returns with the concentration of power in the hands of limited stakeholders makes this an avenue of great future potential if the right indicators can be developed to enable the decisions to be made. The challenge then becomes for the larger tourism companies to cascade their newfound sustainability down to their smaller rivals and, similarly, small businesses that have made clear progress towards sustainability, to provide this information for potential up-scaling to improve the sustainability of the comprehensive tourism system. The arguments for those representing the destination side of the equation, the government, NGOs and local residents are considered in the following chapter.

Public Sector Drivers

4

Introduction

Chapter 3 demonstrated the reasons why business should be motivated to promote sustainability and how the development of indicators can aid this process. In Chapter 4 the reasons for government, NGOs and the community to be involved with the development of indicators are explored. However, unlike in Chapter 3, for this group of actors (nominally referred to as 'public sector') the motivation to promote sustainability is relatively clear-cut. As such, Chapter 4 considers not so much *why* but *how* monitoring can assist government, NGOs and communities to promote sustainability.

There is a noticeable shift in the literature used in the current chapter from a very evidenced-based approach in Chapter 3, to a literature that is based on how systems of government should be organized. The reader is alerted to this characteristic of the literature and encouraged to consider how practical the suggestions for improved participatory systems of governance actually are and the likelihood of such proposals becoming enacted.

How does Monitoring Assist Government?

At a very simplified level, the role of government is to enable its citizens to enhance the quality of their lives. Chapter 40 of Agenda 21 urged governments around the world to develop indicators in order that it could be understood if the quality of these lives was improving or deteriorating. Agenda 21 thus gave rise to a wave of efforts by various governments, at various levels of government to develop indicators to assess the quality of life of their citizens and the sustainability of their economic and social systems. As an example of these efforts made nationally, Box 4.1 lists the quality-of-life indicators developed by the UK government. It is worth noting here that throughout the literature, there appears to be an implicit assumption that monitoring does actually help government. The following section considers not just how monitoring can help government, through improved understanding, tracking progress, initiating dialogue, forming partnerships and affecting policy, but also whether there is any evidence to suggest that monitoring enables government to do its job more effectively.

Box 4.1. Overall assessment of 2003 UK headline indicators of sustainable development.

Headline indicators/change	Change since 1970	Change since 1990	Change since Strategy
H1: Economic output: GDP and GDP per head	✓	✓	✓
H2: Investment: Total and social investment relative to GDP	≈	≈	≈
H3: Employment: Proportion of people of working age who are in work	≈	≈	✓
H4: Poverty: Indicators of success in tackling poverty and social exclusion	✗	≈	✓
H5: Education: Qualifications at age 19	•••	✓	✓
H6: Health: Expected years of healthy life	✓	≈	≈
H7: Housing: Households living in non-decent housing	•••	✓	✓
H8: Level of crime: Robbery	✗	✗	✗
Vehicles and burglary	✗	✓	✓
H9: Climate change: Emissions of greenhouse gases	✓	✓	✓
H10: Air quality: Days when air pollution is moderate or higher	•••	✓	✗
H11: Road traffic: Traffic volume	✗	✗	✗
Traffic intensity	✗	✓	✓
H12: River water quality: Chemical and biological river quality	✓	✓	✓

H13:	Wildlife: Wild bird pop.: Woodland birds	⊗	⊗	≋
	Farmland birds	⊗	⊗	≋
H14:	Land use: New homes built on previously developed land	•••	✓	✓
H15:	Waste: Household waste	•••	⊗	⊗
	Waste raising and management	•••	•••	≋

'Change since strategy' assesses progress since the UK Government's sustainable development strategy in 1999.

Key

✓ Significant change, in direction of meeting objective

≋ No significant change

⊗ Significant change, in direction away from meeting objective

••• Insufficient or no comparable data

Source: DEFRA (2004).

Improve understanding

Based on a major study of quality of life indicators, the New Economics Foundation (NEF) cites five benefits from monitoring and reporting for government, the first of which is the improved understanding which results from efforts to measure sustainability (NEF, 2003). Chapters 1 and 2 of this book demonstrate the evolution of understanding about sustainability in a relatively brief period of time; Chapter 3 demonstrates the conceptualization of sustainability taken by business while the interchange of the terminology between 'quality of life' and 'sustainability' in this chapter demonstrates the imprecision that confounds the topic. Adding to this general lack of understanding about sustainability, the tourism industry is faced with its own public awareness issues, such that at a national level, governments will almost always be more occupied with other areas of public life than tourism. At a regional or local level, the priority tourism is afforded in government attentions may differ, but tourism is still recognized to be a poorly understood industry (Cheong and Miller, 2000). Caffyn and Jobbins (2003) refer to the lack of understanding by the national governments of both Morocco and Tunisia about the consequences of tourism for coastal sustainability. Thomas and Thomas (1996) in a study of the effects of political devolution in the UK demonstrate the lack of benefit for the tourism industry. The authors question whether a lack of understanding about the needs of the industry is to blame for the failure of tourism to benefit from a change in the level of decision making to one, intuitively at least, more suited to recognize the specific needs of the local industry. Hence, any improvement in understanding sustainability that can come from monitoring, particularly as it relates to tourism, should be heartily welcomed.

Track progress

A second benefit of monitoring is the ability for government to track the full extent of its own progress. Governments, as well as citizens, like to see the results of their efforts, and indicators can act as a means for encouragement when times are tough, or to reveal the size and immediacy of a problem when there has been little progress. Yet, an important lesson from this book is how shifts from more quantitative to qualitative approaches to government necessitate a change in thinking about how the contribution of government should be measured. Writing about the contribution of tourism in the future Ryan (2002, p. 24) observes, 'The calculation of returns requires new means of assessment'. If government is acting in new policy areas, then it will need new methods of assessment to capture the effects of its actions.

Enabling governments to track their progress assists governments who feel they are performing well to receive their due plaudits. For example, McMahon (2002) refers to the ability of regional governments to use the results of indicator programmes to demonstrate progress and support bids for national or European level funds. As such, indicators are used as evidence of professionalism and seriousness by government about taking actions with the outcomes transparent to their citizens. If this trend is continued, the development of a programme of indicators can become a pre-requisite to bidding for funding. An important challenge to those charged with developing indicators in the future, is to ensure that the science continues to keep pace with the increased role indicators are being asked to perform.

Monitoring also enables other bodies to track the progress of government aiding the move towards greater transparency in government. There is a strong intrinsic reason to encourage transparency and reduce corruption in government. For example, *The Economist* (2003) discusses the correlation between corruption and environmental performance. If transparency is a key element in the fight against corruption, then monitoring the openness of actions of government can be seen as a crucial element in the country's environmental and social development, and hence provide an instrumental reason to monitor progress.

An instrumental reason that will resonate with politicians is the threat of losing their jobs if they are seen to be performing badly. Monitoring issues of importance to local residents will first identify how closely aligned the efforts of the local government are with the issues of concern for local people, but then also enable the community to track the politicians' performance on these issues. Failure in either regard will provide political opponents with an opportunity to criticize and unseat their rivals through the electorate. NEF (2003) cite the example in the city of Reading in the UK, where an indicator was developed to assess the degree to which social housing matched the demand. The indicator revealed the extent of the problem, which became a central issue in the subsequent election and the governing party lost the election. One of the first things the new ruling party did was to reverse the existing housing policy. The indicator has shown waiting times for social housing have since reduced.

Initiate dialogue

Chapters 6 and 7 refer to the process of 'visioning', a technique that seeks to attain an understanding of the desired outcome from the drive for sustainability. A key task of this technique is the need to initiate a dialogue between the local government and the public about what sustainability actually means, a task indicators and monitoring programmes can assist with. Chapter 6 found that the process of seeking to establish what to monitor through asking stakeholder groups to envision the future improves understanding of sustainability. However, as is also mentioned in these later chapters, the false assumption that the public are waiting to be involved in tourism decisions or any other decisions that affect their lives needs to be exposed. People lead busy lives and may wish to be largely left alone to make their own way in the world, and leave the task to external consultants and government. MacGillivray (1997, p. 261) writes, 'The underlying assumption is that, given adequate information and the associations in which to do so, healthy, wealthy and wise citizens can participate in sustainable development'. Yet some sections of society, indeed some societies, are more politically engaged than others. Marien and Pizam (1997, p. 167) state:

> . . . the typical citizen will participate only in those cases where they feel
> that a particular tourism project would personally and directly affect
> their livelihood, health or quality of life. Therefore the announcement
> or communications need to explain why people should get involved and
> how a certain project may affect their life.

A central part of motivating people may be the provision of information about an issue, of which previously they were unaware, or the creation of linkages between seemingly remote, global problems and day-to-day actions and behaviour.

There is a danger, however, of providing too much information to citizens, such that they receive a never-ending stream of information, a stream so rich that they risk getting completely lost. The IISD (2004a) argue for the right for information in order to make the voter more aware of issues facing them, and in order that the citizen can fairly judge their government's performance. Yet, in addition, the IISD (2004a) stress the availability of indicators is not sufficient in a situation where citizens are flooded by other, equally available but biased information. Instead, democratic institutions must guarantee that objective information is effectively communicated to the voter, against the stiff competition of non-neutral information.

In some areas, the problem of communicating and motivating residents may be made more difficult by previous attempts to generate community involvement that have exhausted the residents, or muddied the waters. The challenge thus becomes to find new ways to bring residents back to the discussion table, a much more difficult challenge, and one that demonstrates the importance of conducting the process properly the first time. Recognizing this situation, Marien and Pizam (1997) ask whether all volunteers should be paid for their time in the same way citizens are paid for jury duty or to be army reservists, recognizing community involvement in the same civic terms.

Develop partnerships

Following moves to strengthen trust and enable dialogue between stakeholders, the fourth benefit of monitoring cited by the NEF (2003) is the ability to develop partnerships amongst these various groups who come forward. Robinson (1999, p. 393) believes collaboration and partnership are '. . . symbolic of new ways of working', while the NEF (2003, p. 9) recognizes the more practical value of partnerships providing '. . . both focus and a platform for collaboration bringing relevant players to one table'. Such a comment reflects the strength of the concept of sustainability in being able to demonstrate shared goals between previously opposing forces, although the 'platform for collaboration' may also reveal differences. Jamal and Getz (1995) believe collaboration theory can greatly assist in achieving a consensus amongst a group of stakeholders. Conversely, Taylor (1995) holds that if disparate groups are able to represent themselves equally, then such will be the spread of opinions that it is inevitable for there to be insurmountable differences. Such a situation does not preclude partnerships being formed, but these are not likely to be one cohesive partnership that includes all stakeholders, rather separate partnerships formed in alliance. This revelation may do little to enhance the consensus of society, but at least potential problems are made obvious before it becomes too late to even attempt to address differences of opinion. Further, problems may arise in cultures that require more consensual politics and are not able to tolerate such division.

Effect on policy

If indicators are to have any value, then they need to be able to influence policy on sustainability. Even if government decides that the way for its citizens to enhance their quality of life is for government to remove itself as far as possible from the policy arena, then a decision has still been made about the kind of policies required to enhance sustainability. Further, if monitoring is able to help government move towards sustainability then there should be some evidence of changes in policy as a consequence of indicator programmes. A 30-month study by PASTILLE (2002, p. 45) of four European cities concluded, '. . . sustainability indicators do not currently have much impact on decision making at municipal level'. Further, the NEF (2003) found in its UK study, 61% of all local authorities surveyed were using indicators of sustainability, but there was little evidence to support the thesis of indicators having led directly to a change in policy. Indeed, of the five benefits identified by NEF, their survey showed indicators were helping to improve understanding about sustainability, were serving to track changes and were promoting partnership, but as well as not having a direct effect on policy, the indicator programmes were not aiding dialogue between stakeholders.

There are a plethora of reasons why monitoring might not have led to a change in policy. One reason might be that the local government already had their policies correctly aligned with the wishes of its community, progress was being shown towards an ever more sustainable future and there was no need for change. Such a situation is unlikely, but the monitoring of progress being made will enable the local electorate to review the efforts made on their behalf and to act accordingly through the political system.

The NEF (2003) proposes that the recency of the indicator movement is another, more likely reason for the lack of effect on policy making. Although the Rio summit was held in 1992, and in the UK alone around 150 local authorities are known to have experience of developing quality of life indicators, the acceptance of indicators has taken a long time to filter through to local government policy making. Indeed, this book itself is testimony to the delay before indicators have permeated the literature of an industry as large as tourism. In addition, the lack of legislative incentive from national government has served to produce a situation where senior local authority managers would be loath to spend scarce resources on non-statutory requirements. The NEF report senior managers who recognize the importance of indicators, but exhibit a lack of 'buy-in' that leaves the programmes looking marginal and unconnected with policy making. Such a position threatens the very existence of the indicator programmes, as their benefits are not being realized, and instead only the expense of running the programme are felt. These practical challenges are discussed further in Chapter 7.

In attempting to explain why monitoring was not impacting on policy making the NEF survey found a lack of vision from the local community and a lack of leadership from the local authorities. To make matters worse, only 27% of the local authorities surveyed believed they were communicating the results of their indicator programmes effectively (NEF, 2003). Monitoring can provide a source of motivation for groups to come forward to engage in dialogue with government. Such energy can be translated into a vision for the region, which provides the local authorities with a mandate to push ahead with difficult decisions. Yet, if there is little support from management, there are no assurances that the right questions are being asked, the indicators are having little effect on policy making and the outcomes are not being communicated properly. There is, therefore a long road to travel before indicators can be said to be fulfilling their potential to help government to promote sustainability.

Despite the pessimism of the results from the NEF, several local authorities have placed great emphasis on monitoring to aid the drive for sustainability. Bell and Morse (1999) discuss in detail the work of Norwich city council through their 'Norwich 21' programme, while Box 4.2 provides the case of Bristol. In common with much of the material for this book, the examples fall outside the realm of tourism, but serve to demonstrate how indicators could be of value to tourism destinations. The Bristol project makes use of indicators measuring different levels of life in the city, and as such is an approach that creates an opportunity for local private-sector organizations, or industries to contribute. If indicators can be determined ranging from European level down to the level of the community, then it would be easier for companies and industries to measure issues important to them, and their impact on issues important to the local community. Doing so would serve to promote discussion about the role of business in society, improve understanding, whilst also monitoring performance. If business or government is not prepared to accept this challenge, then NGOs exist to pick up the gauntlet on behalf of communities and use monitoring to achieve their goals.

How does Monitoring Assist NGOs?

To understand how monitoring can assist NGOs it is important to consider what they do. It is difficult to talk of NGOs in a general sense because of the range of size, scope and aim. However, Korten (1987) believes NGOs today are undertaking work advocating sustainable systems, which have evolved to represent a third generation of activities for NGOs. Korten (1987) describes how NGOs could previously be characterized as being engaged with welfare relief in an essentially fire-fighting capacity, and then there was a general move towards capacity building through encouraging self-reliance, although short of promoting self-determination. For Horochowski and

---

Box 4.2. Monitoring in Bristol.

Bristol began to develop its quality of life indicators in 1993, publishing its first report in 1995. The programme began as a 'top-down' initiative that has been expanded to include a 'bottom-up' methodology for residents to generate ideas and become involved. Crucial to the Bristol project is inclusion of indicators from five different levels of life in the city:

- Level one: European common indicators are measured by the local community to provide comparisons with other cities across Europe.
- Level two: National indicators are measured by central government, while regional indicators are those developed by the Audit Commission in 1999 to a common methodology, but measured by local authorities.
- Level three: Stakeholder indicators were developed from a 'State of Bristol' conference in 1999, which brought key stakeholders together to choose headline indicators for 12 sustainability topics as a framework for the LA21 strategy. These indicators are measured by NGOs, the community and other stakeholders.
- Level four: Ward and city-wide indicators were developed in 1995 and followed public consultation, but is essentially led by local government. There are approximately 60 indicators measured annually and able to be broken down to ward level within the city.
- Level five: Community group indicators were developed in 2001/2002 in partnership with the local newspaper enabling communities to choose, then measure and ultimately disseminate the results of quality of life issues specific to their neighbourhoods.

A strong link between the indicators and effect on policy making is claimed. The NEF (2003) identify the creation of 'Breakfast clubs' in Bristol after a stakeholder indicator was developed to assess the number of under-14-year-olds who went to school in the morning without having eaten breakfast. Measuring this indicator showed variations existed throughout the city and schools in poorly performing regions were allowed to open the school canteen to serve breakfasts. McMahon (2002, p. 185) observes, '. . . professionals and politicians need the public's insight and to reconcile the top-down approach with the bottom-up community-led approach to select and measure relevant indicators'.

Sources: McMahon (2002), NEF (2003).

Moisey (1999), the growth in concerns is caused by the need to address the declining priority of the development agenda and insufficient funds made available by world governments. Similarly, Suresh *et al.* (1999) believe the role of NGOs begins when there is evidence of government absence or failure in an important policy area, combined with an increase in the level of foreign direct investment. Burns (1999, p. 3) writes, 'NGOs can fill the policy vacuum in reconstructing economies or compensate where democratic processes are ineffective'. Such a definition creates a wide opportunity for NGOs. In addition, the increased recognition of the importance and inter-connectedness of the world's environmental, social and economic systems provides NGOs with a strong justification to become involved in the affairs of almost every area of the globe. This section contains itself to considering how NGOs can use monitoring to conduct assessments, improve their advocacy and campaigning, as well as strengthen their justification for involvement around the world.

Conducting assessment

Kousis (2000) studied more than 4500 cases of local NGO mobilizations in Greece, Portugal and Spain to understand the range of actions undertaken. The research showed the very local flavour of most concerns and their largely apolitical character. In terms of resolving their disputes, specific to tourism Kousis (2000, p. 481) observes, '. . . environmental impact assessment studies are among the more important resolutions proposed for tourism related activities'. Scheyvens (2002) believes NGOs occupy an important role in the measurement and dissemination of impacts because of their independent position in tourism development. As an example, Dixey (1999) describes the work that the United Kingdom Centre for Economic and Environmental Development (UKCEED) have conducted in assessing the impacts of tourism in all-inclusive resorts on behalf of, and in conjunction with, British Airways Holidays. The NGO first assessed the impacts of tourism in general and then the impacts caused by the company in particular. In this case, the monitoring is providing information to the company, creating awareness of the problems and enabling action to take place to ameliorate the problem. While it is to be hoped that the impacts identified reflect the perspectives of the different stakeholders, what is interesting is whether the issues identified are addressed in the same order as the community would address the problems. Here the motivations for different stakeholders to promote sustainability may become apparent as the company looks to address a problem with high publicity value and relatively low cost; the NGO might look for a similar impact to be addressed in accordance with their mission, while the local community might prefer to continue receiving income and deal with more esoteric issues at a less pressing moment in time.

Acknowledging the importance of who conducts the monitoring Connolly (1999) suggests an opportunity for NGOs to assist in the training of local citizens to conduct the measurement for themselves. Scheyvens (2002, p. 225) agrees,

> NGOs can . . . coordinate monitoring efforts and pass on appropriate monitoring skills to local people. It can be very empowering for communities to learn to collect and record information on a regular basis so that they build up a database which they can draw upon if they wish to lobby government about concerns they have about tourism development.

Using participatory data collection techniques greatly enhances the learning outcomes of the monitoring process and gives stakeholders a greater involvement in the process. Yet, the appropriateness of participatory data collection will also depend on the technical demands of the methodology selected for particular indicators, as discussed further in Chapter 7.

Mowforth and Munt (1998) recognize the growth in NGOs measuring impacts, but are critical of the belief that NGOs are neutral, questioning whether NGOs in the context of developing countries serve to propagate middle-class western values rather than truly acting on behalf of community development. Having the local community conduct the monitoring still does not guarantee independence, although the local assessors may be free of any potential influence during the monitoring phase. However, Driskell *et al.* (2001) draw attention to the staging of monitoring events for the benefit of visiting NGO staff who seek to monitor a project from a distance. Hence, when NGO staff visit a project, a false impression may be created of the worth of the project. It is important for commentators to recognize that neutrality is very difficult to achieve and that all actors do have interests and may be willing to manipulate results in order to best serve those interests.

A related area of increasing activity for NGOs has been in providing the data for ecolabelling exercises. Font and Buckley (2001) write at length about the central role NGOs occupy in this burgeoning field. There are strong parallels between the role of NGOs, in empowering the consumer through the provision of information via labelling, and the process of empowering communities through information via indicators. The need to make consumers feel as if they can make a difference, to appeal to a sense of self rather than just community and for the NGO to maintain its sense of credibility are all imperative for both approaches. The approach of labelling and monitoring for companies is typical of more positive engagement between the NGOs, business and the consumer, with monitoring and indicators at the core of the relationship.

Advocacy and campaigning

Beyond assessment, NGOs have a need for the kind of information monitoring can provide in order to conduct advocacy work on behalf of community groups, or to enable groups to wage their own campaign more effectively (Azzone *et al.*, 1997). Scheyvens (2002, p. 214) explains, '. . . information is essential to overcome the disadvantage that most local communities face when engaging with the tourism sector'. The final section of this chapter discusses the informational needs of community groups acting on their own behalf, but for NGOs to advocate different values and alternative ways of being, it is necessary to introduce new information to challenge the status quo. Campaigning and applying pressure for a change in policy, or for companies to discuss issues, lobbying, conducting press relations, producing educational material and networking are all designed to strengthen the arm of local sustainability drives, but are dependent on information being available to counter the dominant view (Box 4.3). Indeed, just as monitoring was seen to provide ammunition for political opposition parties to government, so monitoring can provide NGOs and communities with the same kind of weaponry with which to tackle their opponents. By being accepted by a local community, the NGO is able to build a foundation for civic activism and is therefore provided with the mandate to face their foes.

Resisting criticism

MacGillivray (1997) makes what he describes to be a very conservative estimate of the number of NGOs worldwide to be three million. It is unsurprising given this number that criticism exists of the behaviour of some NGOs, criticism that all NGOs need to defend themselves against if they are to be effective in their goals of promoting sustainability (Mowforth and Munt, 1998).

The issue of the legitimacy of NGOs in a community is an important hurdle for many NGOs to overcome. NGOs will pursue a variety of goals that may be religious, political, relate to just one aspect of sustainability or to a broader suite of issues. Yet, as NGOs are likely to be more prevalent in areas where government is failing and institutional mechanisms may not be functioning,

---

Box 4.3.   Tourism Concern.

Tourism Concern is a UK-based NGO that campaigns to effect change in the tourism industry by campaigning for fair and ethically traded tourism. One of its campaigns has been to draw attention to the human rights abuses in Burma since the military junta took power.

In 1996, when the government declared it to be 'Visit Myanmar' year, Tourism Concern met with tour operators to alert them to abuses in Burma and to encourage the end of tours to the country. In 2000, Tourism Concern began to pressure the publishers of UK guidebooks to Burma, and to encourage them to respect the wishes of the democratically elected leader of Burma, and Nobel Peace Prize winner, Aung San Suu Kyi, who appealed for tourists not to come to Burma. Tourism Concern encouraged anyone concerned about tourism to Burma to send a postcard of protest to guidebook publishers. The campaign was mainly targeted at Lonely Planet, and although they refused to withdraw their book, Tourism Concern claims the campaign was a success because of the attention it drew to the issues and the subsequent withdrawal of several major UK tour operators from Burma.

Source: Tourism Concern (2004).

communities are left vulnerable to the aims of NGOs. Driskell *et al.* (2001, p. 85) are very critical of two NGOs who became involved in a project in Bangalore, asking, 'Who is responsible for ensuring that an NGO is actually working in a community's best interests'? They continue, 'Without an effective institutional framework to promote ethics and accountability, there is a very real risk that NGOs can undermine legitimate community interests, leaving local residents without any established mechanism – such as an election – through which they can change the situation' (Driskell *et al.*, 2001, p. 85). Horochowski and Moisey (1999) believe that without full support from the local population the tourism industry will always be able to resist the efforts and campaigns of the NGO. NGOs need to demonstrate that they do have the full support of the local community and are not simply chasing self-serving goals.

Sparrowhawk and Holden (1999) consider the case of Nepal and the risk of having too many NGOs exist in a destination. Such a country can be considered totemic because of its unique natural resources and culture, making fund-raising relatively easier than for other less unique projects. A cynic might question whether the number of NGOs reflected the desire of the donating middle classes of the Western world to preserve the roof of the world for themselves and their progeny rather than donating money genuinely to promote self-determination and a shift to sustainable lifestyles. With less cynicism, Horochowski and Moisey (1999) note how NGO fund-raising benefits from tourists seeing firsthand the problems that NGOs exist to reduce. If tourists are impressed by the work of NGOs in a destination, the visit can act as a method of fund-raising once the tourist returns home (Turner *et al.*, 2001). (Such philanthropic travel is a much under-researched area and with the increase in organizations raising money for various causes this topic would benefit from serious investigation to determine how much money is raised through this means and the optimum means for maximizing donations.) Such a scenario risks the commodification of the problems of local communities in order to secure grants, funds and donations (Mowforth and Munt, 1998), and the extent to which the need to attract funding alters the goals of the project and the kind of projects pursued. In addition, such projects are left vulnerable to changes in fashion by the major donors such as the US Agency for International Development (USAID), Department for International Development (DFID) and the European Union (EU), forcing NGOs to change the projects they support in order to attract funding.

All this criticism ultimately damages the credibility of NGOs, weakening their effectiveness to achieve the genuine goals of self-determination in the local populace. It does, however, strengthen the argument for the need for NGOs to monitor to demonstrate their effectiveness. Indicators can be said to help with this challenge of demonstrating the value NGOs contribute, but indicators can also be shown to precipitate a world where the worth of items needs to be proven. Yet, just as a government needs to demonstrate the strength of the social contract that exists between itself and society, and business is increasingly pressed to demonstrate its links with the wider society (see Chapter 3), so it is reasonable that NGOs should prove to the host society why they should be trusted. Where this cannot be proven, or the relationship is damaged from previous attempts, or the government feels the steps necessary to promote sustainability are too risky for it to take, the community will need to attempt to organize itself to promote sustainability. Although it may be a daunting prospect for a community in a developing country to take on a large tourism organization, the process of monitoring may at least be able to assist.

How does Monitoring Assist Communities?

The book so far has demonstrated the importance of achieving stakeholder involvement in attempts to make a transition to greater sustainability. Business, consumers, government and non-government all have valuable contributions to make, and monitoring has been shown to offer great assistance to each of these groups. However, the common denominator of all stakeholders is the resident or, in its plural form, the community.

Who are the community?

To this point, the word 'community' has been used in an aggregated sense to represent a group of citizens in a given geographical space. However, it should be obvious that to talk of 'a community' in a pluralistic society is facile. Any group of people will not share the same attitude on everything, or indeed on anything and any one person's attitude is likely to change so that they are not even consistent with themselves through time. Understanding this heterogeneity has led to research over the past 25 years, which has examined many different aspects related to residents' perceptions of tourism development. For a more detailed discussion of resident attitudes to tourism development, the reader is directed to seminal works by Belisle and Hoy (1980), Millman and Pizam (1988), Ap (1990) and Madrigal (1995). Historically, much of the research on the topic of residents' perceptions has been atheoretical in nature (Ap, 1990) although the dominant theory to emerge to shape understanding has been social exchange theory. This theory concentrates on the extent to which residents receive something from tourism for the imposition the industry places upon them and recognizes the way people adapt to the inherent power imbalances of development. Haley *et al.* (2005) summarize this literature and argue that despite the absence of an accepted methodology, the key lesson to emerge from the resident attitude research is in moving beyond an aggregated understanding of a community's attitude, cluster analysis has enabled a more sophisticated view of attitudes. The research by Fredline and Faulkner (2000) of resident attitudes towards the Indy Car motorcar race on the Gold Coast in Australia encapsulates much of the research seeking to establish clusters of resident attitudes, and is presented in Box 4.4.

In addition to the heterogeneity of resident attitudes within a community (causing us to question the usefulness of the term 'community'),

---

Box 4.4. Clusters of resident attitudes.

Ambivalent supporter (29%)	Realists (24%)
Gave ambivalent and moderate answers	Acknowledged both the positive and negative impacts of the event
Agreed with community benefits and slightly agreed with short-term negative impact statements	51% worked in the tourism industry and 32% in associated industries
62% lived in the Indy zone	A large proportion were also low-income earners
97% in favour of the race	
60% in favour of the race location	

Haters (15%)	Lovers (23%)
Disagreed with the community benefit statements and agreed strongly with the short-term negative impact statements (especially economic and environmental)	Highly agreed to statements concerning benefits, economic impact and profile for the Gold Coast
	Only group to disagree with the short-term negative impacts
Did not see economic benefits or media potential	100% wanted the race to continue
Mainly older residents, longer time in the location	76% favoured the current location
	38% attended the event and 35% watched it on TV
65% did not want Indy to continue	Similar demographic profile to spectators
None watched the race and 40% left town	

Concerned for a reason (9%)

Were deeply concerned over some impacts but not totally negative overall
They disagreed over the community benefit statements except that Indy had improved the nightlife
Agreed with the short-term negative statements except that Indy led to increased crime
Most lived in Indy location
High-income earners
97% in favour of the race
Most preferred different locations

Source: Fredline and Faulkner (2000).

communities will be involved to differing degrees with tourism development projects. Chapter 7 discusses how to take indicator programmes from
principles to practice, but the following section discusses some of the reasons why it has proven difficult for indicators to empower the involvement
of communities.

Limits to community involvement

A glance through any travel brochure shows increasing reference to intan-
gible elements of the tourism product such as the friendliness of the local
population, and so provides local residents with ownership of an important
element of the tourism product. However, without legal (as opposed to
moral or historical) ownership of the physical resources of the tourism
industry, any involvement in decisions about tourism development is likely
to be variable. The work of Arnstein (1969) and Pretty (1995) demonstrate
the range of involvement it is possible to have in any project. Pretty's
typology of involvement is explained in more detail in Box 4.5, showing
how of the seven stages, only at the final stage can the community be said to
be fully in control, and indeed the first five stages represent consultation
with varying levels of sincerity. Yet, it should not be assumed that full control is the ideal expression of self-determination or indeed the optimum
scenario for every situation. The residents of Bristol (Box 4.2) recognize
that the local authority is in the best position to control the measurement
of issues, although input is needed from the citizenry. The inclusion of
community group indicators enhances the involvement of the public, but,
reflecting the wishes of the community, the programme can be said to be a
long way from being under the control of citizens.

     With varying attitudes and varying levels of involvement, it is inevitable
that some views will be expressed more effectively than others. Yet, Marien
and Pizam (1997, p. 170) reflect a misunderstanding about the ability of
residents to contribute to development projects through existing power
structures, they comment:

> In many tourism communities where there is a local tourist council/
> commission which is mostly comprised of tourism industry representatives
> and elected public officials, it is common to reserve a few seats for citizen
> representatives. Therefore it is possible to say that in such cases decision
> making is shared by officials and citizen groups.

Conversely, where the community cannot lay claims of ownership, the existing power structure is almost certain to be maintained because of the
tokenistic manner in which seats are assigned to community groups, demonstrating Pretty's (1995) 'manipulative participation'. The community is
brought into an industry/government structure, rather than the industry
going to meet the community, so there is a numerical disadvantage, and

Box 4.5. Forms of community involvement.

Manipulative participation	Tokenistic community 'representation' on panels
Passive participation	Community is told what has already been decided
Participation by consultation	Community are asked their opinions, but decisions not required to acknowledge views of community
Participation for material incentives	Involvement through the provision of resources, but not in decision making
Functional participation	Community is involved to facilitate the successful resolution of the project. This involvement may include decision making, but only when necessary to achieve project goals
Interactive participation	Involvement for intrinsic reasons, wide involvement of stakeholders, learning exhibited about the need for appropriate institutions and structures
Self-mobilization	Expert advice is contracted in to help inform decisions taken by the community. Existing power structures are challenged to enable community development

Source: Pretty (1995).

very likely to be a skills disadvantage, informational disadvantage and financial resources disadvantage. As such, it is very difficult to see how power can be seen to be shared. Jamal and Getz (1999, p. 303) note sagely, '. . . the right to participate does not equal the capacity to participate'. Such a situation may also be demonstrated at a national level, where national governments are beholden to large international institutions and organizations; the involvement of the national government may also be characterized as tokenistic. Returning to community involvement, Joppe (1996, p. 476) is unequivocal that because of the way that the consultation process is stacked against the residents, 'citizen participation rarely has an effect on decision making', with the result that residents are reluctant to engage further in the process and become indifferent towards tourism activities (Cheong and Miller, 2000).

Despite this criticism, Tosun (2000, p. 615) believes, '. . . community participation is a tool to readjust the balance of power and reassert local community views against those of the developers or the local authorities . . .' Yet, although there is considerable emphasis on stakeholder participation in the sustainable development literature, indicator development has been relatively slow to involve local residents. This is because early indicator programmes have tended to be conducted at the national or supranational level, dominated by international organizations such as the UN (1996),

Organization for Economic Cooperation and Development (OECD, 1993) and UNEP (1998). These groups have long seen indicator development as a science best left to the experts, indicator data collection as the task of national governments and indicator use as the privilege of the organization responsible.

The lack of participatory involvement and the complexity of monitoring sustainability can lead to a natural inclination to request the assistance of experts in the field. Donaldson and Preston (1995) refer to the 'informational asymmetry' between the two groups, which elevates the role of expert to a position that is often uncontested. The land quality indicators developed by Dumanski and Pieri (2000) are developed in a top-down manner in which experts visit a destination to determine what the problems are and decide what indicators are appropriate to measure these problems. Bell and Morse (1999, p. 27) confirm that this is a typical approach, '. . . for the most part the sustainability indicators, or at least the method for developing sustainability indicators, have been set by outsiders with perhaps a nod in the direction of those the indicators are meant to serve'. Similar issues are raised and discussed in Chapter 8 in relation to the World Tourism Organization (WTO) monitoring programme. Recognizing the potential arrogance of the western scientist, Kay *et al.* (1999, p. 737) write, '. . . decisions must be informed by science, but in the end they are an expression of human ethics and preferences, and of the socio-political context in which they are made. This of course raises the question, who decides'?

The ability to have one's own view of reality accepted as the dominant view is an expression of power and despite Meadows' (1998, p. 25) invocation, 'Indicators for an entire social system should not be determined by a small group of experts . . . sitting together in rooms out of contact with the people who are expected to understand and use the indicators', power structures continue to threaten community involvement in attempts to promote sustainability (Reed, 1997). Kammerbauer *et al.* (2001) describe a project where indicators are identified 'for' local communities and monitoring tools 'provided' to pursue a path to more sustainable development. This paternal desire to steer a community on to the 'right' path is obvious, but the risk is that such actions can be seen as a well-intentioned form of colonialism, but worse, the indicator programme risks failing to be understood or implemented because of a lack of local ownership and involvement in the monitoring process. Ultimately excessive expert input prevents a significant element of sustainable development being accomplished. Hawkins (2003, p. 38) in his Ulysses prize lecture for WTO states categorically: 'failure to include all key stakeholders within a destination is the most common cause of discord and ultimately can lead to failure of a tourism destination.'

Despite this criticism of top-down, expert opinion, Garcia *et al.* (2000, p. 550) believe, '. . . there is also the potential and need to use existing information that is not generally compiled or reported, such as information from fishers, communities and indigenous groups. The value of these expert judgements should not be underrated'. When local experts are used rather than those who come in from outside, beyond improving the quality of the data, the process of indicator development also enhances local capacity and understanding of the issues. If power structures enable local people to become experienced in data collection, so locals become more self-deterministic as information brings with it empowerment. The process of indicator development enables a greater understanding of what is important, and so what needs to be sustained. The ability to measure and the knowledge of what to measure will reduce the reliance on outside 'experts', both in terms of finances and skills. This virtuous circle is discussed further in Chapters 6 and 7.

However, while it is easy to characterize the outsiders as the main threat, power relations also exist within destinations, which can challenge the ability of the community to enjoy the benefits of moves towards greater sustainability. Burns (1999, p. 6) asks, 'To what extent are the most dangerous enemies of sustainable development local elites who exploit their own people'? Hall (1994) refers to the 'big men' of Samoa who he claims dominate the apportionment of tourism's benefits to their own benefit in some areas. Reed (1997, p. 582) observes in the Canadian context that the '. . . local elites were able to retain their influence locally' in the face of increased tourism development. The difficulties, lie in those people deKadt (1979) refers to as 'culture brokers', while Nunez (1989) calls them 'marginal men', to Cheong and Miller (2000) they are the 'power-brokers' and for van den Berghe (1992) they are simply 'middlemen'. Fernando (1995) provides an insiders' critique of the problems of developmental work conducted in Sri Lanka and organized through community involvement, demonstrating still the potential lack of equality in community run developments. Ryan (2002, p. 23) muses, 'Do we exchange the tyranny of the majority under elective representative systems for the tyranny of the vociferous under processes of social involvement'? The first part of this chapter described how indicators can be useful to encourage transparency in government and also within NGOs. If local democracy is failing and communities are not able/willing to resist the imbalance, then social Darwinism will always reward those who are able to think the fastest, speak the loudest, or grab the most. Indicators are able to perform many roles, but unless action accompanies the monitoring, then they will not be able to assist in any change in the status quo. Indeed, if place-based indicators are employed, but the indicators are selected by only a local elite, then indicators may simply serve to perpetuate an existing system. In this instance, more generic, externally developed indicators may serve to shine a light on the shortcomings of a destination. However, the problem with this approach is that such indicators would likely be unwelcome and unsupported, rendering them impossible to implement.

Beyond power, Tosun (2000) describes three potentially severe types of limitations to community involvement (Box 4.6); operational, structural and cultural. Limitations at the operational level are central to this discussion on the role of monitoring because it stresses the lack of information available to would-be participants. Tourism data in developing countries is often insufficient, poorly disseminated and '. . . therefore the low public participation should be expected' (Tosun, 2000, p. 620). Simmons (1994, p. 106) argues that the knowledge of the public is 'at best barely adequate to instil confidence in the soundness of their contribution'. If data are available, but only to those with close contacts, then the knowledge gap is increased, making it more difficult for those excluded from the process to make any contribution. Nettenkoven (1979, p. 143) describes the use by local elites of 'an inexhaustible source of misunderstanding and false information' to further their own ends.

However, although stressing the importance of communities having access to information in order to improve awareness and education, Tosun (2000) fails to consider the value of consulting with local communities before data are collected, in order to determine what issues have greatest resonance with residents and therefore what data need to be collected. In such a way, information can be amassed that is meaningful to residents, rather than likely to preserve the existing structures. This is particularly important given the significant investment a community is required to make in order to advance a programme of indicators. Jamal and Getz (1999) in their study of community involvement in Alberta estimated over 25,000 h of volunteer time had been invested in the process, while Atkisson (1996) refers to the frustration felt by the community at the time it took to make progress. The time required, coupled with the need to acquire skills makes Hart (1997) question why locals in developing countries with more pressing survival problems could be involved even if they wanted to.

Box 4.6. Limitations of community involvement.

Operational level	Centralization of public administration
	Lack of coordination
	Lack of information
Structural level	Attitudes of professionals
	Lack of expertise
	Elite domination
	Lack of appropriate legal system
	Lack of trained human resources
	Relatively high cost of human resources
Cultural level	Limited capacity of poor people
	Apathy and low level of awareness in the local community

Source: Tosun (2000).

Enabling community involvement

The role of indicators empowering communities through the provision of information has been discussed above. Additionally, indicators can assist communities to push towards more sustainable positions through establishing the sensitivity of the community to a development and so helping to initially determine the social capital of the community, as well as the appropriateness of community involvement approaches. Ritchie *et al.* (2002) demonstrate how monitoring in the Banff Bow Valley identified problems with tourism development that will then require further investigation and indicators to assess the effects of amelioration strategies. Had indicators been developed at the outset of the development, the impact may not have occurred, or at least could have been addressed earlier. However, at the outset of the development the rationale for the community to monitor the impact would not have existed. Tosun (2000, p. 627) recognizes the difficulty in introducing such approaches once the power structures in a destination have become set and therefore suggests '. . . deliberate measurements must be taken at the "exploration stage" of tourism developments to empower local people to keep control over tourism development before local destinations become more popular and attractive for large capital owners'. Such a position does not concede defeat in trying to overcome power imbalances in destinations where tourism is more developed, but it does point to a different challenge. The difficulty with introducing impact-related measurement at the exploration stage of tourism development is that the impacts have yet to be felt and there is little motivation for measurement. Stonich (1998) identifies the lack of information that exists before booms in tourism development as being responsible for the inability to provide evidence of the causal connection between the growth of tourism and impacts in the destination. Ryan (2002) also recognizes the inertia to measurement and the reactivity of communities expressing their vision of the future.

Beyond the lack of data at the outset of a project, the role of indicators in enhancing community involvement needs to be assessed stringently to help resolve the arguments over the value of community involvement. The tourism literature is replete with statements as to why there needs to be community involvement if tourism is to be sustainable. Murphy (1985, p. 171) writes, 'Input from concerned community groups could provide a balance to the sustainable tourism objectives of the business sector, and possibly encourage greater variation and local flavour in future projects', while Simmons (1994, p. 98) contends that 'residents of destination areas are being seen increasingly as the nucleus of the tourism product'. More emphatically, Pigram (1990, p. 6) believes, 'Undoubtedly, decision making in the tourism sphere would benefit from public input' and Webster (1998, p. 192) concludes, 'An essential part of the eventual solution is the involvement of those who have a stake in the outcome'.

Against this, Mowforth and Munt (1998) describe the drive for local participation as a 'general fashion', while Taylor (1995) believes that it suits western sensibilities and is politically expedient to know that locals are participating in their own futures and being self-deterministic even when the end result may be indistinct from an externally run tourism development. Whether community involvement does lead to enhanced sustainability, Donaldson and Preston (1995, pp. 86–87) are sceptical, they argue:

> . . . the instrumental case for stakeholder management cannot be satisfactorily proved . . . the ultimate managerial implication of stakeholder theory is that managers should acknowledge the validity of diverse stakeholder interests and should attempt to respond to them within a mutually supportive framework, because that is a moral requirement for the legitimacy of the management function.

They continue, '. . . the notion that stakeholder management contributes to successful economic performance, although widely believed (and not patently inaccurate), is insufficient to stand alone as a basis for the stakeholder theory' (1995, pp. 87–88). If the instrumental reason is to become more powerful, communities need to make themselves more integral to the tourism industry in order to strengthen their role as stakeholders in the success of the tourism industry. Crompton and Ap (1994) demonstrate how residents themselves may be instrumental in discouraging tourism by opposing it or exhibiting hostile behaviour towards tourism advocates and/ or tourists. As discussed above, NGOs have a role in pressuring business to engage with communities.

Brohman (1996, p. 60) is more adamant in his defence of the intrinsic, '. . . the industry ought not to forget that destinations are essentially communities'. Belief in the post-normal science would reduce the extent to which we can believe in instrumentalism, as the link between cause and effect is questioned. Hence, the need for community involvement can be said to come from an intrinsic right to self-determination, which in itself is central to sustainability. If with this self-determination the local community pursues a path contrary to Western advice or expert opinion, then Donaldson and Preston would argue this should be accepted as an example of communities' newly acquired right. It may well be difficult for the developed world to stand back and watch the use the developing world makes of its resources, but such a situation may reveal whether self-determination or preserving the world for the developed world's benefit means most to the developed world.

Yet, although the intrinsic value of community involvement is important, Murphy (1985, p. 171) acknowledges, '. . . participation on a mass scale is an idealistic dream' and even Brohman (1996) accepts the need to measure the effect of involvement on the distribution of benefits in order to add instrumental weight to an argument that otherwise relies on philosophy. Marien and Pizam (1997) argue that indicators demonstrate competence and instil confidence in fellow members of the community, as well as in business, government and other stakeholders. Making the community appear more professional in its dealings with external stakeholders can increase the chance of the group being taken more seriously and their arguments treated with greater weight. Atkisson (1996) describes how the Sustainable Seattle project made people more aware of the issues important to their community, but turned some people into champions for sustainability and an inspiration for the community. All these benefits to the community from monitoring may be universally true, or exist only within the confines of the specific research context. Involvement is after all, a battle between the principle of having everyone involved and the pragmatism of getting the group to agree. What is needed is evidence to strengthen the claims for community involvement and enable positive, instrumental reasons to be cited to advance community involvement. Similarly, indicator programmes need to move forward with the confidence that comes from evidence that they do make a positive difference. The recency of the subject makes this area of research scarce, but this is an important area for future investigation.

Perhaps the most famous example of a community making decisions through the development of an indicator programme is that of Sustainable Seattle. Box 4.7 provides a detailed explanation of how indicators helped the citizens of Seattle to force change in the city and improve sustainability.

Summary

This chapter has shown the reasons why government at various levels, NGOs and the community should be interested in using indicators to promote enhanced sustainability. Governments were shown to use indicators to create and improve awareness, as the initial stage in their dialogue with their electorate. Trust and competence can be demonstrated through indicators tracking progress of the efforts and this help build partnerships whereby governments can be clearly seen to respond to poor indicator results by changing policy. The research presented shows that the final stage of this process is difficult to realize for many reasons, but this policy change and action phase will be the true test of the worth of indicators, as is discussed further in Chapter 7.

NGOs were shown to use indicators to monitor the effects of projects in a region, this information can be empowering for a community in its battle for the kind of development desired. Developing the skills to monitor development was also shown to be empowering as it serves to reduce reliance on outside experts, so reducing the potential for exploitation and well-meaning paternalism. Included in this group must be NGOs themselves,

Box 4.7.   Sustainable Seattle.

The Sustainable Seattle project began in 1990 with a 1-day forum to consider the question 'What legacy are we leaving to future generations?' and by 1996 had been awarded a UN prize for excellence. The initial forum attracted 70 people and led to the 5-year task of developing a set of indicators of sustainability. Sustainable Seattle (1998) believes it achieves its goal of enabling the community to promote sustainability through a three-stage process of improving awareness, assessment and action.

Awareness
Although the initial conference was able to capitalize on the growing environmental concern in the early 1990s, there was a considerable lack of understanding about what sustainability was when the project began. To move forward Atkisson (1996, p. 38) describes how, 'Focusing on the practical question of how to measure sustainability in all its facets, emerged as the best way to explore the issues in more depth and to develop a sense of common understanding'. Through developing indicators the community came to recognize what was important to them, and the indicators they held an emotional attachment with. Guest speakers, round tables and newsletters were just some of the techniques employed to generate enthusiasm and improve awareness to enable the task of choosing indicators to move forward.

Assessment
The final set of 40 indicators was not reached until 1993 and then research began on the indicators to establish historical data and long-term trends. The indicators signal whether issues are improving, worsening or remaining the same. In the 1998 report, 11 were shown to be improving, eight were moving away from sustainability, 11 were neutral and there was insufficient data to show a trend for the remaining ten indicators. Consideration was given during the selection process of dropping indicators where there were no historical data, but the group felt that just because the issue had not been measured previously did not mean it was not important now. Indeed, such indicators showed the importance of the project in measuring what was important rather than simply repeating the actions of the past.

Action
Sustainable Seattle (1998) report six areas where the indicators have had a demonstrable change:

- Public policy – local government policy is now able to be assessed not just by the effect on the indicators when they are measured, but the issues policy addresses can be compared against the issues the project has identified as important. The indicators enable long-term consideration of issues, immune from the political need for more short-term fixes, as well as encourage 'whole system' thinking, rather than policy making that comes from different units of government.
- Local media – although initially uninterested, local print, radio and TV media have become firmly engaged in the process. One of the criteria for indicator selection was that it should have media appeal, with the 'number of wild salmon runs' the most famous. Media have used the indicators as headline

stories to generate understanding and awareness, as well as to exert pressure on the causes of poor performance.

- Business and economic development – business has learnt what is important to local residents and so understands what products it will benefit from bringing to the community. The basis on which business's licence to operate is granted is clear.
- Education – the indicators have focused on linkages between areas of sustainability. Hence, the number of wild salmon is connected to child poverty through school absenteeism and environmental vandalism. This has sent a strong signal to everyone, but particularly children about the potential connection of their actions with damage to the things the community values.
- Civil society – Foundations and philanthropic organizations have used the indicators to set their funding priorities, and use the indicators to arm the community in disputes with local government and business.
- Personal lifestyle – the indicators challenge individuals to view their actions in terms of what society deems to be important.

Undoubtedly, Sustainable Seattle has achieved enormous public involvement, but it is possible to be critical of the extent to which this truly was a development representative of the community, or was instead driven by the passion of a group of citizens from the community. In either case, the project represents perhaps the best example of a large-scale, resident-driven indicator project to promote sustainability and as such it deserves further attention from tourism students. Sustainable Seattle (1998, p. 4) writes of itself:

> The indicators a society chooses to report to itself about itself are surprisingly powerful. They reflect collective values and inform collective decisions. A nation that keeps a watchful eye on its salmon runs or the safety of its streets makes different choices than does a nation that is only paying attention to its GNP.
> The idea of citizens choosing their own indicators is something now under the sun – something intensely democratic.

Sources: Atkisson (1996), Lawrence (1998), Sustainable Seattle (1998).

who can use indicators to assist in their advocacy and campaigning work. Yet NGOs must also be aware of the perils of highlighting some issues in isolation from, and perhaps at the expense of other, wider sustainability issues and conscious of the need to demonstrate their positive contribution to a destination in order to justify their involvement.

The final discussion was of the assistance indicators can provide to a community in their attempts to become more sustainable. Much of the argument centres on the way individuals can be empowered to act for themselves to promote their own vision of sustainability. Questions were raised about how free communities should be to make their own mistakes or whether outside experts can be justified in taking a more controlling role. The chapter also considers whether the lack of instrumental evidence in support of community involvement weakens the argument for this shift.

The example of Sustainable Seattle is one that demonstrates the potential benefits of the citizenry grouping together, creating a shared vision of their future and then working towards that vision. The empowerment provided from the indicators, the ability to track the progress of the efforts as well as the ability to assess the sensitivity of the community to development ultimately gives an example of the role monitoring can play in enhancing community involvement in the push for more sustainable development.

The next two chapters take the reasons why the various stakeholders should be interested in indicators, and demonstrates how indicators can be developed in order to optimize their contribution in terms of a sustainability transition and avoid the many potential pitfalls that have been alluded to here.

III   Monitoring Process

The importance of high-quality, credible information about the state of sustainable tourism in a particular place or business has been highlighted. Indicators are needed to show progress, assess compliance with various regulations, compare actions with policies and identify concerns and priority issues to address. Monitoring systems are needed to convert indicator results into management action.

The third part of the book consists of three chapters. Chapter 5 explores the historical background of monitoring and indicators and reviews some fundamental considerations about indicators and monitoring techniques such as what to measure, how to organize indicators and where to measure. Chapters 6 and 7 focus on the practical aspects of indicator development. Chapter 6 explains the process involved in the design of an indicator programme, the setting of objectives for sustainable tourism and identification of potential indicators for monitoring purposes. Chapter 7 looks at how to convert these measures through efficient data collection and analysis to an action-orientated management response system.

The inclusion of process-based chapters is unusual in a tourism text. Process is usually left for discussion in disparate case studies and seldom emphasized to any degree. This may explain why there is such a dearth of sustainable tourism monitoring projects, or perhaps the lack of projects is the reason there is little knowledge of monitoring processes and techniques. What is clear is that without detailed discussion of monitoring process, progress in sustainable tourism monitoring is likely to continue to be slow, inconsistent and lacking in conceptual basis. What makes this section of the book particularly useful is the way in which it integrates interdisciplinary experience in monitoring sourcing from areas such as recreation, ecology, economics and sustainable development as well as tourism.

In process-based writing there is a temptation to explain monitoring in a step-by-step fashion. The chapters in this book avoid such a one-size-fits-all approach by providing a range of options to consider and alternatives to be used in different situations and at different phases in the monitoring process. The exact techniques used to develop indicators in a particular locality will need to be defined by unique place-based, stakeholder-defined circumstances. If they are to be successful, in view of what is now known about the behaviour of complex systems, they will also need to be adaptive, sensitive to changing situations and designed to maximize learning opportunities for all involved.

The chapters present considerations, issues and challenges faced in indicator development and monitoring in a pragmatic and critical fashion. The reader is left under no false illusions that establishing and maintaining a sustainable tourism monitoring programme is an easy process. Rather than dwelling on the problems, however, these chapters are designed to assist those involved in sustainable tourism monitoring to search for viable solutions and alternative ways forward.

Monitoring Using Indicators   5

Introduction

The previous two chapters have sought to establish reasons why and how stakeholders use indicators in their drive for increased sustainability. Without understanding if there is sufficient motivation to begin the process, there is little value in exploring how a programme of sustainable tourism indicators might be established. It is hoped that the reader is sufficiently convinced of the potential merits of monitoring as an approach to promoting sustainable tourism that we can now turn to the detail of monitoring using indicators.

This chapter begins by exploring the historical background of monitoring and indicators. History provides us with important lessons to learn if indicators are to remain a valuable tool in the pursuit of sustainability. Distinction is drawn between conventional indicators and indicators of sustainability, before examining key considerations for monitoring sustainability. These considerations are multifarious, but are discussed by asking a number of simple questions: what to measure, what type of indicators to use, how to organize indicators, where to measure and how much does it cost. These discussions are exploratory rather than conclusive, and in many ways act as a primer for Chapters 6 and 7, where the practical challenges of indicator development are explained in more detail. Examples of current indicator programmes are provided throughout this chapter to illustrate the monitoring process. However, the chapter concludes with a note of caution, warning against the belief that indicators can solve the problems of sustainability; they are a tool to be used alongside other tools and in conjunction with determination and effort.

©G.A. Miller and L. Twining-Ward 2005. *Monitoring for a Sustainable Tourism Transition* (G.A. Miller and L. Twining-Ward)

Origins of Monitoring

The UK Department of Culture, Media and Sport (DCMS, 1999, p. 3) states the 'aim of indicators is to produce what is measurable and show us something'. Put more simply, 'an indicator is something that helps you to understand where you are, which way you are going and how far you are from where you want to be' (Hart, 1999). Whereas statistics provide raw data with no meaning attached, indicators of sustainable development provide meaning that extends beyond the attributes directly associated with the data.

Death and taxes are said to be the two certainties in life, and monitoring has been used to assess both of these. The Romans conducted census surveys to assist in the accurate collection of taxes, while Carley (1981) reports how mortality rates have been monitored to assess the quality of health provision. However, as populations have grown, so has the need to use indicators as proxies for the actual phenomena that is of interest, and so the problems began. In 1924, Pigou criticized the neo-classical economists for failing to understand that private welfare is not the same as public welfare. In 1934, Kuznets told the US Congress 'The welfare of a nation can scarcely be inferred from a measurement of national income' (quoted in Denny and Vidal, 1998), demonstrating the perceived lack of effectiveness of the indicator (national income) in assessing the issue of interest (welfare). Carley (1981, p. 16) reports of President Hoover setting up a President's Committee to '. . . help all of us to see where the social stresses are occurring and where the major efforts should be taken to deal with them constructively'. Yet the fate of the committee is instructive. The aim had been to collect social data on 32 topics and then to annually report on the progress of the nation on these issues. From 1928 to 1934 this was the case, but with the onset of the great depression in the USA, priorities shifted, the collection of the data was stopped and no further publications came forth.

During the mid-1930s, the prevailing economic conditions of Western economies were such that monitoring was seen as an unaffordable luxury and indicators of social welfare were not developed or used again until the mid-1960s. By the 1960s, there were once again growing levels of affluence and evidence of this national wealth from the success of economic indicators in capturing and relaying key information to decision makers and the general public. Yet the success of the gross national product (GNP) and gross domestic product (GDP) in informing end-users also highlighted their shortcomings in failing to explain the whole picture. Henderson (in Hart, 1999, p. 39) explains, '. . . trying to run a complex society on a single indicator like the GNP is . . . like trying to fly a 747 with only one gauge on the instrument panel'. It is perhaps ironic that the increasing calls for social indicators came as a result of the prominence of economic indicators, but Gross (1966) refers to the way in which these economic measures led to the over-emphasis on monetary issues, something he describes as 'economic philistinism'. (It is an interesting question as to whether the indicators simply reflect the thinking of the time, which was heavily influenced by economics, or whether the indicators came to subvert thinking and influenced the targets to be achieved. Given the rise in awareness of the environment described by Chapter 1, it is reasonable to assume the indicators reflected the wisdom of the time.)

It was understood that the development of social indicators needed to be conducted alongside the traditional economic measures, rather than attempting to replace them entirely. Carley (1981, p. 19) describes how the huge boom in social indicators during the mid-1960s to late 1970s was marked by 'a kind of boundless enthusiasm which envisioned dramatic progress in social measurement and social accounting, translated into almost utopian social planning for a new and improved quality of life'. However, this optimism and recognition of the problem with economic indicators again fell foul of changing economic circumstances in the late 1970s, returning to concentrate on economic measures.

Indeed, it was not until the late 1980s that the sustainable development movement effectively tied environmental conservation with poverty reduction and economic welfare. Since the Rio Earth Summit, many organizations, led by those associated with the UN, have begun to develop indicators as tools for monitoring progress made towards the broad goals of sustainable development (UNCSD, 2001a), amongst them, the very organizations which 50 years ago set the rules on how to take economic measures. Bell and Morse (1999, p. 23) attest, '. . . indicators have been seen by many as the core element in operationalizing sustainability'. Agenda 21 places considerable emphasis on the need to monitor sustainable development using indicators. Chapter 40, for example, notes that indicators can provide a solid base for decision making at all levels. The UNCSD followed up on this interest in monitoring and approved a work programme on indicators of sustainable development at its Third Session in April 1995. This emphasis was reiterated in the 1997 Special Session of the General Assembly (Earth Summit + 5), and again in a UNCSD bulletin, which stresses that indicators are important tools to reduce complexity of information on sustainable development and to support national decision making (UNCSD, 2001b). Box 5.1 discusses the UNCSD programme of work to develop indicators of sustainable development.

As well as the UN, a wide range of other acronymic international organizations, governments, regional authorities, community groups and researchers have contributed to the monitoring literature (OECD, 1993; Hammond *et al.*, 1995; Manitoba Environment, 1997; Peterson, 1997; UK Roundtable on Sustainable Development, 1997; Meadows, 1998; Sustainable Seattle, 1998; US Interagency Working Group on Sustainable Development Indicators, 1998). Among the more established, the OECD (1993) describe their commonly agreed set of environmental indicators for tracking sustainable development in OECD countries in regular reports

---

Box 5.1.   Development of indicators by the UNCSD.

In 1995, the UNCSD approved a programme of work to develop indicators of sustainable development. The main objective of the work programme was to make indicators of sustainable development accessible to decision makers at the national level. There are three phases to the programme:

Phase 1 (May 1995–August 1996): Development of the indicator methodology sheets
Through a series of expert groups, consultations and workshops, methodology sheets were devised for each indicator. The result was published in 1996 for comment, with the aim of producing an accepted and definitive set of indicators by 2001.

Phase 2 (May 1996–January 1998): Capacity building and national testing
Workshops were organized in order to train people in the use of indicators as a tool for decision making and to consider methodological improvements. Countries were encouraged to pilot, test, utilize and experiment with the indicators developed. Many test countries established 'twinning' arrangements with other test countries in order to compare experiences and data.

Phase 3 (January 1999–December 2000): Lessons learned
The testing process was felt to have been successful, with many countries reporting the value of the exercise coming from the process of indicator development as much as the results achieved. Lack of human and financial capacity was held to be a problem, as was the time taken to report on all the indicators. A common problem cited was the need to reconcile nationally important indicators with those important internationally.

Source: UNCSD (2002).

(Box 5.2). Hammond *et al.* (1995) discuss the Dutch and World Resources Institute attempts to develop greenhouse gas indices and Moldan (1997b) acknowledges the efforts of the UK to develop a set of indicators of sustainable development. Box 5.2 provides an example of the OECD approach to indicators.

Monitoring in a tourism context

Despite a traditional lack of data, the tourism industry has monitored destination performance for many years using conventional tourism indicators such as arrival numbers, length of stay and tourist expenditure (Ceron and Dubois, 2003). These figures are easily criticized for the lack of consistent methodology employed by countries to define and count visitors and hence the lack of comparability across destinations. As the WTO has encouraged countries to employ a standard methodology, so the value of longitudinal data has been eroded. Further criticism of these conventional tourism indicators can be directed at the economic and growth-orientated focus of the

Box 5.2. OECD environmental indicators.

The OECD began publishing environmental indicators in 1991; the indicators are sectoral to enable the integration of environmental concerns into decisions affecting entire industries. The OECD points to two major functions of indicators:

- To reduce the number of measurements and parameters that normally would be required to give an exact presentation of a situation;
- To simplify the communication process by which the results of measurement are provided to the user.

The OECD provides the following useful definitions:

- Indicator: a parameter, or a value derived from parameters, which points to, provides information about, describes the state of a phenomenon/ environment/area, with a significance extending beyond that directly associated with a parameter value;
- Index: a set of aggregated or weighted parameters or indicators;
- Parameter: a property that is measured or observed.

Source: OECD (2003).

measures. Despite the rising world interest in the environment during the mid-1980s, the WTO (1985) report into developing indicators for travel and tourism ignores mention of anything but economic issues and continues to broadcast as good news new record numbers of visitors to particular destinations. Still today, the WTO seems to be determined to report to the world how large tourism is as an industry in terms of arrivals and expenditure, rather than in terms of the other contributions tourism is known to make (WTO, 2004a). WTTC pursues a similar strategy, using economic and growth-orientated indicators to advertise the power of the industry and lobby for a greater role in international trade negotiations. The development of the WTTC's Competitiveness Monitor to assess the results of government policy on travel and tourism is heavily skewed towards the development of the tourism industry, rather than the development of the destination (WTTC, 2004). In the same way as GDP has been found to be an inadequate measure of human welfare, therefore, conventional tourism indicators can be seen as inadequate measures of tourism's true performance.

Nevertheless, an increasing number of tourism researchers are stressing the need for the development of more comprehensive sustainable tourism indicators that make the important connection between tourism and the wider economic, environmental and social processes in the destination (Inskeep, 1991; Butler, 1993a; Coccossis, 1996; Dymond, 1997; Goodall and Stabler 1997; WTTC *et al.*, 1997; Mowforth and Munt, 1998; Weaver, 1998; Swarbrooke, 1999; Weaver and Lawton, 1999; James, 2000; Miller, 2001a; Moisey and McCool, 2001; Sirakaya *et al.*, 2001). Despite the attentions of these authors, Weaver and Lawton (1999, p. 21) in their review argue,

'. . . attention to the indicators issue in the tourism literature has not been as great as one might expect, considering its pivotal role in the sustainability monitoring process'.

Moisey and McCool (2001) question how we can possibly know if tourism development is contributing to sustainability without a set of indicators to measure progress. Swarbrooke (1999, p. 355) states that monitoring systems and performance indicators are 'key issues' in the implementation of sustainable tourism, while the more taciturn Goodall and Stabler (1997) suggest the indicator approach can make a useful contribution to sustainable tourism decision making. Weaver (1998, p. 8) explains that the implementation of sustainable tourism is impeded by the current 'unsophisticated state' of understanding with regards to indicators, and Butler (1999, p. 16) suggests that without indicators the term sustainable tourism is 'meaningless'. In the same vein, the Fourth International Forum on Sustainable Tourism Statistics in Copenhagen, 1998, discussed the need for more work on sustainable tourism indicators, and one of the findings from the University of Westminster's 1-day conference on sustainable tourism was the current lack of means to measure tourism's sustainability (James, 2000; Ladkin, 2000).

Notwithstanding the assistance provided by such early monitoring programmes, the shift from using conventional indicators to indicators of sustainable tourism is a difficult one. Sirakaya *et al.* (2001, p. 418) explain the difference between conventional and sustainable tourism indicators: 'Indicators of sustainability for tourism differ from traditional development indicators because they take into consideration the web of complex interrelationships and interdependencies of resources and stakeholder in the tourism system'. Hart (1999) also explains that conventional indicators measure just one variable such as employment, as if it were entirely independent of other variables such as visitor numbers or expenditure. Multi-dimensional sustainability indicators require a more integrated view of the world showing the links between the economy, environment, society and tourism and importantly link with action to enable change rather than just being an indicator of a situation. These differences are contrasted in Box 5.3.

Box 5.3.   Conventional versus sustainability indicators.

Conventional indicators	Sustainability indicators	Emphasis of sustainability indicators
Median income	Number of hours paid employment at average wage required to support basic needs	What wage can buy
Unemployment rate	Diversity and vitality of local job base	Resilience of the job market

Adapted from: Hart (1999, p. 9).

The shift to sustainability indicators involves recognizing that conventional indicators are failing to provide enough information for tourism managers to address the full range of challenges and opportunities facing them. Attaining a wider input of data therefore needs to be coupled with, and will predicate, a more comprehensive understanding of the tourism industry.

Indicator Considerations

The temptation with any approach that purports to provide information is to believe that it will provide all the information needed and as such becomes a panacea. Yet, the understanding that indicators cannot themselves create sustainable tourism is of crucial importance; they are a tool, not a solution, and a technical approach to a very human problem (Ceron and Dubois, 2003). As such, there are many considerations to discuss.

What to measure

Establishing what to measure is as complex as delineating the fluid subject boundaries of sustainable tourism. A key theme of this book is the need for boundaries to be dismantled, enabling students, managers and governments to deliver more comprehensive and sustainable solutions to tourism destinations. Chapter 2 explained in depth about the benefits that can accrue from breaking down the barriers surrounding the study of tourism. Notwithstanding, Miller (2001a) found that a large proportion of tourism academics and experts still feel that tourism should not concern itself with matters 'beyond tourism'. For example, an issue such as equity was felt by some respondents to be important, but mostly not something that the tourism industry should concern itself with.

Consequently, despite the clear demand and progress made in recreation and other fields related to sustainable development, research on sustainable tourism indicators, like other areas of tourism, is still very parochial, constrained as we are by our disciplinary blinkers. Early indicator studies tended to focus more on conventional impact assessment than the achievement of sustainable tourism development and there is a general lack of empirical experience on which to ground the work (Marion, 1991; Crotts and Holland, 1993; Kreutzwiser, 1993; Craik, 1995). Craik (1995), for example, discusses the development of cultural indicators of sustainable tourism and, based on impact research, provides a long list of possible indicators which includes issues such as economic dependence on tourism, degree of public involvement and consultation in planning and management, perceived environmental degradation and conflicts within the community.

Seminal works such as those by Mathieson and Wall (1982), Cohen (1972, 1978) and Butler (1974) have expanded attention for the study of impacts, while the early monitoring work of the WTO also focuses on the management of impacts and the gathering of information that will allow 'decision makers' in the tourism sector to reduce risk to their 'own sector' (WTO, 1993). The University of Waterloo Heritage Resources Centre held a seminar on monitoring, planning and managing tourism and sustainable development in 1991, although few authors got as far as identifying possible indicators or indicator development processes; those that did were inward looking, heavily focused on economic issues and little different from conventional tourism indicators (Nelson *et al.*, 1993).

The paper by Crotts and Holland (1993) can perhaps be seen as an intervening step between conventional and sustainability indicators. The authors took conventional tourism figures and correlated these with quality of life figures already in use in Florida. By including indicators of housing and food costs, local government debt per capita, daily withdrawals from water system, average daily water treatment charges and crime rate, this approach acknowledges impacts and influences beyond the conventionally conceived tourism system. More recently Sirakaya *et al.* (2001) provide perhaps the best account of the need to develop sets of indicators to reflect this expanded range of concerns.

The chapter began by demonstrating the push for the development of indicators because of recognition that economic indicators were insufficient to capture the complexity of the concept of human welfare. If indicators are required to actually measure the phenomena they are intended to, then because we have physical and psychological inputs into our lives, it is axiomatic, regardless of the complexity of the task of measuring, that all aspects must be measured in order to determine quality of life (Carley, 1981). Sirakaya *et al.* (2001) note the need to consider ecological, social, economic, institutional, cultural and psychological dimensions in indicator discussions and highlights the importance of maximizing community participation in the indicator development process. In this respect the paper recommends establishing a community-based structure for indicator monitoring, and provides useful practical advice for how this might be achieved (discussed further in Chapter 6). Yet the research literature invariably stops short of actually implementing the proposed monitoring framework, making it difficult to evaluate the practical implications of the work, a problem explored further in the following two chapters.

What type of indicators?

Connected to the question 'what to monitor' is the decision over the type of indicators and indicator grouping systems to be used. One of the central issues concerns the use of quantitative over qualitative indicator data.

Economic impacts have traditionally been measured using quantitative indicators and were felt to provide an objective measure of the issue under consideration. Objective indicators are taken to mean the counting of specific occurrences or events, while subjective measures, often reflecting social and cultural issues are those of feelings or perceptions based on reports or descriptions by respondents. Thus, quantitative indicators and data have been taken to be objective, rigorous and reliable while qualitative measures have been saddled with the tag of 'subjective' and have been presented as scientifically weaker for it, reflecting a wider debate.

Gallopín (1997) challenges this view and highlights the subjectivity in selecting which phenomena to measure, determining the target value of that attribute and the weighting of simple indicators in any composite scale. For Dahl (1997a) the subjectivity involved with weighting indicators is sufficient that any such approach can be rendered 'suspect'. Nevertheless, the majority of indicators of sustainable development selected are presented as objective, quantitative and normative. Gallopín (1997, p. 17) suggests that this is due to the subject matter, which more naturally lends itself to quantitative measurement, although he acknowledges that this approach will only perpetuate the over-representation of economic data, which in turn lends itself more naturally to quantitative measures.

A further danger of the quantitative indicator, as with much quantitative research, is the pseudo-scientific air afforded to the data because it can be expressed as figures, numbers and charts. Carley (1981) warns of being seduced by the unlikely triumvirate of numbers, statistical procedures and models, while Whitehouse (2003, p. 5) is critical of indicators for creating this 'scientific illusion', which he refers to the 'fallacy of misplaced concreteness' of economics (in Daly and Cobb, 1990). The quantitative traditions of measurement fit comfortably with the Newtonian/Cartesian approach to causality and limit our thinking to what we believe can be proven to be relevant.

Here the debate becomes stuck in a self-perpetuating cycle with a paradigmatic shift needed to open the field to more qualitative issues that are best measured by qualitative indicators. The challenge is therefore to design qualitative indicators that can compare favourably with the more traditionally established quantitative measures so the issues are not dismissed because of the poverty of the measure. It is important to understand that the role of the indicator is not to 'prove' the effectiveness of anything. Indicators do not become invalid if they identify a situation that may have been caused by a myriad of external factors. Hughes (2002, p. 471) states, 'In the absence of certainty about causes and effects, black and white shades off into grey and quantification slides into qualitative judgement. This inconclusiveness undermines the basic function of environmental indicators.' Yet, the role of indicators, as the name suggests, is to 'indicate' whether a situation is moving in the desired direction. The shift to a less linear approach to thinking requires appropriate methods of measurement, and this forces us to consider the value of qualitative indicators, and so lean more heavily on other disciplines to supplement the traditionally quantitative approach tourism researchers have adopted. Winderl (2003, p. 10) reminds us, '. . . the choice of the "right" indicators is an art rather than a science'.

How to organize indicators

Moving on from the qualitative/quantitative dilemma, the more difficult test facing those who wish to develop indicators is to understand how indicators fit together and accomplish their task. There must be recognition that there is an inter-relation between indicators, rather than a belief that indicators are discrete variables, which can be considered separately. Only through testing and logically organizing indicators can this information become available and so future sets and their interconnectivity be improved.

Having a clear, logical framework in place can greatly assist stakeholders to adopt a comprehensive approach to indicator development rather than just drafting a long list of unrelated measures. The indicator categories most commonly used in sustainable tourism monitoring are economic, social, environment, social, cultural and or institutional groupings. Examples of projects adopting this approach include the International FTO ECOMOST study (Hughes, 2002), the Samoa Sustainable Tourism Indicator Project (SSTIP), and the Tourist Optimization Management model (TOMM) Kangaroo Island project. TOMM used economic, market-opportunity, environmental and experiential conditions for Kangaroo Island's tourism sector (Manidis Roberts Consultants, 1997; see Chapter 9). In Samoa, using a thematic approach reinforced the idea that economy, environment and society are of similar importance to the sustainable development of a community but, on the down side, it also suggested these themes are self-contained rather than inherently linked and multi-dimensional.

An alternative indicator grouping system now commonly used for sustainable development monitoring is the Pressure–State–Response matrix (sometimes referred to as the Driving-Force–State–Response (D-S-R)) originally developed by the OECD (1998). 'Pressure indicators' measure human activities, processes and patterns that impact sustainable development. 'State indicators' show the state of a particular aspect of sustainable development at a specific point in time and 'response indicators' measure the willingness and effectiveness of society to provide social and policy responses to the changes in the 'state' of sustainable development (OECD, 1998). The WTO (1996) use this system in their early indicator studies identifying 'warning indicators' and 'pressure/stress indicators' to measure external factors of concern, 'resource state' and impact indicators' to reflect state and effect of current resource use, and 'indicators of management action' and 'management impact'. Although the Pressure–State–Response (PSR) framework is good at breaking down disciplinary boundaries and promoting a more comprehensive, systemic approach, it is often difficult to assign indicators to particular categories, can result in a burgeoning indicator list and be misleading if unfounded assumptions are made about the linkages between pressures, states and responses.

A third possible option in terms of indicator categories is to group indicators according to the specific sustainable development goals they are designed to measure. This is called the goal-matrix framework. The UK sustainable tourism indicator project adopts this approach, using the five indicator categories that coincide with the goals of the UK Sustainable Development Report 'A Better Quality of Life' ('sending the right signals', 'a sustainable economy', 'building sustainable communities', 'managing the environment' and 'international cooperation') (DETR, 1999; Allin *et al.*, 2000). The goal-matrix framework has the advantage of ensuring that indicators are focused on actual community goals and issues (Hart, 1999), but they often also need to be sorted thematically to group common issues together. In this way, it is perfectly possible to combine several different types of indicators at different levels. For example, the UN Indicators of Sustainable Development are sorted by themes, then by chapter headings and goals identified in Agenda 21, and finally using the Driving-Force–State–Response Framework. This system is illustrated in Box 5.4.

Ultimately, the decision on what type of indicator and indicator categories to use will depend on the nature of the monitoring project and the skills and interests of the user group. The PSR indicator categories are more in tune with the comprehensive systemic approach recommended in this book, but they perhaps are best suited to expert developed systems. In contrast, non-expert groups are likely to feel more comfortable with the simple thematic approach. As always, there will need to be a balance between the art and the science, what appears in theory to be the most

---

Box 5.4. UNCSD working indicators.

Theme: Social
Chapter of Agenda 21: 36

Goal	Driving-force/ Pressure	State	Response
Promoting educations, public awareness and training	Rate of change of school age Primary school enrolment ratio Secondary school enrolment	Children reaching grade 5 of primary education School life expectancy	GDP spent on education

Source: UN (1996).

appropriate tool to use, with that which is actually functional on the ground.

Where to measure

In asking where measurement should take place, there are two areas of consideration. The first refers to the practical problems of delineating the physical, sectoral or conceptual boundaries of the area where monitoring will take place; the second, more conceptual set of problems refers to what should be the ideal scale of measurement (local, regional, national, international). Turning to the practical problem of physical boundaries first, it is rare that the pressures, states and responses to a problem neatly adhere to one geographical area (Dumanski and Pieri, 2000). Pollution from British factories causes a change in the state of German and Scandinavian forests, which necessitates a policy response at a European level. Further, an indicator will give different measures according to the area of measurement it is applied to. Sustainable development therefore requires to be measured at a range of geographical areas from local to international. Goodall and Stabler (1997) cite an example of a hypothetical hotel that introduces new energy-saving technology as a cost-cutting measure. However, as a result of advertising its green credentials it attracts more guests, which increases its total energy demand and waste generation, while also adding to the local congestion and air pollution caused by guests travelling to the hotel. If a national scale of measurement is used, and, assuming the increase in visitation is simply redirecting guests from less energy-efficient hotels, there is a reduction in total energy consumed. However, if a local scale of measurement is employed, the energy-efficient hotel may be seen as contributing to a worsening problem. Using a limited scale of analysis, local authorities under pressure to improve air quality, energy usage and waste generation could therefore look unfavourably on energy-saving technology. Chapter 2 demonstrates how a case can be made for a comprehensive approach to sustainable tourism and it therefore follows that this should also apply to monitoring sustainable tourism.

Mowforth and Munt (1998, p. 70) write, 'Too global an analysis ignores local lessons and too local an analysis ignores global questions'. Indeed, monitoring over a larger spatial area does run the risk that important localized conditions will not be recognized, but it does increase the chance that data is already collected by a national or international body. Conversely, indicators measuring impacts at a very local level will be less likely to be measured by larger, external organizations so trend data is unlikely to be available, made up for perhaps by greater local detail.

Invariably, the answer sought is a compromise, whereby attempts are made to preserve local identity with the use of locally specific indicators but to ensure the data can be aggregated to a regional or national level to ensure comparability against regional or national level issues. This is easier said than done, Lawrence (1998), for example, concludes that it is impossible to have a one-size-fits-all approach, while Garcia *et al.* (2000, p. 550) believe, '. . . it may be necessary to agree on a common minimum set of information to be collected', although they concede this is only the case '. . . if the objective is to agree progress towards SD at a regional or global level'. The WTO approach to delineating indicator boundaries is explained in Box 5.5.

The more conceptual issue of what spatial scale should be used to measure sustainability has produced a plethora of opinion and approaches. Moldan (1997a) suggests the need for more indicators at a household level rather than the current preoccupation with national and international level research, while Miller (2003) focuses on the applicability of indicators to the consumer. Dixey (1998) writes of the work UKCEED did at a resort level to indicate pressures, state and responses, while the DJSI concentrates on the corporate group as a whole and how it is performing. Local Agenda 21 has ensured that local and regional authorities around the world are required to provide measures of key issues pertinent to that geographical district and at a UK national level, strong attempts to develop indicators of sustainable tourism by DCMS and indicators of sustainable development by

---

Box 5.5. WTO Guide to delineating indicator boundaries.

The WTO (2004b) recognizes the difficulties of spatial scale and provides the following guide for choosing destination boundaries.

Include key sites and assets
The boundaries should wherever possible surround all of the key assets of the destination.

Try to match existing political and data boundaries with natural and ecological boundaries
Wherever possible, boundaries should be selected which reflect physical or ecological boundaries. The ideal is sometimes attainable by selecting political boundaries which best emulate biophysical ones.

Consider subdividing the destination
In some cases, it may be useful to subdivide the destination into parts for separate analysis, particularly where there are significant differences between parts of the destination such as a core area, where most of the activity occurs, and a peripheral area, which is also clearly impacted or involved.

Consider specific sub-areas for special consideration
Certain areas of a destination will receive different pressures to other areas, and so should be considered 'hot spots' (e.g. the beach, a specific ecological asset). Indicators of the overall destination will not capture the pressures on these areas. Such areas should receive special treatment as a subset of the overall destination.

Source: WTO (2004b).

the Department for Environment, Transport and the Regions (DETR) have been made. Internationally, the European Environment Agency covers European member states, the OECD covers developed countries and the UNCSD takes a global approach to measurement.

Zentilli (1997) believes that this multiplicity of approaches and scales of reference is a strength of indicators of sustainable development, and the many angles researchers have been able to tackle the issue from has all added to the total body of research. Rutherford (1997a) agrees with the need to tackle the puzzle from as many different perspectives as possible and because of the current concentration on national level indicators states there should be more focus on lower level analyses in the future.

In the tourism literature, Weaver and Lawton (1999) identify five possible levels for defining indicators including international, national, regional, local or site-specific for monitoring particular hot spots. Middleton and Hawkins (2000), on the other hand, propose indicators that are developed for use at the local level on the basis that local authorities have closer contact with community stakeholders. The British Resorts Association (James, 2000), also decided local sustainable tourism indicators would be better at demonstrating the relationship between tourism impacts and the community as these occur at the level of a specific site.

We have stressed throughout this book the need to raise and retain local community involvement in the development of indicators; this provides a sense of ownership and control over the development process and the subsequent use of the indicators (Kreutzwiser, 1993; Lankford and Howard, 1994; Webster, 1998). In terms of promoting sustainability, the increased local involvement achieved through the indicator development process, plus seeking to preserve what is special to an area, can be seen as a strong attribute. Box 5.6 summarizes the differences in local and regional monitoring programmes.

An alternative way of looking at the issue, perhaps more conducive to sustainable tourism, is to fit monitoring to the scale of ecological functions. Holling and Gunderson (2002, p. 27) explain further: 'Ecosystems are moving targets, with multiple futures that are uncertain and unpredictable. Therefore management has to be flexible, adaptive and experimental at scales compatible with the scales of critical ecosystem functions'. Perhaps then, there is no single scale at which we can obtain a full understanding of the condition of ecosystems or their tourism relatives. The design of comprehensive multi-scale monitoring systems for sustainable tourism is a long way from reality, but this does not reduce its desirability as a long-term goal. In the meantime, the rather obvious answer to the problem of scale of measurement is that indicators should be developed that fit with the scale of decision making (James, 2000). Hence, global warming is a major global problem that requires global action, and so should be monitored at the global scale by global institutions (Stiglitz, 2002). By contrast, the effect of a change in pub and bar opening hours on crime levels, amount of noise and

Box 5.6. Comparison of local and regional monitoring.

Characteristic	Local monitoring	Regional monitoring
Purpose	Determine the effects of an individual project	Determine the aggregate effect of management activities on the region
Dominant user of information	Local managers and publics	Applicable to all managers and interests in the region
Limitations	Cannot extrapolate findings to other projects or to the region	Cannot describe the consequences of management at the individual site
Site selection	Project or activity of interest	Selected to be representative of the region

Source: Busch and Trexler (2002, p. 91).

congestion are things within the control of local authorities to change and so should be monitored by local level indicators. Depending on the extent of local democratic empowerment, there is always likely to be a slight disparity between the level at which the impact is felt and the level at which a response is possible, but this is an argument for greater political devolution.

How much does it cost?

As more and more development organizations strive to secure funding in a competitive environment, there has been an increasing need to justify resource use and demonstrate tangible results. In the past, donors were satisfied with knowing their funds had been put 'in' to projects and measured these using input indicators (Whitehouse, 2003). Now there is a need to calculate not just outputs (the number of people trained) but actual outcomes (the extent to which, through their training, government offices are working more efficiently). In a rejoinder to Whitehouse (2003), Winderl (2003) states that 2–3% of the cost of any project should be budgeted to monitor effectiveness of how the remaining 97–98% is spent. Alternatively expressed, for a £3 million project, £90,000 would need to be spent on monitoring, or about 5 weeks of a 3-year project. Winderl (2003) believes nowhere near this amount of resources is currently committed to monitoring most major sustainable development projects and that much more resources need to be committed to ensure a high-quality monitoring and evaluation processes. Yet, even with the paucity of resources spent on monitoring, the cost of monitoring programmes can be seen as detracting from money that could otherwise be spent on programmes of action. This unhelpful comparison, between the perceived value of taking action versus assessing the effectiveness of action, will place further pressure on monitoring programmes when resources are limited.

Of course, with perfect resources, each scale of analysis could include measures of everything that was felt to be of importance in assessing sustainability. However, in the real world there is an inevitable trade-off between the need to produce high-quality indicators and build stakeholder involvement, with the need to produce indicators that are cost-effective and can be developed in a reasonable timeframe. This is particularly the case in a world where decisions need to be transparent and return on any money spent, whether it is private or public money, is mandatory. The most likely determinant of whether the indicator process can be cost-effective or not is whether the data are already available through another source, and whether the geographic boundaries for those measures match the intended boundaries for the current project. If not, a new data-collection programme needs to be conducted. The danger is that because of a lack of resources, cheaper methods will be used and the credibility of the programme will be threatened. In the case of developing countries with limited financial and human resources, this also raises the question of whether simple, budget monitoring programmes are worthwhile or whether perhaps the money is better spent upgrading the product. Whitehouse (2003) notes there will always indicators that are easy to measure but essentially trivial, versus the more difficult to measure outcome indicators, which at the same time are much more significant. If the information is to be cost-effective, not just cheap, then those commissioning the research must acknowledge that just as there is an upper limit to what can be spent, so there is a lower threshold of expense below which the information cannot be effectively provided.

How are the data presented?

The purpose of indicators is to simplify complex data for end-users in order to improve the quality of subsequent decisions taken. To do this, the indicators must be clearly understandable. The European Commission (EC), lamenting the state of environmental reporting up to the early 1990s, avers:

> information which is available is often not processed or presented in a
> suitable form for potential end-users – administrations, enterprises and the
> general public – and does not take account of the different levels of
> sophistication or simplification required, nor of the fact that different types of
> decision require different types or levels of information.
>
> (EC, 1992, p. 7.1d)

Similarly, Peterson (1997) believes indicators, as tools within the decision making process, will not be successful unless they are constructed in association with those who will use them. Peterson (1997) advocates, as a minimum, the audience and the intended users of the indicators should determine the degree of aggregation, the number of indicators and the amount of information. These three factors will determine the nature and style of the final indicators. Van Esch (1997) reports how in the use of indicators of sustainable development in the Netherlands, where although there was no direct public input, the indicators were highly aggregated in order to achieve their purpose as a broad communication tool with which to inform the public of sustainability performance.

In order to ensure the target audience understands the indicators of sustainable development, Van Esch (1997, p. 316) believes 'limits should be applied in order to avoid confusion or an overload of information', which would otherwise be the case if reams of non-aggregated data were provided to the general public. Meadows (1998) explains that aggregation is necessary to keep from overwhelming the system with too much detail. The suggestion is that the further data can be aggregated, the wider the understanding and awareness and so the greater the prospect of stakeholders becoming involved with issues affecting the community. Yet, the need to aggregate data must be balanced with the need for detail, as information is inevitably lost as indicators are aggregated. Carley's (1981) concern is that indicators may fall into the same trap as the economic measures suffered, in trying to reduce too much to too little, and oversimplifying the concept being measured. A good example of such a highly aggregated indicator might be the 2004 proposal by the UK Conservative party for a 'tax neutral day', which would be a national holiday to celebrate the symbolic day of the year when UK workers are free of the burden of taxation from government and begin to earn money for themselves. Such a holiday would enable taxpayers to understand more easily if the tax burden they face is increasing or decreasing according to whether the national holiday comes earlier or later in the year. Yet, what such an action ignores is the reason for taxation, so a more useful indicator might be to celebrate the day of the year when the National Health Service meets its target patient waiting time, or the day when class sizes in schools are reduced to a target level. The drive for simplicity and ease of understanding obscures the complexity of the issue.

The ultimate form of data aggregation is the development of indices, whereby the data from indicators are reduced to a single score. A simple example of such an index is the weather forecast, which determines the weather will be 'fine', or 'sunny'. Here, a mass of complex data is reduced to a description the end-user can understand. Quantitative indices can be calculated by weighting indicator results to produce a single overall score. Although these are popular with politicians and decision makers, for many reliant on the weather such as fishermen, farmers and yachties, this level of aggregation may be too basic and not meet their needs. Perhaps the more serious issue, however is the subjective way in which the various indicators are weighted within the index, as a change in the weighting may often produce an entirely different overall score. The risk is that a complex subject like sustainability is reduced to a single score. Hence, as with the *Hitchhiker's Guide to the Galaxy*, the answer to 'the ultimate question of life, the universe and everything' is deemed to be 42, missing the point that it is the complexity of the question that is of importance (Adams, 1996). Whatever the level of aggregation, perhaps the most important requirement is that the subjectivity of the process is acknowledged and any weightings employed made transparent.

However, indicators produce information that is not necessarily 'right' or 'wrong', but requires interpreting, someone to decide if more police officers on the street is a good thing or not (Box 5.7). Nowicki and Nowicki-Caupin (1987, p. 43) refer to the opportunity for political interference, and state with an Orwellian sense of control, 'Information is not neutral – the manner in which it is transmitted determines how it is perceived'. Beyond the ability to interpret data differently, political needs can affect the programme itself. In 1991 the UK government launched and published an annual environmental report with the intention of monitoring the UK government's progress on a number of key indicators, which would then be available for the general public. By 1992, it was discovered that the government of the time was falling back rather than making progress on a number of its measures, and so the programme was abandoned and not published again (McCarthy, 1998). For MacLellan (1999), understanding the political nature of indicators recognizes the difficulty in having indicators employed continuously over a period of time and not just chosen, or deselected, to suit political expediency. Box 5.8 provides an example of how political manipulation can affect indicator results.

Box 5.7. Why combine indicators?

Assessing the state of people and the environment and progress towards sustainable development requires indicators of a wide range of issues. The issues may include health, population, basic needs, income, employment, business success, the economy, education, crime, soil erosion, water quality, air quality, greenhouse gases, protected areas, species diversity, energy consumption, food supply, resources use and so on.

Each indicator can show what is happening to the issue it represents, but unless the indicators are organized and combined in a coherent way, the signals they give will be highly confusing. Some will show good performance, others bad and some are in between. To get a picture of the whole system, it is necessary to combine the indicators, if they are not combined, the indicators produce a lot of noise – a jumbled stream of data – but no clear message. By combing indicators we can make them do more than tell us about the particular issues they represent. They can show if we are making progress toward sustainable development – if we are improving and maintain the wellbeing of people and the ecosystem together.

Source: Prescott-Allen (1997, p. 2).

Box 5.8. Example of political involvement in indicator review.

. . . [I]n the tradition of classifying ketchup as a vegetable – a classic from the Reagan era – the Bush Administration may leave a rich legacy of redefining terms for regulatory purposes. Thought a wild fish is one hatched in the wild? You would be mistaken, according to Bush's environmental stewards. Under a new plan, the distinction between farm-bred salmon, which are later released into rivers and streams, and their cousins hatched in the wild will be removed, instantly raising the overall tally of salmon – and making it more probable that the government will eliminate or downgrade protections for 15 species now sheltered under the US's Endangered Species Act. Such a change is favoured by power and timber companies, whose development plans have been stymied by the government's protective net. Environmentalists complain the action will jeopardize wild salmon.

It is hardly the first example of the Administration's creative wordplay. A recent report by Bush's economic team suggested that burger-flipping jobs, now part of the service sector, ought to be reclassified as manufacturing jobs, a change that would have enabled the White House to claim that manufacturing job losses aren't as bad as they look. Whilst the President may stumble on occasion, his policy formulations often have a way with words.

Source: Fonda (2004).

Thus, the choice can become between the need for scientific accuracy at one end of the continuum, and the need for public/political support and awareness of key issues rather than the set in totality at the other end. Bakkes (1997, p. 379) expresses the dichotomy, 'Indicators are always a compromise. Their design needs to optimise between relevance to the user, scientific validity, and measurability.'

Evaluation

When the process is so long and difficult and requires such significant inputs of human and monetary resources in the early stages, there is bound to be a degree of speculation over whether it is actually worth the effort. Despite the current popularity of indicators, not all scholars are entirely convinced of the worth of the technique (Holling, 1978; Hein, 1997; Meadows, 1998). Meadows (1998) comments that if indicators are poorly chosen, inaccurately measured, delayed or biased, they can result in serious malfunction of monitoring systems, resulting in reactions that are either too strong or too weak and ineffective decision making. In this instance it is clearly better to have no monitoring system than to have an incorrect monitoring system.

However, rather than discouraging investigation of indicator methodologies, knowledge of indicator pitfalls can assist in the development of

innovative solutions and improved monitoring systems. Beyond these technical concerns of indicator development, Hughes (2002) reminds us that
without a moral conviction as well as technical ability, indicators will be
unsuccessful in their efforts. '. . . the continuing search for a technical resolution should not be allowed to mask the moral thrust that lies at the heart
of environmental sustainability' (Hughes, 2002, p. 472). Faith in indicators
should not allow us to relax the need for personal conviction to promote
sustainability – indicators are a tool for our energies, not the energy itself.
If we are committed to sustainable tourism it follows that we are also committed to improving the current imperfect monitoring systems.

The authors of this book have stressed the importance of indicator
development as a process and means to a more sustainable end, rather than
simply as an end in itself. To do this requires not only resources but the
political power to drive it forward and allow useful information to be converted into action. Budiansky (1995, p. 94) is stirring:

> the goals we seek in nature are human goals, goals that reflect an imperfect
> mix of morality and commerce, aesthetics and need, stewardship and politics.
> We might as well admit it and get on with the job. Part of facing up to the
> realities and complexity of nature is admitting that any approach we take will
> be incomplete, imperfect, provisional, and experimental. The important
> thing is to try.

Summary

The challenge of monitoring using indicators presents researchers with a
number of complex issues to address. This chapter has attempted to introduce the historical background to monitoring as well as review some of the
key issues, in order to introduce the reader to monitoring perspectives
prior to the discussion of monitoring techniques in Chapters 6 and 7.

The question of what to monitor is central to the theme of this book.
The authors contend that unless those within tourism charged with driving
the transition to greater sustainability look beyond tourism, then 'sustainable tourism' will always be a parochial subset of sustainable development.
There is enough evidence presented within this book of the dangers of a
tourism-centric perspective hopefully to persuade readers of the need to at
least read beyond the safe confines of the tourism literature. Issues of the
scale of measurement have surely compounded the decision to limit the
subject range of investigations by previous researchers and the importance
of this problem is discussed.

After establishing what and where to measure, the questions become
more technical. The chapter considered the appropriate type of indicator
to reflect the need to measure social and environmental issues, instead of
just provide economic data. How these indicators should be organized and

linked together marks an important difference between conventional and sustainable indicators. Who does the monitoring and how much the monitoring costs will of course influence the way it is conducted, while how the data are presented may determine the way the indicators are received by the intended audience and whether the project continues in the future.

The following two chapters look at practical ways in which the key issues for consideration identified in this chapter can be addressed, taking the reader first through the process of indicator development and then the crucial challenge of indicator use.

Developing Indicators

6

Introduction

As explained in Chapter 5, despite the keen interest and demand for monitoring of sustainable tourism, there are still relatively few accounts of the methodological aspects of indicator development. Most existing tourism monitoring literature focuses either on the need for indicators, critiques of existing indicators or the results of monitoring activities. The process of indicator development is generally left to the technical skill of the researchers involved and seldom critically examined. The reason for this is not just a reluctance to engage in technical and methodological discussions, but is reflective of the early stage of development of indicators of sustainable tourism, the complexity of the process, the small number and relative immaturity of most of the sustainable tourism monitoring programmes currently in existence.

Chapter 5 discussed the historical development of interest in indicators and monitoring and explored some of the general considerations facing monitoring programmes. The focus of the discussion in Chapters 6 and 7 is on the practical aspects of indicator development. The chapters should be considered jointly as together they discuss what are considered here to be six key elements in the indicator development process. This chapter starts with a discussion of how to plan an indicator development programme and design systems for stakeholder participation. With these important foundations in place the focus then shifts to 'scoping' sustainable tourism issues, the process of identifying key concerns and priorities facing the tourism system under study from a variety of stakeholder perspectives. The last part of the chapter addresses the question of how to develop a long list of potential indicators and screen them for technical feasibility, efficacy and user-friendliness. The second three steps covered in Chapter 7 focus on implementing monitoring systems: piloting indicators, interpreting results and using the results.

Ideas are the raw materials from which intelligent place-based responses to monitoring can take root and grow. This chapter aims to present those engaged in indicator development with ideas and options to consider. The methodologies explored are not a prescriptive formula for indicator development but need to be reflected upon and adapted to suit the circumstances in which the monitoring is to take place. Consistent with the central tenets of this book, the authors encourage a comprehensive sustainable development approach to indicators, a keen appreciation of the involvement of a wide range of stakeholders in the process and a willingness to experiment, learn and adapt to changing situations in tourism destinations.

Planning for Indicator Development

Planning for the phased development of indicators of sustainable tourism is a crucial, but often overlooked first step towards the establishment of an effective monitoring process. As explained in Chapter 5, it is easy to become so fixed on the initial task of developing indicators that the ongoing implementation of monitoring results is ignored. Whilst the indicators need to be carefully designed and suited to the specific local circumstances, it is just as important that they are designed as part of an integrated planning system so the results feed naturally into decision making channels and make a difference to the way tourism is managed.

There are two main considerations in the planning stage, designing the indicator programme and making arrangements for stakeholder participation in the monitoring process.

Phases of development

As explained in the introduction, many tourism authors recommend the development of sustainable tourism indicators (Inskeep, 1991; Butler, 1993a; Coccossis, 1996; Dymond, 1997; Goodall and Stabler, 1997; WTTC *et al.*, 1997; Mowforth and Munt, 1998; Weaver, 1998; Swarbrooke, 1999; James, 2000). However, few discuss the technical aspects of indicator development or monitoring. One of the few existing tourism-based accounts of the phases in development of an indicator programme is the WTO's *Indicators of Sustainable Development for Tourism Destinations: a Guidebook* (WTO, 2004d). Developed by a large expert advisory panel, this guide identifies 12 steps to indicator development and use, grouped in three phases as discussed in Chapter 8 (Box 8.3).

Additional assistance in indicator development can be found from recreation management techniques as many of these include indicator development in an integrated planning process. Limits of Acceptable Change (LAC), for example, developed by the US Forest Service, was designed as a tool for planning and managing visitation to wilderness areas (Stankey *et al.*, 1985). It involves local residents in the identification of key issues affecting an area, the development of indicators and decisions about how much change is acceptable. Monitoring is used to identify the difference between the current situation and acceptable levels of activity, so that action can be taken to close any gap that may have emerged. In this way the results of monitoring feed directly into the planning process.

A simpler, less expensive and faster-to-implement surrogate of LAC is the Protected Areas Visitor Impact Management Planning Process (PAVIM). It incorporates impact problem analyses, the flexible selection of strategies, and public involvement but replaces the indicators and monitoring steps with a problem analysis step using an expert panel (Farrell and Marion, 2002). Another off-shoot of LAC is the Tourism Optimization Management Model (TOMM), discussed in Chapter 9, incorporating the identification of alternative development scenarios, identifying and monitoring indicators, and using the results to direct management responses (Manidis Roberts Consultants, 1997). What is common to all these approaches is the focus on minimizing visitor impacts, encouraging public involvement and shared learning, and using monitoring as a tool to identify when a management response is required.

Further assistance in the planning of an indicator programme can be sourced from the sustainable development literature. The Bellagio Principles, developed in 1996 as part of the IISD's Measurement and Indicators Programme, provide a useful starting point in this respect. They are a set of 10 principles developed by practitioners and researchers from around the world to synthesize insights from practical ongoing efforts in order to guide the entire indicator development process from design of indicators through to the communication of results (IISD, 2004a). Principle 1 deals with the starting point of any assessment through the establishment of clear vision and goals. Principles 2–5 focus on the content of the monitoring, stressing the need to merge a sense of the whole system with understanding of priority issues. Principles 6–8 look at the process of monitoring, and 9 and 10 the ongoing challenges with the implementation of a monitoring project. The inclusion of principle 10, the building of institutional capacity, is an often overlooked but particularly important element in the case of developing counties. The principles are summarized in Box 6.1.

The principles provide a useful set of guidelines, very much in line with the comprehensive, adaptive and stakeholder-driven process recommended in this book, as they span the whole monitoring cycle from planning to ongoing management. Nevertheless, they are principles to consider rather than step-by-step instructions.

Box 6.1. Bellagio Principles for measuring progress towards sustainable development.

Principle	Explanation
Guiding vision	Be guided by a clear vision of sustainable development
Holistic perspective	Take a whole-system perspective
Essential elements	Consider all aspects that contribute to human well-being of future and current generations
Adequate scope	Incorporate a long-term time span and set study boundaries large enough to include local and long-distance impacts on people and ecosystems
Practical focus	Indicators should be limited in number, focused on key issues, use standardized measurements and have clear targets, ranges or thresholds
Openness	Use terms, methods and data that are clearly understood or explained
Effective communication	Clearly address the needs of the target audience
Broad participation	Obtain broad representation of key grass-roots, professional, technical and social groups, as well as decision makers
Ongoing assessment	Be interactive, adaptive and responsive to change; adjust goals, frameworks and indicators as new insights are gained; and promote collective learning and feedback to decision making
Institutional capacity	Ensure sufficient institutional capacity to collect data and undertake necessary maintenance and documentation of monitoring system

Source: IISD (2004a).

Perhaps the most comprehensive discussion of sustainable development indicators and their development is provided by Meadows (1998), reporting on a 5-day workshop on indicators by an international network of sustainable development scholars (The Balaton Group). The report identifies ten steps to indicator development, summarized in Box 6.2. Of particular note is the establishment of a small working group of stakeholders to facilitate indicator development (1), the review of existing indicators and data (4), convening a participatory selection process (6), undertaking a technical review (7), publishing and promoting the findings (9) and regularly updating the work (10). These steps are a valuable reference for those developing indicator programmes, but as with the WTO and other indicator work, the Balaton Group unfortunately omits the conversion of indicator results into action and a review and evaluation of indicators.

Adaptive management, introduced and explained in Chapter 1, suggests a more complete monitoring cycle. Although there is no fixed set of

Box 6.2. The Balaton Group approach to indicator development.

1. **Select a small multi-disciplinary working group:** a combination of experts and non-experts from the community or audience to use the indicators.
2. **Clarify the purpose of the indicator set:** whether they are meant for education, decision making, planning, project management.
3. **Identify the community shared values and vision:** these are the aspirations of the community for whom the indicators are intended.
4. **Review existing models indicators and data:** working group examines other indicator projects and data availability and sources.
5. **Draft a set of proposed indicators:** working group draws on their own knowledge to draft first set.
6. **Convene participatory selection process:** draft indicators need to be assessed by a process section of the community, providing an education opportunity, getting local input and gaining local trust and ownership.
7. **Perform technical overview:** knowledgeable people sort through indicators for technical aspects such as measurability, relevance, etc. and reduce the long list.
8. **Research the data:** indicators are revised as the realities of data collection become apparent.
9. **Publish and promote indicators:** indicators are converted into striking graphics, clear language and effective communication campaign
10. **Update the report regularly:** steps 8 and 9 need to be regularly repeated to show change over time.

Source: Adapted from Meadows (1998, pp. 26–27).

steps for this process, it is often conceived in the form of a six-step cycle that starts by assessing the problem through a series of stakeholder workshops to model the existing system, define community values and explore management options (Fig. 6.1; Nyberg, 1999; BC Ministry of Forests, 2004a). This is followed by the design of indicators, their implementation and the use of results. The last two steps involve evaluating and adjusting the actions and indicators based on lessons learned, prior to the next round of problem assessment.

There are several strengths of the adaptive management process, particularly in a developing country setting. First, it is a flexible learning cycle that can be applied to virtually any project from monitoring to strategic planning. Secondly, it stresses the organizational learning aspects of monitoring, building the capacity of human resources both within and outside the organization involved. Thirdly, it shows clearly and visually that designing the indicators is only a part of the job – the real challenge is in the monitoring, evaluation and adjustment. Finally, it provides a tool uniquely suited to cope with complex non-linear system change discussed in Chapter 1.

Although there is no indicator development process that is appropriate to all situations, based on the work explored above, six key elements in the

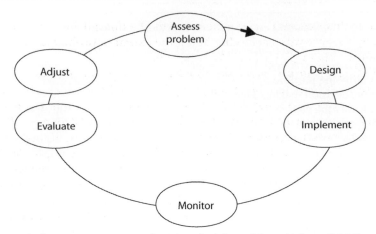

Fig. 6.1. Adaptive management framework. Adapted from Nyberg (1999).

process are described in Chapters 6 and 7. These include: (i) planning; (ii) scoping issues; (iii) identifying indicators; (iv) monitoring; (v) analysing results; and (vi) implementing change. Deciding on the phases of development that are to be used is the first part of the planning process; the second half involves making the arrangements for stakeholder participation.

Arrangements for stakeholder participation

While Chapter 4 considered the more philosophical problems of stakeholder involvement, this section examines the practical realities of involving stakeholders in the indicator development process. Options explored here include expert panels (real or virtual), advisory committees, working groups, participatory workshops and consultative sessions.

The Balaton Group suggests selecting a small, multi-disciplinary working group made up of key stakeholders. A similar approach is recommended in PAVIM, where an expert panel is selected based on their knowledge of the impact problems and or experience in resolving similar problems in other protected areas (Farrell and Marion, 2002). Members of the panel can range from local residents, to scientists, or agency or NGO representatives, or even national or international consultants selected specifically for their expertise related to the specific protected area problems. They explain that 'experts' often provide more objective and independent advice, can apply experience from other areas, disseminate new decision making and management tools, diagnose and analyse problems, and be instrumental in finding optimum solutions. However, they also recognize some of the potential problems discussed in Chapter 4, pointing out that experts can be biased by their background and experience, which may or may not translate or apply well to situations in other countries or regions. Additionally they note that experts can be expensive, may be unavailable when needed, and may disagree with each other about the extent of problems and how to best address them (Farrell and Marion, 2002).

WTO tends to use larger stakeholder workshops for indicator development, often divided into 'break-out groups' for specific activities. The TOMM project discussed in Chapter 9 has a Management Committee, and the Samoa indicator project reviewed in Chapter 10 uses a 12-member Project Advisory Committee (PAC). There is also scope for the use of Internet and e-mail to create virtual stakeholder participation. For example, in 2002, WTO organized an international web-conference conducted through e-mails to facilitate access to stakeholders who could not attend regional indicator meetings. Similarly, in 2003, the Australian Department of Industry, Tourism and Resources conducted online consultation with a large number of stakeholders to seek comments on their tourism white paper (www.industry.gov.au).

Regardless of whether the group is real or virtual there are a number of questions to consider with regard to its composition, summarized in Box 6.3.

As a result of this advice, five types of members are suggested here (for a more extensive list of potential stakeholders, see Box 8.4):

1. Members of the local community.
2. Industry representatives: if possible representatives from private sector associations.
3. Policy makers: those charged with policy decisions.
4. Administrators: those managing the indicator development process and facilitating the working group.
5. Experts: those with specific skills relevant to the nature of the project.

On the question of how to manage the group, the WTO (2004b) regard openness and transparency as essential, and suggest the provision of forums, meetings and discussion opportunities, where all interested stakeholders can identify their interests and concerns. They highlight five considerations that can affect the management of participatory processes:

*   Timing: consultation processes that begin too soon after the start of the programme may cause participants to question why they are there, whilst those starting too late into the process risk accusations that decisions were made without them.
*   Frequency: too-frequent gatherings can result in participant burn-out; too infrequent can end in loss of interest.
*   Duration: consultation needs to be ongoing, ideally from the project conception to its implementation.
*   Consultation techniques: large workshops with small breakout groups used to identify and prioritize issues managed by facilitators who integrate stakeholder feedback at each stage in the work.

Box 6.3.   Questions to consider in making arrangements for stakeholder participation.

How many members are needed?
Too many members can make it difficult to reach a consensus; too few members can put the project's viability at risk if some members drop out. WTO (2004b) recommend eight to ten participants in a group led by a facilitator with a mix of expertise from local officials, to industry, academics, consultants and experts from other countries.

What specific and general skills do members need?
The Balaton Group Study recommends that the best progress be made on indicators when multi-disciplinary experts on the subject are mixed with non-experts. This way experts supply the technical know-how and bring scientific credibility to the selection process, and the non-experts ensure they stay focused on the key issues, make the indicators simple and understandable, and are more open to creative linkages that will capture the big picture (Meadows, 1998).

Who will manage the working group and implement members' suggestions?
It is important to involve an organization's senior staff, otherwise policies may be subsequently be forgotten and not implemented (Bramwell and Sharman, 1999).

Who will be using or learning from the results of the indicator study?
Bramwell and Sharman (1999) also note the importance of including in the working group those who will provide information about the likely practical issues of implementation.

What balance of gender, ethnicity, age, place of residence and experience is appropriate?
This will depend on the nature and scale of the monitoring project, but should be give consideration in the selection of members.

Are different types of participation suitable for different phases in the work?
Rather than being rigidly fixed, there is also potential for the working group to change during the indicator development process. There may be a much broader group of stakeholders involved initially, to identify key issues, and then a smaller, more specialized group for the collection of the data, analysis of results and decisions regarding appropriate action.

- Size: large groups are inclusive but reduce the capacity to reach consensus. Small groups can be very time consuming and may not be sufficiently inclusive.

Other important issues have been raised by Wight include how much political 'top-down culture' and influence there is in the process design, selection of stakeholders and the issues raised, and managing the issue of technical translation in locations where the language of the stakeholders differs from that of the monitoring facilitators (P.A. Wight, Edmonton, 2004, personal communication). Farrell also raises concerns about the impact of 'group think', the situation that may arise when groups get too friendly and wish to give a show of unanimity. In such situations Farrell believes groups may not reflect the possibilities of individual thought, but instead something not far off the status quo, ruling out possible new and valuable directions of thought (B.H. Farrell, Arrowhead, 2004, personal communication).

Despite the attention and praise given to stakeholder participation in the literature, in reality, convincing people to participate, attend meetings or join committees is not always straightforward, nor is gaining their confidence and maintaining their interest. In some areas, Wight notes, stakeholders have been tapped again and again and, as a result, in some situations such as northern Canada, Aboriginal people demand large cash payments to attend stakeholder meetings (P.A. Wight, Edmonton, 2004, personal communication). In other situations, tourism stakeholders may be busy business people with their own responsibilities and time restraints, who would prefer external consultants to take on the responsibility monitoring project.

Clearly, rather than one form of stakeholder input being appropriate, it is often a question of what is acceptable in any given situation. Involving 'everyone' can be seen as having democratic appeal, but the consequence would be unwieldy committees, representation of those with too little technical knowledge, too much focus on immediate interests and extremely time consuming. Appropriate stakeholders will be dependent on the nature, scope and scale of the project, with the definition of 'appropriate' varying throughout the stages of the project. As such, it is potentially dangerous to present a list of stakeholders and recommend their involvement.

Scoping Issues

The second important step in the development of a monitoring programme is to identify the central point of reference for indicators – the question of what is to be measured. The process of identifying a small number of priority issues to address from a broad range of potential problems is generally referred to as scoping (Department of Lands, Surveys and the Environment and the South Pacific Regional Environment Programme, 1997). Allin *et al.* explains: 'Perhaps the most crucial stage in the development of indicators is to define what those indicators should represent, i.e. to define the themes and topics that constitute sustainable tourism' (2000).

Several different approaches to scoping are possible incorporating stakeholder views, secondary information or a combination. In an EIA, scoping normally involves consultations with the main development partners in order to establish and prioritize a checklist of issues to address. Similarly Peterson (1997) suggests stakeholder workshops can provide the appropriate forum for scoping activities, and MacGillivray and Zadek (no date) recommend soliciting broad community input using questionnaire surveys. In contrast, the World Economic Forum (2001) scoped key issues for their environmental sustainability index based on a review of environmental literature, supported by statistical analysis. The US Interagency Working Group on Sustainable Development Indicators (1998) conducted a literature review followed by a series of thematic meetings to identify issues currently affecting the economy, environment and society in the USA. The MEA focuses less on the process and more on the need interact extensively with the intended users of the assessment and modify the scoping document based on their review (MEA, 2002).

The approach favoured here uses a combination of primary and secondary data as recommended in adaptive management; first synthesizing existing knowledge and identifying knowledge gaps, then assessing stakeholder views in one or more facilitated workshops, and finally analysing the information and producing the master list of key issues. These elements are shown in Fig. 6.2 and explained below.

Secondary sources

The extent of the review of secondary sources will depend on the spatial (international, national, local) and conceptual (tourism-centric/interdisciplinary) scale of the project. Indicators developed at the international level can be based primarily on international level reports on sustainable development and tourism from key organizations such as the UNCSD and the WTO. At the national level, indicator projects can source key issues from existing national tourism plans, state of the environment reports, economic plans and social studies where these are available. At the local, village or individual business level, however, scoping tends to be less reliant on secondary information and more reliant on stakeholder and community input often guided by national concerns.

Whatever the physical extent of the study (international, national, local) reviewers of secondary sources face a common difficulty of how to get access to the necessary information, what to look for and how to identify key issues and concerns, and extract useful material from what may be a huge number of documents and reports (sometimes in a foreign language). Finding and comprehending key secondary sources may be a significant challenge for community groups, outsiders and those working in a different language through a non-technical intermediary. Consequently, in many developing country situations, the literature review may be best assisted by local experts particularly in the case where an indicator working group has been set up. The task of identifying and analysing appropriate literature can then be divided between the groups according to areas of expertise. Another simpler method, where the working group consists predominantly of non-experts whose language may not be the reporting language, is to select just one up-to-date and broad-ranging document as the

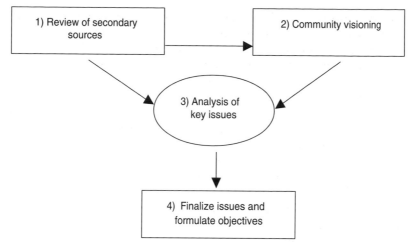

Fig. 6.2. Scoping process.

foundation for the project, such as the current tourism plan (if it has a sufficiently comprehensive focus), state of environment report or the local
Agenda 21 report. This provides a substantial shortcut to indicator development, effectively linking the programme with a parent scheme, which,
ideally would have already been through a wide consultative process. This
was the case for the TOMM Kangaroo Island project, for example, where a
considerable amount of community-based planning consultation had
already been undertaken prior to the monitoring programme and was
therefore used as the basis for the project (Manidis Roberts Consultants,
1998). The approach is also recommended with PAVIM, and has been
shown to work well where time, money and expertise are in short supply
(Farrell and Marion, 2002).

Community visioning

Whereas reviews of secondary sources highlight what are generally considered to be the technical or scientific issues facing the sustainable development of an area or community, community visioning can be an effective
method of validating and prioritizing the issues on the basis of local stakeholder priorities and concerns.

The concept of community visioning was developed in the USA to aug-
ment more traditional forms of planning. It involves citizens coming
together to articulate core community values, identify emerging trends and
issues, build consensus on future directions, and develop specific strategies
and actions to achieve goals over time (Ames, 2003). Several different
methodologies can be used for this process, including consultative meetings, questionnaires and advisory panels, and sometimes a combination of

methods is appropriate, depending on the scale and nature of the project and the cultural and educational background of the stakeholder involved. In the South Puget Sound area in Washington State, for example, a core group of 20 people met over an 8-month period to describe their vision of a sustainable community and they developed a set of indicators to show how the community matched this vision (Hart, 1999).

A variation on this approach, the focus group technique, is well suited to the oral collective culture found in many small island developing countries. The purpose of focus groups is to enable participant to generate ideas in a group setting, sometimes coming to a consensus and other times agreeing to differ. Clark *et al.* (1998, p. 138) explain: 'The technique is supposed to encourage not only an exchange of views and ideas, but also the production of new ideas as a consequence of the public sharing and assessing of the ideas of others. Each member of the group is free to argue, disagree, question, and discuss the issues with others in the room.' One important benefit of this approach is the social learning that takes place as a result of the exchange of ideas not normally voiced in the community.

A variation on focus groups, the nominal group technique, is recommended by WTO (2004b) as a means to select key issues for concern for indicator development. According to Ritchie (1985) this involves assembling a group of experts who are invited to reflect individually on a particular issue and record their thoughts. These are then introduced to the group and participants are asked to establish privately the relative importance of each suggestion. The results are coordinated to produce the most popular suggestions with additional rounds of voting and consideration possible if the initial list is large in number or broad in scope.

In situations where people tend to have less time to participate in public meetings, a questionnaire-based approach may be more practical, either using a self-administered postal questionnaire, telephone or face-to-face interview. Clark *et al.* (1998) recommends the use of face-to-face interviews, noting how they allow the interviewer to build rapport with respondents, probe for answers, strengthen open-ended questions and ask supplementary questions in order to clarify responses. Fowler (1993) agrees that personal interviews are probably the most effective way of enlisting cooperation for most populations. One of the weaknesses of these approaches, however, is that the learning outcomes are minimized, as the information flow is individual and predominately one way. This problem is addressed by the Delphi Method, a technique that, like the nominal group technique not only elicits information on particular subjects but gives individuals the chance to refine their initial responses on the bases of group input (Kaynak and Macauley, 1984). This can be done either in a physical group or as a postal survey like that used by Miller (2001a) to assess expert opinion on the criteria and selection of indicators for monitoring sustainable tourism.

Whichever technique is chosen, it is unlikely that the whole population can be sampled, in which case either a random or purposeful sampling may be employed. Where time and funds are limited, purposeful sampling has the advantage of quickly identifying individuals who are especially knowledgeable and insightful in particular areas giving special attention in the research process (Ward *et al.*, 1999). Random sampling, however, may be a more objective option, which helps avoid the risks of over-representing the views of one group, perhaps the eloquent, knowledgeable and opinionated.

During the visioning process, inevitably discussions will run deeper than just the list of key issues. In order to avoid losing all the other information collected during scoping activities, it is useful to organize and document this for later reference. Box 6.4 gives an example of how additional information on two key issues from the SSTIP was documented.

As can be appreciated from Box 6.4, an issue list is not the same as a list of problems or pressures. Wight explains that whilst problems can create a sense of negativity and despair, issues provide a sense of what has to be overcome to achieve a particular goal providing direction for positive action (P.A. Wight, Edmonton, 2004, personal communication). Similarly WTO (2004b) highlights the benefits of positive issues that can enthuse and motive communities rather than belittle them. Hawkins (2003, p. 37) puts the point very clearly:

> Too often we define a problem as an obstacle, a hindrance, or a constraint that stops us from doing what we want to do. We need to define a problem as the gap between where we are now and where we would like to be. Once that is determined we can address the gap by identifying realistic options and alternatives available to close the gap.

Whatever form the visioning process takes therefore, it is important that participants be encouraged to identify positive future outcomes or the conditions to make a desirable future possible rather than simply produce a long list of complaints.

Box 6.4.   Example of key issue table.

Key issue	Pressures/impacts	Current state	Management response
Forest conservation	Logging for commercial and agricultural use, cyclone damage	Deforestation is widespread and many protected forests are at risk	Village conservation areas have been established in some areas with ecotourism as income generation
Clean water	High water usage, demand currently exceeding supply	Poor state of pipes, lack of rainwater collection	Protection of catchment area and measures to reduce consumption

Analysis of key issues

Armed with the lists of key issues from the secondary sources and community visioning process, the indicator working group, researcher or organization involved faces the challenge of how to combine, filter, prioritize or
otherwise reduce the list of issues to a manageable number, from which to
develop the indicators. The WTO (2004b) recommend the initial analysis is
probably best undertaken by the project facilitator or manager followed by
a workshop to rank issues either through a show of hands or star-rating system often used in the nominal group technique. In many cases, they note,
issues of great interest to stakeholders may be outside the realm of tourism
such as keeping a school open or reducing heart disease, and consequently
may be better referred to other agencies that have the mandate to respond.
Achieving a balance between the focus on the tourism sector and incorporating a comprehensive sustainable development approach is therefore a
significant challenge.

Once this is completed to the satisfaction of those involved, and a key
list of issues has been produced, it is quite logical and possible to move
directly on to the development of indicators. However, one useful extra
step at this point is to use the issue list to formulate a set of 'objectives' for
sustainable tourism. Whereas issues tend to represent the situation at a
particular point in time, objectives are more future-focused and suggestive
of possible management responses or actions. Consequently, the objective
can have much wider use, providing a direction for future sustainable
tourism strategies and, in so doing, effectively solving the problem of defining sustainable tourism in the local context, which has so burdened the
sustainable tourism debate to date.

The formulation of objectives can either take place in the same forum
as the issue identification or on a subsequent occasion. In the SSTIP
discussed in Chapter 10, initial drafting of objectives was undertaken by
indicator advisory panel in small focus groups and later reviewed by a wider
group of stakeholders. In larger projects or developed world situations,
this process may also be quite possible using the Internet. Despite being
described here as an extra phase, this process should not be undervalued.
Having a clear set of objectives for sustainable tourism opens the door for a
range of projects such as the development of a tourism plan or strategy and
in so doing also widens stakeholder understanding of what sustainable
tourism means in their particular context.

Whether or not objectives are defined, at the end of the scoping
process is marked by the achievement of a clear vision of what is important to sustainable tourism in a particular country, place, community
or business. This then provides a solid foundation for the identification
and design of indicators that are reflective of the opinions of local
stakeholders.

Identifying Indicators

Once the key issues and objectives for sustainable tourism in the country, community or business are agreed upon, the identification of indicators should be a relatively simple task of matching the indicators with appropriate measures. However, inevitably the theory is complicated by a number of practical realities. First, as yet there is no existing master list of sustainable tourism indicators, so extensive secondary research is required to avoid re-inventing the wheel. Secondly, issues are specific to particular sites, ecosystems and regions many of which may not have been previously monitored and so many indicators will need to be developed from scratch. Thirdly, the indicator identification process is complicated by the considerations discussed in Chapter 5, as well as concerns over the number and type of indicators to use, data availability and resources, many of which will have place-specific rather than generic answers.

Developing an indicator long list

There are two main steps required to develop an indicator long list: a review of monitoring literature, and then a stakeholder or expert group brainstorming session to fill the gaps. The aim of this literature review is to identify indicators used in other related projects that could feasibly be adapted for the particular programme under review. These can be sourced from tourism or sustainable development monitoring literature or indeed any of the multitude of disciplinary areas linked to tourism (economics, environment, social studies, politics, institutions, culture) and are relevant to the key issues identified.

As discussed previously, literature reviews inevitably favour expert input. Specialists tend to have greater access to information on related monitoring programmes and will be better able to extract useful indicators than non-experts. For community and non-expert indicator working groups, it may be easier for the project facilitator to review related literature and develop a master list for stakeholders to select from. Although many of the indicators sourced from the literature review might not be selected in the end, they serve as a useful starting point for generating new indicator ideas.

The second phase of indicator generation involves brainstorming to produce new indicators that are more relevant to the objectives and key issues to be measured. This is the opportunity for broad stakeholder input that can help enhance the project's legitimacy and popularity in the community. Brainstorming can be defined as 'a non-committal way of exploring views and options and gathering multiple ideas on a given issue or problem' (Borrini-Feyerabend *et al.*, 2000, p. 69). It involves generating ideas in a group setting, reviewing the results with the group, sorting the ideas, highlighting differences of opinion and resolving these so that a long list of indicators is drawn up to the satisfaction of the group.

To assist the brainstorming process, it is useful for stakeholders to not only be equipped with the result of the literature search of possible indicators but also some generic guidelines regarding the desirable characteristics of the indicators. Long lists of desirable indicator criteria exist and are discussed in the following section on screening, but these are too technical to use in the first round of brainstorming without risking dampening the enthusiasm of participants. The most important considerations at this stage are simply that the indicators are relevant to the key issues or objectives they are designed to measure, simple to understand and likely to be feasible for the organization involved in the monitoring programme to collect data on. Sirakaya *et al.* (1999) provides a list of five general points to consider shown in Box 6.5.

Screening indicators

Once a long list of indicators has been produced based on the literature review, brainstorming and crude indicator review above, the indicators are ready for the more detailed and technical screening process. One of the first questions to be raised in this respect is, 'how many indicators are really needed?'

There is clearly no ideal number of indicators. Just as an attempt to cover all aspects of sustainable tourism with only a few indicators is

---

Box 6.5.   Guidelines for indicator brainstorming.

- Indicators must be created to cover the entire spectrum of socioeconomic, cultural, natural and political environments at the local, regional, national and international levels.
- The number of indicators must be manageable and be implemented with ease at the destination and community level.
- Community participation must be maximized in order to reflect the visions and values of a community-based destination, and a long-term welfare-view of the destination is required in order to facilitate long-term sustainability.
- Indicators must have a high degree of reliability, predictive capacity and integrative ability.
- The process of developing indicators cannot be haphazard in that it requires a systematic approach to developing indicators that are robust, measurable, affordable and able to provide an integrated view of specific and overall conditions pertaining to the sustainability of the destination and its natural and cultural resources.

Source: Sirakaya *et al.* (1999, p. 419).

unrealistic, a list of more than 100 indicators would, in most situations, be impractical. Hart (1999) suggests that the number of indicators that a community selects depends on the size of the community, the number of critical issues, and the resources available to track and report on the indicators. She notes that the final list should not be so short that critical problems or areas are overlooked, or so long that measuring and reporting them on an ongoing basis is an overwhelming task. Wight adds that the purpose of the indicators and method and frequency of data collection will also affect the number of indicators, e.g. the use of predominantly pre-existing data collection methods means that a long list may be less overwhelming (P.A. Wight, Edmonton, 2004, personal communication).

Sustainable development projects have had a tendency to use large numbers of indicators for monitoring purposes. The 1997 State of Environment Monitoring requirements for Pacific Island countries included 563 indicators. The United Nations Department for Policy Coordination and Sustainable Development developed a draft list of 130 indicators to measure progress towards sustainable development (UN, 1993; Moldan and Bilharz, 1997). The UK Roundtable on Sustainable Development (1997) identified 150 indicators for measuring sustainable development in the UK. The US Interagency Working Group on Sustainable Development Indicators (1998) managed to keep their total number of indicators down to 40, but MacGillivray and Kayes (1997) argue that even 40 is too many and will result in confusing information, and a lack of popular appeal. Over the past decade, there has been increasing understanding that more is not necessarily better, and sometimes fewer, more multi-dimensional indicators are of more use than large numbers of conventional indicators (McIntyre, 2000). In this regard, UNEP in the Global Environment Outlook programme is steering towards considering five key issue indicators within nine environmental themes.

Sustainable tourism indicator programmes have been generally more successful in limiting the number of indicators used. WTO (1996), working on the WTO sustainable tourism indicator project, suggest using 11 core indicators supplemented by additional site-specific indicators not exceeding 25 in total. CAG Consultants (Allin *et al.*, 2000), were commissioned to produce the smallest set of indicators possible to measure sustainable tourism in England, and ended up with 21. James (2000), commenting on efforts by the British Resorts Association to develop sustainable tourism indicators, suggests 12 to be about the right number of indicators for measuring tourism impacts and good management practice amongst local authorities. Newman *et al.* (2001) started with 30 indicators but narrowed this down to six representing the social, resource and management conditions of Yosemite wilderness. There is therefore no magic number of indicators. Too many detract from the overall effect and may confuse stakeholders, too few risk not showing the whole picture, and, in fact, preoccupation with any ideal number is an unnecessary distraction. For most sustainable tourism projects, 10–15 indicators seems to be considered appropriate, with smaller localized projects using the lower end and national level projects the upper end.

Once the target number or range is decided on, the purpose of the indicator screening is to reduce the long list to within reach of this target number. As noted in the previous section, there is no lack of information about the qualities of a good indicator; indeed nearly every indicator report contains a list of desirable indicator characteristics.

The Bellagio Principles, shown in Box 6.1, note the need for indicators to be holistic in perspective, adequate in scope, practical in focus and incorporate broad and effective participation (Hardi, 1997). OECD (1998) highlights the need for policy relevance, analytical soundness and measurability. MacGillivray and Kayes (1997) emphasize relevance, reliability, availability and popularity. Logical framework approach advises that indicators should be SMART, i.e. Simple, Measurable, Accessible, Relevant and Timely (Norwegian Agency for Development Corporation (NORAD), 1997).

Similar criteria have been used to develop sustainable tourism indicators. WTO (2004b) highlighted five indicator criteria: relevance to the issue; feasibility of obtaining and analysing the information; credibility of the information; clarity and understandability to users; and comparability over time. Examples of more comprehensive lists of indicator criteria are provided in Box 6.6.

Like long indicator lists, whilst extensive lists of indicator criteria may be useful to review, they are impractical to implement, as it is virtually impossible to find indicators that meet all the criteria. Meadows (1998, p. 18) comments: 'Having made a list like the one above, the typical indicator study group disbands, encouraging someone else to come up with actual indicators that meet all these wonderful criteria. Or alternatively, the study group proceeds to recommend a long list of indicators that don't meet the criteria.' Nevertheless, there are clearly some indicator criteria that are more essential than others, some that are technical requirements and others that are more qualitative such as whether the indicator is understandable for user groups.

The initial technical screening is probably best undertaken by the project facilitator, expert working group or project management team using a clear list of criteria to assess each indicator in turn. Box 6.7 provides an example of a technical indicator screening table based on the work of Miller (2001a).

The screening table identifies nine questions to be asked of the indicators, each with a simple yes or no response. Using a similar approach, CAG Consultants (1999) developed a table with potential indicators listed horizontally and indicator criteria listed vertically, revealing how each indicator performed on each criterion. Indicators could then be scored as good, moderate or poor according to how they performed on these criteria. WTO (1996) provide another alternative: ranking indicators using a high, medium and low scale as to how well they match certain criteria. Hart

---

Box 6.6. Examples of sustainable development indicator screening criteria.

UNCSD indicator criteria (UN, 1996)
- National in scope
- Relevant to the main objective of assessing progress towards sustainable development
- Understandable, clear, simple and unambiguous
- Conceptually well founded
- Limited in number, remaining open-ended and adaptable to future developments
- Broad in coverage of Agenda 21 and all aspects of sustainable development
- Representative of an international consensus, to the greatest possible extent
- Dependent on data which is readily available or available at reasonable cost/benefit ratio

Furley *et al.* (1996) indicator criteria
- Be easy to identify and measure
- Be functionally important in the ecosystem
- Have a high imputed value
- Have modest technical requirements
- Be sensitive to the stress in question
- Have mechanisms whose response should be understood
- Be quick to respond
- Be low in ambiguity

Meadows (1998) indicator criteria
- Complementing: interesting, exciting and suggestive of action
- Clear in content: simple and understandable language and units
- Clear in value: no uncertainty about which direction is good or bad
- Sufficient: not too much information to comprehend
- Policy relevant: for all stakeholders in the system
- Democratic: people should have input into indicator choice and access to results
- Appropriate in scale: not over- or under-aggregated
- Feasible: measurable at reasonable cost
- Timely: compliable without long delays
- Supplementary: should measure what people can't measure for themselves
- Hierarchical: so a user can get details if needs be but also get the message quickly
- Participatory: should make use of what people can measure
- Physical: use of volume units not prices
- Leading: to provide information in time to act
- Tentative: up for discussion, learning and change

(1999) suggests that each indicator be given a numerical score according to its fulfilment of the indicator criteria, and only those scoring over a particular threshold are accepted.

Yet, a problem with these systems is that they presume each criterion for selecting an indicator to be of equal importance, which is clearly not

Box 6.7.   Technical screening table.

		Yes	No
Name of indicator			
Type of indicator			
Page number			
1	Is the indicator applicable to tourism?		
2	Is the indicator a complete indicator?		
3	Is the indicator applicable to all types of tourism?		
4	Are the data for the indicator easily obtained?		
5	Is the calculation required for the indicator simple?		
6	Is the indicator understandable?		
7	Is the data objective, quantifiable and reliable?		
8	Does the indicator point towards sustainable development?		
9	Can the indicator be measured on an ongoing basis?		
Links to other indicators			
Notes			

Source: Miller (2001a).

always the case. In view of this problem, a two-phase technical screening was carried out by Miller (2001a), whereby all indicators needed to show themselves to be relevant to tourism and measurable on an ongoing basis (criteria 1 and 9 in Box 6.7), but not necessarily simple or quantifiable (criteria 5 and 7). This is similar to the method used by the Samoa Indicator Project, discussed in Chapter 10, where some criteria were seen as 'essential' whereas others were labelled 'preferable'.

In addition to the technical screening process, as many indicator programmes shift from top-down to a 'local benefits first' approach there is enhanced understanding of the importance of creating public confidence in the process and striking a chord with the user group by employing terms, units and concepts with which people can become familiar (Hart, 1999). For example, citizens of the US city of Seattle selected 'salmon runs in local rivers', as a key indicator of sustainable development, demonstrating the important role of salmon in the region's cultural heritage (see Chapter 4), whereas in Santiago de Chile, people were more interested in the amount of traffic and levels of air pollution in the city judged by whether or not they could see the Andes mountains through the city smog (Sustainable Seattle, 1998; MacGillivray and Zadek, no date).

Having the ability to select or de-select indicators on the basis of public interest and opinion is a seemingly broad and democratic process, but it does open the screening process to possible bias and political influence. However, this is unavoidable regardless of the system used. Simply undertaking the process is part of the solution and the discussion and dialogue initiated along the way will help generate learning-based solutions. As Winderl (2003, p. 10) explains, it is simply a reminder that indicator development is often more of an art than a science:

> Although most indicator-people will agree whether a particular indicator is better or worse, there is no systematic way to decide among indicators which are equally good or bad. In short: far from being science, the development of indicators is art combined with a large portion of systematic, logical think, and an even larger portion of common sense.

Box 6.8 highlights the difficulties and frustrations felt by the Balaton workshop members in trying to select appropriate indicators.

Box 6.8. The indicator challenge.

Having tried the exercise, however, the Balaton workshop members found ourselves in sympathy with others who have failed to come up with perfect indicators. It was easier to complain about other indicators, to spew out theoretical list of hundreds of (mostly immeasurable) indicators, or to philosophize about the Ideal Indicator, than it was to produce a limited, comprehensible number of compelling, effective indicators.

Our understanding is imperfect, our worldviews get stuck, systems are complex, people disagree, we fall back on our narrow specialties, we fail to summon the enormous creativity we need. One wants to throw up one's hands and do something easy.

To keep ourselves from ducking the difficulties, some of us created, at irregular intervals throughout the workshop, an imaginary challenge to come up with ten, just ten, crucial indicators we would recommend to the nations of the world, 'or else be shot at dawn' . . . If you aren't too dignified, I would recommend the 'ten indicators or be shot at dawn' exercise when you find yourself bogging down. Otherwise it is too easy to indulge in theorizing or politicizing or some other evasive activity.

Source: Meadows (1998, pp. 18–19).

Summary

Monitoring is now an integral component of many government, business, community and planning activities and there is increasing pressure on both public and private institutions to evaluate their performance using indicators. Despite this increasing demand, there is still a lack of understanding of the importance of the process of indicator development and the benefits to be derived from adopting a comprehensive, adaptive and stakeholder-driven approach.

This chapter has sought to fill this gap, drawing on information from multi-disciplinary sources to bring together a range of technical options for the first three phases of the indicator development process; planning for indicator development, scoping issues and identifying indicators. A number of issues are raised in this discussion, including the importance of recognizing the phases of development of indicators within an integrated monitoring cycle; the value of forming an indicator working group made up of both experts and non-experts; and the benefits to be derived from community visioning and stakeholder involvement in indicator selection. The subjective nature of screening indicators has been discussed. This is an area where it is important to recognize the limitations of indicators and to seek to build a more established methodology, rather than portraying the development of indicators as a perfect science. As has been stressed throughout the book, adaptive management encourages us to take a chance, try new methods and experiment with alternatives. Inevitably mistakes will be made along the way, some things will simply not work out, important lessons will be learned, and improvements will be made as a result.

Chapter 7 investigates how a set of indicators can be converted into a sustainable tourism monitoring system that can be used to assist a transition towards sustainable tourism.

Implementing Monitoring Systems   7

Introduction

This chapter examines some of the conceptual, practical and technical challenges involved in converting a set of issues and indicator ideas into a viable sustainable tourism monitoring system. It explores the implementation process that takes individual measures of sustainability and enables a country, business or village to use them to make more informed decisions about future plans and policy making.

The chapter starts by exploring the question of how to formulate indicator definitions, develop a reliable monitoring methodology and collect baseline data. Next, the chapter discusses the interpretation and communication of results with reference to targets, ranges and critical thresholds. The final section examines the challenges involved in establishing and internalizing an institutional framework to convert indicator results into management responses and ensure the ongoing review and maintenance of the monitoring system.

In keeping with the themes of the book particular emphasis is given to maintaining a comprehensive sustainable development focus, incorporating a high degree of stakeholder participation and developing adaptive monitoring systems that can be improved over time. As a result, the authors touch on a wide variety of interdisciplinary techniques and approaches – many from sustainable development monitoring. As with the previous chapter, the processes described are options to be considered and adapted to suit the changing circumstances of the destination rather than a rigid set of steps to follow.

Piloting Indicators

The purpose of the indicator screening process described in the previous chapter was to eliminate any indicators that were either not technically feasible or lacked public appeal, and a variety of methods were described for this undertaking. Up to this point, however, the indicators have only been discussed in theoretical terms, so the purpose of piloting is to convert them into practical monitoring tools. The two most important parts of the piloting process are discussed here: indicator fine-tuning and data collection and management.

Indicator fine-tuning

WTO (2004b) describes indicator refinement as a process that forces comparison between what is desired and what is practical. This often results in substituting some indicators with others that are easier to support given current availability of information. In practice, this involves undertaking a technical review of each indicator, addressing any specific difficulties presented by the indicator, formulating the precise indicator wording and associated definitions, and making preliminary suggestions in terms of monitoring methods and protocols.

Indicator fine-tuning is a time-consuming process, but ensuring indicators are precisely formulated at the start can save a great deal of time and money by helping to avoid the collection of unnecessary information in the data collection phase. The kinds of questions that need to be asked about each indicator include the following:

- What is/are the variable/s to be measured?
- What information/data is already available on this/these variable/s?
- Where will the data come from?
- Who are the people with greatest knowledge about this data?
- How do they think this data can best be collected?
- What is the precise technical description of the indicator?
- What do all the terms in the indicator wording actually mean?
- Is the indicator wording sufficiently tight that it cannot be misinterpreted?

Researching responses to these questions in technical areas such as sewage treatment systems or satellite accounting may involve meetings with the indicator working group, specialists from different fields and analysis of technical literature on areas that may be outside the project facilitator's knowledge. For example, if the proposed indicator concerns the percentage of hotels treating their sewage, there is a need to define what 'treating' involves, research the type of systems used in the destination and get advice about which one is most environmentally friendly and appropriate for the location. There may also be a need to define 'hotels' or suggest a more all-embracing term such as 'tourist accommodation providers'.

Fine-tuning therefore involves research similar to that described above, for each indicator. In some cases information uncovered during this phase will necessarily result in the decision to drop a particular indicator or change its focus. Even with the most detailed screening process, what might appear in theory to be the appropriate indicator or monitoring protocol, may in practice prove quite impractical, prohibitively expensive, unreliable or culturally inappropriate.

Adaptive management techniques and concepts are particularly useful in these circumstances. Adaptive management suggests that indicators are never cast in stone: they are drafted, redrafted and improved as new information and resources become available. In some instances this may require selecting the second choice indicator and in other cases it may require going back to the drawing board and brainstorming to find an alternative indicator, rescreening and fine-tuning. Time and patience at this stage are likely to be rewarded by more resilient indicators later on. By the end of the fine-tuning a great deal of useful background information should have been gathered on each indicator which needs to be carefully documented in order to maximize learning outcomes of the process.

Data collection

One approach to data collection is that each indicator becomes a project in its own right, involving the identification of independent data sources and development of specific data collection methods. However, the dangers here are that the comprehensive focus of the work is lost and sustainable tourism becomes nothing more than a list of independent indicator projects. It is suggested here that there are significant efficiencies to be gained by viewing the indicator list in its entirety, integrating and rationalizing data collection methodologies and enabling groups of indicators to be researched together. In this way the collection and identification of common data sets such as 'tourist accommodation facilities' is facilitated and survey methods can be more easily designed to collect information for more than one indicator simultaneously.

Indicators can be grouped thematically or by data type (quantitative or qualitative) but perhaps the most effective initial division is between those requiring primary and secondary data. Primary surveys (which can cover all themes and data types) are, in general, more costly, time-consuming and demanding on human resources than secondary surveys, so existing sources should normally be considered first. In many cases this can be achieved without compromising indicator reliability or focus, either by combining data collection for several indicators into one survey, or by finding alternative secondary sources of data. For example, if a visitor questionnaire is required for one indicator such as tourist satisfaction, it may also be possible to use this to gather information about the number of tourist crimes that take place or the level of service in hotels, depending on the indicators that have been selected. There is, therefore, often a need for a trade-off between the desire to use primary research to secure up-to-date, specific data, with the greater speed and lesser cost with which secondary information can normally be obtained. Peterson (1997, p. 133) echoes the warnings in Chapter 5 on this subject: 'The temptation to submit "any old data" because it is readily available has to be avoided'.

The actual data collection process is designed and undertaken in a similar way to other visitor research initiative, using local expertise where possible. Using participatory data collection techniques can greatly enhance the learning outcomes of the monitoring process and gives stakeholders a greater involvement in the process (see Chapter 4). For example, the Iguazu Forest Natural Reserve in Brazil uses tourist guides to identify animal activity and other indicators of the state of fauna and flora (Aguas Grandes, 2004). Although problems were initially experienced with the regularity and accuracy of the indicators, there were very clear benefits for those guides involved, enabling them to provide greater information to tourists and encourage improved tourist behaviour (WTO, 2004b). Clearly, the appropriateness of participatory data collection will depend on the technical demands of the methodology selected for particular indicators.

Methodological options for the collection of primary data may include telephone interviews with tourism establishments, face-to-face interviews with tour operations, site surveys, aerial photography, water sampling, coral reef monitoring, local community surveys or focus group meetings. Visitor questionnaires using open-ended questions have been found to work well to assess satisfaction either independently or when added to an existing survey. Low-cost alternatives to visitor questionnaires may also be considered such as the 'diary approach' developed for use in Yosemite Wilderness by Newman *et al.* (2001). For larger-scale projects, Langaas (1997) recommends the use of geographical information systems (GIS) to improve the spatial understanding of indicators, provide a more integrated response and help with the organizing of large data sets. The main advantage of GIS being its ability to perform visual overlays enabling the results of multiple sets of data to show simultaneously how particular areas are affected. In the Yosemite example above, for example, Newman *et al.* (2001) also used GIS analysis to develop overlay maps to display current and desired conditions of their indicators.

In terms of secondary data, contact points will need to be established and perhaps, where information is of a sensitive nature (for example inland revenue data, company registration or average wages), inter-departmental agreements should be drawn-up for the sharing of information. WTO (2004b) suggests that in some cases a 'data alliance' may be necessary where the supplier obtains some advantage from their provision of data such as marketing opportunity or compensation for their time and effort. Even at this point it may be necessary to reconsider the selected indicator if the practice of data collection becomes too problematic. Box 7.1 provides a summary of data collection considerations.

Monitoring sustainable tourism indicators results in the accumulation, over time, of a large amount of information on the tourism system under study. Careful consideration of data management is therefore also an important consideration during indicator piloting. Despite the large array of high-tech data management solutions available, Marion (1991) considers simple computerized databases are often the most effective and accessible methods of storing and analysing data. The simpler the system, the more accessible it will be for a wider range of stakeholders, removing the need for costly expertise to input and update the system to reflect changes and improvements made over time.

If there are just a small number of indicators, say less than 20, one of the simplest and most commonly available tools is a Microsoft EXCEL spreadsheet. This can be prepared to display the following information about each indicator:

Box 7.1. Data collection considerations.

1. It is valuable to integrate sustainable tourism indicator monitoring with other regular cycles of information collection in the business or community. This will help create efficiencies within the organization and enable the indicators to become integral rather than extra parts of the tourism planning process.

2. It is important to consult with both experts and non-experts in design of the data collection methodology. Experts are good at providing the technically correct solution and non-experts at being realistic about what is feasible given existing resources and what the general public are likely to understand and relate to.

3. Involving as wide a range of potential information users in the data collection process as is logistically possible (without compromising accuracy) helps to enhance the social learning outcomes to the monitoring project, provides ownership, builds expertise and interest in the project and often results in a more robust monitoring process.

4. It is essential that data collection techniques are carefully documented, as without standardized techniques and carefully defined and documented procedures, changes in the personnel could lead to a situation in which managers are unable to continue monitoring or to interpret previously collected data.

5. Finally, it is important to note that there will be no right and wrong ways of collecting data. Any particular indicators can have different and complementary methods of measurement and the best method will depend on resources, time, place and other local circumstances.

Adapted from: Marion (1991).

- Precise indicator wording;
- Desired trend;
- Data requirements;
- Data sources;
- Data collection process;
- Sample size;
- Results;
- Contact person;
- Useful references.

In addition, or as a more visual alternative to the database, Manidis Roberts (1997) recommends the use of a reporting chart system where the progress of each indicator can be tracked visually on a graph so that their performance can be compared with the acceptable ranges (see next section) and trends over time can be appreciated at a glance. An example is provided in Fig. 7.1.

An additional consideration in data collection is the potential dilemma between the need to develop longitudinal data and the need to produce indicators specific to the problems facing a place or community at a particular point in time. In this context it is useful to remember that sustainability is not a static concept: people's attitudes and environment condition change over time. Consequently indicators selected to monitor sustainability need to be updated on an ongoing basis, and as a problem is reduced in acuity, such as with incidences of smallpox, then it may cease to be measured. Although this inevitably means valuable time-series data will be lost, there is little point in measuring indicators that are no longer relevant when other issues may urgently require attention (there is further discussion of this in the review section at the end of the chapter).

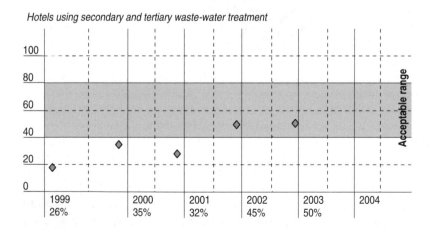

Fig. 7.1. Acceptable ranges. Adapted from: Manidis Roberts Consultants (1997).

Finally, indicators must be able to produce data in a timely manner (Peterson, 1997, p. 133).

Interpreting Results

We live in an information-based society. Stakeholders of all types are increasingly bombarded with statistical data and, as a consequence, need to take great care with the interpretation and communication of indicator results. Various techniques may be used to assist the effective interpretation and communication of indicator results, one of which is benchmarking.

Benchmarking

The results of indicator monitoring are not always self-evident, and will be of little value unless they can be accurately interpreted and understood. It needs to be clear to the indicator working group and the users of the monitoring data what it means if 76% of sampled accommodation facilities recycle their biodegradable wastes and whether or not this requires a management response. To facilitate the interpretation of indicator data, benchmarks, baseline, target or critical limits can be established.

A baseline normally represents the agreed starting point for the monitoring process, often the first year for which data has been collected. The indicator result is then interpreted based on the degree of variance from the baseline. Busch and Trexler (2003, p. 4) explain baseline monitoring as 'the determination of the initial status of the system to be evaluated at a given point in time'. This works well as long as it is clear to the target audience that the baseline may not necessarily represent a desirable state, as critical limits may, unknowingly, already have been exceeded in particular areas (Weaver and Lawton, 1999). The other difficulty of this approach is that baseline alone does not indicate when action is needed, just when the previous status quo is reached or exceeded. In order to gain clarity in this respect a second point of reference is needed. This can take the form of a threshold or target.

The UNEP (1997) describes a threshold as a cut-off point beyond which some type of severe consequence reveals itself, be it ecological (i.e. the point at which pollution of a stream leads to chronic loss of fish life) or social (i.e. disputes reach the point where users are obliged to take legal action). Scheffer *et al.* (2002, p. 196) call it a 'switch' which they explain as follows: 'Sometimes the ecosystem may seem untouched by increasing stress until it suddenly collapses to another state when certain threshold values are passed'. Identifying such a critical point in advance, can serve as a type of early-warning system, alerting managers to the potentially drastic consequences and irreversible changes that may occur if certain boundaries are crossed, and enabling them to take action before serious threats to sustainability occur (WTO, 1996, 2004b). Whilst intuitively attractive, this approach appears scientifically flawed in view of what is now known about uncertainty and the behaviour of complex systems (see Chapter 1; Ludwig *et al.*, 1993, NRC, 1999). Goodall and Stabler (1997) explain that even for areas as well researched as water quality, it is very difficult to determine critical loads or threshold levels for particular indicators because of limited scientific understanding and absence of data, reflecting many of the criticisms of tools such as carrying capacity (Mathieson and Wall, 1982). An alternative management approach to thresholds is to view them as the trigger-point for management response, a point which calls for action even if the action is just examining the issues more closely, getting more information and ensuring the drastic consequences described above do not occur.

In contrast to thresholds, targets focus on the need to reach or exceed a desirable goal. For example, the target percentage of children over 6 years old in primary education may be 99%. The IHEI, an online database hoteliers can use to compare aspects of their environmental management with an industry average for a similar type of hotel, uses this type of generic approach (Middleton and Hawkins, 1998). Nevertheless, over-emphasis on measurable targets also brings its problems. Whitehouse (2003) outlines the risks inherent in 'indicatorism', and Miller and Twining-Ward (2003) warn of the dangers of 'targetitus', where an excessive focus on reaching the target blinds project managers from actually using the data to help move towards sustainable tourism. At worst, the pursuit of targets affects the policy decisions made, with the attainment of the means, becoming more important than the end.

An alternative interpretive solution more in line with the adaptive approach advocated in this book is to identify a fluid range of targets, an 'acceptable range' that can be used in an experimental manner, and adjusted as and when new information becomes available. The concept of 'acceptable ranges' or conditions was developed for the TOMM project based on LAC explained in the previous chapter. TOMM (see Chapter 9) describes an acceptable range as a goal or a set of conditions, which, in a given situation, represents a 'desirable state' (Manidis Roberts, 1997). Once the range is established, managers then compare the actual result with the range in order to assess whether or not a response is required. The range may be identified either using stakeholder consultations to establish how much social and ecological change in a particular area is viewed as acceptable under current conditions (Cole and McCool, 1997), or using a multi-pronged approach involving previous research, personal observations and the advice of experts in various fields (Manidis Roberts, 1997, p. 23).

Despite the subjectivity, which appears to be unavoidable in benchmarking activities, the advantage of the approach is that it provides a relatively simple, and easy to visualize indication of whether the indicator result represents a positive or negative state in relation to a particular sustainable tourism objective. Rather than trying to identify a magic number as a trigger point for a management response, it recognizes that there are likely to be a range of situations that may be appropriate under different circumstances and require different types of responses.

Figure 7.1 shows how, using acceptable ranges, Manidis Roberts Consultants developed reporting cards for each indicator on Kangaroo Island designed to provide a 'quick and easy' opportunity to detect trends and interpret results.

In reality, the semantics are confusing, and benchmarks, thresholds, targets and ranges are often used interchangeably to mean the point at which action should be taken. Whichever term is used, there are some common difficulties, which are summarized here:

- If the ranges are set too low, the outlook becomes too rosy, sends 'business as usual' signals to the industry and may result in unsustainable practices not being identified soon enough. Conversely, if the ranges are set too high, too many indicators fail and the situation could appear so daunting that there is a risk nothing would be done at all.
- There are some indicators for which the desired direction of trend in results will be ambiguous. For example, whilst a drop in tourism's contribution to GDP of below 10% in the context of an acceptable range of 15–20% is regarded as less than optimal, it could simply mean that other areas of the economy were performing strongly, which in itself would not be cause for concern. The classic example is whether an increasing number of police officers is indicative of increased or decreased security.
- Whilst for environmental indicators there may be a relatively objective scientific basis for setting targets or limits (e.g. proven level of air pollution which causes respiratory illnesses), social and economic limits are more value-laden and indicators must be relative to each society's concepts, goals and values (Dahl, 1997b).
- Benchmarking is inherently subjective. Different people will inevitably see the same result with different eyes, as the setting targets requires value-judgements that are unavoidably culture-bound.
- Ranges need to be updated to take account of pressures faced. If current policy actions seem to be ineffective, or new threats emerge, then what is an acceptable range of pollution, tourists, etc., may need to be revised.

Given these impediments, it is important to avoid misplaced confidence in benchmarks, and ensure the shortcomings of the particular mechanism adopted are openly admitted. Noon (2003, p. 45) observes, 'Acknowledging uncertainty up front is critical because such incomplete knowledge is an explicit risk that can be addressed in the decision process. Despite this uncertainty, monitoring programs are of limited value if trigger points or critical distributions have not been identified.' It is therefore important to realize that although baselines, thresholds, targets and acceptable ranges provide a useful point of reference for analysing indicator results, they are not an alternative to critical evaluation of the absolute data or in-depth investigation of possible causal factors, a topic returned to later in this chapter.

Indices and aggregation

Despite the need to adopt a comprehensive approach to monitoring, the complexity of aggregating data to create indices means the results of sustainable tourism indicators are most commonly presented independently. There are two main problems with this: first, it makes it difficult for managers to assess the overall sustainability performance of the location, community or business (although this does militate against the temptation to 'score' sustainability in destinations), and second, it can lead to a disjointed programme of action for sustainability. Rutherford (1997a, p. 149) clarifies the dilemma:

> One of the challenges of sustainable development indicators work is the requirement, on the one hand, to determine the direction the whole system is moving in order to understand at the macro level whether it is sustainable or not and hence to set macro policies to correct the situation, and on the other hand, to provide adequate information for decision making at the micro level, where action really counts.

Rather than dissection and then reintegration of results, Rutherford recommends a holistic approach, seeing the whole from several different perspectives in order to gain greater understanding.

Another interpretive option is the identification of 'keystone', critical or headline indicators. Like its biological equivalent, 'keystone species', are an indication of the overall well-being of the ecosystem. It may be possible to identify a number of keystone indicators such as tourist satisfaction and local satisfaction that can be regarded as indicative of the overall well-being of the tourism system. Keystone characteristics might include: stability, public resonance, simplicity and indicators that are multi-faceted. Although this will be difficult to find initially, over time, the most valuable three or four indicators will become clear and can then be used to help managers assess progress towards sustainability, identify uncertainties and make suggestions for appropriate management responses.

Aggregating indicator results by describing results in a collective fashion, or quantitatively using an index is also a popular interpretive tool. Aggregation can be undertaken either for all indicators together based on the number of indicators reporting good or bad news, or in thematic categories (e.g. overall results from environmental or economic-focused indicators). Both types of aggregation raise technical problems as the MEA (2004) notes:

> It is enormously challenging to measure the overall 'condition' of an ecosystem. Unlike a living organism, which might be either healthy or

unhealthy but can't be both simultaneously, ecosystems can be in good condition for producing certain goods and services while in poor condition for others . . . Typically, we manage ecosystems to increase the production of one or more goods and services, such as food or timber, at the expense of others such as water quality or biodiversity. We thus make conscious and unconscious trade-offs between the capacity of the system to support different goods and services.

One example of a highly successful index is the South Pacific Applied Geo-science Commission (SOPAC) Environmental Vulnerability Index. The index was developed in response to a call made in the Barbados Plan of Action for Small Island Developing States to develop a composite vulnerability index that incorporates both ecological fragility and economic vulnerability (Briguglio, 2004). The purpose of the index, conceived in 1985 but produced for the first time in 1992, is to highlight the underlying economic and environmental fragility of small states. Box 7.2 provides further information on the index.

However, like other indices such as university rankings, most liveable city or most corrupt country, SOPAC's also has a number of weaknesses principally associated with: the subjectivity in the choice of variables, absence of data for some areas and inconsistent measurement. An additional difficulty with any type of quantitative aggregation, as discussed in Chapter 5, is assigning appropriate weightings and the fact that detail is lost and results can be strongly influenced by one outlying positive or negative result.

Despite the difficulties noted above, a popular index used for tourism purposes is the Blue Flag beach programme that involves the aggregation

---

Box 7.2. SOPAC's Vulnerability Index.

SOPAC's Vulnerability Index is designed to draw attention to the issue of economic and environmental vulnerability of small island developing states (SIDS), less-developed countries (LDCs) and other vulnerable countries. It presents a single-value measure of vulnerability that can be considered with regards to the allocation of financial and technical assistance or for assigning special status to vulnerable countries and is also being considered by the United Nations Committee on Development Policy as a possible criterion for classification as a least developed country.

It provides a predictive value for identifying vulnerability issues, types of hazards and approaches to stewardship of the environment of a state, identifying problem areas for external assistance, and a performance indicator for donor funding. The index can be used as a measure of change in environmental vulnerability if repeated assessments are made (every 5 years) and is also a practical tool for raising awareness of environmental vulnerability and the actions that increase or decrease it.

Source: Briguglio (2004).

of complex indicators into a simple yes/no result – the beach either has a blue flag or does not. Another programme that has received international attention is the Green Globe 21 certification programme, which enables hotels and other tourism businesses to assess their environmental performance and access a large amount of environmental information on line. These two certification programmes are described in Box 7.3.

Both the programmes described above employ standard thresholds and indicators so are comparable internationally but at the same time are not reflective of place-specific sustainability issues. The Green Globe tends to focus on the big five operational issues: energy, water, waste, sewage and social issues. Although it has a useful contribution to make, and some tourism authorities have bought into the programme, there are also many who are sceptical of the commercial ambition of the company, and concerned about the implications of Green Globe potentially gaining a monopoly over global tourism certification.

Box 7.3.   Blue Flag and Green Globe 21.

Blue Flag Programme

The Blue Flag programme is owned and run by the independent non-profit organization, the Foundation for Environmental Education (FEE). The Blue Flag Campaign is an environmental initiative for the certification of beaches and marinas. The programme started in Europe in 1987 and had awarded almost 3000 beaches by 2004. Blue Flags are awarded based on achievement in four areas: water quality, safety and services, environmental management, and environmental education and information.

FEE has been cooperating with the UNEP and WTO on extending the campaign to areas outside Europe, among other them several Caribbean countries.

Green Globe 21

In 1994, the WTTC launched Green Globe, a worldwide environmental management and awareness programme for the travel and tourism industry. Their Green Globe 21 (also called GG21) is an accreditation programme that is based on Agenda 21. Companies and destinations can be taken through an assessment, benchmarking and certification process that will lead them to become a certified Green Globe company or destination. Travel agents and tourists see certification by Green Globe as a guarantee of being environmentally 'safe'. Green Globe can only consider certification of a destination if there is a leading institution that has planning and regulatory authority and is also involved in the development and management of tourism. There are four different kinds of Green Globe standards: company, community, international ecotourism, and design and construct, each with their own set of standards. Green Globe has 500 participants in over 100 countries.

Sources: Blue Flag (2004), Green Globe (2004).

Communication

Documenting and communicating indicator results are important but under-utilized elements of the monitoring process. Indicators can be brilliantly designed and piloted, but if the results are poorly portrayed or not effectively communicated, their impact will be minimal. There is therefore a great need for effective and skilled communicators to convert indicator data to information on which decision making can be based.

WTO (2004b, p. 4) comment that many managers operate in an environment that can be considered 'data-rich but information poor'. Meadows (1998, pp. 77–78) explains further:

> Long lists of numbers may underlie an effective instrument panel, but the most immediate indicators need to be graphic, sensual, real, compelling. Perhaps they need not require a corps of bureaucrats to obtain or maintain. People with training in advertising, public relations, focus groups, graphic art may be more helpful than people with expertise in database management.

Instead of tables and graphs, she suggests it may be useful to experiment with colours, icons and symbols that convey poor, average or good indicator results in a highly visual manner. Maps can also be an effective means of reporting indicator results such as densities of tourism development, or areas of high water usage allowing particular hot spots or regional problem areas to be identified (WTO, 2004b). GIS have the potential to become an increasingly important communication tool in this regard, improving spatial thinking and awareness (Langaas, 1997).

In the context of monitoring sustainable tourism indicators, the WTO (2004b) suggests the means of presentation of results should depend on the users; for some users bar charts might be most effective and for others simple use of symbols is more appropriate. The SSTIP initially experimented with the use of a traffic light coding, whilst the Kangaroo Island TOMM project used simple shapes to present their data. Other icons are generally used for ecocertification, and benchmarking programmes such as Green Globe and Blue Flag use green leaves, globes or keys to indicate overall business fulfilment of environmental criteria, providing an aggregated indication of the whole result.

In Fig. 7.2 Garcia *et al.* (2000) demonstrate the results of their indicator programme using a kite diagram to compare actual scores against 'ideal' scores, or targets. The diagram aggregates indicator results using a complex mathematical formula to provide a very simple but highly visual tool. The example shown in the box suggests that human well-being in terms of revenues and jobs is doing better than the ecological well-being, and that the state of the nurseries may be bordering on a concern. The main benefit of the kite diagram is that it enables users to immediately draw broad conclusions from a long list of confusing and sometimes contradictory

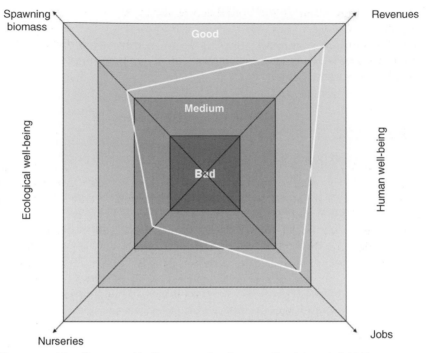

Fig. 7.2.   Kite diagram of indicator results. Source: Garcia *et al.* (2000).

indicator results. It does this by converting the results into a common currency relative to their performance.

A further extension of data presentation possibilities is the use of computer software to enable end-users to select and weigh indicators according to their own interests. Kerr (1997) discusses the computer-aided simulation programme of the IISD in Canada, designed to enable local communities to track their progress towards sustainability. The software enables communities to compare their results against other communities on standardized issues or against the national trend. The benefit of such an approach is its flexible and interactive nature, allowing and encouraging public support for the programme itself through simulated 'what-if' scenarios. More recently the IISD has completed a similar project, which is designed to present indicators in the style of a car dashboard in order to portray the speed at which different countries are travelling on their economic, environmental, social and instrumental issues based on the UN's core set of sustainability indicators (IISD, 2004b). At the first level, the dashboard aggregates the results of more than 100 sustainability indicators across more than 100 countries giving them a simple colour-coded score in relation to their environmental, social, economic and institutional sustainability. At the second level, each sector area such as the environment is disaggregated to show colour-coded scores for its key indicators. Despite the political and visual attractiveness of this approach, the results can be somewhat confusing, and with such a large number of indicators condensed into a small diagram risks loss of interesting detail in a very broad-brush approach.

Indicator Use

The final link in the monitoring chain is the question of what to do with the results. If the monitoring process is to be successful it is essential that there is a clear link to implementation (see the research by NEF in Chapter 4). Busch and Trexler (2003, p. 10) put the point very clearly 'Monitoring is an empty exercise, no matter how well conceived, if it does not tie into the policy making or management process'. Indicator use is the process that ensures that monitoring is not simply an information generating activity, but a proactive sustainable tourism management tool that is used to improve the way tourism is managed in a particular place. The NRC (1999, pp. 3–4) also highlights the importance of this stage:

> Ultimately, success in achieving a sustainability transition will be determined not by the possession of knowledge, but by using it, and using it intelligently in setting goals, providing needed indicators and incentives, capturing and diffusing innovation, carefully examining alternatives, establishing effective institutions, and, most generally, encouraging good decisions and taking appropriate actions.

Planners are perhaps one of the most common users of indicator results. In many countries the long-term master plans are being replaced by short-term strategic planning which requires a continuous stream of up-to-date information about the performance of the tourism system. In Samoa, for example, the indicator results were used as a basis for the impact management section of the tourism plan, providing a much more comprehensive pool of information for the planners to work from than would otherwise have been the case. Policy makers are also keen users of monitoring data. The North Sydney Council in Australia used social and economic indicators as the basis of its Cultural Tourism Plan. Indicators also can be used for site planning, to assess which locations are best for new resort development, for establishing criteria for a sustainable tourism competition, to justify applications for donor funds for particular activities or in an effort to avoid or at least put off the regulatory mechanisms. One of the most effective ways to ensure indicator results are actually used to change the way tourism is managed is to develop an implementation framework as an integral part of the indicator development programme.

Implementation framework

An implementation framework is an established process for converting indicator results into management responses. Very few monitoring programmes seem to include this important link but examples of action-based frameworks can be found in recreation literature. For example, in the LAC framework, indicators are not seen as an end in themselves, but as part of an ongoing process that involves the identification of social and eco-logical conditions, investigation of causal factors and the design and imple-mentation of appropriate management action (Stankey *et al.*, 1985; Marion, 1991). This LAC process is shown in Fig. 7.3.

Although the LAC process is a good example of how monitoring can be integrated in a planning cycle, it is still a little top heavy. The top three boxes in the figure remain static whilst the bottom half changes, which could result in a mismatch between management objectives and conditions on the ground.

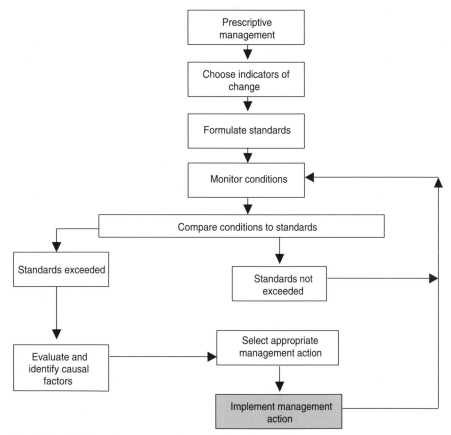

Fig. 7.3. LAC implementation framework. Adapted from: Marion (1991).

A more balanced implementation framework is suggested by adaptive management in Fig. 7.4. The adaptive management framework incorporates many of the monitoring functions discussed in this chapter; design and protocols (fine-tuning) is followed by data collection and interpretation and then communication of the results (interpretive reports, publications, public access). In addition, the framework incorporates two phases of review and improvement in each cycle. Following the data collection, monitoring and modelling advancements are used to improve the design and monitoring protocols. Then, when the reporting is completed, the adaptive management analysis involves the identification of areas where management responses are needed prior to a second review of the indicator design and monitoring protocol.

The two most important elements of the implementation framework are therefore regarded as management responses and the review. These are explained further below.

Management response strategy

One of the advantages of using acceptable ranges, and other interpretation tools discussed above, is that they give a clear indication of when policy intervention or a management response is called for. This can be referred to as a 'trigger' for action. In the example in Fig. 7.1, for the first 3 years the result was outside the acceptable range. Based on the principles of adaptive management, this should then trigger the development of a number of management responses. The responses can be tested and the most successful adapted (based on lessons learned) in order to give an improved result the following year. This type of cycle is shown in Fig. 7.5. The diagram, based on the monitoring of the US Northwest Forest Plan, illustrates the simplified

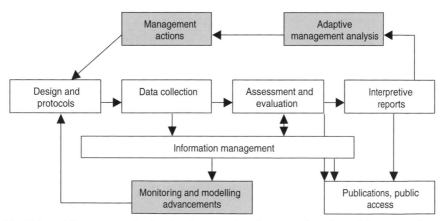

Fig. 7.4. Adaptive monitoring implementation framework. Adapted from: Trexler and Busch (2003, p. 420).

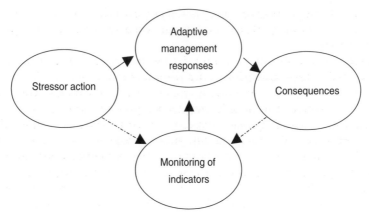

Fig. 7.5.   Management response cycle. Adapted from: Noon (2003).

relationship between environmental stressors, adaptive management practices and anticipated ecosystem responses. Attributes that are predictive of
the changes in ecological conditions are selected as the indicators and management responses are selected to reduce the particular stress and improve
the consequences.

As explained in Chapter 1, assessing the impact of management
responses is complicated by the fact that in non-linear systems outputs are
often quite out of proportion to inputs both in time and space, making pre-
diction as well as cause–effect relationships impossible to define with any
degree of certainty. Scheffer *et al.* (2002, p. 196) explain:

> . . . it is often assumed that the impact [ecosystem response to human use]
> will simply increase more or less smoothly with the intensity of use. However
> the evidence is accumulating that the response to increasing stress is
> frequently far from smooth. Sometimes the ecosystem may seem untouched
> by increasing stress until it suddenly collapses to another state when certain
> threshold values are passed.

In addition to system uncertainty, lack of knowledge can also confound the
search for appropriate responses. Hughes (2002) gives the example of
coral bleaching where there still exists some scientific uncertainty over
the combination of causes of this process, making management response
problematic.

Nevertheless, adaptive management is specifically designed to deal
with such uncertainty and limited knowledge. Instead of immediately
identifying a solution to a particular stress, more information is gathered,
techniques are piloted and lessons learned from the results are used to
reduce systemic uncertainty and provide adaptation to the most productive responses. In this way, management develops an experiential
learning cycle in which a broad range of stakeholders, not just those at the
top, are involved in assessing the effectiveness of various alternative

strategies. Using this approach, models of how the system functions can be improved as new information from research and monitoring is fed into the system.

One useful option to consider during this process is to draw up a list of potential action strategies for each indicator in advance, based on discussion with the indicator working group and local experts. These can be included in a manual of monitoring techniques and once poor results are reported and an investigation of possible causes has been completed, management can consider choosing one or two projects from the list of action strategies to be trialled for integration into the tourism strategy and undertaken as separate projects. In the case of too many indicators falling short of their thresholds, and too few resources to implement management responses, there may be a need to prioritize those requiring immediate action. An example of hard and soft management response options for a wastewater indicator are provided in Box 7.4.

Box 7.4. Example of management response to wastewater indicator.

In a situation where an indicator on the percentage hotels treating their sewage outflows gave a result well below the acceptable range. Several questions will need to be addressed:

- What is the main reason why hotels are not treating their sewage?
- How can this situation most efficiently be reversed?

To assist with the answering of these questions, both hoteliers and wastewater treatment specialists will need to be consulted and possible management responses (hard and soft) lined up for consideration and prioritization by the indicator working group.

The soft options to consider might include:

- Conduct environmental awareness programmes for hoteliers;
- Organize competition for environmentally friendly hotels;
- Provide tax holidays for import of secondary and tertiary technology;
- Provide free technical advice on the upgrading of sewage systems.

Harder options could include:

- Place a ban on one-chamber septic tanks in some areas;
- Draw up proper regulations for hotel wastewater treatment.

During the first year of poor results, it might be decided that environmental awareness campaign or training for hoteliers should be run; year 2 might offer special deals for those (particularly in low-lying wetland areas) willing to change their sewage systems. With monitoring undertaken annually, the results of these actions can be tested and compared, allowing project managers to assess how actions actually affect indicator results and build their knowledge of system behaviour.

Review and evaluation

The aim of the review process is to look again at the monitoring programme in the light of the initial and ongoing data collection and analysis and make any necessary improvements to the indicators or monitoring protocols. Acknowledging the indicators are unlikely to be perfect first time around and having the flexibility to expect and adapt to change is important especially given the dynamic nature of tourism systems. Situations change, stakeholders learn and new data becomes available over time. The NRC (1999, p. 265) report:

> . . . indicators used to report on a transition to sustainability are likely to be biased, incorrect, inadequate and indispensable. Getting the indicators right is likely to be impossible in the short term. But not trying to get the indicators right will surely compound the difficulty of enabling people to navigate through a transition to sustainability.

Indicators therefore need to be regularly reviewed to ensure they reflect the changing circumstances of the location under study.

The review process is an essential part of the monitoring cycle and the most important phase in adaptive management. WTO (2004b, p. 45) explains:

> As the issues which destination managers must address change, so do their needs for indicators. With use, it will become clear which indicators are serving the purpose well, and which will need to be updated or even replaced. While there is certainly a strong reason to retain indicators, as they are likely to become more useful over time as the record becomes longer, it is still worthwhile to revisit indicators every few years seeking improvement.

Monitoring programmes therefore need to be designed to anticipate the development of improved methods and sampling designs and better scientific knowledge on particular issues. Some of the questions that the indicator working group need to address in their evaluation of indicators are shown in Box 7.5.

Box 7.5.   Questions to ask during an indicator review.

- Is the indicator still measuring the issue it was designed to measure?
- Is the issue being measured still important to sustainable tourism and worth measuring?
- Are there changes that need to be made to the data collection process in the light of lessons learned?
- Is there now new information or technology that could influence the relevance or suitability of the indicator or data collection method/units?
- Has the indicator result been useful in the design of a sustainable tourism action plan?
- Is the threshold/target/acceptable range/trigger still considered suitable in the light of recent results?

The review of the indicators can take place at several levels: the indicator working group, project managers and the general public. WTO (2004b) suggests the performance of the sustainable tourism indicators should be evaluated by additional indicators focusing on components such as level of awareness of indicators, level of use (frequency of reporting), impact of the indicators and continuing commitment to the programme. Trexler and Busch (2003, p. 412) recommend a multi-level review process, 'Multi-level review is one mechanism to engage stakeholders throughout the process, including review and comments by independent panels of scientific or management experts'. The results of the review process can then feed directly into the monitoring procedures. This may mean that some indicators are dropped and new ones suggested in their place that also need to be screened, fine-tuned and piloted prior to the next round of monitoring. Busch and Trexler (2003) suggest that over time there may be a transition towards monitoring fewer or simpler indicators although they warn how a reduction in the number of indicators runs the risk that an oversimplified picture may emerge. Similarly, WTO (2004b) observes that the same indicator might serve different purposes or their role might change over time. They give the example of an indicator of stress on the system that can later serve to measure the effects of a management response. Over time the stability of the indicator set and monitoring protocols is likely to improve and the benefits of change will need to be carefully balanced with the benefits of consistently monitoring the same indicators in the same way over an extended period of time. At the same time it should be remembered that retaining an indicator or a specific data collection technique which has become irrelevant or has been usurped by other more pressing concerns simply for the sake of providing longitudinal data over a number of years is unlikely to assist a location move towards greater sustainability.

Maintaining the Monitoring Programme

Once the initial challenge of establishing indicators and monitoring methods is completed, there is the ongoing issue of how to ensure that monitoring is maintained in the long term. Although the process itself has been shown to be a useful one during which stakeholders identify their vision for sustainable tourism and how they wish it to be measured, if the monitoring is not kept up, the long-term effects of the work will be minimal.

The Resilience Alliance stresses the need to develop new institutions and institutional strategies with sufficient flexibility to adapt to change (Resilience Alliance, 2004). This is supported by the experiences highlighted in the case study section of this book. Consequently, it is recommended that rather than remaining as an 'indicator project', once established, the indicators and implementation frameworks become internalized in some manner so that the 'monitoring programme' becomes integral to management practice. This can take place at the level of a tourism business where monitoring becomes part of an annual reporting process, or at a national level when monitoring results become the drivers of action strategies and budgetary allocations for sustainable tourism.

Maintaining the interest of stakeholder groups after the indicator development process is completed is also a key challenge. WTO (2004b) suggest that commitment is the key, that indicators need to become part of a planning process for the destination, and by so doing they 'enter the public domain'. Marion (1991) suggests staff training is an essential means of creating commitment, improving monitoring procedures, internalizing the process so they become tacit knowledge and building an appreciation of quality. In more isolated locations there are the practical difficulties involved in gathering stakeholders together and the cost involved in travel to consider. Adaptive management puts the focus on organizational learning and stakeholder involvement; using monitoring as a tool to learn more about the complex tourism system, getting people involved and sustaining interest this way (Resilience Alliance, 2004).

Having a clear schedule for monitoring activities that can be incorporated into already existing data collection processes can also help with institutionalizing the monitoring system. The monitoring schedule will depend on the purpose of the particular indicator programme whether it is annual, to coincide with other reporting requirements of the business, organization or community, or biennial. Biennial monitoring allows greater time for the implementation of action plans and effects to been felt but annual or even biennial monitoring provides more detailed information, and faster development of trend data, important where the pace of change is rapid. In some monitoring projects, where more resources are available for the first few years, more frequent monitoring may initially be possible for some of the indicators, providing a good initial baseline from which to reassess acceptable ranges, targets or thresholds. This can then change to annual or biennial monitoring once the indicators are shown to be working well and collection systems have been optimized.

Summary

Designing and implementing a monitoring system is a complex process that involves ongoing challenges. Monitoring sustainable tourism is not a project to be undertaken lightly or without due planning, resources and consideration of how the results will be used. However, if the implementation process is successful, tourism organizations, businesses or communities will gain a valuable tool to assist them learn more about the system they are operating and understand how to move towards greater sustainability on an ongoing basis.

This chapter has demonstrated how a set of draft indicators can be converted into an operational system for monitoring progress towards sustainability in a particular place, business or community. In doing so, it has bridged the frequently ignored gap between indicator development and indicator use, presenting readers with a number of alternative monitoring processes to consider. Key issues raised include the value of involving a wide range of stakeholders in data collection, the importance of communicating indicator results in a simple, clear manner in order to maximize stakeholder learning opportunities, and the value of integrating monitoring into the tourism planning and policy-making process.

Throughout the chapter emphasis has been placed on adaptive monitoring strategies that value experimentation, learning and the need to adapt indicators and their monitoring protocols based on lessons learned. These have served to highlight why the success of a monitoring programme should not only be judged on the indicators it produces, or the visual results it presents, but in the knowledge it generates and the alternative options and action for sustainable tourism it results in. Information creates empowerment, ensuring clear messages reach local stakeholders, assists them to take a more active role in the tourism development process.

Research on sustainable tourism indicators is still rather exploratory, and this chapter does not provide all the answers or indeed ask all the questions. As with other newly emerging areas, a degree of trial and error is to be expected in all monitoring activities. Systems will be established, mistakes made and lessons need to be learned that hopefully will enable the monitoring agency to perform more effectively in the future. Over time, the development and implementation of monitoring systems is likely to become easier as standardized sustainable tourism indicator sets are produced and data collection methodologies facilitated. Whilst this will be a significant time saver, it cannot be a substitute for effective community visioning, screening, the identification of local place-based data sources and the needs and preferences of user groups.

IV   Introduction to Case Studies

The practical mechanics of monitoring can be discussed and the process of indicator development detailed, but it is not until the indicators are put to the test that the real costs, benefits and constraints to implementation become clear. Tourism systems are complex and constantly changing; they are location-specific and defy 'one-size-fits-all' type solutions to planning, monitoring and practically any other type of management. Consequently, one of the most effective ways to study monitoring issues is to look at specific case studies in some depth.

The following case studies present a wide range of monitoring experiences from international level in the case of the WTO indicator programme to regional with the TOMM Kangaroo Island Project and national in the case of the SSTIP. Whilst these first three case studies examine monitoring from a destination perspective, the Tour Operators' Initiative provides a useful demonstration of how monitoring is applied at a sector level to tour operators. Throughout the case studies, attempts are made to demonstrate how the key issues raised in this book namely the need for a comprehensive, stakeholder-driven and adaptive approach to monitoring, work in practice. All the case studies include extensive discussion of the processes used to develop the monitoring programmes, participation of stakeholders and the results of the programmes and an evaluation and review of lessons learned. This is designed to be of assistance to other destinations, sectors or organizations who may be interested in establishing their own indicator programmes and can benefit from the lessons of hard experience.

The WTO case study clearly shows the evolution of the sustainable tourism indicator process over the last decade in terms of process, indicators and stakeholder participation. The TOMM Kangaroo Island case study discusses some of the very real practical, institutional and resource-based challenges faced by the community of Kangaroo Island as it attempts to effectively manage its own change process through an ongoing monitoring programme. The Samoa study highlights the involvement of stakeholders in indicator development and shows how adaptive management can be used to help bridge the gap between indicator results and management responses and improve the learning outcomes of the monitoring process. Both Kangaroo Island and Samoa demonstrate the principles of adaptive management, and both recognize the need to change and adapt over time and to address issues facing tourism in a comprehensive systemic fashion. Finally, the Tour Operators' Initiative reflects on the challenges of promoting corporate social responsibility amongst tour operators and demonstrates how indicators can be used to improve the sustainability performance of the tourism sector.

Review of these cases reveals that the challenges of gaining sufficient stakeholder interest, enthusiasm and loyalty are not to be underestimated. However, when it comes to practical obstacles, it is the maintenance of the monitoring programme over time that seems to be the greatest hurdle. Nevertheless, it is important to remember that all the projects discussed are relatively recent and as TOMM notes, in reality, such an extensive integrated monitoring process takes time to gain momentum and stakeholder confidence.

The World Tourism Organization   8

Introduction

The WTO was one of the first international level organizations to develop and use indicators as an instrument to monitor and measure sustainable tourism and as such, it is apt that it should be the first of the case studies presented in this book. Since 1993, the WTO has organized sustainable tourism monitoring pilot projects in different parts of the world where WTO consultants have worked together with national and local tourism managers to develop indicators for particular sites. Since 2003, when the WTO became a UN Specialized Agency, the organization has been analysing the experiences from these case studies and workshops and combining these with results from other countries and advice from indicator experts throughout the world. Consequently, the WTO has become an important resource and first point of reference for any project involving sustainable tourism indicators.

The first part of the chapter outlines the background to WTO monitoring. From this foundation, the evolution of the WTO indicator development process and indicator identification is examined, showing the changes in approach and methods that have taken place since 1993. Two of the WTO case studies are then examined in more detail – Sri Lanka (2000) and Croatia (2001) – in order to see how the process works in practice. The final part of the chapter examines the strengths and weaknesses of the WTO monitoring programme. It concludes that WTO has made a significant contribution to the field of indicator development, being both a catalyst and frontrunner for monitoring projects worldwide, but also critiques the programme for its lack of commitment to long-term stakeholder

©G.A. Miller and L. Twining-Ward 2005. *Monitoring for a Sustainable Tourism Transition* (G.A. Miller and L. Twining-Ward)

involvement and its failure to effectively implement and maintain the monitoring schemes.

Background to WTO Monitoring

Sustainable tourism development has been one of the WTO's core programme activities since the 1992 Earth Summit in Rio de Janeiro. The WTO has been the executing agency for many projects worldwide and given technical assistance to a number of countries, often in cooperation with the UNDP. In the 1990s, the primary focus was environmental aspects of sustainable tourism but in recent years the WTO has expanded its attention to include poverty alleviation. It has been responsible for many publications on sustainable tourism and has organized multiple summits and seminars to create awareness and increase the knowledge of member states of this area.

Conscious of the need to assess progress towards sustainable development, following the Rio Summit, the World Tourism Organization established an international taskforce to develop sustainable tourism indicators through their Tourism and the Environment Committee. The chair of this new committee was Dr Ted Manning, principal of Consulting and Audit Canada. The taskforce consisted of 13 consultants, government officials and researchers from North America and Europe (WTO, 1993). The goal of the taskforce was to produce a list of indicators to help identify emerging concerns and to assist tourism managers to recognize potential problem areas. The initial results from the group were reported in a publication entitled *Indicators for the Sustainable Management of Tourism* (WTO, 1993). The report discusses the need for indicators, and proposes a preliminary list of indicators and a framework for indicator selection.

In this first report, the international taskforce focused primarily on indicators that would measure the impact of tourism on the natural and cultural environment. The potential indicators were divided into those intended for national use and those for local or 'hot-spot' application and then tested for usefulness in five locations worldwide: (i) Prince Edward Island, Canada; (ii) Los Tuxtlas, Mexico; (iii) The Netherlands; (iv) Florida Keys National Marine Sanctuary, USA; and (v) Villa Gesell and Peninsula Valdes, Argentina.

As a result of the pilot studies, the taskforce defined a list of 11 core indicators (Box 8.5) that was to be supplemented with issue-specific indicators relating to specific destination types. The core indicators were intended to be used by all destinations and consisted of indicators that would give a 'tourism decision maker' a base level of management information. The destination-specific indicators were further divided in two categories:

- Supplementary ecosystem-specific indicators, which could be used in specific ecosystems (e.g. mountain regions, coastal zones or urban environments); and
- Site-specific indicators that were developed for a specific location.

The WTO then produced *What Tourism Managers Need to Know: a Practical Guide to the Development and Use of Indicators of Sustainable Tourism* in 1996. The book identifies a set of core indicators, suggests different destination-specific indicators, provides the results of the pilot studies and is written for tourism industry decision makers in order to assist them work towards enhanced sustainability. These new indicators and the related methodology were further developed and tested in Balaton, Hungary (1999); Mexico (1999); Villa Gesell, Argentina (2000); Beruwala, Sri Lanka (2000); Kukljica, Croatia (2001) and Cyprus (2003). The case studies were more comprehensive than the initial pilot studies and in both Hungary and Mexico, the WTO consultants organized workshops to demonstrate to regional tourism managers the process of developing indicators. Participants were asked to discuss their destination's development issues and decide on which key indicators should be selected. The workshops attracted regional attention with tourism managers from six Central American and Caribbean nations participating in the Cozumel workshop, while in Argentina, seven South American countries participated. The principal goal of the workshops and case studies was to expand the understanding and awareness of sustainable tourism indicators internationally, and following each of the studies, the WTO consultants improved and updated their methodology based on lessons learned.

The most recent addition to the WTO indicator publications is *Signposts for Sustainable Tourism: a Guidebook for the Development and Use of Indicators of Sustainable Development for Tourism Destinations* (WTO, 2004b). This new text incorporates the WTO's 10 years of experience in the field and has the input of more than 60 experts working on sustainable tourism indicator development in 20 countries. The guidebook is intended to act both as a resource book and a practical handbook for the development of indicators within a tourism destination. The stated objective of the work was to 'create an enhanced process or suite of processes/tools which can serve as a practical guide for destination managers and destination management organizations' (Consulting and Audit Canada, 2003, p. 4). The publication consists of two volumes, the first of which explains the process, practice and implementation of indicators with numerous practical examples and the second of which is practical step-by-step field guide for developing sustainable tourism indicators.

Examination of the 1993, 1996, 2004b and 2004c WTO publications reveals the evolution of the WTO monitoring techniques and practices from stand-alone expert-developed indicators to indicator programmes that are more integrated into local planning processes and developed using participatory methodologies.

Indicator Development Process

The primary focus of the first WTO publication on sustainable tourism indicators in 1993 was identifying an initial list of indicator ideas. In contrast, the 1996 guide *What Tourism Managers Need to Know* offered for the first time a method for indicator development itself, outlined in Box 8.1.

This method was further refined during the case studies held between 1996 and 2001 and reduced to the seven phases shown in Box 8.2.

While at this time the first phase of the process tended to be executed by the WTO consultants with minimal local support, phases 2–4 utilized the input from various local stakeholders during workshop sessions facilitated

---

Box 8.1.   Indicator development process, 1996.

Phase 1: Setting the boundaries of the site study – determine the physical boundaries of the study site.
Phase 2: Identifying site attributes – identification and description of the tourism assets.
Phase 3: Identifying current key issues – identification of environmental issues on the site.
Phase 4: Selecting indicators for use – identification of core and supplementary indicators.
Phase 5: Determining data sources – determine the availability of the necessary data.
Phase 6: Data collection and analysis.
Phase 7: Evaluation of results – identification of benchmarks against which indicator measurements can be compared.
Phase 8: Revisiting key issues – identification of possible new issues for inclusion in subsequent monitoring.

Adapted from WTO (1996).

Box 8.2.   Indicator development process, 2001.

Phase 1: Research and organization.
Phase 2: Risk and issue identification.
Phase 3: Development of candidate indicators.
Phase 4: Selection of priority indicators.
Phase 5: Refinement of key indicators.
Phase 6: Implementation.
Phase 7: Monitoring and evaluation of results.

Source: WTO (2001b).

by WTO consultants. During the selection of the priority indicators (phase 4) participants were asked to rate candidate or potential indicators based on two dimensions: importance to tourism decision making and urgency of need. Each one was then screened using five criteria: relevance, feasibility, credibility, clarity and comparability. Steps 5–7 required rating each indicator using a five-star system (five stars for the most important, one for the least), and this was undertaken as a group. When their relevance had been determined, a process of refinement took place to determine who would use the information, who would provide it, how it would be treated, the level of detail needed, how accurate the data was, and how current the information must be to affect decision making. The final implementation and monitoring phases were executed by the local tourism managers, with some initial guidance from the consultants.

As a result of the experience gained during the implementation of the case studies, the Taskforce saw the need to broaden the indicator development programme in order to involve local tourism stakeholders to a much greater degree. Manning (1999, p. 180) explains the reasoning behind this change:

> Only through a participatory approach, involving the industry, the tourists and the various elements of the host community or region, is it possible to determine what range of values is relative to the assets. Further, it is only through a participatory approach that it is possible to determine which values are negotiable, and which are not.

Consequently, the new model, developed in 2004, uses 12 sequential steps subdivided into three main phases: research and organization, indicator development and implementation (Box 8.3). Not only does the 2004 process include greater opportunities for participation, it also puts more emphasis than previously on indicator use.

During phase one of the new model, the boundaries of the destination are set, all major stakeholders are identified and an initial meeting is organized to identify the destinations assets and issues. Another part of this first phase is the identification of common goals for the destination and the determination of its long-term vision. Information is gathered through interviews with all major stakeholders before the initial formal meeting takes place. The main difference between this process and the 1996 method is the development of the long-term vision of the destination to act as a point of reference for the indicators.

Phase two of the process involves the development of the indicators at a concentrated 3-day workshop. The goal of the first day meeting is to choose and rank issues. These are then grouped thematically into four categories: economic, environmental, social and management, and ranked in order of importance. During day 2, the participants identify the indicators to measure the selected issues and research potential data sources. The indicators are further rated using five evaluation criteria (relevance, feasibility,

---

Box 8.3.   Indicator development process, 2004.

Phase One: Research and organization
1. Definition/delineation of the destination.
2. Use of participatory processes.
3. Identification of tourism assets and risks.
4. Long-term vision.

Phase Two: Indicator development
5. Selection of priority issues and policy questions.
6. Identification of desired indicators.
7. Inventory of data sources.
8. Selection procedures.

Phase Three: Implementation
9. Evaluation of feasibility.
10. Data collection and analysis.
11. Accountability and communication.
12. Monitoring and evaluation of results.

Adapted from: WTO (2004b, p. 24).

---

credibility, clarity and comparison). Day 3 then involves reaching an agreement on the implementation of the selected indicators and the possible sources of information and support for each indicator. According to the WTO (2004b), the workshops can help to accelerate the indicator development process (which could otherwise take months to complete), create local support and form a strong basis for the implementation phase of the monitoring programme. This may be so, and a shorter period certainly makes it easier for the consultants, but whether 3 days' deliberation is really enough to support a destination-wide monitoring programme may require further research and follow-up of these case studies.

However, it is the third and final phase of the WTO process that still seems relatively undeveloped. This involves first identifying data sources, costs, characteristics, frequency of data collection and other technical requirements in order to generate a plan for the implementation of each of the selected indicators. Then the final step is to evaluate the results and set up a process for the ongoing collection of indicator information over time. Despite the great improvements in this area since 1996, the programme is still weak in this area and in transforming indicator results into action and improved management. Chapter 4 demonstrates that this is a problem common to many indicator programmes and, although this does not excuse it, it does highlight the need to find a workable solution. The problem is due, at least in part, to the tendency of WTO to focus on 'establishing indicators' rather than 'maintaining the monitoring', and symptomatic of organizations and agencies that work to short-term timeframes and project-based budgets, and actively avoid ongoing commitments. Although this

---

Box 8.4. List of potential stakeholders.

Public sector
Municipal authorities
Regional authorities
Various levels of government responsible for tourism and its key assets
Other ministries and agencies in areas affecting tourism

Private sector
Tour operators and travel agents
Accommodation, restaurants and attractions, and their associations
Transportation and other service providers
Guides, interpreters and outfitters
Suppliers to the industry
Tourism and trade organizations
Business development organizations

NGOs
Environmental groups
Conservation groups
Other interest groups (hunters, fishers and sports/adventure associations)

Communities
Local community groups
Native and cultural groups
Traditional leaders

Tourists
Organizations representing tourists in the region and point(s) of origin
International tourism organizations

Adapted from: WTO (2004b, p. 27).

---

situation is understandable, without a long-term commitment to monitoring, many learning as well as research opportunities may be missed, and knowledge on how to maintain monitoring programmes over time will be lost. Notwithstanding these shortcomings, the 2004 publication includes some useful features, such as the many case and varied case studies, examples and boxes of useful information, including a list of potential stakeholders at local destinations, shown in Box 8.4.

WTO Indicators

Having reviewed the evolution of the indicator development process, it is now useful to assess the progress WTO has made in terms of indicator formulation. Based on their pilot studies, the WTO 1996 Taskforce chose a set of core indicators that were practical enough to be used by most destinations, but would also provide enough information to assist with sustainable tourism decision making in specific destinations. The 11 core indicators focus principally on the environmental impact of tourism, and indicators that are relatively easy to quantify. These are explained in Box 8.5.

From Box 8.5, it can be seen that indicators 2, 3 and 4, which measure the level of stress, use intensity and social impact of tourism, are all quite similar, based on the concept of carrying capacity (see Chapter 2). While these indicators can show trends over time, the results are difficult to analyse and compare with other destinations and the concept of carrying capacity itself is now recognized to be of dubious validity. Other indicators such as indicator 6 (waste management) seem to be too simplistic to address properly the complex issue of waste management and tourism. Surprisingly, there is little focus on the economic aspects of sustainability, which is usually a primary

---

Box 8.5.   WTO core indicators, 1996.

Indicator	Specific measure	Explanation
1. Site protection	Category of protection according to IUCN index	Classifies the site according to categories produced by International Union of Nature and Natural Resources (IUCN)
2. Stress	Tourist numbers visiting site during specific period	Measured by the number of people who visit the site during a specific period of time (per annum/peak month)
3. Use intensity	Intensity of use in peak period (persons/hectare)	Measures the potential levels of overuse of the site and its resources as the ratio of the number of people on the site divided by the site area
4. Social impact	Ratio of tourists to locals (peak period and over time)	Measured by dividing the number of visitors at peak season by the number of permanent residents of the site
5. Development control	Existence of environmental review procedures or formal site controls	A ranked indication of the level of development of control (1–5) where 1 indicates no control and 5 indicates a high degree of control
6. Waste management	Percentage of sewage from site receiving treatment	Calculated by dividing the amount of sewage treated by the total amount of sewage produced at the site. The necessary data are usually available from sewage and water authority facilities

7. Planning process	Existence of organized regional plan for tourism	Like the development control indicators, this indicator rates the planning process on a scale of 1–5 where 1 indicates no formal planning process for tourism development and 5 indicates an extensive process
8. Critical ecosystems	Number of rare/endangered species	The indicator is numbered based on three levels of species at risk: endangered, vulnerable and threatened. A change in the number suggests that species have been eradicated, stressed or preserved
9. Consumer satisfaction	Level of satisfaction of visitors measured with questionnaire	This indicator measures the quality of the tourism site as perceived by the visitor. Tourists are asked: (i) to rate their holiday experience, and (ii) whether they would recommend the destination to their friends
10. Local satisfaction	Level of satisfaction by locals measured with random sample questionnaire	Measures the level of satisfaction of the local population. Residents are asked: (i) their opinion of tourism in the country, and (ii) whether they would like to see more, less or about the same level of tourism in the future
11. Tourism contribution to economy	Proportion of total economic activity generated by tourism only	Measures the dependency of the local economy on tourism and risk to the economy and the environment should tourism decline for some external reason

Adapted from: WTO (1996, p. 12).

target of WTO monitoring. The WTO dropped their last indicator, 'Tourism contribution to local economy', from the initial list of core indicators, perhaps because it was seen as ambiguous, either indicating improved performance of tourism or increased dependence, or also because it could prove to be too difficult to collect or too sensitive to political interference. Whatever the reason, there is a risk that if economic issues are removed from the process it becomes less comprehensive, and also less attractive for tourism authorities as for many, assessing the economic impacts is the primary motivation for monitoring.

Following the development of the core indicators, one of the objectives of the pilot and case studies was to develop composite indices that could be used in each destination. Preliminary studies in Argentina (WTO, 1996) made an attempt to identify the components that would make up the indices. While there were some common indicators identified for measuring carrying capacity as well as site stress, the first results showed that it would be problematic to determine a standard list of indicators for site attraction. The case study in Kukljica, Croatia (WTO, 2001b), showed again that carrying capacity is difficult to quantify, and the weighting process necessarily subjective, requiring frequent adjustment. Similar results were found for the level of site stress. While the different indicators can be used as a warning sign for reaching site stress thresholds, the specifics of each and every destination defy the one-size-fits-all approach. Given the attention destinations pay to creating a distinctive identity, it is of little surprise that different indicators are required to capture the variety between destinations. So while the efforts made by WTO to develop a more uniform approach via these indices are acknowledged, the diversity of destinations around the globe means that common indices may be of little value to the local tourism authorities.

A more successful idea has been to create ecosystem-specific indicators. The taskforce identified eight different ecosystems along with their respective key tourism issues, and developed specific indicators for each different ecosystem. The eight ecosystems with supplementary indicators are directed at: coastal zones, mountain regions, managed wildlife parks, unique ecological sites, urban environments, cultural sites (heritage), cultural sites (traditional communities) and small islands. For each ecosystem, the main issues were identified, indicators selected and possible measures suggested. Sites could decide to use more than one set of ecosystem-specific indicators if they felt other indicators to be applicable. Box 8.6 provides an example of ecosystem-specific indicators for the coastal zone.

In the 2004 guidebook, the WTO has defined a new approach to indicator development. Instead of the core indicators and ecosystem-specific indicators, a set of 12 baseline issues and 20 related indicators are suggested (Box 8.7). Like the core indicators of the 1996 publication, the baseline issues and indicators are those that are considered to be the most common and suitable for almost all destinations, allowing for international comparison. These include general tourism business indicators such as seasonality as well as the economic indicator previously excluded.

Including baseline issues, the WTO developed a total of nearly 50 issues each with 10–15 sub-issues and 25 suggested indicators applied to 18 different types of destination from small islands to theme parks, providing an immense, and rather overwhelming monitoring resource of more than a thousand potential indicators. The issues are divided into four sub-groups: economic, social and cultural, environmental, and managerial. The example provided in Box 8.8, 'Host community well-being', shows the level of

Box 8.6. Example of supplementary ecosystem-specific indicators for the coastal zone.

Issue	Indicators	Suggested measures
Ecological destruction	Amount degraded	% in degraded condition
Beach degradation	Levels of erosion	% of beach eroded
Fish stocks depletion	Reduction in catch	Effort to catch fish
		Fish counts for key species
Overcrowding	Use intensity	Persons per metre of accessible beach
Disruption of fauna (e.g. whales)	Species counts	Number of species
		Change in species mix
		Number of key species sightings
Diminished water quality	Pollution levels	Faecal coliform and heavy metals count
Lack of safety	Crime levels	Number of crimes reported
		Water related accidents as % of tourist population

Source: WTO (1996, p. 44).

Box 8.7. Baseline issues and suggested indicators, 2004.

Baseline issue	Suggested baseline indicator(s)
Local satisfaction with tourism	Local satisfaction level with tourism (questionnaire)
Effects of tourism on communities	Ratio of tourists to locals
	% who believe that tourism has helped bring new services or infrastructure
Sustaining tourist satisfaction	Level of satisfaction by visitors
	Perception of value for money
	% of return visitors
Tourism seasonality	Tourist arrivals by month or quarter (distribution throughout the year
	Occupancy rates for licensed (official) accommodation by month
	% of all occupancy in peak quarter (or month)
Economic benefits of tourism	Number of local people (and ratio of men to women) employed in tourism
	Local GDP and % contributed by tourism
	Revenues generated by tourism as % of total revenues generated in the community

continued

Box 8.7. *Continued.*	
Baseline issue	Suggested baseline indicator(s)
Energy management	Per capita consumption of energy from all sources (overall, and by tourist sector – per person day) % of businesses participating in energy conservation
Water availability and conservation	Water use (total volume consumed and litres per tourist per day) Water saving (% reduced, recaptured or recycled)
Drinking water quality	Percentage of tourism establishments with water treated to international potable standards Frequency of water-borne diseases: percentage of visitors experiencing water-borne illnesses during their stay
Sewage treatment (wastewater management)	Percentage of sewage from site receiving treatment (to primary, secondary, tertiary levels) Percentage of tourism establishments (or accommodation) on treatment system(s)
Solid waste management (garbage)	Waste volume produced by the destination (tonnes) (by month) Volume of waste recycled (m^3)/total volume of waste (m^3) (specify by different types) Quantity of waste strewn in public areas (garbage counts)
Development control	Existence of a land use or development planning process, including tourism % of area subject to control (density, design, etc.)
Controlling use intensity	Number of tourists per square metre of the site (per km^2 of the destination) – mean number/peak month average/peak Total tourist numbers (mean, monthly, peak)

Source: WTO (2004b, pp. 244–245).

information provided on each indicator and how each specific indicator is part of a larger set that addresses an issue.

The 2004 WTO guidebook therefore describes the issues and indicators in much more detail than previously and includes of number of practical examples of implementation. It offers users more options and greater flexibility to develop their own indicators, using WTO indicators simply as an aid. With the addition of visitor exit questionnaires and indicator development workshop, this provides a much more comprehensive set of monitoring tools than has been seen before (WTO, 2004b). However, there is also a downside to the extensive nature of this work, namely its complexity

---

Box 8.8. Example of baseline indicator.

Sociocultural sustainability: well-being of host communities

Issue
Local satisfaction with tourism.

Components of the issue
Problems or dissatisfaction.
Level of community satisfaction.

Indicator
Local satisfaction level with tourism (and with specific components of tourism) based on questionnaire.

Reason for use of this indicator
Changes in level of satisfaction can be an early warning indicator of potential incidents or hostility and a means to obtain information about emerging problems or friction before they become serious. It is a direct measure of actual opinion.

Source(s) of data
Some information would be obtainable through interviews with officials or use of focus groups; the most effective way is through a community questionnaire. An annual questionnaire with questions on specific issues of local concern should be used.

Means to use or portray the indicator
Both overall level of satisfaction and changes over previous years are useful measures.

Benchmarking
The best comparative use of these data is at a local level. Comparing two or more similar communities in the same destination or measuring trends over time in overall satisfaction levels, and importance of specific irritants.

Adapted from: WTO (2004b, p. 56–57).

---

and size, both of which may be off-putting to first time users. Such a huge list of indicators, many of which may be good ideas but have been neither tried nor tested, risks misleading and confusing tourism managers. This is not helped by the uncritical approach adopted, which risks downplaying the challenges of monitoring and the multi-author nature of the text, which has resulted in variation in the quality of the different sections. The real test of the indicators and methodology developed is, however, in their implementation.

WTO Implementation: Cases

As mentioned earlier, the WTO organized five workshops and case studies between 1999 and 2001. Most of the case studies were undertaken in areas where tourism is a relatively new phenomenon and tourism planning is not well developed. The experiences of each case study have contributed significantly to the evolution of the WTO monitoring programme, but this chapter will focus on the two most recent WTO case studies: Sri Lanka (2000) and Croatia (2001).

Beruwala, Sri Lanka

Beruwala consists of two villages, Moragalla and Kaluwamodera. The area is approximately 15 km² and located on the west coast of Sri Lanka, 60 km south of Colombo. In 1998, the Beruwala area had a collection of 13 hotels and 12 licensed and unlicensed guesthouses along the beach in the two villages. The total population of both villages is approximately 45,000. At the time of the study, Beruwala had about 1300 rooms available for accommodation and a total of 583,469 guest nights (data from 1999). Of these guest nights, over 90% were by international tourists, primarily interested in sun and sand, although there are many cultural and ecological attractions nearby.

There were two objectives for the WTO case study of Beruwala: (i) to determine the key risks to the sustainability of the tourism industry in Beruwala, and (ii) to use this study as a demonstration of the identification, evaluation and use of indicators of sustainable tourism in general. The WTO used the seven-phase 1996 process for indicator development shown in Box 8.2. While the consultants, with assistance of members of the Sri Lankan Tourism Board, did the field work and site interviews, the actual selection of the indicators was carried out by the local workshop participants. During the 3-day workshop, the participants were briefed about the process and the criteria, presented with key destination facts and given a site visit to the key areas of concern. Then, in three working groups, the participants focused on the development of candidate indicators. The groups adopted almost all of the WTO core indicators with the indicators relating to waste management, planning processes and development control being regarded as the most significant. The ecosystem-specific indicators identified were the coastal zones and the local communities' indicators. Participants also added some site-specific indicators addressing, for example, their concern about the growing number of package tourists staying at the site. The identification of priority indicators took place in smaller working groups, assessing each candidate indicator relative to five criteria: relevance, feasibility, credibility, clarity and comparability (over time and between destinations). After refinement of the key indicators during a further workshop, they were prioritized using the five-star system (five stars allocated to the most important and only one to the least important indicators), those allotted five stars have been shown in Box 8.9. Overall, there are a large number of indicators, some of which are relatively easy to quantify, and some of which require extensive and costly primary research, which may be outside the capacity of the local authorities. The final list of selected indicators was divided into six different categories: environment, society, economy, product quality, management and community planning. The WTO suggested separately measuring certain indicators for some specific 'hot spots' within Beruwala, which included the beachfront area and the lower reaches of the Bentota River where tourists from the adjacent resort use the river. It was suggested that for these areas indicators such as intensity of use should be measured to supplement the destination-wide indicators.

At the time of the indicator project, there was no significant planning in Beruwala and no authority to oversee data collection. Additional challenges came in the fact that the consultants left before the data were collected by the local authorities. The strengths and weaknesses of the indicators and their methodologies are seldom seen until they are properly

Box 8.9. Beruwala indicators list.

Environmental issues	*Indicator*
Waste management	Water quality (*E. coli*, biochemical oxygen demand, heavy metals)
	Number of truck loads of garbage removed from beach/day
Seawater quality	Water contamination in river and off the beach
Sewage systems	Volume treated
	Volume discharged by hotels (treated or untreated)
River and beach erosion	Changes in vegetation coverage and
Loss of soil/sand	beach configurations (using aerial photographs)
Lack of drainage	Number of flooding events/waterlogged areas
Tourist environmental awareness and expectations	Measures of tourists' environmental awareness and expectations (see also Social issues – B)
Drinking water contamination	Freshwater quality (including bacterial counts, hardness, heavy metals)
Social issues	*Indicator*
Local involvement in tourism industry	Percentage of all direct tourism jobs held by local residents
Unemployment	Statistics from census/government surveys

continued

Box 8.9.   *Continued.*

Economic issues	*Indicator*
Tourist numbers (baseline data)	Tourism industry statistics: totals, occupancy levels (by month)
Lack of dependable hotel supply and materials from local suppliers	Purchases Number of contracts with local suppliers
Wages in tourism relative to other sectors	Salary scales

Product quality issues	*Indicator*
Tourist safety	Percentage of tourists comfortable leaving hotel at night No. of daytime complaints to police/Ceylon Tourism Board regarding safety Exit survey of tourists perception of safety (theft, harassment, vehicle safety, danger, etc.)
Touts/beach boys	No. of complaints regarding harassment
Exposure to Sri Lankan culture	Complex indicator of cultural integrity of tourism offerings (classification system)
Scarcity of 'real' high quality products	Percentage of tourists who are satisfied with their level of contact with Sri Lankan culture during their visit
Access to destination Road congestion	Time to get to destination
Access to health facilities	No. of complaints from operators (and tourists) about health care facilities
Perceived quality of tourism product	Attitude survey on perception of value for money
Quality of the beach experience	Garbage counts/quantity of garbage and other waste on beach (see also environmental issues) Tourists perception of cleanliness of beach

Tourism management issues	*Indicator*
Unlicensed and uncontrolled tourist services	Enforcement of licensing
Density of motorboats on Bentota river	Number of boats (each type) on river at peak time (See also environmental issues – A)

Density of boat traffic in mangroves	Number of boats (per hour) in mangrove on peak days
Stray animals (also a quality of tourism issue)	Animals loose on beach/ in hotel grounds (count)
Community planning issues	*Indicator*
State of planning for Beruwala	Presence/absence of integrated plan (including key elements)
Public access to beaches	Access roads per km of beach Local perception of level of access to beach for community
Environmental awareness	Level of pollution on riverbanks Local awareness (and tourist awareness) of environmental issues

Source: WTO (2000).

piloted and in this case implementation revealed difficulties in data collection, ambiguity in indicator wording (is a larger number of garbage trucks removing rubbish from the beach an indication of a move towards or away from sustainability?) and differences in definitions, which might well have been resolved had the process not been so rushed. In terms of participation, although each working group reflected a mix of expertise including local officials, politicians, industry participants, academics, consultants and other relevant experts, of the total number of 35 participants, 18 were Sri Lankan Tourist Board representatives and only two participants were direct representatives of the site itself. The remainder represented the national government hotel schools and consultants, suggesting a group unrepresentative of the destination. As a result of the Beruwala case study, the following points are highlighted:

- Full local participation is essential, not only to identify issues, but also to create ownership of the overall process.
- Workshops are a useful tool to involve stakeholders and acquire access to local expertise but care is needed in ensure the right mix of representatives depending of the focus of the project (site/ national).
- Piloting indicators and data collection is an essential part of indicator development, which allows for fine-tuning and standardization of definitions, data sources and methodologies.
- Specific heavily used sites within a destination, so called 'hot spots' benefit from separate indicator measurement.
- Indicator selection needs to be realistic in terms of the capacity of the local authority to implement the indicators.

The destination choice for this case study and workshop is interesting as the destination was at a critical stage of tourism development at the time. However, the lack of planning and authority at the site obviously diminished the opportunity for actual implementation of the indicators. A cynic might question whether implementation of the monitoring scheme was ever actually intended, or whether indeed it was developed merely as a demonstration project for WTO purposes. Either way, without follow-up and ongoing support it seems unlikely that this project will maintained in the long term.

Kukljica, Croatia

The Kukljica case was the last in the 1996–2001 series of case studies that the WTO engaged in. Kukljica is located on the island of Ugljan, part of the Ugljan and Pasman island destination off Croatia's Adriatic coast and is considered an emerging tourism destination. The two islands are connected by a bridge and can be reached from the mainland via two ferry lines. Each island is about 70 km^2 in size and has a total of about 11,000 inhabitants according to the 1991 census. Tourism on the islands consists mainly of sun- and sea-orientated experiences primarily during the summer months of July and August. The island of Kukljica has many small guesthouses but only one main resort. Of the 7000 beds available to tourists, more than 4500 are in privately owned rooms and flats.

The main objective of the Kukljica study was to determine the current and potential risks to the sustainability of the tourism industry in the area. The WTO consultants on this case study were the same as those who had worked on the Beruwala case study, and again WTO used the regional workshop approach to demonstrate the identification, evaluation and use of indicators. The workshop was attended by experts from seven Mediterranean countries as well as a strong contingent of Croatian and local stakeholders. The Minister of Tourism and local officials were also present during the workshop. The logistics of the workshop were as follows:

- A site visit to the key areas of concern and presentation by local officials and experts to provide participants with an in-depth understanding of the area.
- Three different working groups, each with a mix of local and international participants created a list of the issues or risks to the destination.
- Using the nominal group technique, small groups worked on short-listing issues and selecting the key areas of concern.
- In small groups, the participants selected the potential indicators that would respond to the key issues based on the WTO criteria for indicator selection and evaluation worksheets. The results were then discussed by the larger group.

- Open session by participants to discuss development of future recommendations for the site, other island destinations in Croatia and other Mediterranean countries.

As in the Sri Lankan case, most of the WTO core indicators were considered useful by the selected group, supplemented by the ecospecific indicators for coastal zones, small islands and local communities. Indicators relating to social values, access, waste management, planning processes and development control were considered most important for the specific destination. Other indicators that were found particularly important were those that focused on employment in the tourism industry, benefits to the local economy, and the maintenance of the islands' image as a clean, unspoiled destination. As with the previous case study, Box 8.10 only shows the indicators given a five-star priority rating.

In contrast to the Beruwala case, data specifically relating to the tourism industry were readily available and reliable, collected at the municipality level. The WTO consultants made three preliminary recommendations: first that the municipalities agreed on a set of indicators to be used on a regular basis from the list, secondly that another meeting should be arranged where the findings and recommendations of the case study and the workshop would be presented to the stakeholders in the industry, and thirdly that the report should be translated into the local language to increase stakeholder support.

The Kukljica case suggests that when most workshop participants are economically dependent on tourism, the focus tends to be on achieving economic tourism growth. The indicators and monitoring therefore risk justifying further growth rather than acting as an effective form of development control. The use of environmental indicators was also somewhat limited and superficial in this case, focused on determining customer satisfaction with the environment as opposed to measuring the actual environmental condition and tourism's impact on this. Perhaps this highlights the need for expert input and screening of the selected indicators, in order that the full range of environmental viewpoints be represented and demonstrate the consequences of a growth-oriented approach. Other points worthy of consideration in this case include whether the involvement of political figures such as a Minister of Tourism contributes or detracts from the process. Such high-level appearances might do much to boost the perceived importance of a workshop, but government presence may also reduce the willingness of participants openly to speak their minds about particular issues.

Evaluation

The WTO has put more time, resources and effort in developing sustainable tourism indicators that any other organization. As a result of its

Box 8.10.   Ugljan–Pasman indicators list.

Cultural integrity issues	*Indicator*
Identification and protection of key cultural and historic sites	Inventory of cultural sites prepared and maintained Availability of information on sites
Local attitude towards tourists and tourism	Local attitudes

Employment and economic welfare issues	*Indicator*
Local involvement in tourism industry	Unemployment statistics Local residents employed in tourism Ratio of local employees to total population
Quality of accommodation	Price of accommodation (average Kuna/night) Opinion of quality

Stability and seasonality issues	*Indicator*
Low numbers of tourists out of peak season	Number of tourists over year
Quality of tourism product	Perception of quality experience by tourists

Physical planning and control issues	*Indicator*
Income sources for municipalities	Sources of income for the municipalities
State of planning for the islands	Planning of destination
Ease of access to the islands	Number of ferry trips per day Price of ferry trips Frequency of hourly crossings
Access to sites	Volume of tourism Signage Organized access

Management of resources and the environment issues	*Indicator*
Maintaining clean environment and image	Tourist opinions on seawater quality Garbage levels on shoreline Clean image of island

Adapted from: WTO (2001b).

ongoing efforts, there is clearly improved understanding and greater awareness of how as well as what to monitor. Over time, the WTO method has evolved from a mainly environmentally focus to a much wider and more integrated approach demonstrated in the 2004 publication.

Of the 11 core indicators suggested in 1993, seven measured environmental impact, three measured social and cultural impacts and only one focused on the economic issues (and was later dropped). The 2004 list of 50 issues including 12 baseline issues and almost a thousand indicator ideas. While some indicators from the original list are included in the baseline issues, there are also many new issues such as energy management and tourism seasonality that emerged as important as a result of the case study experience. There is now more focus on the scarcity of certain resources such as energy and water and on the quality of the environment, highlighting such issues as sewage treatment, solid waste management and the quality of drinking water. These are examples of cross-cutting issues that can become very important and tangible for both the local population and tourists alike. Noteworthy is the fact that most issues are measured now by more than a handful of indicators giving destinations greater choice. However, the complexity of the indicators has generally also increased, perhaps making it less accessible to the uninitiated. Another concern is that many of the indicator ideas are just that, ideas from a wide range of experts that have yet to be piloted, refined and tuned to the realities on the ground.

Sharing experiences and knowledge among member states appears to have been a guiding priority of the WTO indicator work and also a key strength of the process. This has been accomplished by developing practical instruments, testing them on individual destinations and then modifying them on the basis of lessons learned. In this way, knowledge gained at one site can be used by many other countries, and their practical experiences can help to improve the instruments on an ongoing basis.

However, there is still a question mark over the actual implementation of the use of the WTO indicators as little follow-up appears to have taken place. Although the WTO 2004 guide places greater emphasis on the implementation phase of indicator development than the 1993 and 1996 documents, to date the organization has allocated few resources to implementation and even at a theoretical level, there is still no mention as to what should be done with the results of the indicators besides reporting them. If the indicator results are not converted into action, they function only as an interesting source of information, not a useful planning tool. Whilst it is possible to sympathize with short-term budgeting and political horizons, it is argued here that moving towards greater sustainability is not likely to be achieved by increasing awareness of indicators but by converting indicator results to action on an ongoing basis. Clifford (2002) stresses that the indicator development process may be more important than any of the specific indicators that are defined, indeed, if the outcome of the monitoring process is not used, the motivation to continue monitoring will inevitably wane. Although the new WTO resource book concludes that indicators are tools, not one-time procedures, and therefore must be used and shared to empower destinations to improve sustainability, there is little advice as to how this could be carried out.

In terms of stakeholder involvement, although not always as broad and inclusive as Box 8.5 recommends, the WTO process has made some distinct improvements. During the original case studies, the majority of the preparation was carried out by the WTO consultants, but the new guide book and field guide should be able to assist local tourism managers to execute this process with a minimum of external assistance. As discussed in Chapter 4, the absence of an experienced facilitator could slow down the process; it could also mean that the overall process would benefit from a stronger sense of local ownership and therefore have better prospects for long-term survival.

Nevertheless, the case studies have shown that local site-based tourism operators do sometimes miss out in favour of national, regional, international and politically well-connected representatives. Perhaps one reason for the composition of the group is that these were demonstration projects designed to give indicators and monitoring maximum regional exposure. Another is the intensive 3-day workshop format. Although this short time-frame is well suited to politicians and consultant schedules, it may not be convenient for local stakeholders or conducive to considered in-depth review and analysis of issues and their indicators. Any process that seeks to achieve local ownership needs to move at the speed with which this ownership develops and stakeholders feel comfortable. Local stakeholders cannot be made to own a programme within 3 days to suit the consultant. Ownership must evolve and it will always be difficult to set a timetable to this. Perhaps even more crucially, such an intensive workshop does not allow for piloting the indicators or the first round of data, which is typically where the problems and challenges emerge and indicators may have to be substantially reworked or even dropped.

A further point of note is that WTO decided to focus their initial case studies in destinations with a relatively underdeveloped local planning system. It must be questioned whether destinations that do not have a current tourism plan have sufficient human capacity to complete the process once the consultants have left. If not, the indicator development process risks raising unrealistic expectations and failing to be implemented. Linked to this is the question about whether scarce resources should actually be spent on monitoring in such situations or whether they may be better spent on upgrading the airport or other necessary infrastructure. This suggestion is perhaps surprising to find in a book on the importance of monitoring, but researchers must also be realists and sometimes it may be necessary to develop crucial infrastructure before monitoring visitor satisfaction.

Notwithstanding these criticisms, the new 2004 resource book gives destinations much more support in indicator development by providing examples of possible questionnaires for specific indicators. With this assistance, it appears likely that even destinations with limited resources would be able to choose a small number of indicators that are most important for the site and be able to monitor these. Box 8.11 summarizes the strengths and weaknesses of the WTO approach.

Box 8.11.   Strengths and weaknesses of WTO approach.

Strengths of WTO's efforts

- Creates awareness, understanding and publicity for sustainable tourism and monitoring
- Builds on lessons learned in various case studies world wide and adapts the process as a result
- Allows for individualized approach to the destination whilst at the same time providing opportunity for international comparison
- Is comprehensive, covering all of the key issues
- The process is evolutionary even if the monitoring is not
- Provides destinations with the starting blocks of a monitoring system to enable them to continue the work
- Provides the most widely documented accounts of the development of sustainable tourism indicators to date

Weaknesses of WTO's efforts

- The 3-day workshop, a rushed process, seemingly designed around consultant schedules, which may not allow stakeholders sufficient time to engage in the process or time to pilot and refine indicators and the methodologies for collecting data
- The justification for the indicators is focused on the use of the results for improved decision making yet the focus of the process is exclusively on the development of indicators, not their use
- The case studies require commitment that neither WTO nor destinations appear to be able to maintain in the long term
- The multi-author 2004 text is too long and many 'indicator ideas' have not been tried, tested or refined
- There are no documented WTO examples available of indicators that have been implemented and used
- All the case studies were in relatively undeveloped tourism destinations so may not necessarily apply to mature mass tourism destinations
- The programme does not effectively link sustainable tourism monitoring to the overall tourism planning process despite suggesting this is important
- Method does not provide user to link the indicator results into an action plan

Adapted from: Bakker (2003).

Summary

Between 1992, when the first WTO taskforce started to work on indicators for sustainable tourism, and 2004, with the publication of the new resource book, the WTO has evolved considerably. The workshops have been essential in increasing the knowledge and awareness about indicator development in the field. Using that knowledge and sharing the experiences with other experts all over the world has advanced the study of sustainable tourism indicators. The improved indicator development process and the baseline issues are likely to prove an invaluable tool for destinations that are ready to implement indicators of sustainable tourism with limited outside resources, making it much easier than starting from scratch. From the first attempts, the level of participation as well as the complexity of the indicators has increased and the case studies from Sri Lanka and Croatia clearly demonstrate how the process has improved.

This chapter has shown how the resources at the disposal of the WTO have enabled it to build on previous attempts and to learn lessons from actual case studies. In this way, the indicator development process for the WTO can be seen as dynamic, although the irony is that the lack of attention to implementation and maintenance means the indicator programmes in the case study destinations are often unable to evolve further. The WTO approach has also sought to increase the range of stakeholders involved in indicator development, and although further progress needs to be made, the principle of local representation has been acknowledged. Less positively, the chapter has been critical of the intensive workshop approach, the lack of attention to implementation, the lack of application to mature tourism destinations and the separation of the monitoring process from the planning system.

Future research might profitably focus on documenting the implementation and findings of indicators that have already been put into practice. Key questions which need to be answered concern the effects of the indicators over time, the actions taken as a result of indicator measurements and the contribution indicators make to the quest for greater sustainability.

Tourism Optimization Management Model

9

Introduction

Kangaroo Island is the third largest island off the coast of Australia and is 155 km long and up to 55 km wide. The island retains 47% of its original native vegetation, of which 50% is conserved in National and Conservation Parks. There are just over 4400 people living on Kangaroo Island with a significant and increasing number of non-resident landowners.

The island is home to abundant native wildlife, such as wallabies, echidna, Kangaroo Island kangaroos, dolphins, Australian sea lions, fairy penguins and a variety of birds. It is a place of fresh air, safe communities and diverse landforms and is recognized as a tourism icon destination by the South Australian Tourism Commission (SATC) on the basis of its wildlife and its superb natural environment (SATC, DEH, 2003). In 2003 150,915 people visited Kangaroo Island, of which 26% were international visitors (TOMM, 2003).

The growth of tourism to the island has introduced new external demands on Kangaroo Island. On the one hand, tourism is assisting with economic diversification with many island residents looking towards tourism as a means of enhancing their economic base. On the other, the island is vulnerable both ecologically and socially and the 'sense of place' sought by the broader and global visitor market is potentially at risk, depending upon management actions and developments pursued. Tourism developments to date have generated both internal pressures as well as opportunities for the local community. The people of Kangaroo Island see prosperity in tourism, but know that what they have is a unique resource that must be managed carefully if it is not to be destroyed. They are working hard to find the delicate balance between development and conservation.

This chapter highlights how the community and governing agencies of Kangaroo Island have collaborated to address the issue of tourism impacts on the community, economy and environment of the island. It draws on the practical experience of implementing sustainable tourism at a community level and considers what changes and challenges are required if local communities are to implement, maintain and monitor sustainable tourism in the long term.

Background

Kangaroo Island's tourism product has been recognized as being largely based around small-scale, unimposing, yet accessible accommodation and experiences that showcase the Australian wildlife in its natural habitat. In 1991, the Kangaroo Island Tourism Policy (Kangaroo Island Tourism Policy Working Party, 1991) and later the Kangaroo Island Sustainable Development Strategy (Kangaroo Island Sustainable Development Committee, 1995) both reinforced this position with vision statements that stressed Kangaroo Island as one of the 'world's pre-eminent nature-based tourist destinations'. Their visions are of 'a strong, rural industry selling' its products to domestic and overseas markets, providing a 'high quality of life for residents', and a 'well-managed natural environment'.

This vision was supported by a set of community values, which had already been identified through previous planning projects over a number of years (PPK Planning, 1983; Kangaroo Island Tourism Policy Working Party, 1991).

These values were very similar to the characteristics and experiences sought by visitors to the island and emphasized (Manidis Roberts Consultants, 1997, p. 15):

- Expansive and relatively unchanged rural and natural landscapes (particularly the coastline);
- Abundant and highly visible wildlife;
- A safe, clean and healthy environment;
- Relative solitude through a small and sparsely spread population;
- Unpretentious and relaxed lifestyle;
- Strong sense of community and common bond with the land and its heritage.

The island's key competitive advantage lay in its 'intrinsic appeal of a large island where the impact of human activity is relatively low, the large proportion of island reserved as protected areas, the name "Kangaroo Island" for the international market, and the relative proximity to Adelaide . . .' (Manidis Roberts Consultants, 1997, p. 16).

In 1995, visitation increased to over 150,000 visits and day trips appeared to be on the rise due to the introduction of a fast ferry service from the mainland (Centre for Tourism and Hotel Management Research, Griffith University, 1996). It became evident that without clear observation and understanding of the motivations and changes brought about by the tourism industry, visitor impacts both on the environment and community, coupled with economic worries and emigration of youth could easily take their toll on the future sustainability of the island.

To manage the potential demand for the island in a sustainable manner, a management system was required which would value and ensure the health of Kangaroo Island whilst providing an accurate picture of tourism impacts, both positive and negative, on the community, environment, economy and visitor experience. The 'coming together' of key government agencies and community groups to develop a unified strategic direction to address the changes being ushered in by tourism, was a critical stage that provided an opportunity to initiate long-term attitudinal change. It required an acknowledgement that Kangaroo Island was experiencing a variety of impacts from tourism development and that informed, collaborative and integrated communities stood a better chance of managing this process of change if they had access to relevant and timely information on the health of their community. Such an approach was considered of value to the local community and Island's tourism industry through increased market knowledge, information about the health of the community, environment and economy and increased international reputation. This approach also potentially provided benefits for the wider industry and government beyond Kangaroo Island, as the process could be replicated elsewhere.

From the consultation process, it became apparent that for the community of Kangaroo Island effectively to manage its own change process and future tourism activity, there were going to be several factors critical to achieve sustainable success, including: access to information on a regular basis; the ability to monitor trends within the industry, visitor market, community, economy and environment; and a collaborative approach based upon a shared vision.

The TOMM Project

The challenge facing Kangaroo Island was how to monitor and check the health of the industry and the resources it depends upon. In the past, industrial health has often been considered in terms of identifying positive and negative impacts and measured against the impacts tourism generates (Hall, 1995). Well-known impact assessment frameworks include carrying capacity, LAC and more recently the Visitor Impact Management Model (VIMM) (Wight, 1998), aiming to minimize negative ecological impacts, and have been in existence for over 30 years. More recently, with the increasing attention to incorporating sustainability into development, the need for the tourism industry to assess its health and the well-being of the resources on which it depends to a broader extent has grown more apparent.

A broader and more integrated approach was tested through the development and implementation of TOMM (Manidis Roberts Consultants, 1997), created especially for monitoring and managing tourism on Kangaroo Island. Specifically, TOMM was designed to: monitor and quantify the key economic, marketing, environmental, sociocultural and experiential benefits and impacts of tourism activity; and assist in the assessment of emerging issues and alternative future management options for the sustainable development and management of tourism activity (Manidis Roberts Consultants, 1997).

The TOMM was developed not only to monitor tourism activity but also to assist people and management agencies in particular, and make better decisions about tourism. The project report states clearly:

> TOMM should be used to help change the culture of the tourism industry and its stakeholders. This can be done by generating tangible evidence that the viability of the industry is dependent upon the quality of the visitor experience it generates, and the condition of the natural, cultural and social resources it relies on. As this cultural change is generated, more people will understand how tourism can become healthy and of genuine benefit to all.
>
> (Manidis Roberts Consultants, 1997, p. 9)

TOMM was originally developed as a monitoring programme, based upon a series of indicators, covering:

- The health of the economy;
- The number and type of tourists visiting;
- The health of the environment;
- The type of experience visitors are having;
- The health of the community.

However, as the project has evolved, this focus has enlarged to a project that not only highlights the benefits of tourism, but a project that actually demonstrates that communities and individuals can take action to facilitate attitudinal change to promote more sustainable tourism given sufficient time, energy and resources. The vision of TOMM is to be a centre of excellence and inspirational leader in destination management:

> Kangaroo Island will be Australia's number one responsible nature-based tourism destination. We will achieve this through our commitment to a collaborative monitoring and management system, which will lead to sound decision-making based on relevant information and knowledge. TOMM will be a long-term process for working for the people and environment of Kangaroo Island. It will bring about a cultural shift in the way people think about and manage tourism, taking into account environmental, social and

economic factors. As a result of its success, TOMM will continue to attract the resources to create and ensure a healthy destination.

(TOMM, 2004)

The TOMM Committee is comprised of representatives from the Kangaroo Island Council, Kangaroo Island Development Board, Tourism Kangaroo Island, Department for Environment and Heritage (DEH) and the SATC. The committee successfully accessed funding from the Office of National Tourism to implement and test the TOMM on the island with a view to its implementation in other locations globally. Through ongoing visitor exit surveys, resident surveys and strategic planning workshops with both the TOMM Management Committee and community, the original values have evolved as guiding principles for the TOMM process and now include:

- Sustainability;
- Conservation and environment;
- Effective communication;
- Innovation;
- Teamwork;
- Integrity;
- Commitment;
- Leadership;
- Partnership;
- Persistence;
- Passion and commitment;
- Continuous improvement.

The incorporation of these values as guiding principles in the strategic decision making process of all Island government agencies is considered to be a critical step in making progress towards a more sustainable tourism system. This integration has yet to be fully achieved and will form the basis of the TOMM activities in future years. However, as with the values identified through the original TOMM consultation, there is a very close match between the expressed community values and those of the visiting public. This has been demonstrated through the annual resident survey and visitor exit survey programme.

The TOMM Development Process

In contrast to management frameworks such as LAC and VIMM, where the focus is on setting limits to manage impacts, the TOMM involves the community in envisioning optimal and sustainable outcomes for tourism and the community, from which acceptable ranges or scores for each indicator are drawn up. During the development of a tourism management framework for Kangaroo Island, background research on existing models was carried out. Through this and the consultation process, a number of issues and questions were identified that highlighted an evolution of previous tourism management models. These issues and challenges are shown in Box 9.1.

TOMM adopts an integrated approach to tourism management and alleviates concern regarding limitation of tourism growth, by:

• Avoiding use of the terms 'impact' and 'limits' which the tourism industry interpret as discouraging growth and thus business;
• Focusing on the entire tourism system rather than just its ecological and market components;
• Providing for the involvement of all stakeholders, through a partnership approach and grounding the systems within community processes;
• Serving a multitude of stakeholders, operating at a regional level over a range of protected area and private land tenures (Twyford, 2001).

A central feature of the TOMM concept was the inclusion of a management response system, which alerts key stakeholders, including the community, to those indicators that are not performing within their acceptable range, or to other potential issues that may merit additional monitoring. In theory, with active involvement of all key management agencies on the island and ongoing dialogue with the island community, this cause/effect/response relationship allows for effective and timely management action. It also results in the evolution of a sustainable tourism model in line with the changes occurring within the island community.

The development of the TOMM required extensive consultation to identify the values of the community, which informed the development of potential indicators and became the first of a three-stage process made up of a context analysis, a monitoring programme and a management response system (Manidis Roberts Consultants, 1997). The development of the TOMM approach is represented in Fig. 9.1.

Context analysis

The context analysis identifies the current situation of tourism activity within the destination, including trends, tourism growth, tourism product, market opportunities and community values. It also identifies alternative scenarios for the future of tourism, all of which are then used to develop optimal conditions that tourism should aim to create. These optimal conditions form the basis of the tourism indicators.

Using a scenario-based planning framework, various options were projected for tourism growth on Kangaroo Island and each considered the potential impacts and associated information that was required in order for the community and its governing agencies to effectively manage this change.

Box 9.1. Perceptions, challenges, questions and planning issues for tourism on Kangaroo Island.

	Perception	Challenge, questions, planning issues
Economic	Tourism should make money, it is a business	How can yield be maximized?
	Tourism provides economic benefit to the region	How can this investment flow into other industry sectors?
		How can employment opportunities be maximized?
	Tourism attracts finances from outside of the region	How can tourism provide long-term employment and training opportunities?
	Tourism creates employment	
		How can issues of seasonality be overcome?
Market opportunity	Tourism should grow and be developed	How is market data integrated into small business marketing?
	State and federal bodies set the market	How are state and federal market campaigns linked to regional marketing opportunities?
	Any market segment is good	How can the proportion of visitors that match the environmental/cultural profile be increased?
Environmental	Tourism has only negative impacts on natural resources	How is impact on natural resources minimized?
	The region is 'clean and green'	How can tourism contribute to best practice environmental management?
		How are visitors and operators educated regarding environmental issues?
		How is sustainable development attracted and encouraged?
		How are existing operators and businesses encouraged to adopt best practice environmental business principles?

continued

Box 9.1. *Continued.*

	Perception	Challenge, questions, planning issues
Experiential	This region is different from other tourism regions Visitor satisfaction is good	How can this region provide a unique experience Is marketing and promotion matching visitor experience?
Sociocultural	The region has no control over tourism once it starts Tourism will impact on the community's way of life	How do residents feel they can influence tourism decisions? How are opportunities provided for residents to have input into tourism decisions? How does tourism contribute to and enhance community well-being?
Integration	Tourism should be sustainable. Tourism should be constructive and link with all stakeholders, including community, conservation groups, industry, government and economic development and planning agencies Tourism should contribute to a community's well-being, and have positive outcomes for the environment	How does the tourism sector engage with other sectors? How can tourism be monitored and managed to ensure the health of the industry and the resources it depends upon? How are outcomes to be measured and reported on? How can benchmarks be established?

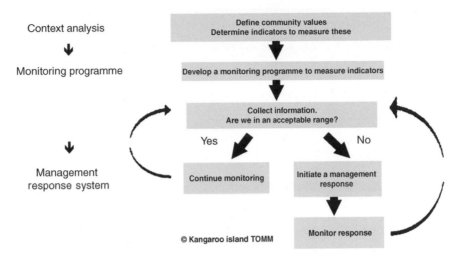

Fig. 9.1. The TOMM approach.

The scenarios considered included:

- A significant increase (15% per annum) in tourism demand to visit Kangaroo Island;
- A significant decrease (15% per annum) in tourism demand to visit Kangaroo Island;
- A significant increase in interest to visit Kangaroo Island from the international market;
- A decrease in annual overnight stays and an increase in day visits;
- Significant investment commitment in a new tourism product;
- Single operator in area of key service provision (Manidis Roberts Consultants, 1997).

Using these scenarios, community values and an assessment of the tourism product, Manidis Roberts projected tourism growth rates of 8.8% and 10% reaching 333,000 and 4000,000 visits respectively in 2004/05. They also summarized the market needs of three market segments as shown in Box 9.2.

From this information, the results of community consultation, previous tourism planning documents and the National Ecotourism Accreditation Program benchmarks, a series of draft optimal conditions were established for Kangaroo Island. A selection of these conditions was identified as being suitable for integration into the TOMM model and formed the basis of the TOMM monitoring programme. Box 9.3 identifies the original optimal conditions selected.

Monitoring programme

The monitoring programmes associated with the TOMM are fundamental to its success and have been developed in accordance with the identified

Box 9.2.   Tourism market needs from Kangaroo Island.

State market	Opportunity to increase knowledge of state Food and wine Fishing Bush walking Child-focused activities Evening entertainment Interaction with locals and other visitors
National market	Opportunity to increase knowledge of country Wildlife viewing Coastal environments Living history Recreational opportunities Food and wine Arts and craft Comfortable weather
International market	Visit natural environments Visit a local farm Opportunity to participate in local events Arts and craft Food and wine Interact with locals Photographic opportunities

Adapted from: Manidis Roberts Consultants (1997).

optimum conditions (Box 9.4) and based upon a series of indicators that enable measurement of how close the current situation is to the optimal or desired conditions.

Over 60 indicators were initially identified through a series of workshops with industry, government and community representatives, and assessed based upon the following criteria (Manidis Roberts Consultants, 1997):

- Degree of relationship with actual tourism activity (needs to be clear);
- Accuracy (need to be represented accurately);
- Utility (what additional insight does it generate?);
- Availability of data (it is more feasible if the data already exists or are accessible); and
- Cost to collect and analyse (ideally, the indicator requires minimal additional cost to collect and analyse).

Box 9.4 highlights the indicators that were eventually chosen for the Kangaroo Island TOMM.

Based upon the optimum conditions, an acceptable range was identified that provided a realistic measurement for each indicator based upon the best information available at the time, including previous research,

Box 9.3. Original TOMM optimal conditions.

Environmental	The majority of the number of visits to the island's natural areas occur in designated visitor service zones
	Ecological processes are maintained or improved (where visitor impact has occurred) in areas where tourism activity occurs
	Major wildlife populations attracting visitors are maintained and/or enhanced where tourism activity occurs
	The majority of tourism accommodation operations have implemented some form of energy and water conservation practice
Economic	The majority of visitors to Kangaroo Island stay longer than 2 nights
	The growth of local employment within the tourism industry is consistent
	The tourism industry undergoes steady growth in tourism yield
	Seasonal fluctuations in the number of visits are limited and relatively smooth
Market opportunity	Operators use market data to assist in matching product with market segment opportunities
	There is integration of business, regional, state and national tourism marketing programmes for Kangaroo Island
	A growing proportion of visitors come from the cultural/environmental segments of the domestic and international markets
Experiential	Tourism promotion of wildlife experiences in Kangaroo Island's natural areas is realistic and truthful to that actually experienced by most visitors
	The visitor experience is distinctly different from other coastal destinations in Australia
	The majority of Kangaroo Island visitors leave the island highly satisfied with their experience
Sociocultural	The majority of residents feel they can influence tourism related decisions
	Residents feel comfortable that tourism contributes to a peaceful, secure and attractive lifestyle
	Residents are able to access nature-based recreational opportunities that are not frequented by tourists

Source: Manidis Roberts Consultants (1997).

Box 9.4.   TOMM optimal conditions and indicators.

Optimal condition	Indicator
Environmental	
The majority of the number of visits to the island's natural areas occurs in designated visitor service zones	The proportion of Kangaroo Island visitors to the island's natural areas who visit areas zoned specially for managing visitors
Ecological processes are maintained or improved (where visitor impact has occurred) in areas where tourism activity occurs	Net overall cover of native vegetation at specific sites
Major wildlife populations attracting visitors are maintained and/or enhanced where tourism activity occurs	Number of seals at designated tourist sites Number of hooded plover at designated tourist sites Number of osprey at designated tourist sites
The majority of tourism accommodation operations have implemented some form of energy and water conservation practice	Energy consumption/visitor night/visitor Water consumption/visitor night/visitor
Economic	
The majority of visitors to Kangaroo Island stay longer than 2 nights	Annual average number of nights stayed on Kangaroo Island
The tourism industry undergoes steady growth in tourism yield	Annual average growth in total tourism expenditure on Kangaroo Island per number of visitors
The growth of local employment within the tourism industry is consistent	Annual average growth in direct tourism employment
Seasonal fluctuations in the number of visits are limited and relatively smooth	Annual variation in room nights sold between peak and low season
Market opportunity	
Operators use market data to assist in matching product with market segment opportunities	Number of operators using market data in Kangaroo Island and operator plans
There is integration of business, regional, state and national tourism marketing programmes for Kangaroo Island	Number of cooperative marketing campaigns such as joint brochures and advertisements
A growing proportion of visitors come from the cultural/environmental segments of the domestic and international markets	Proportion of visitors that match ATC cultural/environmental segmentation profile The number of visits to Kangaroo Island

---

Experiential

Tourism promotion of wildlife experiences in Kangaroo Island's natural areas is realistic and truthful to that actually experienced by most visitors	Proportion of visitors who believe their experience was similar to that suggested in advertisements and brochures
The visitor experience is distinctly different from other coastal destinations in Australia	Proportion of visitors who believe they had an intimate experience with wildlife in a natural area
The majority of Kangaroo Island visitors leave the island highly satisfied with their experience	Proportion of visitors who were very satisfied with interpretation provided on a guided tour

Sociocultural

The majority of residents feel they can influence tourism related decisions	The proportion of residents who feel the local community can influence the type of tourism on Kangaroo Island
Residents feel comfortable that tourism contributes to a peaceful, secure and attractive lifestyle	Number of petty crime reports committed by non-residents per annum
	Number of traffic accidents involving non-residents per annum
	Proportion of the community who perceive positive benefits from their interactions with tourists
Residents are able to access nature-based recreational opportunities that are not frequented by tourists	Proportion of residents who feel they can visit a natural area of their choice with very few tourists present

Source: Manidis Roberts Consultants (1997).

---

observations and estimations from those with experience in the field and community. The indicators have subsequently been refined as more knowledge and market data are gathered and new monitoring opportunities arise. The indicator programme will continue to be refined and improved as the TOMM knowledge base increases and new monitoring programmes and data collection techniques become available.

Whilst the subjective element of the acceptable range component of the TOMM may be considered one of its weak points, the purpose is to provide a focus for the monitoring programmes and enable the reporting of impacts within a range as determined to be acceptable by the stakeholders. Obviously, these ranges will change over time and will elicit ongoing debate, given that an acceptable impact for one group may be unacceptable to another. However, using this approach does provide a picture of the impact of tourism over time and enables the community to comprehend the changing trends that the industry inevitably brings with it.

Collection of the actual data through a series of monitoring programmes is the final element of this second stage of the TOMM process. In terms of resourcing, this stage represents a major component of the process. Whilst each monitoring technique was assessed against the criteria used for the TOMM indicators, preference was given for those techniques using existing systems and initiatives (Manidis Roberts Consultants, 1997). The two major monitoring systems identified for development were a visitor exit survey and an annual resident survey. To date, these have been undertaken by external research agencies contracted by the TOMM project, whilst additional data gathered from existing research conducted by agency partners and local authorities have been collated by the TOMM Project Officer.

Management response system

The TOMM management response system assesses information from the monitoring programmes and compares these with the optimal conditions. The interpretation of this information allows the stakeholders to identify problems, areas of opportunity and potential actions required to address these. The Management Committee then alerts responsible government agencies or community groups to a desired course of action.

Trends generated through the indicators are reported through survey results and also visually represented by way of simple charts showing if the optimal condition was met or not. This is shown by a tick to indicate the condition has been met (inside the acceptable range), a cross to represent the condition has not been met (outside the acceptable range) and a question mark to indicate that the data were not sufficiently clear to suggest either way. Box 9.5 highlights examples of the reporting system.

The management response system is ultimately the most important element of the TOMM as it generates tangible evidence of the TOMM process and ensures government agencies, community groups and individuals are kept informed and alert to potential tourism impacts. However, in practice, it is the hardest of the three TOMM components to implement. Nevertheless, there have been some success stories as shown in the outcome column of Box 9.5. These include the initiation of the 'stay another day' programme, research into the relationship between seal and visitor behaviour, an educational programme being developed to assist in managing the impact of cars on the hooded plover, raising of awareness regarding visitor behaviour around wildlife and the sealing of key roads around the island.

Although TOMM was developed and first implemented on Kangaroo Island, the progression and effective implementation of management responses have been slow, leading to criticism from some sectors of the community. This has meant TOMM has faced a battle to survive as it has grown, changed shape and concentrated on ways of ensuring its maintenance in the long term. As the issues of resourcing are resolved, the focus will shift from survival to effective and improved implementation.

Box 9.5. Examples of TOMM reporting system.

Optimal condition	Indicator	Acceptable range	Result 2001	Outcome
Examples of economic indicator results				
The majority of visitors to Kangaroo Island stay longer than 3 nights	Annual average number of nights stayed on Kangaroo Island	3–5 nights	✔	Tourism Kangaroo Island initiated a 'Stay another day' promotional campaign to encourage visitors to stay longer on Kangaroo Island
The tourism industry is undergoing steady growth in tourism yield	Annual average growth in total tourism expenditure on Kangaroo Island per number of visitors	4–10% annual average growth	✔	Continuation of current monitoring programme
Examples of environmental indicator results				
Major wildlife populations attracting visitors are maintained and/or improved in areas where tourism activity occurs	Number of seals at designated tourist site	0–5% annual increase in numbers sighted	?	Research is currently being undertaken in relation to seal and visitor behaviour at Seal Bay Annual surveys of the hooded plover indicate that there is impact on this species. There is a current debate on the island regarding the presence of cars on beaches in which the plover nests. A local environmental group have been included in an education programme in partnership with the DEH to assist in managing this issue
	Number of hooded plovers	0–5% annual increase in numbers sighted	✗	

continued

Box 9.5. *Continued.*

Optimal condition	Indicator	Acceptable range	Result 2001	Outcome
Examples of market indicator results				
A growing proportion of visitors come from the cultural/environmental segments of the domestic and international segments	Proportion of visitors that match the cultural/environmental profile	60–80% of total visitors to Kangaroo Island	✔	Continuation of current monitoring programme
	The number of visits to Kangaroo Island	0–7% annual growth in the number of visits	✔	Visitor numbers increased to Kangaroo Island by 8.6% in 2001–2002 with a 0.8% increase in 2002–2003. This change may have been prompted by the occurrence of significant international events such as terrorism
Examples of experiential indicator results				
The Kangaroo Island visitor experience is distinctly different from other coastal destinations in Australia	Proportion of visitors who believe they had an intimate experience with wildlife in a natural area	70–100% thought it was very important	?	Ongoing education is being undertaken amongst tourism wholesalers by Tourism Kangaroo Island in an effort to educate them regarding the best times to view wildlife. Similarly, local tour operators are extending touring programmes in peak summer periods to enable visitors to see the mostly nocturnal wildlife

Examples of sociocultural indicator results

Residents feel they can influence tourism related decisions	% increase in residents stating that they can influence tourism related decisions	70–100% of residents	(?)	Better articulation of questions relating to how residents feel about tourism in future surveys
Residents feel comfortable that tourism contributes to a peaceful, secure and attrac-tive lifestyle	Number of petty crime reports committed by non-residents per anrum	10–25 crime reports	(?)	Ongoing liaison with the local police department on the island is underway with the aim to refine this indicator to reflect current data collection processes
	Number of traffic accidents per annum	50–80 vehicle accident reports	➹	Given the extensive gravel roads on the island, TOMM data have been used to access additional funding to seal certain key sections of roads on the island

TOMM Results

A major challenge for models such as TOMM is the ability to satisfy agency and individual needs for immediate and short-term results. Like all monitoring programmes, TOMM is a long-term process in which reliable and informative trends that provide a picture of tourism's overall well-being are gained over a period of time. Amongst some stakeholders, there is a perception that the Kangaroo Island TOMM is still not 'working'. This criticism has centred on the false expectation that TOMM will immediately provide answers to many of the tourism questions that are being asked. To date there has also been some frustration caused because not all of the identified indicators are being fully reported.

In reality, such an extensive integrated monitoring process takes time to gain momentum and stakeholder confidence. Monitoring methods, indicators and optimal conditions all have to be refined to suit the practical reality of implementation on an ongoing basis. For example, in the case of the original TOMM indicators, the language used to define the indicator was not sufficiently rigorous to enable accurate reporting, and consequently some of the TOMM indicators currently in use differ from those originally devised. A reduced number of indicators are being actively monitored through a variety of mechanisms, including a TOMM-funded visitor exit and annual resident survey, and environmental monitoring funded by the DEH as part of their ongoing operations. In reality, it is unlikely that TOMM will itself develop and maintain monitoring programmes for all of the identified indicators, due to inevitable resource constraints. Effective partnerships are critical and make the best use of the resources Kangaroo Island has available.

Nevertheless, TOMM is producing valuable results over and above the information reported through the indicators. This information is being used by key government agencies on and off the island as well as some sectors of the island business community within their strategic business planning. In a report on the comparison of tourism management models in Australia, Pearlman noted that whilst the collection and reporting of data was initially sluggish and the environmental indicators rather weak, he did point out that the TOMM was beginning to develop 'a broad information database that is relevant to industry and the community' (Pearlman, 2002).

The TOMM on Kangaroo Island is currently reporting on indicators outlined in Box 9.5 and is undergoing a review of data sources and indicators with the view to enhancing data reporting based upon its acknowledged weaknesses. The examples given in the table relate to information gathered and reported on in 2001.

TOMM Implementation

The implementation of TOMM has seen and overcome many challenges. The progression from a conceptual model to a working project has high-lighted many issues and TOMM has evolved as a consequence. The evolution, development and successful implementation of TOMM are a result of the passion and commitment of the people involved in the process. As the full implementation of TOMM continues on Kangaroo Island, so will the evolution of the TOMM process.

Institutional arrangements and management structure

The TOMM is made up of partners from State and local government, community-based environmental groups and tourism industry representatives. Government agencies have become involved with TOMM as it provides them with valuable data on the effect tourism has on their individual operations. The TOMM Management Committee consists of representatives from key Island government agencies, community and industry representatives. Government agencies that are funding partners are also entitled to nominate a representative to sit on the TOMM Management Committee. All groups that fund TOMM and therefore form part of the Management Committee are signatory to a memorandum of understanding that assists in clarifying their roles and responsibilities. To date, industry and community have been represented by persons who have been involved with the TOMM process since its inception. The Management Committee has considered a nomination and election process for these positions and also considered increasing the number of representatives. The aim of these proposals would be to increase awareness of TOMM and engage the community and industry further. The TOMM Management Committee structure is outlined in Fig. 9.2.

The administrative element of the TOMM process is managed by the Kangaroo Island Council, and the TOMM Project Officer is employed part-time by the Kangaroo Island Council. Originally, this position was contracted and administered by the DEH; however, it was felt that the Kangaroo Island Council was more representative of the community and therefore should have greater ownership of the process. Management models such as TOMM require on-the-ground drivers as well as pro-active, passionate management committee members. Staffing of the Kangaroo Island TOMM to date has been part-time; ideally, however, TOMM requires two staff members covering indicator analysis and research as well as community engagement, marketing and strategic planning.

The Kangaroo Island Council, Kangaroo Island Natural Resources Board, Kangaroo Island Development Board and Tourism Kangaroo Island are all locally based organizations responsible for the economic, environmental and social development of the island. Tourism Kangaroo Island is the only

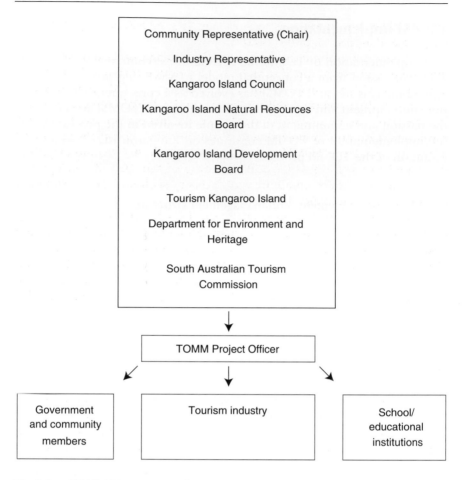

Fig. 9.2.   TOMM Management Committee structure.

agency specifically responsible for marketing and promoting tourism to the island. The SATC and DEH are state government agencies. DEH have a regional office on Kangaroo Island and manage a number of tourist sites within the National Park reserves on the island, whilst the SATC is based in Adelaide and a representative attends TOMM meetings and provides a link to state-based tourism activities.

The tourism industry and community have representation on the Committee and provide a vital link to the residents and business operators on the island, encouraging them to use the TOMM data within their individual business planning processes. All positions, other than the Project Officer, are volunteer posts. The Committee meets at least bimonthly, with sub-committees working via e-mail and meetings to progress specific issues and actions. Each member of the TOMM committee is expected to play an ambassadorial role within their respective sector, both in terms of accessing opportunities for funding as well as ongoing education regarding the purpose and aspiration of the TOMM.

The broader community both on and off Kangaroo Island have input into the operations of the Management Committee through their respective representatives, directly with the TOMM Project Officer through its main street office, via the feedback forum on the TOMM website and during the many community workshops held to discuss the results of each survey period. Community engagement is considered an essential component of the success of the TOMM and as such, a specific strategy was originally developed to ensure broader understanding of the TOMM concept and integration into the community and industry sectors. The consultation process is depicted in Fig. 9.3.

One of the main challenges facing the TOMM process is the ongoing maintenance of communication with stakeholders given the limited time resources of the Project Officer and Committee members. Ideally, this type of model requires both the expertise of a data analyst/project administrator as well as a marketing/communications officer to ensure that each component of the process is being effectively addressed. Ultimately this challenge is linked to adequate resources.

Funding

Initial seed funding of AUS$54,000 was accessed through the Office of National Tourism (now Department of Industry Science and Resources) in 1997, to develop the original TOMM concept and commence phase one of implementation. In the past additional funding has been provided by:

- Office of Workplace Relations and Small Business to assist with business expansion based upon increasing tourism growth;
- Kangaroo Island Wilderness Tours were the first private contributors to the TOMM project on Kangaroo Island;
- Adventure Charters of Kangaroo Island provided assistance to the TOMM project in 2000 and has continued to provide in-kind and financial support; and
- Previously the Kangaroo Island Health Service and Agriculture Kangaroo Island (Non-Government Peak Body) have been partners to the TOMM.

Currently, TOMM relies on core funding from partner agencies ranging from annual contributions of $5000–15,000. Core funding has been provided until 2004/05 by the following stakeholders:

- Kangaroo Island Council;
- Kangaroo Island Development Board;
- Tourism Kangaroo Island;

Objective: Awareness building leading to participation and engagement

Primary Target Markets:

Kangaroo Island	Globally
Island-based government agencies	Ecotourism associations
Tourism operators	Australian Tourism Commission
Retail and business sector	State and local tourism agencies
Local area schools	Educational sector

Consultation Strategies

- Development of a business plan to clearly outline the path of TOMM

- Community meetings to introduce and explain the TOMM concept

- Formation of business networks through the Kangaroo Island Development Board to promote TOMM and use of the data it creates

- Guest speaking and educational projects with local schools focusing on youths' perspectives and ideas regarding sustainable tourism – this included development of an educational kit

- Presentation of papers at ecotourism conferences around the world

- Development of news briefs containing TOMM data relevant to the business and community of Kangaroo Island

- Regular presentations to the Island Government agencies and community groups and contact with core global agencies interested in the concept

- Sponsorship by the Islander Newspaper of a regular column on TOMM called 'Beating the TOMM'

Future activities include:

- Maintenance of the TOMM website

- Formation of Ambassadors to speak on behalf of TOMM and maintain local enthusiasm and feedback

- Improved educational campaigns for local schools both on Kangaroo Island and South Australia

Fig. 9.3.   Communication strategy.

- Kangaroo Island Natural Resources Board;
- DEH;
- SATC.

Currently the Kangaroo Island TOMM has committed funds and support to implement:

- Annual visitor and resident surveys;
- Environmental data through the DEH;
- Social data through the Department of South Australian Police and their crime/traffic statistics;
- Regular review of indicators to ensure they are relevant to the changing needs of the destination, whilst maintaining continuity with existing agency data collections;
- Analysis and interpretation of the data in formats that are easily understood and considered relevant to the particular target audience.

The Kangaroo Island TOMM and its administration has been able to maintain its operations as a result of committed long-term partners, advisers and project managers in addition to project specific funding accessed in association with other government agencies. A project such as TOMM will always have ongoing resource requirements, and a sustainable funding mechanism for TOMM is being sought, to alleviate its reliance on support from stakeholders and grants. The presence of a 'driver' is vital in this respect and the various Project Officers associated with the TOMM have successfully accessed grants through Federal and State Governments to undertake project specific work. For example, the Office of Workplace Relations and Small Business provided a grant to assist local businesses expand their operations using TOMM data within their business planning processes.

However, long-term success of the TOMM process will only be achieved when a sustainable funding source can be identified and the reliance upon government funding reduced. Whilst this is a logical progression, the actual implementation of the concept is proving to be far from simple, despite a range of opportunities being considered including corporate/philanthropic donations via tax deductibility status, commercial partnership opportunities and a visitor levy. The process of implementation has to recognize the intrinsic value of identifying shared understanding, respect for others values and opinions, access to diverse and stable funding sources, rigorous indicators and information dissemination, and above all, the nurturing and support of those passionate individuals that make up the team of committed partners (Jack and Duka, 2004).

Evaluation

Despite the number of tourism management models that have been created and continue to be developed, McArthur (2000) highlights the apparent lack of information relating to the adoption, implementation and performance – successful or otherwise – of previous models, most of which were traditionally focused on the heritage resource as the central pillar in the management process and relied upon heritage managers for their implementation (McArthur, 2000). He argues that the costs of this are:

- A limited awareness, involvement and ownership of the models by the various stakeholders they were designed to serve;
- A limited degree of understanding about the real characteristics and capabilities of the models among those they were designed for (predominantly heritage managers);
- A limited commitment among heritage (resource managers) to utilize and/or adapt the models for their own use.

In the movement towards sustainable tourism, the development of the TOMM, with its integrated focus across all stakeholders, the formal management response structure and active implementation and ownership building within the community, offers a tangible and practical example of the ongoing development, implementation and testing of a sustainable tourism management model applicable to heritage areas and communities globally (Jack and Duka, 2004).

Committing to ongoing integration of data

A key component of the TOMM concept is a management reporting process that addresses the issues generated from ongoing trend data relevant to the destination. An essential component of this is the integration of key TOMM data into agency management systems. This is a challenging process not only in terms of accessing funding for ongoing monitoring and research but also in terms of ensuring indicators, optimal conditions and acceptable ranges are relevant to the current community and agency environment. The process also needs to ensure that the management response system is pro-active and where possible integrated into existing data collection and reporting systems and strategic planning processes undertaken by other agencies, particularly government.

The integration of TOMM data into key agency processes has taken time and still requires ongoing collective responsibility within the culture of partner agencies and their representatives. TOMM will continue to advocate that these philosophies and relevant TOMM data are reflected in strategic plans and day-to-day decision-making processes. This will take time and depend upon the attitude of the agency representatives towards the value of the TOMM process and data generated through the TOMM surveys.

The integration of this information will ultimately affect the management response component of the TOMM process. When all agencies are pro-actively using and applying TOMM data, there may be much greater interest in addressing problems and opportunities as they arise. To date, the TOMM data are included in the following strategic planning processes:

- Kangaroo Island Integrated Strategic Tourism Plan (in preparation);
- SATC Strategic Plan (2004);

- Responsible Nature-based Tourism Strategy 2004–2009: SATC and DEH South Australia;
- Kangaroo Island Development Board Strategic Plan (2003–2008);
- Kangaroo Island Natural Resource Management Investment Strategy (2003);
- DEH, Kangaroo Island Regional Strategic Plan (2003–2004, in preparation);
- Tourism Kangaroo Island Strategic Plan (2004, in preparation).

Creating and maintaining awareness

Any long-term community-driven project not only has to deliver outcomes but also has to promote these to an audience, thereby creating a demand for the project and its results. Creating awareness of the Kangaroo Island TOMM project, enrolling people into the concept and generating a sense of excitement, inspiration and enthusiasm has been as integral to the process as collecting data and strategic planning.

An important element of this has been the need to broaden the mainstream concept of community. There have been many different 'communities' involved in the Kangaroo Island TOMM process, all of which require different approaches with regards to information dissemination, awareness raising and involvement. The resident community is the reason why the model was originally developed and requires ongoing communication through workshops, presentations, newspaper stories, posters, representation at local shows and attendance at events. Within the resident community, it is acknowledged that different levels of stakeholders exist, and only over time will all community residents gain an understanding, appreciation and find application of the TOMM data useful.

Government agencies on and off island similarly are a major focus of the TOMM process, with communication being established through meetings, conferences, establishment of TOMM as a case study for their own promotional efforts and ongoing representation by TOMM advocates. The educational sector has proved to be very fertile ground for the dissemination of information regarding TOMM. Schools both on and off the island have been approach through 'guest speaker' opportunities, the establishment of projects such as 'Our Island' where students were asked to depict what they loved about Kangaroo Island, the provision of student work experience within the TOMM office and the integration of TOMM data into curriculum programmes. The tertiary sector has likewise been keen to include the TOMM model within tourism degree courses that address sustainable tourism management. Work experience places are provided to university students and greater links are being forged with agencies such as the Cooperative Research Centre for Sustainable Tourism, the University of South Australia and the WTO.

Whilst the tourism industry both on and off the island has been slow to become actively involved in the TOMM process, it is beginning to gain greater awareness and application, particularly through the activities of Tourism Kangaroo Island, the SATC and via application in other destinations such as the Sydney Quarantine Station.

A new 'community' that may increasingly demand contact is that of the global visitor to Kangaroo Island. As international visitation increases, the potential for visitors to generate an attachment to the island increases, as does their desire to know more about the sustainable development of the destination. Communication to inform visitors of the work being undertaken by the Kangaroo Island community has taken place via exit information, including posters and displays, representation at trade shows through local tourism operators and the linkage with recognized codes of ecotourism practice.

Creating opportunities for the development of skills capacity and social capital

The implementation of the Kangaroo Island TOMM process has not only begun to generate trend information on the economic and environmental aspects of Kangaroo Island, but is also facilitating the development of indicators that reflect the social and cultural characteristics of the community. This information ranges from data that highlights the number of volunteer hours residents contribute to community causes through to the educational level and ownership of computers amongst households. When pieced together and integrated into other information from the health and education sector, these data tell a variety of stories regarding the relationships, social bonds and daily challenges that help or hinder people working together. Knowledge of this nature can, and has, assisted in social programmes aimed at community health and development, leading ultimately to the strengthening of social capital. The establishment of a community development officer position within the Kangaroo Island Council is a good example of how the work of various community groups, coupled with information generated through TOMM resident surveys, facilitated the formation of this part-time position. Long-term, responsible tourism management requires the presence of strong social and community capital, which in turn sustains the core values of trust, integrity, reliability and honesty, all of which are central to the success of the relationships required to manage programmes such as TOMM.

The Kangaroo Island TOMM experience may shed some light on the elements needed to facilitate the realistic implementation of sustainable tourism management at a destination and community level. Whilst the Kangaroo Island TOMM has enjoyed some success, it has required an enormous ongoing belief and commitment in the process, as well as ongoing resources at an operational level.

Lessons Learned

The Kangaroo Island TOMM process has highlighted two distinct yet equal areas that require attention, if community-driven projects such as this are to make a long-term difference in the area of sustainable tourism. These are some of the pertinent operational and attitudinal issues (Boxes 9.6 and 9.7).

Summary

The catalyst of increasing visitor numbers and the recognition that the core values of the island and its community were potentially at risk due to increasing tourism pressure, facilitated the development of the TOMM. This process brought together key stakeholders involved in the governance of the island, residents and those from the tourism industry. The opportunities presented by such a catalyst may not always be acted upon within the community context, but they do continue to surface until some action is taken to address them. Kangaroo Island had previously considered the sustainable development of tourism and its impact on the resources of the island, yet it was not until its impact became more tangible that the concept of a tourism management model was implemented.

The TOMM is now an important and integral process in the governance and management of Kangaroo Island. It has begun to demonstrate that, at a local community level, partnerships can realize economic, environmental and social development, given sufficient time, resources and the attitude to succeed. TOMM has also added to the theoretical approach to sustainable tourism management at a destination level with the focus on integrating the social, environmental and economic values of a destination rather than considering the impacts at a site-specific level. Through the integration of these elements, the TOMM provides an ever-changing picture of the effects of tourism on Kangaroo Island and links these with the broader strategic planning and management processes within the destination. Ideally, indicators and monitoring programmes used by a TOMM will be integrated into existing and potential monitoring systems of other government agencies, thereby providing an integrated island 'health report' that addresses not only tourism but other essential industries and environmental/social/economic characteristics. This longer-term possibility is reliant upon the shared agreement of indicators, monitoring processes and reporting mechanisms as well as the obvious elements of funding, human resources and management support.

Box 9.6.   Operational issues.

Operational Issues

1. Indicators
- Ensure data are collected in an appropriate and consistent manner. Engagement of local tourism business will occur when data are available and can show trends.
- Data are only of value if they can be applied and used by others. Data cannot be the sole focus of the process even though agencies may see it this way.
- Communication of the findings in a format and language understood by the intended audience is essential.
- Review existing data collection systems to see how they can be applied, do not reinvent the wheel.
- Review indicators on a regular basis for relevance to both the destination, and audience needs and integrate into existing information systems.
- Align indicators and data collection processes with other models where applicable so a global comparative study may be possible.
- Ensure the development of indicators meet the long-term needs of the community, not just funding agencies.

2. Marketing
- Establish a marketing budget to enable the production of promotional tools such as a website, posters, fliers, news articles and conference papers.
- Promote the process and its outcomes (positive and negative) on an ongoing basis. Outdated information may reflect badly on the success of the process.
- Do not try to engage everyone at the same time. Identify target markets and work towards engaging the entire community in the long term.
- Work collaboratively and collectively with government and non-government agencies and community groups to ensure a mutually beneficial approach for all involved.
- Document the process being undertaken for future reference and application elsewhere.
- Demonstrate how people can become involved in the process, and detail what they can do to help, e.g. a TOMM Tool Kit.

3. Human resources
- Requires a staff of at least two people (data analysis/administration plus marketing/representation) as well as a committed project driver/champion/chair.
- Burnout of key drivers (Project Officers and Management Committee) is a very real issue and can destroy a project. To avoid this recognize the signs of burnout provide support and identify the achievements of those involved through marketing initiatives.
- Ensure some continuity of key individuals especially on the management committee, to maintain institutional memory that will in turn ensure the process remains on track.
- Appoint staff/advisers/management committee with the passion, interest and willingness to invest their time in seeing the process succeed. They will be your greatest ambassadors.

4. Governance
- Independence of a board/management committee is important to its ability to comment on issues relating to the status of tourism and the island in general.

- The TOMM process, as well as the outcomes of the TOMM research, have to be trusted and non-politically influenced.
- Agencies/partners have to believe in the long-term process and articulate this belief within the public arena.
- People will always question if the process is working. Project managers need to demonstrate that the process runs through a natural lifecycle and urge stakeholders not to panic or lose confidence when stagnation hits, rather use this to evolve the concept.
- Cultural change amongst government agencies, communities and individuals takes time. Do not worry if integration into management does not happen immediately; remember this is a long-term process.

5. Funding
- Access to sufficient resources continues to be a major focus for the Kangaroo Island TOMM and demands a great deal of time and energy. These resources are the most tangible evidence of the success or otherwise of the process; however, they have the capacity to slow the momentum and enthusiasm for the project in the short term.
- Think creatively, commercially and collectively regarding funding arrangements to ensure the implementation of TOMM. Traditional funding sources may not be sufficient to maintain the operational costs in the long term.
- Be prepared. Develop a business plan and funding outline.
- Encourage government agencies to allocate funding to TOMM as a standard operational cost rather than through annual funding rounds. This will also ensure they remain committed to and involved in the process.
- Funding alone will not assure the success of a TOMM, funding is only one aspect of the process.
- Value-add access to funding and link projects where possible.
- Always factor in an administrative element to funding submissions. These projects do not happen without a driver.

6. Monitoring
- Maintain a record of successes, lessons, contacts, promotional exposure. This will help when needing to establish a business case.
- Create additional indicators to monitor the implementation process, e.g. the number of government agencies incorporating TOMM into their strategic planning, the number of successful initiatives by government agencies that have used TOMM data.
- Encourage partners/government agencies/community groups/industry to use monitoring results for their own promotion. They again act as excellent ambassadors.

Box 9.7.   Attitudinal issues.

- Whilst there are tools and techniques that will assist in the implementation of TOMM attitudinal issues such as identifying and harnessing attitudes; building relationships as a positive force towards implementation can be essential in successfully implementing sustainable tourism management models.
- To establish a process such as TOMM, community, government agencies and individuals will be asked to develop an agreed set of values that help guide the destination or community towards a shared understanding of its sense of place, its future direction and the various constraints in which all players are working.
- Understanding and having empathy for the limits of each player within the sustainable management process provides the basis for understanding behaviour and responses. This can be useful to help to reduce conflicts through the partnership process.
- Similarly, the community will be asked to commit funding to the process over a long time period. The funding of sustainable tourism management models such as TOMM requires financial support to fund research, marketing and administration. However, they also rely heavily on non-financial resources such as time, networks and expertise. These are resources, which cannot easily be bought, yet are critically important to the success of partnerships (Jack and Duka, 2004).

After 4 years, the impact of TOMM is becoming evident. Results are being generated and used by key government agencies and community groups on the island, as well as within the broader business community. Some of the original indicators are yet to be reported on and it is acknowledged that those currently being monitored may require ongoing review to ensure they continue to meet the needs of the island community. However, the recognition that it is a useful start should not be undervalued. The data generated to date are providing a picture of the impacts of tourism and represent a far superior base of local knowledge than previously existed prior to the implementation of TOMM.

TOMM offers an organic approach to sustainable tourism management. Those involved from the commencement of the concept have not only had the capacity to hold on to a vision for a period of time but to display an understanding of the lifecycle, politics and manner in which people operate and the impacts this might have on the process. With the increasing pressure for short-term outcomes, driven by short-term funding programmes, it is often the community members themselves that have the stamina and long-term vested interest in seeing the process succeed. These key people also have the patience to allow the process and its players to evolve as needed rather than expecting results over night. Those involved with the Kangaroo Island TOMM are proactive about developing the model as it is their community, livelihoods and local environment that is at stake from the increasing tourism interest in the destination. The collaboration of government agencies and community groups as well as individuals that have characterized the TOMM since its inception remains as a central component of the ongoing nature of the TOMM process.

Theoretical concepts behind sustainable tourism management will continue to evolve, but the TOMM process represents an important step in the understanding and knowledge of how local communities can realistically implement these concepts within the constraints of funding, human resources and short-term time frames. Management models such as TOMM can succeed at a local level, if the process is allowed to evolve in the long term. Kangaroo Island has succeeded not because it is an island, rather it is due to the shared commitment to achieving a vision and the ability of those involved to be flexible and ensure open communication amongst key stakeholders.

If community partnerships such as the Kangaroo Island TOMM are to work at a national and global level, governments have to create enabling institutional contexts to facilitate this happening. This includes making funding available, as well as pushing government departments to work in a more cohesive manner, ultimately leading to changes in public policy. The shifts in organizational attitude and culture that have taken place within government agencies and community groups on Kangaroo Island ultimately have to be replicated on a much broader scale.

Samoa Sustainable Tourism Indicator Project

10

Introduction

The Samoa Sustainable Tourism Indicator Project (SSTIP) is the only known example of the use of sustainable tourism indicators in the South Pacific. Developed by the author in collaboration with the Samoa Tourism Authority (STA) and a multi-disciplinary Project Advisory Committee (PAC), the indicators were designed to help policy makers move towards more sustainable tourism in the country. The project demonstrates the very real challenges of not only developing an indicator programme but also implementing and maintaining one over time. It illustrates how indicators can be developed in a comprehensive and participatory fashion, they can be agreed on by stakeholders and written into tourism planning processes, but their ongoing survival is reliant on a complex and unpredictable set of occurrences.

The chapter is divided into three parts. The first section briefly describes the background of the South Pacific and then introduces the context of Samoa and the development of tourism in the country. The second section explains the establishment of the SSTIP, and the process of indicator development applied to the case of Samoa. It details the scoping of key issues, selection of indicators, piloting and monitoring of indicators, analysis of results and design of an implementation framework to convert results into action. The third section evaluates the indicator process and outcomes, identifying costs and benefits of monitoring and exploring some of the reasons why the Samoa indicator project has not yet fulfilled its potential.

The chapter serves to highlight the application of many of the theoretical principles explained in Part One of this book, namely a sustainable

©G.A. Miller and L. Twining-Ward 2005. *Monitoring for a Sustainable Tourism Transition*
(G.A. Miller and L. Twining-Ward)

development approach, using participatory methodology and applying adaptive management techniques.

Context

The clear-cut geographical boundaries of islands have long led geographers, anthropologists and biologists alike to recognize them as useful spatial laboratories. Wilkinson (1989) was able to produce a bibliography of over 600 references of research related to tourism in island microstates. King (1997) notes that research on an island enables theories to be tested and processes observed in the setting of a semi-closed system and Filho (1996) suggests it is easier to assess the effectiveness of policy decisions and techniques to implement sustainable tourism within the confines of an island.

Less widely acknowledged are the challenges of conducting research in small, isolated communities with strong traditional culture. On small islands, the business and policy environment is likely to be less diverse than on mainland masses, dominated by a few well-connected people and difficult for an outsider to join (Crocombe, 2001). This is especially so in Samoa and other parts of the South Pacific where kinship and blood ties are close, and personal favours and preferential treatment for those of chiefly status are an accepted part of everyday life (Hess, 1990; Fairbairn *et al.*, 1991).

The South Pacific

The South Pacific Region spans 22 countries and territories shown in Box 10.1. This includes countries north of the Equator such as the Federated States of Micronesia, the Marshall Islands and Guam and Papua New Guinea in the west, but excludes Hawaii and Easter Island (SPREP, 1992; Crocombe, 2001).

Together, these countries have a combined Exclusive Economic Zone (the oceanic zone over which a country has jurisdiction including control over fishing) of almost 30 million km^2, covering almost one-eighth of the earth's surface. However, the large size is deceptive, as only 1.8% of this area is land, and the region supports a population of just 6.8 million people, 70% in Papua New Guinea, the largest of the islands (UNDP, 1999).

Present-day economies of the countries in the region are very much dictated by their physical environment. The continental islands like Papua New Guinea, export amongst other things, gold, copper, sugar, coffee, cocoa, palm oil and forest products and have fairly well-developed manufacturing, service and tourism sectors (Crocombe, 2001). Some of the high volcanic islands such as Samoa, French Polynesia, Fiji and the Cook Islands

Box 10.1. South Pacific Island States: cultural groupings.

Island groups	Countries included
Micronesia	Federated States of Micronesia, Guam, Kiribati, Marshall Islands, Nauru, Northern Marianas, Palau and Tuvalu
Melanesia	New Caledonia, Papua New Guinea, Solomon Islands, Vanuatu and most of Fiji
Polynesia	American Samoa, Cook Islands, French Polynesia, Niue, Pitcairn Island, Samoa, Tokelau, Tonga, Wallis and Futuna and eastern parts of Fiji

Source: after Page (1996).

are also beginning to focus on service industries and have attempted to develop specialized regional exports such as citrus fruits, copra, cocoa and vanilla, whilst the smaller coral atolls are generally restricted to coconut products, fish and, in the case of Nauru, phosphates.

The lifting of preferential trade agreements, combined with some of the constraints of small size and isolation noted in Box 10.2, make it difficult for these islands to find profitable export markets, and tourism is being increasingly recognized as a potential tool for sustainable development in the region. Yet, as has been discussed at length by other authors such as Briguglio *et al.* (1996), Butler (1993b) and Milne (1997), tourism can also threaten small island sustainability. Examples abound of tourism increasing economic leakages because of high dependence on imported goods and Britton reports on the tendency of the industry to employ foreign labour, especially in senior positions (Britton 1982, 1987). Environmentally, tourism can put pressure on limited resources such as fresh water and land, especially in coastal zones (Farrell, 1986). There are also strong social and cultural traditions that risk commercialization (de Burlo, 1996). Box 10.2 outlines the six key issues to be discussed at UN Barbados +10 meeting in Mauritius in 2004, perceived as those most likely to affect the abilities of small island countries to pursue sustainable development.

These hazards make it even more important that tourism is developed in a manner and scale that is compatible with available human and physical resources and is sensitive to pertinent environmental and social issues. Samoa is one country in the region that has taken active steps towards monitoring the sustainability of their tourism industry.

Samoa

Samoa is one of ten Polynesian states located approximately midway between New Zealand and Hawaii, just east of the International Dateline.

Box 10.2.   Key issues facing small island developing states.

1. Trade: small size and isolated location combine to render island economies highly dependent on external markets for imports.
2. Tourism: when not properly managed, tourism is fraught with hazards for small island states in a number of ways including stress on freshwater and other natural resources.
3. Freshwater: because of increasing development, growing populations and little catchment areas, many small islands have insufficient freshwater resources.
4. Climate change: Sea level has risen 10–20 cm in the last century; if this continues, when combined with extreme weather, land and freshwater supplies are adversely affected.
5. Energy: small island developing states are dependent on imported petroleum products, making up a significant percentage of imports.
6. Transport and communications: distance and isolation have resulted in high transport costs and communications infrastructure is often poorly maintained.

Source: UN (2004).

Samoa's nearest neighbours are American Samoa (unincorporated US territory) to the east, Fiji to the west, the Kingdom of Tonga to the south, and Tokelau and Tuvalu to the north, meaning both geographically and culturally that the country is 'the heart of Polynesia' (Fig. 10.1).

The country consists of nine islands of which only four are permanently inhabited: Savaii, Upolu, Manono and Apolima. The population is estimated at 177,000, with 72% living on the island of Upolu, home to the international airport and capital, Apia (Government of Samoa, 2001). Despite being under the administration of several countries through its history, culturally, Samoa never lost its independence, and the *fa'aSamoa*, the Samoan way of life, is still a dominant influence on all social and economic activities, centred on the village and dominated by the chiefly hierarchy (*fa'amatai*), extended family (*aiga potopoto*), ceremonial gift-giving (*fa'alavelave*) and customary land ownership (which prevents the sale of traditional land and has a significant impact on tourism development). Samoa's economy was formerly dominated by copra, cocoa, taro and rubber, but falling world prices in the post-colonial era made this policy problematic. In the decades since independence, Samoa has sought, with some considerable success, to diversify its largely agrarian economy, and tourism, commerce and manufacturing are now dominant contributors to the GDP.

Tourism in Samoa has its origins in the late 19th century but, conscious of the potential impacts of tourism on the traditional culture, the Government maintained a slow and cautious attitude to tourism development up until the early 1990s, when financial difficulties (the result of two major cyclones and a disease that devastated the country's staple crop) left the

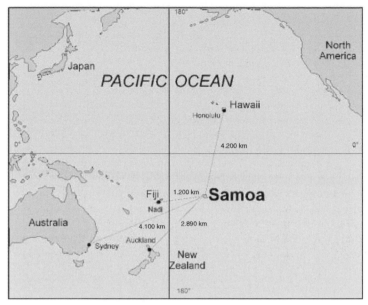

Fig. 10.1. Location of Samoa in the South Pacific.

country with few other economic options. The Government then began making a concerted effort to attract foreign investment and supported the elaboration and implementation of the 1992–2001 Tourism Development Plan (Government of Samoa and TCSP, 1992). Combined with the pioneering efforts of the private sector in setting up the first few beach hotels and tour operations, and the large numbers of visiting friends and relatives (VFR) (Samoans living overseas returning for family gatherings), international arrivals reached 92,313 in 2003 as shown in Box 10.3.

The main attractions of Samoa for foreign visitors are the country's natural beauty (beaches, reefs and rainforests), the friendliness of the people, the tropical climate and the traditional Samoan culture (SVB, 2000a). The country has the additional attraction of traditional beach *fale* (hut) accommodation, popular with both backpackers and VFRs, and providing a ready source of income for coastal villages. Over the last few years, marine tourism and ecotourism have become important tourism activities including surfing, sea kayaking, diving and game fishing. Despite these developments the relative absence of high-quality beach resorts (due to customary land tenure, natural hazards, cultural constraints, and political and institutional indecision) means Samoa is still some way off optimizing its tourism potential. Scheyvens (2004, p. 1) describes the situation as follows:

> Samoa has a wide range of cultural and natural attractions, yet successive governments have not sought to 'cash in' on these by actively pursuing growth of the tourism industry. In fact, there has been ambivalence about tourism

Box 10.3. Tourism arrivals to Samoa, 1994–2003.

Source markets	1994	1995	1996	1997	1998	1999	2000	2001	2002	2003	% of 2003 total
American Samoa	21,482	23,817	24,138	23,729	30,062	31,099	30,063	31,016	31,803	30,166	32.7
New Zealand	16,857	17,709	20,617	19,655	20,627	23,248	22,818	23,337	23,790	26,974	29.2
Australia	6,796	6,816	7,789	6,940	7,886	9,311	10,954	11,224	11,438	12,101	13.1
USA	7,832	6,202	8,018	6,628	7,770	7,932	9,032	8,467	8,720	8,545	9.3
Other Pacific island	4,927	4284	4,692	3,764	4,261	4,781	5,503	5,355	5,904	6,286	6.8
UK	928	1,238	1,103	1,204	1,238	1,588	2,092	1,722	1,480	2,092	2.3
Other Europe	1,942	3,017	2,006	1,617	2,173	2,331	2,520	2,147	2,086	1,837	2.0
Germany	2,472	2,696	1,690	1,673	1,506	1,541	1,784	1,928	1,196	1,207	1.3
Japan	1,016	836	1,016	879	892	812	713	718	577	683	0.7
Canada	599	254	416	328	267	320	390	370	375	406	0.4
Other countries	2,238	1,523	1,670	1,543	1,244	2,161	1,819	1,979	1,591	2,016	2.2
Total arrivals	67,089	68,392	73,155	67,960	77,926	85,124	87,688	88,263	88,960	92,313	100

Sources: SVB (2000a) and STA and Government Department of Statistics (2004).

development which is strongly tied to Samoa's history of resistance to outside interference in their country and culture.

A positive spin-off from this policy is that local participation in the industry is still high, and that the kind of dependency on foreign investors and expatriate staff that has been experienced by destinations such as Fiji does not exist in Samoa (Twining-Ward and Twining-Ward, 1998). On the reverse side of the coin, many of the facilities are right on the beach, run by families who have little knowledge of environmental or social issues related to tourism and inadequate resources to finance appropriate sewerage.

Indicator Project

The idea for the SSTIP emerged during 1998 as a result of a review of tourism plans and policy documents from around the region. These documents revealed that many island states in the South Pacific such as Samoa, Niue, Tonga and Fiji have made public commitments to the sustainable development of their tourism sectors but there are few tools currently available to assist them (Government of Samoa and TCSP, 1992; UNDP, WTO and Government of Niue 1997; Government of Tonga and TCSP, 1997). It was against this background that this researcher began working with the STA (known at the time as the Samoa Visitors Bureau, SVB) in September 1998, to establish a project that would develop a practical and user-friendly monitoring system to assist Samoa in their transition towards sustainable tourism.

The STA were enthusiastic about getting involved in such a project, and took up the management of the project in November 1998 in collaboration with the researcher. After reviewing recommendations from other indicator projects they resolved that a small multidisciplinary PAC should be established to collaborate with STA on the work.

PAC

The advisory committee had a dual purpose: first, to ensure wide stakeholder representation in the project and secondly, to advise STA in areas that were important to sustainable tourism development but outside the normal activities of STA namely, environmental, cultural, social and economic matters.

In deciding the potential composition of PAC, a number of stakeholder groups were considered. First, STA, as the implementing agency, would clearly need a strong presence on the committee. Secondly, the tourism industry of the islands of Upolu and Savaii, which were likely to be involved in the monitoring and interested in the results were important

partners to have on board. Thirdly, the regional environmental organization (South Pacific Regional Environmental Programme, SPREP) and a
number of government departments showed interest in the work and were
likely to be key providers of information and data. Fourthly, the National
University of Samoa and the University of the South Pacific had a stake in
the project due to the research component of the work. As shown in
Fig. 10.2, the final PAC consisted of 12 members broadly divided by
expertise and experience into five subgroups.

Nine PAC meetings were held during the 16-month project development phase of the work, facilitated by the researcher with assistance from
STA staff. Each meeting lasted approximately 2.5 h. In addition to the main
meetings, the PAC was on occasions divided into specialized working
groups in order to assist on particular tasks such as questionnaire design,
indicator brainstorming and fine-tuning.

One of the most important initial tasks of the PAC was to identify the
objectives and goals of the project so the work could be planned accordingly.
The PAC opted to start by developing a clear understanding of what sustainable tourism meant in a Samoan context. Consequently the first phase of the
work was to formulate a set of clear Samoa sustainable tourism objectives.
The idea was that from these objectives, a robust set of indicators could be
derived. Then, to assist STA managers interpret indicator results and take
appropriate action, an implementation system was deemed necessary.

The goals of the project were therefore threefold and drawn up as
follows:

- To establish exactly what sustainable tourism means in the context of
  Samoa by formulating a set of clear objectives;

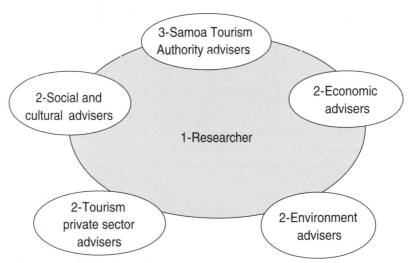

Fig. 10.2.   Project advisory committee composition.

- To identify, select and pilot a set of robust sustainable tourism indicators to monitor progress towards the objectives;
- To set up an effective implementation system to assist with the interpretation of indicator results and the translation into tangible action projects.

These steps are explained below.

Sustainable tourism in a Samoan context

International definitions for sustainable tourism provided a helpful starting point, but if the sustainable tourism indicators were to be relevant to the situation in Samoa, it was clear that they needed to reflect Samoan priorities and concerns and be founded on a sound understanding of the challenges facing sustainable development in Samoa. In order to develop a clearer understanding of what sustainable tourism meant in the Samoan context, a multi-stage process was developed, incorporating the collection of both primary and secondary information, the analysis of key issues and then clearly describing objectives (Fig. 10.3).

Information on sustainable tourism development issues facing the country was collected from three main sources. First, a focused literature review was conducted in order to collate existing knowledge on sustainable tourism development in Samoa. Then, a series of key informant interviews was carried out in order to incorporate specialist knowledge in particular areas, and finally a series of village surveys was organized to enable the PAC to incorporate the views and concerns of those living in rural areas.

The literature review commenced with a careful selection of the most relevant and up-to-date sources of secondary information on sustainable development in Samoa conducted by the researcher with the assistance of PAC members. As a result of the literature review and subsequent PAC analysis, 34 key sustainable tourism development issues were identified. In order to find out more about these issues, a series of in-depth key informant

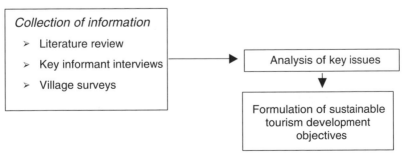

Fig. 10.3. Process used to identify Samoa's sustainable tourism objectives.

interviews were conducted. Thirty potential key informants were identified with expertise in one of the four main project themes (environment, economy, society and culture and tourism) using a stratified snowball sampling technique (identifying a member of the population of interest and asking them if they know anybody else with the required knowledge). In interviews that averaged 45 min in length, participants were asked about what they saw as the key issues facing the sustainable development of Samoa and their relevance to tourism. As a result of the interviews, 22 key issues were identified, many like deforestation and over-fishing reiterated, and those issues found from the review of secondary sources were clarified.

The third data collection technique used was the village surveys, designed to ensure the priorities and concerns of those living in rural areas were also taken into consideration in the formulation of sustainable tourism objectives. Four villages were selected using a semi-stratified sampling frame: Matautu-tai, Maninoa, Saluafata in Upolu, and Fatuvalu in Savaii. In total, 100 household interviews and 12 focus group meetings were conducted. Respondents were asked about their social and economic priorities, as well as their perception of the impacts of tourism in their village.

Once these three stages of information collection were completed, the results and issues identified were then analysed and combined, and those that appeared under current conceptions to bear little direct relevance to tourism (e.g. lifestyle, diseases, political freedom) were eliminated. As a result of this process, 12 key issues for sustainable tourism development in the country emerged and were grouped into environmental, economic, social and tourism concerns.

In terms of environmental issues, forests, reefs, waste and water were found to be the main areas of concern.

- The degradation of land and coastal resources through deforestation, and subsequent downstream effects such as increased runoff, soil erosion, siltation and reduced fresh water supplies is accelerating.
- Destructive inshore fishing practices such as dynamiting and coral crushing also threaten the marine ecosystem, as does development in and around mangrove forest areas.
- As the urban population grows so does the demand for imported foods and the resultant increase in non-biodegradable waste is a significant issue compounded by the lack of suitable landfill sites and difficulties of recycling on small islands.
- Finally, the demand for treated water is currently greater than the available supply, leading to inevitable water shortages and health risks as untreated river water is added to mains water supply to make up the shortfall.

Key economic issues identified were centred on employment and the balance of payments:

- The increasing gap between urban and rural incomes, particularly with the shift from a mainly subsistence to a predominantly cash-based economy was found to be of concern to residents in both areas.
- Traditional methods of income generation are unable to keep up with the demands of education, healthcare, church and family needs, resulting in increasing reliance on cash remittances, especially from New Zealand, and migration to urban areas in search of paid employment.
- There is also a concern about the country's narrow economic base making the economy vulnerable to external shocks and balance-of-payments deficits, hence the need to diversify into the tertiary sector, providing a more enabling environment for investment and boosting exports.

In terms of social and cultural challenges, education, traditions and performing arts and crafts were the main areas raised:

- Lack of trade or professional training has restricted the ability of those living in rural areas to benefit effectively from tourism.
- Culturally, there is some concern that the power vested in the village *matai* (chiefs) and respect between youth and elders is now being challenged through changes in dress and behaviour codes.
- Tourism provides one such influence so the general feeling is that care needs to be taken properly to orient and educate tourists about appropriate codes of conduct in villages.

Finally, with regards to tourism development, the quality of the tourism product and its management was of great concern:

- Tourist facilities and infrastructure are still under-developed in Samoa, reducing its ability both to compete effectively as a Pacific island tourist destination, and to attract sufficient numbers of holidaymakers.
- Sustainable tourism awareness and practice amongst the tourism industry is still fairly low and this was also identified as a concern.

Although the process of collecting and analysing key issues was lengthy, taking almost 5 months to complete, it was an extremely useful undertaking, resulting in considerable learning for all involved and turning sustainable tourism from an abstract concept to something that had real meaning for stakeholders in Samoa. It also enabled tourism in Samoa to be conceptualized not as a separate industrial sector but as an integrated complex system where changes in one part would inevitably influence the other parts. To assist this understanding and to enable the visualization of tourism in Samoa as a system, a system diagram was constructed, not an entirely comprehensive system as explained in Chapter 1, but a diagrammatic interpretation of the 12 key issues (Fig. 10.4).

Examination of the issues explained above enabled the researcher, the PAC and STA to develop a very broad understanding of where tourism

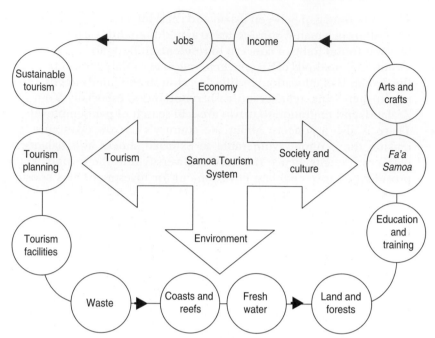

Fig. 10.4.   Key issues for the sustainable development of tourism in Samoa.

fitted with the other sustainable development concerns in Samoa. It was clear that the objectives would have to be formulated to bridge the gap between what are conventionally understood as tourism issues and other areas. The way this was done in the case of Samoa was to clearly link the key issues with the 12 main objectives and then to develop two or three sub-objectives for each issue. In this way, the linkage between the sustainable development and tourism issue was more precisely highlighted. These three levels of system information are shown in Box 10.4. Review of these key issues, objectives and sub-objectives below will give readers a sense of the broad interpretation of sustainable tourism that seemed appropriate in Samoa, a small island where the interconnectivity between environmental, economic, social and cultural aspects of sustainability is very close.

Samoan-style indicators

With Samoa's sustainable tourism objectives as a foundation, the next step for the monitoring project was to identify existing and/or develop new indicators to measure progress towards the sustainable tourism development objectives. Selecting indicators entailed both PAC brainstorming and then screening the potential list.

Box 10.4. Key issues and objectives for sustainable tourism in Samoa.

Key issues	Objectives	Sub-objectives
1. Forest resources	Encourage the conservation of land and in particular forest resources	Encourage the participation of village communities in conservation programmes Promote the careful use of tourism as an income generating activity for conservation areas and other natural areas under protection
2. Coastal environment, particularly coral reefs	Promote the careful management of coastal and marine resources with special focus on coral reefs	Encourage the participation of village communities in marine conservation programmes Promote the careful use of tourism as an income generating activity in coastal areas
3. Waste and pollution	Encourage the use of proper waste management practices at both the national and village level	Enhance village awareness of appropriate waste disposal methods Encourage the tourism industry to adopt appropriate solid and human waste management practices
4. Water quality and usage by tourism industry	Stimulate appropriate employment and income-generating opportunities in rural areas	Work together with responsible agencies to upgrade the quality and reliability of water supply especially to rural areas where tourism is being developed Promote measures to increase efficiency of water use particularly by the tourism industry
5. Tourism employment and income in rural areas	Stimulate appropriate employment and income-generating opportunities in rural areas	Support the participation of village communities in appropriate tourism income generating activities Encourage tourism operators to use locally produced goods and services Create opportunities for increased tourist spending
6. Tourism contribution to national economy	Diversify the national income base	Encourage local entrepreneurship and initiative in all facets of the tourism industry
7. Training, education and awareness	Promote appropriate training and education, especially in rural areas	Provide and deliver appropriate tourism awareness information, especially to villages where tourism is already being developed Ensure formal tourism training is readily accessible to young people, women and those living in rural areas Ensure sustainable tourism practices are an integral element in all formal tourism education

continued

Box 10.4. *Continued.*

Key issues	Objectives	Sub-objectives
8. Respect for the *fa'aSamoa*	Foster respect for the *fa'aSamoa* in all activities	Develop tourism activities which provide opportunities for learning about the *fa'aSamoa*
		Identify and address potential conflicts between tourism and the *fa'aSamoa*
9. Participation in arts and crafts	Encourage and promote widespread participation and skills in performing arts, crafts and other cultural practices	Take steps to maintain and rejuvenate traditional performing arts and other cultural practices
		Support the development of high-quality crafts as well as their potential for income-generation
10. Tourism facilities and services	Improve the quality of the tourist experience through the upgrading of tourist attraction sites, facilities and services	Support efforts to enhance the quality of tourist attractions, particularly those of historical and cultural significance
		Seek to upgrade the quality of tourist facilities and services
11. Planning and development of tourism	Ensure tourism development is carefully planned and of a scale and form compatible with the natural and cultural environment	Ensure national-level tourism planning and policy is environmentally and culturally appropriate, carefully implemented and monitored, and developed in partnership with stakeholder groups
		Evaluate all applications for new tourism development in terms of their environmental and cultural compatibility
		Take special care to safeguard critical natural and historic landscapes from inappropriate development
12. Sustainable tourism awareness and practices	Enhance awareness and adoption of sustainable tourism principles and practices	Enhance the awareness and commitment of government departments and NGOs to sustainable tourism
		Encourage and support the tourism private sector to employ sustainable tourism practices and technologies in their businesses

The aim of the brainstorming process was to think up four or five poss-ible indicators to measure progress towards each of the objectives. Mem-bers first brainstormed the indicators in small groups and, later the whole PAC group met to discuss and decide on the working list of indicators that would go for further screening. The brainstorming was kick-started with the review of secondary sources on indicators, which provided a base list of 32 possible indicators that PAC members then reviewed, added to and changed. As a result of this process, most indicators identified during the literature review were heavily edited or rejected and others were suggested that were more appropriate to the issues facing Samoa (Twining-Ward and Tuailemafua, 2004). A total of 279 indicators were considered during PAC discussions across the four areas of the project, but only 57 were recom-mended by PAC members for further screening.

Armed with a list of potential indicators, the next important task was to screen the indicators to assess whether they were likely to be measurable, and suited to the circumstances in Samoa, and, by rejecting those that were not, reduce the number of indicators to a workable set of between 12 and 24. First, a two-phase technical indicator screening was undertaken along the lines suggested in Chapter 7. All indicators were required to receive a 'yes' for questions 1–6 and at least two out of four 'yes' answers for ques-tions 7–10. Those that did not meet this criterion were eliminated (Box 10.5).

Eighteen of the 57 short-listed indicators were rejected completely during the technical screening process, and a further four indicators rejected after some further research, leaving a final list of 35 indicators to be tested for their appeal and interest to stakeholders in Samoa. For this task, the original key informants with the addition of a number of tourism industry members were provided with a scaled questionnaire on which they could indicate on a Likert scale of 1–5, the extent to which they agreed or disagreed with the use of a particular indicator. In making their decisions, respondents were asked to consider whether they regarded the indicator as interesting, clear and useful in the management of sustainable tourism in Samoa. They were also given the opportunity to make any additional comments or suggestions for improving the indicator list. As a result of this process, 24 indicators were selected and approved by the PAC at a meeting held on 14 September 1999. The realities of the piloting process, discussed below, resulted in four more indicators being dropped such as rural tour-ism employment and tourism businesses located outside of Apia. The final 20 indicators are shown in Box 10.6.

Review of the indicators above show that there was much greater emphasis given to environmental than economic monitoring in Samoa. Each of the four environmental key issues was allocated two indicators, one with a general sustainable development focus, and one with more of a tour-ism focus. This was because there was very little existing information on the relationship between tourism and the environment in Samoa, and also

---

Box 10.5.   Technical screening questions used for Samoa's indicators.

1. Is the indicator clearly focused on the corresponding objective?
2. Is the proposed data collection method likely to produce reliable and objective data?
3. Is the data collection feasible in terms of both human and financial resources of SVB?
4. Is the indicator likely to be useful over a number of years?
5. Is it clear which direction of change is designated as acceptable?
6. Does the indicator have national relevance?
7. Do historical data exist for this indicator?
8. Does the indicator use secondary as opposed to primary data?
9. Does the proposed data collection method involve the participation of agencies and individuals other than STA?
10. Is the indicator simple to calculate and easy to understand?

---

because there was some uncertainty about which indicators would prove the most useful. Similarly with the social and cultural indicators, the PAC was not entirely confident with the choice of indicators so it was felt better to have a few more with the idea that the list could be reduced to a core of 15–16 following the piloting or first round of monitoring.

Moving from indicator identification to monitoring requires a series of steps as outlined in Chapter 7, the most important being definition–formulation, data collection and data management. In order to ensure that terms used in the indicators, such as 'holidaymaker' or 'marine tourism', 'biodegradable waste' were understood in the same way each time the indicator was used, precise definitions were needed. Some of these were technical in nature such as 'safe water' defined as 'World Health Organization (WHO) standard requirements for microbiology, $1/100$ *E. coli* of Total Coliform'. By contrast, non-technical terms were defined in a Samoan context, e.g. a holidaymaker was a 'visitor who checks the box "pleasure" on their arrival card, as the main purpose of their visit to Samoa'.

In the collection of data, each indicator became a mini research project in its own right. For the indicators relying on secondary information, official letters requesting the necessary information were sent to relevant government departments, and then followed up in person. For the primary data collection, a survey of 25 accommodation facilities, 21 tour operators, 20 attraction sites and three craft markets was conducted. The first two of these activities were conducted using telephone interviews, the attraction site inspection was undertaken by a PAC survey team using a standardized evaluation sheet, and the craft market survey was a manual counting exercise conducted by the researcher.

Data management involved two main undertakings, an indicator database and the writing of a manual of monitoring techniques. The database had to be simple enough to be managed by non-specialists and quick to

---

Box 10.6. Final list of Samoa's sustainable tourism indicators.

Environment	**1.** % of villages important to tourism participating in land and forest conservation programme
	2. % of all holidaymakers to Samoa going on nature tours
	3. % of coastal villages important to tourism participating in marine conservation programmes
	4. % of all holidaymakers to Samoa taking part in marine tourism activities
	5. % of tourist accommodation facilities using secondary or tertiary wastewater treatment systems
	6. % of tourist accommodation facilities recycling their biodegradable wastes
	7. % of villages important to tourism in the Samoan Water Authority (SWA) sampling programme, whose water meets SWA quality standards
	8. Average volume of water used per guest night in hotels with water meters
Economy	**9.** % of full-time jobs in tourist accommodation facilities that are located in rural areas
	10. % of newly registered tourism businesses, compared to other newly registered businesses
	11. % of GDP generated by tourism businesses
Society and culture	**12.** % of villages important to tourism included in tourism awareness programmes
	13. % of full-time tourist accommodation employees who have been on training courses during the year
	14. % of hotels and tour operators consistently providing visitors with information about village protocol
	15. % of traditional events in the Teuila and Independence Festivals programmes
	16. % of stalls in the three main markets selling handicrafts as the main product
Tourism	**17.** % of the top 20 most visited attraction sites rated either good or excellent in terms of their services, facilities and environment
	18. % of newly registered tourist accommodation facilities that have had an environmental assessment conducted
	19. % of key tourist sites and landscapes damaged by inappropriate developments (on a cumulative basis)
	20. % of tourism operators adopting sustainable tourism practices

---

update. Based on the advice of Marion (1991), the following information was included in the Samoa indicator database:

- Indicator descriptor – summarized indicator wording (i.e. hotel wastewater treatment);
- Precise indicator wording and necessary definitions;

- Data collection technique – step-by-step instructions of how data should be collected;
- Data set – the whole population for the particular indicator (where feasible, otherwise list of those sampled);
- Sample size – actual number from the data set for which data was available (expressed as a percentage of the whole data set);
- Results – percentage of the sample size with the desired characteristics (in this case secondary or tertiary wastewater systems).

As part of this process, a manual of monitoring techniques was drawn up, detailing the procedure for collecting data on each indicator and including questionnaires to be used and evaluation sheets. A shorter form of the manual was later published as an indicator handbook (Twining-Ward, 2003), designed to assist other small island countries in the Pacific to develop sustainable tourism indicators.

Results of Samoa monitoring

In order to assist STA to interpret indicator data, based on the TOMM experience discussed in the previous chapter, the PAC decided to identify 'acceptable ranges' for each indicator. An acceptable range represents what is considered a 'desirable performance' from a particular indicator, e.g. 60–80% of hotels composting biodegradable waste was identified as the acceptable range for indicator 6, so based on this yardstick the indicator result of 76% was rated 'acceptable'.

The ranges were decided on the basis of baseline results, expert opinion and information from other areas where similar indicators have been monitored. They were a compromise between the ideal state (in most cases 100%) and what is a realistic target given the current baseline. The acceptable ranges for each of the indicators are shown in Box 10.7.

As shown in Box 10.7, just one of the 20 indicators achieved a result that was better than the acceptable range (the number of tourism operators informing guests about cultural protocol, 72%). Eight of the indicators gave results that fell inside the acceptable range. Of these, the proportion of hotels composting their organic waste scored the highest – 76% (although rural hotels did a lot better than urban hotels in this respect; Twining-Ward and Tuailemafua, 2004). Of the 11 'poor' indicator results, the most critical was that only 8% of sampled accommodation facilities were found to be using secondary or tertiary wastewater treatment. This is of particular concern given the number of hotels located in low-lying areas of Apia and in the coastal zone where the danger of ground water pollution through flooding and seepage from septic tanks is at its highest. Another related area of concern is water quality. As only half the villages important for tourism have safe drinking water, there is a real health risk to both tourists and local residents. Even a few cases of water-borne disease, if reported

Box 10.7. Results of Samoa indicator monitoring 2000.

	Result	Acceptable range	Performance
Environmental sustainable tourism indicators			
Tourism village participation in land conservation	26%	50–75%	Poor
Tourist participation in nature tourism	8%	20–40%	Poor
Tourism village participation in marine protection	42%	50–75%	Poor
Tourist participation in marine tourism	23%	20–40%	Acceptable
Hotels using secondary or tertiary sewage treatment	8%	30–50%	Poor
Hotels composting their biodegradable waste	76%	60–80%	Acceptable
Tourism sites passing SWA water quality tests	50%	70–90%	Poor
Water usage per guest night in hotels (in litres)	928*	500–1000	Acceptable
Economic sustainable tourism indicators			
Proportion of hotel jobs in rural areas	48%	40–60%	Acceptable
Proportion of new businesses focused on tourism	4%	10–20%	Poor
Contribution of direct tourism businesses to GDP	4%*	10–20%	Poor
Social and cultural sustainable tourism indicators			
Villages included in tourism awareness programmes	28%	25–50%	Acceptable
Hotel staff going on training courses	27%	25–50%	Acceptable
Tourism operators informing tourists about village protocol	72%	50–70%	Good
Proportion of traditional events in Tourism Festivals	50%	50–70%	Acceptable
Proportion of handicraft stalls in the markets	21%	20–40%	Acceptable
Sustainable tourism indicators			
Evaluation of quality of key tourist attraction sites	35%	60–80%	Poor
New hotels undertaking environmental assessment	33%	90–100%	Poor
Tourist landscapes under threat from development	20%	0–5%	Poor
Tourism operators using sustainable tourism practices	48%	60–80%	Poor

*These are data from 1999, not 2000.

by the international media, could seriously damage Samoa's image as a safe
and family-friendly destination (Twining-Ward and Butler, 2002).

Improvements were also found to be urgently needed at attraction
sites, as 20% were considered by tour operators to have deteriorated during
the year and only 35% scored a 'good' or 'excellent' rating on the SVB
attraction evaluation form. The number of tourists participating in nature
tourism (8%) was also found to be very low, and given the need to provide
nearby villages with a financial incentive to continue conserving their natural resources, further work is need to make these areas more accessible and
tourist-friendly.

When analysed in terms of the four project themes (economy, environment, society and culture, and tourism), none of the tourism sector indicator results were inside the acceptable range, whereas all the results from the
social and cultural indicators were rated either 'acceptable' or 'good', and
three of the eight environmental indicators were rated 'acceptable'. Of the
economic indicators, two were rated 'poor' and one 'acceptable'. Without
more longitudinal data, it is difficult to analyse the results in much greater
depth than has been attempted above, but with more than half of all the
indicators showing 'poor' results, and many of those rated as 'acceptable' at
the bottom of their acceptable ranges, it is apparent that improvements are
needed.

To make these improvements, monitoring needs to be closely linked to
action (see Chapter 7). The challenge in Samoa was to ensure poor indicator results triggered appropriate action on the ground. This was achieved
using a six-phase implementation framework similar to those discussed in
Chapter 7. This is shown in Fig. 10.5.

- Phase 1 involved monitoring the indicators and inputting the results
  into the indicator database.
- Phase 2 involved comparing results with acceptable ranges and divid-
  ing the indicators into three groups according to how they performed
  (poor, acceptable, good).
- Phase 3 required research into possible causes of poor performance. Three questions were investigated: Have the data been
  properly collected? Have there been any significant changes in the
  data set or sample size? What external factors, if any, have affected
  the indicator?
- Phase 4 involved deciding on the appropriate management responses
  to address areas of poor performance. The indicator handbook
  included a list of potential actions to adopt for each indicator should it
  show an unacceptable or unexpected result.
- Phase 5 was to prioritize and publicize the indicator results and action
  projects in an effort to attract funding. This was achieved in the form of
  a status report detailing indicators results and proposed actions in a
  four-page colour newsletter (SVB, 2000c).

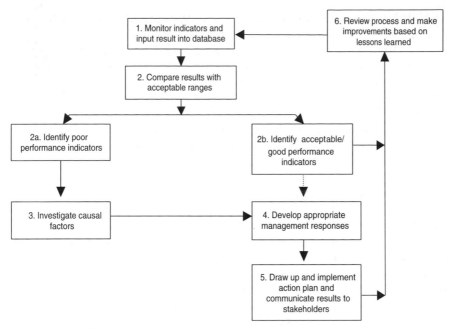

Fig. 10.5. Implementation framework.

- Phase 6 was then to review the results of implementation, re-monitor the indicators and repeat the whole cycle, adapted on the basis of lessons learned.

Evaluation and Review

Providing critical evaluation of the Samoa project when the author has been so closely involved with its development has proven challenging and the reader is encouraged to apply their own critical review of the work. The Samoa project adopted the three central pillars of sustainable tourism noted at the beginning of this book: a comprehensive sustainable development approach, a participatory methodology and the use of adaptive management. The following section considers the strengths and weaknesses of the project in terms of the process, the indicators themselves, the outcomes and current status of the work.

Process

The use of a comprehensive approach in the SSTIP is best illustrated by the interdisciplinary PAC and the broad range of key issues and corresponding objectives that were identified. Having the interdisciplinary

PAC helped the STA Authority to address tourism issues in the context of the broader social and economic situation in the country, especially important given the close inter-linkages of these elements on small islands. The Committee members came from a wide range of back-grounds and experiences and were able to keep the project in touch with its main stakeholder groups. One weakness of this arrangement was that the tourism industry was only represented by two members rather than being instrumental in the whole process. However, at the time the tourism industry associations in Samoa were not well organized or capable of carrying out such a project, whilst the STA was relatively well funded, respected and had a broader overall reach.

The use of adaptive management in the Samoa project is best illus-trated through the cyclical, learning-based approach to monitoring. Whereas most monitoring projects such as the WTO system discussed in Chapter 8 tend to focus on indicator development *per se*, the rather unique element of the Samoa project was that an implementation framework was incorporated in the work in order to move on from indicator results into action. This effectively converts a simple information generating process to an adaptive learning cycle incorporating four elements, monitoring–analysis–adaptation–improvement. Nevertheless, linking information too closely to action also has its share of difficulties. The inevitable subjectivity of acceptable ranges leaves the project exposed to criticism, political influ-ence and differing interpretations of results. There is also the difficulty of establishing with any degree of certainty, causal factors for particular issues as discussed extensively in Chapter 7. Furthermore, focusing too much on poorly performing indicators could result in resources being diverted from other worthwhile projects, which may have greater potential for effecting sustainability. In summary, however, the Samoa approach represents a rela-tively simple step-by-step process, which, whilst focused on Samoan reali-ties, could conceivably be adapted to suit other small islands in the region. Likely adaptations would be to ensure the methods used for stakeholder involvement are compatible with the norms and value systems in the place under study, and that the study boundaries are appropriate to the size of the destination and the level of development of its tourism industry.

Indicators

The robustness of the Samoan indicators is difficult to assess as they are place-specific and there is only one complete set of baseline data on which to base their performance. However, as with the objectives, a strength of the indicator set was their comprehensive coverage of sustainable development issues, making a public statement about the important linkages between tourism and other aspects of life in Samoa, and their logical connection with Samoa's sustainable tourism objectives. Having a comprehensive set of indicators helped STA to appreciate better the interdependence of tourism on other services and resources in the destination, and establish contacts and partnerships with a wider spectrum of stakeholders. The organization not only learned a lot about environmental, economic and cultural issues normally outside of its mandate, but also had a far greater combined effect on sustainable tourism development than would otherwise have been the case had they remained in a narrow, industry-orientated cocoon.

The benefit of developing indicators in the context of particular connections, salient components and relevant processes, was that they became truly place-specific, and allowed the Samoa project to gain much more local respect than it would have done had indicators, less pertinent to the Samoa situation, been imposed from outside. The indicators reflected issues stakeholders in Samoa saw as important and were monitored using techniques that stakeholders could understand, had the resources to undertake and capacity to manage. Conversely, the Samoa focus of the work might be conceived as a weakness by those more interested in destination comparisons. The selection of rather unconventional indicators such as the 'Proportion of traditional events in tourism festivals' meant that probably initially, such new indicators risked losing credibility and resonance with those tourism industry players who still conceive tourism in narrow sector-specific terms.

Outcomes

Another way of evaluating monitoring systems is on the basis of whether or not the information generated has actually been useful. The fact that this type of evaluation has not yet taken place in the WTO work was seen as a major weakness in Chapter 8. For the Samoa Project, tangible outcomes were always a main strength of the approach with the emphasis not so much on what the indicators or results were, but on how they could be used to enhance the sustainability of tourism in Samoa.

The implementation framework identified ten priority areas for action, seven of which have since been completed. A workshop has been held for conservation area managers, National Beautification Committee inspection procedures improved, and a new attraction site information brochure produced for tourists. A training manual for both tour guides and attraction site managers has also been developed, a workshop held for hoteliers on sustainable tourism practices, and a committee formed concerning the economic monitoring of tourism (Twining-Ward and Butler, 2002). The sustainable tourism objectives have also been put to a number of uses, appearing in the STA corporate plan (SVB, 2000b), the Government's Economic Strategy (Government of Samoa, 2002) and guiding the vision and impact management aspects of the 2002–2006 Samoa Tourism Development Plan.

Current status

Despite all the work that went into the SSTIP during 1999 and 2000, the project is currently in limbo with little progress having been made since the completion of the first round of monitoring. The reasons why this is the case are likely related to changes in personnel in STA, loss of momentum as a result of the new tourism plan and the loss of the original project driver. These factors are explained here followed by some suggested solutions.

Over the period 2000–2003, considerable organizational change took place in STA involving new management, a reduction in budget and a new tourism plan. In this reshuffle process, all three of the STA managers involved in the monitoring project moved on to jobs elsewhere, resulting in considerable loss of capacity and institutional memory. The change in leadership led to a U-turn in STA priorities and this, combined with a 10% reduction in the total budget, meant the indicator project has understandably ended up fairly far down the list of management priorities. The development of the Samoa Tourism Development Plan 2002–2006, although clearly demonstrating the use of indicator results, engaged STA to such an extent over the period 2001–2002 that all other projects had to be set aside and the monitoring has yet to be resumed.

The departure of the author, who had been the principal driver for the project, has been an additional setback. Despite considerable time and effort spent on building capacity of STA to take on the monitoring role, personnel changes continually thwarted attempts to transfer project ownership, and to escape from the perception, on the part of critics, that the project was externally conceived and driven.

Lessons Learned

One of the principal lessons learned was that if monitoring is going to be maintained over time it needs to become an integral part of the planning process. In the case of Samoa, explicit objectives were formulated but have so far failed to be internalized, perhaps because they did not sufficiently engage the STA as an organization. As a result, the monitoring appears externally conceived, an add-on to the activities of the planning division, and an item that may be easily cut when resources and expertise are limited. Baumard's (1999) explanation of tacit versus explicit knowledge sheds light on this problem. According to Baurmand, tacit knowledge (knowledge internal to the organization) is much more resistant to change than explicit knowledge, and he suggests the more people that have this tacit knowledge, the stronger the resistance will be to change. In order to ensure monitoring is fully incorporated in an organization's activities, therefore, a deeper type of capacity building may be necessary, more like an organizational learning, that will need to come from within the organization itself.

The second lesson learned from the Samoa project was the importance of effective communication. Although the Samoa project produced a Status Report, it did not make as much use of the local newspapers, schools, industry association meetings and Internet communication as it might have done. Given the need to differentiate the tourism product offered from other island neighbours, information on the monitoring programme could also have been used as a marketing tool. Generating public interest in the monitoring process can help create a demand for the data and the impetus to continue monitoring. If industry stakeholders are used to receiving updated reports on sustainability every 6 months, they begin to expect these and complain when they cease. The Kangaroo Island TOMM project reported in the previous chapter is a good example of how communication with local government, educational institutions and the international community can help further the aims of the project. Similar processes in Samoa would likely help further the project.

The third issue highlighted here is the importance of maximizing tourism industry participation in the monitoring of sustainable tourism. In 1999, the tourism industry associations in Samoa were not well developed and consequently industry only played a minor part in the PAC. Times have changed in Samoa, and were the project to be renewed, a much closer linkage between the industry and the monitoring project would now be possible. Not only would this help build capacity and understanding of sustainable tourism in the tourism industry but it would also assist in moving the project more towards a self-regulating type approach.

Fourthly, the issue of external project drivers is one to be reconsidered. Project drivers are essential but can also make the project vulnerable if too much knowledge is concentrated with one or two individuals as was the case both in Samoa and the TOMM project on Kangaroo Island (Chapter 9). In order to avoid this situation, TOMM suggests recognizing signs of burnout and providing support in advance, as well as acknowledging the achievements of those involved. Lessons from the Samoa project are to spread the load and ensure external project facilitators are partnered with suitable long-term local counterparts.

In this context, it is useful to reflect on how the principles of adaptive management explained in Chapter 1 might assist the project to move on from the current impasse. Holling's adaptive cycle (Fig. 1.2) suggests how systems can get so over-connected that one small change (in this case perhaps the organizational reshuffle in STA or loss of the project driver) can tip the balance and result in a new and different cycle. Rather than trying to ignore, avoid or prevent such inevitable change, Holling (2001) recommends that efforts are made to learn from the experience and as a result build monitoring systems that will be more resilient next time around. People will always move on and organizations will change so perhaps an important lesson to learn is to spread the load, expect change and adapt to it. Stakeholders must learn to operate in a context of non-linearity, with the expectation of a transition towards sustainability even if such a universal change of viewpoint may take decades to implement. A slow, step-by-step series of changes over a number of years is the best that can be expected in terms of new knowledge being absorbed. Adopting this learning-based adaptive management approach presents a real opportunity for the SSTIP, one that when current constraints are removed, the project can re-emerge, stronger for the passing of time and experience, better integrated into the STA planning process. The next iteration should emerge with improved communication, greater industry participation and organizational under-standing of how to manage the complex Samoa tourism system.

Summary

This chapter has examined the role of indicator development and use in the sustainable development of tourism in a small island country in the South Pacific. The chapter started by outlining the context of tourism in the South Pacific, looking at the geographical and economic circumstances that make reliance on tourism one of the few development options for many countries in the region. Given the ecological and cultural vulnerabili-ties of small islands, sustainability is very much at the forefront of many of their tourism policies but there are still few tools to assist small island coun-tries make progress on this front. The SSTIP was conceived with this prob-lem in mind: to see how indicators could be developed in a small island context and whether they would be useful tools in the journey towards greater sustainability.

The case study has revealed that the process of developing indicators can be an enlightening one, particularly if a comprehensive approach to sustainable development is adopted and a wide range of stakeholders are involved. Indicator results can help with tourism planning as well as the development and funding of sustainable tourism action projects, by provid-ing a clear justification for why a particular project is being targeted (based on a poor indicator result). The indicators themselves and development systems are likely to become more sophisticated over time as experience increases and there is greater documentation of what does and does not work and improved applications of technology for monitoring. This will enable greater confidence in the process, the integration of monitoring within tourism and planning systems and a much shorter lead-time between project initiation and the system being up and running.

The long-term monitoring of the indicators will always be a challenge open to the unpredictable nature of the complex tourism system. Funding priorities change, as do project personnel. Increasing the number of groups which take ownership and an active stake in the work would seem to increase the project's chances of long-term survival, as would widely communicating and publicizing the project.

The case study showed that if a suitable implementation framework is put in place a clear connection can be made between indicator results and sustainable tourism practice. It has also demonstrated how the process of establishing key issues and objectives for sustainable tourism can be an important learning experience for all involved from which numerous spin offs are possible. The Samoa project was novel and experimental in a number of ways and consequently had very few projects on which to base its planning and design. Given these experiences and lessons learned, further application of the lessons learned here and elsewhere is needed so that the task of identifying appropriate indicators and developing monitoring systems becomes progressively easier over time.

The Tour Operators' Initiative for Sustainable Development

11

Introduction

Tour operators have long been regarded as the weakest link in sustainable tourism stewardship, often claiming that they do not have direct impacts outside their office and brochure production, and instead that it is their suppliers who are responsible for the impacts (Carey *et al.*, 1997; Curtin and Busby, 1999; Aronsson, 2000; Gordon, 2001a; Klemm and Parkinson, 2001). Tour operators have also claimed that they are market-driven organizations that only respond to sustainability requirements when there is a competitive advantage linked to it. Adventure and ecotourism have been seen to be the first segments to rise to the challenge/opportunity of corporate understandings of sustainability, albeit often exploiting the destination's resources rather than preserving them (Cater and Lowman, 1994; Engeldrum *et al.*, 1998; Hall and Lew, 1998b; Neil and Wearing, 1999).

Against this backdrop, this chapter reviews the progress and reflects on the challenges of promoting corporate environmental and social responsibility amongst tour operators, through the efforts made by the Tour Operators' Initiative for Sustainable Tourism Development (TOI). The TOI is a network of tour operators who seek to improve their environmental performance and to incorporate sustainable development principles in their business operations. The TOI was created in response to a growing awareness on the part of some more proactive tour operators that their success depends on a clean and safe environment.

The TOI members recognize that tour operators play a central role in the tourism industry. As intermediaries between tourists and tourism service providers, tour operators can influence consumers' choice, the practices of suppliers and the development patterns in tourism destinations. This unique role means that tour operators can make an important contribution to furthering the goals of sustainable tourism development, protecting the environmental and cultural resources on which the tourism industry depends for its survival and growth. This is not new knowledge; what is new is to hear a group of tour operators acknowledging this position and then working towards these goals. While there is increasing evidence of good practice in the tourism industry, this has not been widely adopted across the sector as relatively few tour operators have had the management tools or experience to design and conduct tours that promote sustainable tourism (Hawkes and Williams, 1992; Gordon, 2001b; Tapper, 2001). Some of the large operators involved in the TOI have previously demonstrated that they can improve their sustainability records and enhance their overall businesses (see Luck, 2002, for examples of the two largest German operators TUI and LTU; and Mowforth and Munt, 1998, for British Airways Holidays and Thomson Holidays). Yet, through the TOI, all members now aim to develop and use these tools in their own operations, and encourage other tour operators to do the same.

Background to the Scheme

The TOI was formally launched in March 2000, following nearly 2 years of preparations involving the founder members. The Initiative is voluntary, non-profit, and open to all tour operators, regardless of their size and geographical location. As of August 2004, it brings together 25 tour operators, including the Initiative's founder members – TUI Group, TUI Northern Europe, LTU Touristik, VASCO, First Choice, British Airways Holidays, Aurinkomatkat-Suntours, and Hotelplan. The TOI is supported by the UNEP, UNESCO and the WTO. The goals of the Initiative are to share information, demonstrate best practices, and raise awareness of environmental and social issues that affect the tourism industry. With this Initiative, tour operators are committing themselves to working with others through common activities to promote and disseminate methods and practices compatible with sustainable development (Box 11.1).

To integrate sustainability into their businesses, tour operators need to consider environmental, social and economic aspects at all stages of the process of developing a holiday package. There are many previous experiences of individual tour operators working for sustainability; yet one of the challenges remains to attain compliance with sustainability guidelines throughout the sector (Sirakaya, 1997; Sirakaya and Uysall, 1997; Sirakaya and McLellan, 1998). The emphasis in this chapter is how tour operators as a sector have mapped out the key areas where they have impacts, developed indicators to reflect their sustainability, and are making progress to report on their attempts to be more sustainable. While each company has an

Box 11.1. The Tour Operators' Initiative approach to sustainability.

The TOI's mission is:

- To advance the sustainable development and management of tourism; and
- To encourage tour operators to make a corporate commitment to sustainable development.

The Initiative addresses ways to decrease negative impacts on the environment, culture and communities in tourism destinations, and to generate benefits for local communities and the environment, through the design and operation of tours and the conduct of tour operators' business activities. Members of the Initiative should strive to adopt best practices in their internal operations, their supply chain, and at destinations. Among the ways to do this are:

- Making exchange of information easier;
- Developing new management tools and adapting existing ones to the industry; and
- Providing a forum for dialogue with other partners.

Members will assess progress on a regular basis and create partnerships to address common issues. Broadening support for sustainable development among other players in the tourism sector, including tourists involves:

- Cooperating with business partners, regional and national governments, NGOs and other groups with a common agenda on specific activities and projects; and
- Working to increase awareness among tourists, other segments of the tourism industry, and local communities and people.

The TOI is also dedicated to establishing a critical mass of committed tour operators through:

- Increasing the visibility of committed tour operators and creating an image of the Initiative as a world leader in the area of environmentally, socially and culturally responsible tourism;
- Increasing the membership of the Initiative; and
- Establishing partnerships with other organizations that contribute to achievement of these objectives and strengthening links with regions through tour operators' associations and the UNEP, UNESCO and WTO networks.

individual responsibility to address the challenges of sustainability, sectoral approaches and tools can effectively complement the efforts of individual companies and create synergies throughout the industry. One of the major achievements of the TOI is the development of the tour operators' performance indicators, which supplement the 2002 Global Reporting Index (GRI) Sustainability Reporting Guidelines. The GRI is a cross-industry international framework to standardize corporate reporting accounts and raise their quality and rigour to the level of financial accounts (Ranganathan and Willis, 1999; Sustainability and UNEP, 2000; GRI, 2002; Line *et al.*, 2002; Waddell, 2002; Willis, 2003). The tour operators' supplement to the GRI framework is the result of a 9-month process that included numerous meetings and online exchanges with UNEP (acting as the TOI Secretariat) with the GRI acting as facilitators, and the active participation of stakeholders deemed relevant by the tour operators and the secretariat.

The members of the TOI agreed that the best way forward was to develop a 'sector-specific supplement' to the GRI's core sustainability reporting performance indicators (these are included in the GRI Sustainability Reporting Guidelines), that apply to all industry sectors. The development of the tour operators' sector-specific performance indicators had to take into account three main considerations. First, the supplemental indicators had to complement the performance indicators contained in the existing 2002 guidelines. Therefore, the supplement aimed to capture issues that were either essential components of sustainability unique to tour operators, or relevant to numerous sectors, but of critical importance to tour operators' sustainability performance. The second consideration was the recognition of the 'middle-man' role of tour operators in the tourism industry. As tour operators do not deliver services or produce physical products, clearly defining the boundaries of responsibility was considered a necessary first step in the process. The third consideration was that the lack of examples of sustainability reports in the sector meant that the performance indicators could not be based on existing practices.

A Multi-Stakeholder Working Group on Sustainability Reporting was created to develop a common framework for sustainability reporting guidelines for the tour operator's sector, within the context of the GRI. Not only is it a GRI requirement that a multi-stakeholder Working Group needs to be created, but the GRI has strict requirements on how Working Groups are to be set up and run, including requiring them to be co-chaired with one industry and one civil society co-chairpersons, and to include representatives of all major groups relevant to the sector for which guidelines are being developed. The Working Group comprised not only selected members of the TOI (11 outbound and two inbound tour operators) but also representatives of other major groups relevant to the tour operator's sector, such as NGOs (four), trade unions (one), hotels (three), cruise lines (one), airlines (one) and local authorities (two). Within the private tourism sector, representatives from a range of different types of tourism businesses were included in the Working Group to reflect differences in their size, type of holiday packages offered (and hence type of customers) and destinations served, all of which are important factors in influencing the ways in which these different businesses operate. Overall, the Working Group had a total 30 members, and was coordinated by UNEP and the GRI, supported by two consultants.

The Multi-Stakeholder Working Group held three consultation meetings of 2 days each, in November 2001, and February and April 2002. During the first meeting, Working Group members focused on identifying (using a 'gap analysis') the sustainability issues specific to the tour operators' sector that were not sufficiently addressed by the core GRI Sustainability Reporting Guidelines. Based on this, a first draft of tour operator-specific indicators was developed. This draft was further discussed and developed during the second and third meetings of the Working Group, leading to the production of revised drafts after each meeting. Comments were also sought from other organizations and individuals, utilizing the TOI website to post drafts following the first and second Working Group meetings, as well as sending drafts electronically to key organizations. All comments received were circulated among the members of the Multi-Stakeholder Working Group as well as posted on the website. The Working Group agreed at its third meeting to submit the final draft that it produced to the GRI Board of Directors for approval; this was completed in May 2002. In November 2002, the GRI published the Tour Operators' Sector Supplement for use with the GRI 2002 Sustainability Reporting Guidelines. The resulting indicators are designed to demonstrate how tour operators have performed in putting their vision and strategy for sustainable development into practice.

The rest of this chapter discusses the indicators chosen and reporting approach developed in relation to the key operating areas where tour-operating companies can integrate sustainability into their operations. This achieves two purposes, first to present the agenda that tour operators have set themselves to move towards more sustainable tourism, and second to reflect on the many challenges for tour operators to both manage this agenda and report on the outcomes.

Development of the Scheme

The performance indicators themselves are grouped under generic GRI 2002 indicators, and supplemented by tour operator-specific indicators. The Tour Operators' Sector Supplement includes 57 indicators exclusively relevant to tour operators, in addition to the 97 core GRI 2002 indicators, grouped under environment, social and economic performance. It is important to note that the measures developed for these areas under the GRI guidelines cover both quantitative and qualitative measures, and address both performances achieved and the processes, such as management and monitoring systems, that are necessary for delivery of improved sustainability performance. The Working Group felt that the quantitative indicators would enable the GRI guidelines to cover actual results achieved, whilst the qualitative indicators would allow for recognition of other pro-sustainability actions taken by suppliers that were not suitable for quantitative comparisons. Similarly, the group also decided that it was important to have indicators of the processes in place to monitor for continuous improvements in sustainability performance. The five areas under which the TOI divides its 57 indicators are:

- Product development and management – planning tours and selecting holiday package components that minimize environmental, economic and social impacts;
- Internal management – taking into account sustainability principles in the management of human resources, office supplies and production of printed materials;
- Contracting with suppliers – integrating sustainability principles into the selection criteria and service agreements of suppliers;
- Customer relations – guaranteeing privacy, health and safety standards, and providing customers with information on responsible behaviour and sustainability issues at their destinations;
- Relations with destinations – supporting destination stakeholders' efforts to address sustainability issues and financially contributing to conservation and development projects.

Product management and development

Product management and development includes a range of indicators relating to the choice of the destination as well as the type of services. These indicators are grouped here under destination framing, destination selection process, understanding the impacts on holiday products and changing the design of holiday products. The actual indicators recommended for reporting by the TOI under this heading are presented in Box 11.2.

Destination framing requires each tour operator to report on how they define the geographical unit considered as destination (country, region, city/town, municipality) and the services included in a holiday package. Reporting on the percentage of business in the destination shows how important the destination is to the operator, while reporting on the market share shows how important the tour operator is to the destination. In justifying the *destination selection process*, tour operators are expected to illustrate the sustainability principles taken into account in the selection and/or de-selection of destinations. Policies can be generic or specific, varying according to the type of packages and the destinations, to take into account specific needs and impacts. The policies could refer to choosing destinations with good environmental and social management records (or the avoidance of destinations where it is evident there is uncontrolled growth or impacts).

A tour operator's performance is also linked to how far the company invests in *understanding the impacts on the visited destinations*. Performance in this aspect is related not only to the issues for which information is gathered, but also to the methods that are employed to gather that information. In particular, the indicators focus on issues identified, percentage of destinations for which information has been gathered, source of the information and how often the information is reviewed. Tour operators must also demonstrate that they understand their impacts at the destination level. One

Box 11.2.   Product management and development (PMD) indicators.

PMD1   Indicate percentage of reporting organization's business (by passengers carried) and market share in operating destinations

PMD2   Describe policies on selecting, developing and deselecting destinations based on environmental, social and economic issues

PMD3   Describe key environmental, economic and social issues identified in destinations and types of information gathered

PMD4   Indicate percentage of destinations in which organizations operate for which issues (PMD3) have been identified, and percentage of reporting organization's business this represents (by passengers carried)

PMD5   Describe types of approaches taken in gathering information (PMD3) and rationale for applying an approach to a given destination

PMD6   Indicate length of time over which this information (PMD3) has been collected, and the frequency with which it is updated

PMD7   Quantify overall economic, environmental and social impacts of typical holiday products

PMD8   Describe changes in design of holiday packages and other actions to address key environmental, economic and social issues (see PMD3) of destinations

PMD9   Describe measures to maximize economic benefits to destinations

significant lesson to be learned from these indicators is recognition of the effort invested in measuring and monitoring impacts, using a mix of quantitative and qualitative indicators, generated by the various components of the holiday packages. This is considered as a key step in being able to eventually revise the design of holiday products to reduce their impact. It requires tour operators to understand the impacts, determine the level of significance of the different impacts, and concentrate on those that have the highest impact, and then identify measurement methods using a systematic methodology that can be reproduced in a variety of destinations to allow comparability. Quantification of the impacts is shown to be a complex exercise, and the process will need to be progressive. It is expected that in the initial period of reporting each operator will test a range of methods until they identify the most suitable for their products, consider the use of already-published sources of data, undertake staff training on the methods or organize the subcontracting of the measurement of the impacts. The range of impacts that could be measured is vast and part of this process will also include selecting significant and prioritized impacts that can be used as totemic indicators of the tour operators' pursuit of sustainability at the destination level.

A further important part of reporting involves showing how the operator is *changing the design of holiday products*, on the basis of information collected on impacts. Understanding and quantifying the impacts of holiday products provides evidence for assessing the 'level of sustainability' of the current holiday products, and moreover enables considering alternatives that can reduce negative impacts and maximize the positive benefits of each holiday overall. The corporate social report should extend to highlighting the changes made to their holiday products, and specifically highlighting the measures designed to maximize the economic benefits to destinations. It is expected this will include accounting for the choices available for a particular holiday component, the methods used to consider the impact of each alternative and the rationale for the choice made.

Internal management

The second aspect of tour operators reporting is internal management. This covers all the operations and activities that take place in the headquarters or country offices such as the use of office supplies, production of brochures and direct employment. The GRI 2002 Guidelines have an extensive set of indicators at this level as they began life as an index for the manufacturing industries, and these are organized around the three principal pillars (economic, environmental and social) of sustainability. The indicators from the tour operator supplement to the GRI are shown in Box 11.3.

Economic impacts are generally covered through traditional financial indicators that assess the profitability of an organization and are used to communicate this information primarily to management, shareholders, and the wider investment community. These data are important to present a broad picture of the size and structure of the tour operator and can be used to demonstrate the financial benefit of tourism to the destination.

The GRI provides an exhaustive list of *environmental indicators* to measure performance on areas of direct responsibility for the tour operators. As the GRI have been developed with the manufacturing industries in mind, their guidelines provide templates for energy and water protocol. Tour operators' indicators address the environmental issues associated with promotional materials and customer documentation and the policies in place to minimize impacts in these areas. Firms are encouraged to have policies, take actions and keep evidence of reducing environmental impacts. In particular, they are invited to report on their policies related to the production, distribution and use of promotional material and customer documentation; quantify the total use of paper by type and environmental quality; and the proportion of material that is certified to an environmental standard. In addition to the production phase, reporting tour operators are also asked to report on both their policies for reusing and recycling the above mentioned documents, and on the percentage of travel agents that tour operators have successfully involved in implementation of reuse and recycling programmes.

Social performance issues are mainly covered through general GRI indicators, sorted by a number of GRI technical protocols that are available on the GRI website (http://www.globalreporting.org). The indicators for tour

---

Box 11.3. Internal management (IM) indicators.

IM1 Provide evidence of recruiting local residents (including destination nationals) for destination posts including management positions

IM2 Describe existence of policies and programmes to address the physical and mental well-being of staff at headquarters and destinations

IM3 Describe types and mechanisms of training on environmental, social and economic issues by category of employee

IM4 Describe policies and actions in place to accommodate cultural customs, traditions and practices of staff throughout the organization

IM5 Describe policies to minimize the environmental impacts associated with the production, distribution and use of promotional materials and customer documentation

IM6 Indicate total quantity (tonnes or kg) of material used by type (e.g. paper, plastic) and environmental quality (e.g. recycled content), for the production of promotional materials and customer documentation

IM7 Indicate percentage of promotional materials and customer documentation that are produced in accordance with an environmental standard

IM8 Describe policies and targets for redistribution, reuse and recycling of promotional materials

IM9 Indicate percentage of total travel retailers that agree to adopt policies and practices on reuse and recycling of promotional materials

---

operators here refer to UN and International Labour Organization (ILO) conventions. For example tour operators would be expected to report on their awareness of the requirements of the ILO Declaration on Fundamental Principles and Rights at Work, 1998, and show how this is implemented in their workplace.

The complexity of reporting on all these issues should not be underestimated, since it involves tour operators in the collection and aggregation of information from their suppliers as well as internally. This requires dialogue with suppliers, as well as training, and although the amount of time this requires per supplier is relatively small, for tour operators with many suppliers, this can be a major exercise, and also requires development of internal systems to manage and collate the information that is collected. To facilitate this, the TOI is developing a series of support mechanisms to facilitate the collation of information, to provide templates that can be used for reporting, and to assist in training. For example, the TOI has prepared 10 fact sheets on key sustainability issues (biodiversity, climate change, water and waste, human rights, etc.), a module on poverty alleviation, and a training kit on environmental and social corporate responsibility for tour operators to deliver internal staff training.

Supply chain management

As intermediaries between tourists and tourism service providers, tour operators bring together a variety of tourism-related services to form a complete holiday package, which is then marketed to customers either directly or through travel agents. Each package holiday generally consists of accommodation (often including some food provision), transport both to and from the destination, ground transport within the destination, and events or activities such as excursions and social activities. As most services are provided by subcontracted companies, tour operators may often have only indirect control of the environmental and social impacts of their holidays. Despite this, consumers expect the tour-operating companies, from which they buy their holidays, to ensure that those holidays meet certain standards in addition to offering quality and value for money. Miller (2003) demonstrates the growing willingness of UK tourists to pressure their tour operator to ensure action on some environmental and social issues. Pressure is also likely to come from insurance companies and financial institutions, as discussed in Chapter 3. For tour operators, who offer products comprised almost entirely of contracted goods and services, this means that effective implementation of their sustainability policies requires close working with suppliers to improve sustainability performance in all the components of a holiday throughout the life cycle of a holiday package. As Box 11.4 shows, this is the area with the greatest number of indicators, reflecting its importance and complexity.

Supply chain management addresses actions related to the selection and contracting of service providers, using the purchasing power to improve sustainability requirements, as has previously been done to improve health and safety requirements and quality. As with the two previous areas for reporting, indicators relating to supply chain management require the operator to lay out policies, identify impacts, put programmes in place, measure change and report on efforts made. The main goal is to work on product/service stewardship across the entire life cycle of the holiday package – to design packages with acceptable economic yields, lower environment and social burdens, and to be able to communicate with confidence on the sustainability profile of holiday services. In this area, the indicators are grouped under three headings; supply chain management policy, policy implementation, and continuous support.

Operators are asked to report on their *supply chain management policy*, highlighting how environmental, social and economic sustainability is integrated in the choice of suppliers. A policy is important because it states the tour operator's intent and helps to communicate it to the relevant parties, since the sustainability policy may establish certain criteria that will be taken into account when the operator contracts with its suppliers. The ability to introduce sustainability requirements in purchasing policies depends on the stability and power balance in supplier–purchaser relationships. To report on contractual agreements confidentiality could be a problem, but

Box 11.4. Supply chain management (SCM) indicators.

SCM1   Describe the supply chain management policy, objectives and targets on environmental, social, and economic performance

SCM2   Describe processes through which suppliers, by type, are consulted during development and implementation of the supply chain management policy, described in SCM1

SCM3   Describe issues identified through supplier consultation and actions to address them

SCM4   Describe processes through which suppliers, by type, are engaged in the implementation of the supply chain management policy, described in SCM1

SCM5   State joint actions taken with suppliers, by type, to support improvements in suppliers own environmental and social performance

SCM6   Describe progress in achieving objectives and targets related to supply chain policy

SCM7   Indicate percentage of suppliers, by type, subject to supply chain management policy

SCM8   Indicate percentages of suppliers, by type, subject to supply chain policy that have a published sustainability policy, implemented a sustainability management system and/or have a staff person with management responsibility for corporate sustainability

SCM9   State types of information requested from suppliers, by type

SCM10 Indicate percentage of suppliers, by type, subject to supply chain management policy that provided the requested information

SCM11 Indicate percentage of suppliers, by type, subject to supply chain management policy whose environmental, social and economic performance has been reported

SCM12 State actions taken by the reporting organization in response to suppliers' reported performance (as per SCM11), by type of suppliers

SCM13 State actions to inform suppliers of customers' requirements

SCM14 State contracting policy and how it is communicated to suppliers

SCM15 Describe joint initiatives with suppliers to improve environmental, social and economic conditions in destinations

SCM16 State benefits for the reporting organization from implementing the sustainable supply chain policy

sustainable issues are generally regarded as non-competitive, enabling suppliers to report freely on agreed terms. A good supply-chain management policy should address the nature of the businesses, such as issues associated with the selection and packaging of holiday services, and should convey a strong and clear message to suppliers on what is expected from them. Operators are encouraged to report on consultations that they may have with suppliers on writing the supplier policy, on the issues identified by suppliers and on how this consultation has informed the policy written. Suppliers' consultation can be in a variety of formats, from informal discussions to consultation through focus groups for each destination, to reviews of draft policies.

Implementation starts getting suppliers to acknowledge, assess and report on their impacts, develop systems to manage them, and make measurable improvements in key areas. The indicators are designed to measure the operators' ability on these aspects, requesting information on what mechanisms have been adopted to support integration of sustainability aspects in their suppliers' activities. These might range from adopting measures to raise suppliers' awareness about what issues are important, to assisting them from a technical perspective, to promoting the best performers and finally to contracting only with suppliers that have met set environmental, social and economic standards. It is expected that different firms will start at different levels, depending on their past history, and on the types of tourism and suppliers with which they are involved, but that there will be continuous improvement. The basis of the TOI is cooperative in helping to facilitate progress by members, and in sharing best practices. In addition, peer pressure within the group, and the public scrutiny to which the tourism sector is subject, provide strong positive momentum to the members.

Beyond the mechanisms to encourage suppliers to meet sustainability targets, TOI members need to assess how effective they are being in receiving and using information from their suppliers. This effectiveness is measured by the percentage of suppliers that have provided information on their own performance, if this information has been verified, and what actions have resulted from the tour operators' side. Quantitative data can be illustrated with examples of actions taken to enable and support their suppliers to be more sustainable.

The last step of the implementation stage is demonstrating how operators respond positively to those suppliers that are proactive towards their sustainable supply chain management measures. Noteworthy performers can be rewarded with longer contracts, more favourable prices and payment conditions, increased volumes of business, further training and education programmes, assistance with equipment upgrading and property refurbishment, and joint projects to maintain destination quality, experiences comparable to those in other sectors (Krause *et al.*, 1998). They may also choose to highlight the sustainable service providers in their holiday brochures and websites, which will give the tourists a chance to directly reward these businesses with their custom.

After implementation, *continuous development* needs to be reported across a range of supplier development activities (Krause, 1997). Here three aspects of support for suppliers are identified: communication of expectations, joint actions to improve sustainability performance and efforts to raise awareness of benefits from sustainability improvements by suppliers. Supplier development programmes are an essential part of the implementation of programmes for improved performance in accordance with an operator's expectations and policies in this area. Such programmes also have a strong pedagogic and motivational value for suppliers, backed up by an important economic incentive. While the power relation may encourage setting high targets, it is important to use the supplier development programmes to agree upon realistic objectives and targets from both a tour operator's and its suppliers' perspectives (Krause, 1999).

Supply chain management is probably the most complex of aspects for sustainability reporting, because of anti-competitive practices of tourism businesses in the originating markets including tour operators' use of power over local suppliers, demanding higher quality for lower prices, limiting the ability of small firms to negotiate their futures (Diaz-Benavides, 2001; Tapper, 2001; Bastakis *et al.*, 2004). This will need to change if suppliers are actively to engage in addressing requirements for sustainability improvements that are made by operators. Any change will also need to be accompanied by greater stability in contractual relationships, appropriate pricing and more active promotion of sustainability improvements by tour operators as a whole. Trust resulting from secure income streams, stable contracts and foreseeable contracting conditions including prices are a prerequisite (Font *et al.*, 2004).

Customer relations

The sustainability concerns in customer relations relate to the provision of information on sustainability issues and raising awareness of these issues amongst customers. This goes beyond the traditional tasks of ensuring the health, safety and data security of customers, and that the content and quality of holiday services are in accord with the way in which they are described, advertised and marketed. Health and safety *per se* are already regarded as part of mainstream quality management, and management of sustainability issues often begins by building on health and safety systems, property audits conducted during supplier selection and contracting, and other management systems that are already in place. Reporting in this area within the GRI framework is organized under the headings of awareness raising and feedback, customer health and safety, characteristics and advertising of products and services, and respect for privacy, as seen in Box 11.5.

Tour operators are expected to report on actions to *raise awareness* of sustainability with customers. Evidence in this aspect is more widely available, and usually less confidential than for other aspects such as supply chain management. These range from leaflets, notices, fact sheets and in-flight videos, to records of how sustainability elements are introduced in the welcome meetings by each destination representative. Equally the operator can keep records of how they collect feedback from visitors on sustainability issues to communicate to local authorities and service providers at the destination.

GRI indicators on *product information and labelling* translate easily and directly to holiday promotion materials. They cover policies and

---

Box 11.5.   Customer relations (CR) indicators.

CR1   Describe tools and measures used by reporting organization to raise consumers' awareness of suppliers' environmental, social and economic performance

CR2   Describe tools and measures used by reporting organization to raise the consumers' awareness of destinations' environmental, social and economic issues

CR3   Describe tools and measures used by reporting organization to raise consumers' awareness of sustainable holidaymaking

CR4   Describe means to invite customers' feedback on economic, environmental, and social issues related to the holiday product and actions taken to respond to feedback

CR5   Indicate percentage of total feedback received, related to economic, environmental and social issues

CR6   Provide evidence of consultation with destination stakeholders and suppliers on how the destination and services are portrayed to customers

CR7   Indicate number of complaints from destinations' stakeholders and holidaymakers regarding misleading and inaccurate representation of destinations

---

procedures employed to ensure that promotional material is in keeping with the characteristics of the destination, and that claims of sustainability, either self-assessed or the result of gaining sustainability labels and awards, reflect the reality of the product. In this area, there is scope to emphasize the mechanisms by which tour operators have consulted with destination stakeholders to ensure brochures and any communication campaigns reflect the realities of the destinations and products they are marketing. Various indicators can be used to measure tour operators' performance on these aspects, for example, by recording what percentage of hotels have seen the brochure pages where they feature, and agree with their contents, and the percentage of tourist offices that have seen and agreed to the description of the destination in the tourist brochures. Both the general GRI and the tour operator-specific indicators highlight the importance of reporting on the management actions taken to keep *advertising* in line with relevant legislation, and to keep records of those occasions where advertising standards might have been breached – perhaps due to poor product descriptions – and of any complaints from stakeholders in the destination. Reports on performance can also make mention of prizes, awards and labels received for sustainability in general, or for particular environment and social reasons, and the criteria that were met to receive this award.

For any private company, *customer satisfaction* is a key element of the financial viability of the business, so assessing customer satisfaction should be almost a standard procedure in tour operating to improve service quality. Mechanisms for measuring satisfaction could include the use of questionnaires, random interviews, and written feedback received on service and destination quality. There is also the choice to highlight specific efforts that tour operators make to invite feedback on environment and social aspects of the holiday experience as part of their customer satisfaction tools. Such efforts also help to promote and raise awareness of sustainability among customers.

Finally, operators are requested to report on how they *respect customer privacy*. As more and more transactions are carried out online, and electronic crimes are ever increasing, taking care in the management of their electronic databases on customers, becomes important. This includes identifying legislation on consumer privacy that is relevant to their country of operation, and describing the systems that they have in place to comply with this legislation. This data could be complemented with information on complaints received on breaches of consumers' privacy. To report on this aspect, records of complaints including litigation regarding breaching consumer privacy should be kept.

Cooperation with destinations

Cooperation with destinations is a broad subject that goes far beyond the production and delivery of a tour operator's holiday package. This allows tour operators to report on efforts made to establish partnerships, assist in community development and undertake philanthropic activities, as seen in Box 11.6.

A number of environmental and socioeconomic impacts arising from product development and management take place outside the boundaries tour operators feel directly responsible for. However, these are impacts that if addressed effectively would improve the tourist appeal of a destination or product. Reporting can therefore include the ways in which the operator engages with destination stakeholders – including local authorities, local communities and the private sector overall – to address these issues, from informing each other of impacts, to more developed, long-term partnerships. The variable nature of partnerships means that no specific reporting format is recommended, and instead tour operators should record the number of partnerships entered and the level of detail available on both the actions taken and the outcomes achieved. Specific elements of the relationship can include the policies to manage impacts on communities in areas affected by an operator's tours, policies to address the needs of indigenous people, or jointly managed community grievance mechanisms.

The reporting of the procedures and criteria for selecting projects and organizations to which *philanthropic and charitable donations* are made, helps to ensure that money is well targeted to bring change. Indicators are provided on both the overall value and scope of the philanthropic and charitable donations. In addition to reporting on the total value of funds

Box 11.6.   Cooperation with destination (D) indicators.

D1   Describe ways reporting organization engages with destination stake-
       holders to address issues, including those identified in PMD3
D2   Describe measures taken to identify and offer commercial opportunities
       and assistance to non-contracted suppliers that support community
       development
D3   Describe procedures and criteria for selecting projects and organizations
       to which philanthropic and charitable donations are made
D4   Indicate total funds (in cash and estimated value of in-kind contributions)
       for conservation and social development projects
D5   Describe programmes for philanthropic and charitable donations in
       relation to conservation and community development projects
D6   Provide evidence of benefits generated (in D4 and D5), particularly at
       destinations, in support of community development, biodiversity conser-
       vation and other social, economic and environmental improvements at
       destinations

distributed, in cash and in estimated in-kind donations, operators may also report on the sources of donations (including those made by their clients as well as by a company), on the types of projects to which funds are donated, and on the location and nature of organizations receiving the funds. There is also scope to provide further details of specific projects and the benefits that they are generating, although this will generally be qualitative data, not comparable across projects. Where organizations are supported over a number of years, written records of the benefits over time will often provide a better indication than one-off reports.

Implementation and Evaluation

This chapter has so far presented the agenda that TOI and the wider stake-holder group have set to assess sustainability performance in the tour-operating sector, in the form of the expected reporting indicators. This framework allows a company to reflect on the goals set by itself and its peers and report on progress made towards them.

In setting indicators for sustainability performance for tour operators, compromises are necessary between what is desirable and what is achievable. The GRI is a bold attempt to develop measures that contribute to achieving this, and is much more detailed than previous reporting mechanisms. Only time will tell whether the expectations and numbers of indicators are actually realistic, and in the meantime they set valuable benchmarks against which tour operators can assess they performance.

By requiring multi-stakeholder input to the development of sustainability indicators, the GRI process itself aims to ensure that the compromises are credible. The advantage of the indicators developed here is that they are the result of long-term commitment from a number of organizations that work regularly in related projects. The TOI is still young and so any evaluation may be too soon to fairly judge the potential for the scheme. However, the aim of this chapter is to demonstrate the direction the TOI has taken and stress the need for examples of best practice in developing indicators for use by the commercial sector tourism industry.

Very few attempts have been made previously to set sustainability indicators for tour operators, and when this has taken place these tend to focus more on processes than on actual performance standards (Font and Bendell, 2002). TOI members see reporting as a process by which to become accountable internally, not as a marketing benefit. By working in this way the process could be more inclusive of a wider range of firms without a tradition of sustainability actions, but with strong management commitment to show progressive improvements. What is yet to become apparent is the success of the Initiative in attracting smaller tour operators, to see whether, given the financial and human resources necessary to develop indicators, these smaller operators can put the same emphasis on internal accountability over marketing benefits.

Measuring and monitoring sustainability performance for tour operators is no easy task, particularly when it is one of the first service sectors to attempt this. Consequently flexibility is allowed to tour operators in the choice of which indicators to report on, the expectation being that they will first choose a limited number, and gradually will add others that are most relevant to their specific business activities. In addition, information on the tour operators' profile and their institutional arrangements to plan, manage and implement sustainability priorities provide a clear backdrop against which the performance indicators can be presented. The important point to note is that the TOI approach is very different to those that seek to set standards and lead to externally recognizable certificates of sustainability. Certification works on the basis of the 'haves' who are certified and the 'have-nots' who are not. Certification is seen as a marketing tool and once it is achieved there may be little motivation to continually improve sustainability performance unless standards of certification are tightened. In contrast to this approach the TOI process is seen as evolutionary, tour operators gradually increasing the number of indicators they report on. Members of the TOI experiment with the development and implementation of a range of actions and frameworks to make positive progress towards improvement of sustainability performance whilst also increasing the knowledge base of the organization in this regard. For any given topic, tour operators have agreed to choose from the same set of indicators, and so that comparisons of performance can eventually be made. The approach taken by the TOI supports change of internal practices of the tour operators, a more lasting approach than simply raising a self-congratulatory flag or externalizing sustainability through fundraising for destination-specific projects.

For any company to ensure that activities targeted towards sustainability are comprehensive, credible and lead to long-term positive changes, it is important that they integrate sustainability principles into corporate policy and management systems, and monitor and report on their performance. Sceptics may question the motivation and capacity of tour operators to actually meet these requirements given the cut-throat nature of the business and technical expertise required to monitor many areas. Yet, embracing the challenge and learning about impacts is already a major step forward for a sector that has historically denied their responsibility, only using the environment for marketing purposes and consequently often blamed for corporate greenwashing. The indicators are designed as inspirational learning tools; they set the path for improvement as well as a method to check progress through comparing published company reports. The next few years will witness tour operators experimenting, and often struggling, with the praxis of social and environmental accounting, auditing and reporting. For the TOI, the immediate challenges are to increase the number of companies that report on at least some aspects of their sustainability performance, to assist those who have already made a start, to encourage a more systematic approach to reporting and to address the issue of how to provide support to smaller tour operators who may wish to take part in the scheme. While the number of companies using the GRI framework to report is growing fast, their number is still fairly small in comparison with the size of the sector (Mordhardt *et al.*, 2002). Reporting is proving a challenge for tour operators, requiring many internal changes to the company structures for data collection. At the time of writing this chapter, only the Swiss operator Hotelplan (http://www.hotelplan.ch/umwelt/) had published a complete report taking into account the full GRI.

The TOI is a unique example of the development of indicators to operationalize and measure corporate environmental and social responsibility of tour operators towards sustainable development. Its strengths are that tour operators themselves have recognized the need to act and have set themselves challenging indicators that go far beyond anything previously designed. Its weaknesses are in the dominance of larger operators, the complexity of the reporting recommendations and the current ad-hoc nature of much reporting. To be able to report on sustainability performance in this area, companies need to establish mechanisms to promote performance improvements as well as to measure them in a standard manner. Not only does this take considerable time, it presents two significant challenges for the industry. The first of these is for tour operators to adapt their internal processes so that each builds in sustainability into operations, both where they have full control (as in a vertically integrated tour operator with their own transport and hotels) and where they work with contracted suppliers. This requires considerable dialogue and training within tour operators so that existing systems can be enhanced to incorporate sustainability criteria, e.g. by adding some basic environmental and social performance criteria into the contracting process. Equally, suppliers will need to be engaged in a programme of dialogue and training, which will involve a significant resource and logistical challenges.

The second challenge is to find effective ways to work with the very large numbers of suppliers with which most tour operators, large and small, are involved. Both these challenges require experimentation to find workable solutions, and it is likely that a variety of approaches will be necessary to match the diversity within the tourism sector itself. Understandably much of this experimentation and adaptation is likely to take place away from public gaze, and as in other sectors, tour operators are likely to wait until they feel confident that they have effective frameworks in place before they report fully on all aspects of sustainability. The key for the members of the TOI will be to find the right balance between behind the scenes development and implementation of improvements, and public reporting. Reporting in general, and for tour operators specifically, is work in progress; having now set the agenda and acknowledged the responsibility to take action, the next few years will tell up to which extent they can be implemented.

Summary

This chapter has described how tour operators have joined together to tackle the problems they understand their business causes for destinations around the world. Chapter 3 considered the range of forces that could motivate the commercial sector to pursue a sustainability agenda and it is likely that many of the reasons discussed will be relevant in varying degrees to the members of the TOI. However, an aim of the programme is to raise worryingly low levels of awareness about sustainability and show how short-term publicity cannot be the motivating force for the considerable investment of time and effort made. Indeed, that the programme exists at all is no small achievement and a testimony to a more genuine recognition of the need for, and potential of, a transition towards more sustainable tourism. In an incredibly competitive industry with often very thin profit margins, the partnership between a range of stakeholders is all the more impressive for the central role sharing information and best practice plays in the TOI.

The background to the scheme demonstrates how these stakeholders have come together and lists the main organizations included. One judge of the success of the TOI will be how effective it is in encouraging smaller tour operators to join or to develop their own methods of monitoring. Small and medium-sized enterprises have long argued it is the responsibility of larger tour operators to show leadership and to commit their more considerable resources to the problems of sustainability. In the TOI, the largest of Europe's tour operators have made considerable investment and returned the challenge to their smaller rivals to follow suit.

By linking with the GRI, the TOI has made progress in drawing the tourism industry in line with efforts in other industries. In this way, progress in indicators of sustainability in other industrial sectors can be readily introduced to the tourism industry. Given the late start the tourism industry has made to monitoring, it would be appropriate for real commitment from the tourism industry now to result in progress that is fed back across previously confining boundaries.

The chapter focused on presenting the range of indicators decided upon by the TOI. These have been presented under five areas of management: product management and development, internal management, supply chain management, customer relations and cooperation with destinations. After the detail and definition of the case studies presented so far, it may seem disappointing that the TOI does not commit to targets and acceptable ranges. This is a challenge for the future and one the TOI will have to grasp if the programme can continue to have credibility in the future. For the moment, it is difficult to evaluate the success of the programme in effecting change, beyond the fact that the existence of the programme is in itself an indicator of change.

Acknowledgements

A special thanks to Sarah Raposa and Sean Gilbert from the GRI Secretariat and Oshani Perera for their input and support in all phases of the process. The Tour Operators' sector supplement is the result of the work of many individuals that sat around a table and discussed face to face what sustainability means for tour operators. Discussions were not always smooth – but always constructive. A special thanks to: Jane Ashton, First Choice Holidays; Gregorio Austria, City of Puerto Princesa; Adama Bah, Gambia Tourism Concern; Dirk Belau, International Labour Organization; Ellen Bermann, Viaggi del Ventaglio; Ramon Botet i Pont, Lloret de Mar (Spain, Costa Brava); Elizabeth Carroll-Simon, International Hotel & Restaurant Association; Carolyn Cresswell, P&O Princess Cruises plc; Karen Fletcher, International Hotel Environment Initiative; Graham Gordon, Tearfund; Gabriele Guglielmi, Filcams CGIL Nazionale (Italy); Kaspar Hess, Hotelplan; Isabelle Hustache Bennani, Dynamic Tours; Jan Jackson, British Airways Holidays; Lotta Sand, TUI Netherlands; Andreas Museler, LTU-Touristik GmbH; Homar Nawaz, Tourist Board of Sri Lanka; Victoria Newton, British Airways; Nico Visser, Travel Unie Nederland; Pierre Orsoni, Telefono Blu, SOS Turismo Consumatori; Paul Matell Scandinavian Leisure Group; Keith Richards, Association of British Travel Agents; Tom Selanniemi, Aurinkomatkat-Suntours; Jamie Sweeting, Conservation International; Justin Woolford, WWF UK.

Conclusion

The conceptual starting point and common thread throughout this book has been that a transition towards sustainable tourism development can be greatly facilitated by an interdisciplinary understanding of sustainable development. Too often in the past, sustainable tourism has been interpreted as an alternative to mass tourism, or as a niche activity closely related to ecotourism. Such narrow product-based approaches fail to recognize the contribution tourism can make to sustainability, and in misappropriating the debate, denies tourism the wealth of inter- and transdisciplinary knowledge that would help provide a more sophisticated study of tourism.

This book has demonstrated how the viewpoints and methods that have contributed to the contemporary ideas and continuing evolution of sustainable development can also advance our understanding of sustainable tourism. We have also suggested how the concepts, tools and management strategies used to implement sustainable development can provide vital clues for the transition towards sustainable tourism.

The first part of the book traced the origins of both sustainable development and sustainable tourism in their own milieux, demonstrating the close interrelationship between the two concepts and exploring current issues and critiques. Based on this investigation it was suggested that the study of sustainable tourism suffers from a lack of synthesis, interdisciplinary exchange, a failure to pay more than lip service to stakeholder participation, and a lack of understanding of the behaviour of non-linear complex systems. As a result, three recommendations are made that subsequently form the guiding principles for the study.

First, sustainable tourism needs to be appreciated in broader and more comprehensive terms as a complex adaptive system in which inter-linked environmental, economic, social and cultural forces, as well as those of tourism are at play (Inskeep, 1991; Hein, 1997; Abel, 2000).

Secondly, sustainable tourism needs not only incorporate effective stakeholder participation but also be a stakeholder-driven process that reflects the place-based needs and priorities of people in the study location (Dasmann, 1984; NRC, 1999).

Thirdly, in the context of new understandings of the unpredictability of complex systems, sustainable tourism tools and techniques need to be adaptive and incorporate social learning as an integral component (Lee, 1993; Gunderson *et al.*, 1995a; Laws *et al.*, 1998; NRC, 1999; Kates *et al.*, 2001).

Using these guiding principles, the second part of this book explored the motives both the private and public sector might have for pursuing sustainable tourism, and looked at how monitoring can assist governments, NGOs and communities move towards their sustainability goals. These motives were shown to be multifarious, but while there is frequent discussion within tourism of the role of government, NGOs and local citizens can play in promoting sustainable tourism, the role of the consumer, financial industries and even corporate responsibility has been largely ignored in the literature. The importance of principle was stressed in an attempt not to acquiesce completely to the instrumentalist view. Yet, whether it be dogma or pragma, without understanding what motivates all stakeholders to pursue sustainability, attempts to monitor sustainability will be futile.

Part III of the book reviewed both the principles and techniques involved in indicator development. In keeping with the themes of the book, these chapters draw on the both the experience of the authors and research by colleagues in other disciplines. Carter *et al.* (2001) in their excellent critique of tourism research identify the absence of practitioners writing as a weakness, leading to a lack of consideration of the management of tourism. Addressing this criticism, Part IV of this book has benefited from the contribution of authors intimately involved in the hands-on development of monitoring programmes. It is hoped that mixing academic and practical insight has produced four carefully selected case studies that are of value to the reader and add praxis to the book.

The aim of this final chapter is to provide a commentary on the guiding principles employed throughout the book and then to reflect on the contribution of monitoring and indicators before considering possible future directions for the subject.

Commentary on Guiding Principles

A study of the current work in sustainable development reveals that many of the serious threats facing humanity are multiple and cumulative and to address them requires synthesizing several otherwise discrete fields of study (ESA, 1995; NRC, 1999; Kates *et al.*, 2001). Applying integrated knowledge from widely disparate sources to tourism is interpreted as adopting a comprehensive approach, the purpose of which is to embrace and synthesize all relevant components of human and biophysical systems in order to enhance understanding of tourism.

For some time, there has been discussion about the need for more comprehensive and integrated approaches to tourism planning (Murphy, 1985; Inskeep, 1991; Manning, 1998). Nevertheless, there are still barriers to the adoption of a fully comprehensive approach to the study of tourism, such as the large proportion of tourism academics and experts who still feel that tourism should not concern itself with matters 'beyond tourism' (Miller, 2001a). However, the book has shown how adopting a comprehensive, transdisciplinary stance to monitoring means that indicators can make a public statement about the important linkages between tourism and other aspects of sustainable development. A comprehensive approach helps break down the barriers between departments and organizations, and establish contacts and partnerships with a wider spectrum of stakeholders. In the collection of monitoring data, investigation of causal factors and the implementation of action projects related to indicators, it obliges the monitoring organization to collaborate with a wider range of stakeholders and departments. The organization will not only learn as a result, but also have a far greater combined effect on sustainable tourism than would otherwise have been the case if they remained in a narrow, industry-orientated cocoon.

In many ways, the argument for a more comprehensive view of tourism is the least contentious of the themes presented in this book. It seems difficult to advocate a narrower view of anything in an era of expanding horizons. Yet, it is relevant to then consider why we do not have a more comprehensive approach to tourism? In part the answer will lie in the difficulty of reading material outside our field of expertise and acquiring new skills. Disciplinary backgrounds will encourage us to certain conceptions of problems, which can work against other approaches to thinking. Tourism researchers based in management or hospitality schools will be exposed to different techniques and approaches than those in schools of environmental sciences and recreation. With an increasing tendency of tourism schools to adopt the former stance there is a very real risk that tourism will become disconnected with its geographical, anthropological and sociological foundations. Whatever the orientation of the department, however, perhaps the common denominator of a drive towards a more comprehensive approach to tourism is the need for academics of whatever background to rise from their comfort zone and draw knowledge, approaches and topics from a much wider sphere into tourism.

The second conceptual principle for the book was discussing the opportunities and potential benefits of involving a range of stakeholders in the process, wherever possible in the driving seat. From recognition of the democratic right of citizens to be involved through to the financial advantages of community involvement, the book has presented many reasons for stakeholder involvement. Chapters 3 and 4 in particular examine why sustainability and monitoring benefits from our involvement, through our many roles as consumer, employee, shareholder, voter, member of civil society or just resident. In the case study section of the book, the roles of stakeholders are particularly highlighted. On Kangaroo Island, the TOMM process relies on a stakeholder management committee to identify areas where action needs to be taken as a result of the monitoring. In Samoa, stakeholders were actively involved in the identification of key issues and selection of indicators. In Chapter 11, the TOI has a guiding committee reflecting their patronage and cooperation with NGOs, but in order to enable a real transition towards sustainable tourism, the group of stakeholders may need to be more broadly drawn. Similarly, in Chapter 8, there was criticism that the range and make-up of stakeholder groups involved with the WTO indicator programme was restricted because of the intensive timetable for the work. As a consequence, external consultants set up the work in a short space of time and it was then difficult for the local user group to maintain the project momentum once the consultants had left. The TOMM project concludes that with the increasing pressure for short-term outcomes, driven by short-term funding programmes and political agendas, it is often the community members themselves that have the stamina and vested interest in seeing the process succeed. Project drivers may need support to sustain their enthusiasm as well as patience to allow the process and its players to evolve as needed.

The case studies also revealed that, despite the romanticized view of stakeholder participation depicted in much tourism literature, the reality is that many stakeholders, in both the developed and developing world, are busy, professional people who have little time to attend stakeholder workshops and meetings, and may well prefer a consultant to do the leg work. Those who do decide to participate may have vested interests in doing so which may be at odds with sustainable tourism objectives and priorities. However, when successful, there is little argument over the value of engaging stakeholders in the development and monitoring of sustainable tourism indicators. What is important is that the literature shifts from rousing descriptions of what should happen to a more sophisticated discussion of what does and can happen, as well as what goes wrong. Examples of successful community involvement are so difficult to find that it is clear there are significant problems in operationalizing the concept. Honest accounts of these problems are needed in order to evaluate if the concept is so stricken with problems that it needs to be reviewed, or if strategies can be devised to achieve its significant potential.

The third important conceptual issue discussed in this book was that rather than operating as simple, predictable linear systems where inputs are proportional to outputs, all human and natural systems can now be thought of as complex adaptive systems, in a constant state of flux and self-organization. To make progress in the face of such uncertainty, adaptive management has been found to be a valuable technique allowing managers progressively to learn more about the systems they manage through trial and error, close stakeholder involvement and continuous monitoring.

Adaptive management differs from normal management practice in the way it incorporates an ongoing process of experimentation, monitoring and adaptation as part of a continual social learning process (the sharing and building of knowledge and expertise between stakeholders within the community or social setting) (Parsons and Clark, 1995). The strong emphasis adaptive management puts on engaging stakeholders and the progressive accumulation of knowledge helps make monitoring an on-going learning and action-oriented process. It also assists in making the important connections between information collection and management action, which has been shown to be a common failing of monitoring programmes.

As with the other guiding principles, as well as benefits there are in-evitably challenges involved in the implementation of adaptive manage-ment. In business, the pressures to maintain short-term share prices, deliver 'quick fixes' and to be seen as successful all militate against experimenta-tion in favour of more tried and tested paths. For some managers, particu-larly when times are hard, experimentation may be seen as a high-risk strategy they can ill afford, but on the other hand, maintaining the status quo may be even more risky. Such organizations, Westley (1995) notes, become increasingly resistant to new sources of information, and manage-ment systems may become disconnected from the environments they seek to manage. She explains, 'Crisis is needed to shake such conclusive ideolo-gies, and organizations in this state are prone either to crisis or demise' (1995, p. 401). Resistance to change and adaptation may therefore work against the successful transition to sustainable development. However, adaptive management is a collectivist tool requiring partnership and collab-oration, but Chapter 3 demonstrated the difficulty for business of employ-ing a collectivistic tool within Hardin's view of an individualistic society. Chapters 6 and 7 also explained how it takes more time to experiment, eval-uate, adapt and review following adaptive management rather than taking a more linear approach, although the long-term lessons learned can create significant savings by identifying more efficient technologies and better ways of doing business. There is clearly more research to be done in this area. While the benefits of a 'learning organization' are clear and have already been applied in many areas from medical practices to car manufac-turer and high technology, research is now needed to see how it can apply to the tourism industry.

Discussion of Monitoring and Indicators

The tourism industry has long suffered from insecurity about its commercial status. This lack of confidence seems to manifest itself in an almost obsessive output of figures stating tourism to be the world's largest industry and optimistic projections about future growth prospects. The drive for indicators might fit well with the attempts of the industry to prove itself to be serious and mature, and to be an industry worthy of the same regard as its more established industrial peers. Chambers (1989, p. 130) observes, 'Within and between professions, status and respectability are sought and can be gained through quantification, mathematical techniques and precisions. Professions or disciplines which develop or adapt skilled techniques of measurement move upwards.'

Nevertheless, outside the traditional economic areas of jobs and income, the commercial tourism industry does not have an impressive record. Although there are some excellent examples of tourism making a strong commitment to a more sustainable tourism industry, research has been cited throughout the book, particularly in Chapter 3, showing the tourism sector overall as something of an industrial laggard in terms of sustainable development. For the industry to be able to post continuous growth figures, the unwritten licence to operate that exists between businesses and societies needs to be continually renewed. Here, indicators can be of great assistance in equipping industry to demonstrate the contribution it is making to society, rather than relying on exaggerated claims of importance. Yet indicators can only measure what performance there is. For indicators to present a picture of a responsible industry will require the tourism industry to become more responsible; indicators alone cannot be seen as evidence of action, there is a need now to walk the talk. Notwithstanding these concerns, the TOI and other case studies in this book should be applauded for the pioneering steps they have taken in aiding sustainable tourism's transition from a fuzzy concept to something measurable. The challenges of so doing at such a time are not to be underestimated.

Although experience in sustainable development and other fields is relatively advanced, indicator development as applied to sustainable tourism is still in its infancy. As a result of the relative immaturity of the sustainable tourism monitoring, there is no existing master list of sustainable tourism indicators from which measures can be selected; therefore many indicators will have to be designed from scratch. More examples of indicator programmes are needed – particularly more examples of cooperation between industry, local communities and researchers. These do not need to be 'successful' to be worthy of reporting; indeed there are often more lessons to be learned from things that have gone wrong, from those that have tried and failed, than in exaggerated reports of success. The benefits of honest, critical analysis and reporting are clearly shown in the case study section of this book and are essential if lessons learned are to broaden our collective understanding of monitoring processes. Given the lack of tourism practitioners writing on tourism research, the bulk of this challenge must fall to tourism students and academics to conduct and/or report on practical research on indicator programmes (Carter *et al.*, 2001).

It has been shown that indicators cannot be a goal in their own right. Whitehouse (2003) cites an apocryphal example of shoe factories in the old Soviet Union that had targets to produce shoes, but no specification that these should be pairs of shoes. As it took time to change the machines from making left shoes to making right shoes, the easiest way to meet targets was to continue producing only left shoes! In another more recent example, it was exposed that clinicians in the UK have adjusted the order in which they treat patients to assist in meeting government imposed targets for waiting time to see a doctor (Hinsliff, 2003). Similarly, the Research Assessment Exercise of UK Universities has been accused by Members of Parliament of leading to a distortion of research and ruining academic careers as members of staff with limited publications are re-designated as tutors in order that the output of 'research-active' lecturers at the university is not negatively affected, striking particularly hard on women in higher education (BBC, 2004). As a technical approach to a very human problem, indicators cannot themselves create sustainable development, sustainable tourism or sustainable anything. They give us only a partial description of the bigger picture, like the five blind men giving different descriptions of the same elephant because each can feel only a small part of the whole animal. This problem of the partial view is compounded by the conviction with which indicators seem to propagate 'the answer'; each man sure of his description of the elephant because the 'evidence' is before him. Gunderson and Holling (2002) and Hein (1997) correctly note that we should be wary of simple prescriptions that replace uncertainty with the apparent certitude of precise numbers.

Such examples reflect poorly on the concept of indicators and monitoring leading to criticism of indicators for getting in the way of doing the job properly, meanwhile costing time and diverting resources away from the central element of the task. The case studies also revealed several potentially formidable barriers to indicator development, including time and language constraints, know-how, and extensive financial and personnel resource requirements (e.g. employee training and data collection and the need for highly competent protected area planners, meeting facilitators, and technical and scientific experts). Time can be a key constraint in much of this work because process takes time especially when it is stakeholder driven. In resource-poor destinations, advanced monitoring techniques using ambitious, highly technical indicators are unlikely to help or be implemented on a long-term basis. It was suggested in Chapter 5 that if information is to be cost-effective, not just cheap, then those commissioning the research must acknowledge that there is a lower threshold of expense below which the information cannot be effectively provided. Significantly more funds need to be invested in research into indicators of sustainable tourism. Other industries have enormous research and development costs, with large amounts of money committed to collaborative ventures with universities and other organizations. Yet, the commercial tourism industry will argue that its small margins, and particularly in recent years its vulnerability to external events has meant it is impossible to fund research on monitoring. Such a position links back to the claims of the industry to be a full-grown, mature member of the industrial community. After all, Chapter 3 found that size alone does not make an industry responsible, it is the way it behaves that defines its sovereignty.

A final lesson to be learnt from the case studies and examples in this book is the pivotal role of stakeholder support for indicators. Having the patronage of industry, government and residents has been shown to increase the likelihood of maintaining the monitoring programme in the long term, but it also serves to strengthen the indicators developed from the start. The Samoa case, for example, showed that no matter how well the indicators may be thought out, if industry and government are not fully committed to the programme, then the programme comes under threat. Similarly, the credibility of the TOI project may be diminished in the future by the lack of resident input from the destinations affected by tourism. The importance of having a project champion and driver – someone who pushes the project forward and stands up for monitoring resource allocations – has also been identified, along with the very real risks of over-reliance on one manager resulting in possible burnout and consequent loss of project momentum. Both the Sustainable Seattle example and the TOMM project demonstrated that long-term, responsible management requires the presence of strong social and community capital, which in turn sustains the core values of trust, integrity, reliability and honesty, all of which are central to the success of the relationships required to manage monitoring programmes in the long term.

Further Avenues to Explore

In order for indicators not to become tarnished as an instrument of excessive intrusion into the working practices of professionals, or to be seen as an instrument of unwarranted bureaucracy, there is a need for more research into a number of areas. First, more practical and long-term indicator studies leading to further cases need to be reported in the literature. Perhaps even more than this, however, there is a need for considerably more research on the use of indicator data to assist in the journey towards sustainability.

The second fertile area for research is into the efficacy of indicator programmes: establishing what contribution indicators make to the movement towards greater sustainability. It is entirely possible that just as with alternative tourism, ecotourism and carrying capacity, indicators prove to be an ineffective tool in the drive for sustainability and are rightfully consigned to the bin of 'bad ideas'. However, the literature produced by tourism academics on these alternative forms of tourism has been vital for the development of the subject, just as an expanded literature on indicators will surely prove to be.

A third area of valuable research is in establishing the way in which indicators fit with other tools for promoting sustainability. There is obvious relevance to the move towards greater self-regulation, certification of tourism destinations and tourism products and competitions for responsible behaviour. As tourism planning moves from long-term master plans to short-term strategic planning, the integration of adaptive management and monitoring techniques becomes extremely relevant, providing the information necessary to make decisions on policy change.

Other considerations to explore include the implications of scale for monitoring, whether, for example, a localized place-based approach can show itself to be more successful than efforts at a larger spatial scale, and how approaches may be up- or downscaled. Global indicators are the option advanced by the WTO, while the TOI present their industrial scale indicators. In the case of a small island country like Samoa, with a very low level of tourism and clear geographic resolution, it was possible to develop place-based indicators. However, in the instance of a larger country, particularly one that exhibits a wider variety of ecological and social conditions, or has a more developed tourism industry, a regional approach, like that adopted for Kangaroo Island, might be more appropriate. Although the case study section has endeavoured to cover a wide range of scales, it has not identified an example of a sufficiently developed local-level sustainable tourism-monitoring project to include. It is hoped that this book will inspire such work with the emphasis on stakeholder involvement that is particularly well suited to the development of local level indicators where the community concerned takes the lead role.

As monitoring becomes less specialized and involves more local stakeholders, so the need to model possible future outcomes becomes more pressing. This fits well with the study of ecosystems, where the logical progression of adaptive management is the development of scenarios and systems analysis. The Tourism Futures Simulator used in the Douglas Shire Region of North Queensland is a good example of such an attempt at modelling (Walker *et al.*, 1999). Another is the Dynamic Simulation Model of tourism on the Yucatán Peninsula, which shows how relationships between the economy, environment and population change over time and how factors not directly related to tourism, such as safety and popularity of other areas, affect the industry (Kandelaars, 1997). Both these programmes demonstrate the need for more research into the role technology can play in monitoring sustainable tourism. This book has tended to emphasize simple, low-cost solutions that are applicable to a wider range of developed and developing world situations. However, recent innovations such as those offered by the Global Scenarios Group or the 3-D digital imagery technology developed by GEO-3D, may offer significant potential for sustainable tourism monitoring (GEO-3D Inc., 2001). The use of the Internet and/or CDs to produce interactive models can bring indicators to life, increase their relevancy to the user and so encourage their usage, such as with the sustainability dashboard developed by the IISD and discussed in Chapter 7 (IISD, 2004b).

Beyond research into monitoring, research needs to be directed towards the development of more comprehensive, integrated and whole ecosystem ways of studying tourism. This will necessarily involve greater interdisciplinary understanding and exchange of ideas, and the need for more researchers to be generalists, wearing several hats at once rather than maintaining a strictly mono-disciplinary outlook that excludes much of the big picture (Holling, 1993). In this light, the emergence of the new field of sustainability science warrants special consideration (NRC, 1999; Kates *et al.*, 2001; Sustainability Science Forum, 2002). Similarly the implications of complexity and complex system dynamics for tourism management offer many new and exciting avenues for further research and study, which could conceivably lead to a reconceptualization, or at least a much broader and more integrative approach, to the study of sustainable tourism in years to come (Farrell and Twining-Ward, 2004).

Final Summary

This book has taken a broad interdisciplinary approach to the challenge of monitoring sustainable tourism and tackled the problem from many different angles in order to appeal to and be useful for a wide range of readers. Whilst not all the chapters reflect the use of non-linear techniques to the same extent, in many parts of this book, readers have been introduced to a new way of looking at old problems. The approaches presented have the potential to be applied to a much wider field in the future. The focus of the work has been on the use of monitoring as a tool to facilitate a sustainability transition. The idea of a transition or journey towards sustainability has been stressed, a journey which changes in relation to place, scale, time and numerous other factors still yet to be explored. The results show that monitoring, the supply of information and data about sustainability using indicators can help managers adapt to and prepare for change rather than simply react to problems as they occur. In addition, it can help build the case for operational and product change in tourism businesses and support government interventions in some areas.

Much more remains to be explored both in terms of non-linear science applications to tourism as well as indicator development and monitoring techniques. This book has simply touched the surface of the debate, but small steps when joined by others and maintained over time can slowly help the field move forward. The case has been made for monitoring from a variety of angles and it is hoped that this will provide a valuable resource to work from in future studies. In the short term, system monitoring can warn of imminent changes that may be avoided. In the longer term, more thorough understanding of the behaviour of the system may be developed, enabling managers at a variety of scales, to build system resilience, adapt to change, keep abreast of new thinking and monitor for a successful transition towards sustainable tourism.

References

Abel, T. (2000) The complex systems dynamics of a development frontier: the case of eco-tourism on the Island of Bonaire, Netherlands Antilles. Unpublished dissertation, Department of Anthropology, University of Florida, Gainsville.

ABI (Association of British Insurers) (2001) *Investing in Social Responsibility. Risks and Opportunities*. ABI, London.

ABP (2004) About ABP. Available at: www.abp.nl (accessed 9 September, 2004).

Adams, D. (1996) *The Hitchhiker's Guide to the Galaxy*. Random House, New York.

Adams, W. (1990) *Green Development: Environment and Sustainability in the Third World*. Routledge, London.

Aguas Grandes (2004) Aguas Grandes Turismo. Available at: www.aguasgrandes.com (accessed 10 May, 2004).

Allin, P., Bennett, J. and Newton, L. (2000) Defining and measuring sustainable tourism: building the first set of UK indicators. *Proceedings of the 5th International Forum on Tourism Statistics*. Glasgow Caledonian University, 19–23 June.

Ames, S. (2003) How to design, implement and manage an effective community visioning process. *Training Workshop for Community Visioning: Planning for the Future of Local Communities*, 23 April, Perth.

Andrews, K. (1980) *The Concept of Corporate Strategy*. Dow Jones, Irwin, Illinois.

Ap, J. (1990) Residents' perceptions: research on the social impacts of tourism. *Annals of Tourism Research* 17, 610–616.

Arnstein, S.R. (1969) A ladder of citizen participation. *American Institute of Planners Journal* 35, 216–224.

Aronsson, L. (2002) *The Development of Sustainable Tourism*. Continuum, London.

Atkisson, A. (1996) Developing indicators of sustainable community: lessons from Sustainable Seattle. *Environmental Impact Assessment Review* 16, 337–350.

Ayensu, E., Van Claasen, D., Collins, M., Dearing, A., Fresco, L., Gadgil, M., Gitay, H., Glaser, G., Juma, C., Krebs, J., Lenten, R., Lubchenco, J., McNeely, J., Mooney, H.,

293

Pinstrup-Andersen, P., Ramos, M., Raven, P., Reid, W., Samper, C., Sarukhan, J., Schei, P., Galizia Tundisi, J., Watson, T., Guanhua, X. and Zakri, A. (1999) 1999 International Ecosystem Assessment. *Science* 286, 685–686.

Azzone, G., Brophy, M., Noci, G., Welford, R. and Young, W. (1997) A stakeholders' view of environmental reporting. *Long Range Planning* 30, 699–709.

Bakker, M. (2003) A pre-study on the potential use of sustainable tourism indicators for the Island of Bonaire, N.A. Unpublished special advanced project for Master of Science, New York University, New York.

Bakkes, J. (1997) Research methods. In: Moldan, B. and Bilharz, S. (eds) *Sustainability Indicators: Report of the Project on Indicators of Sustainable Development.* John Wiley & Sons, Chichester, UK, pp. 379–389.

Bastakis, C., Buhalis, D. and Butler, R. (2004) The perception of small and medium sized tourism accommodation providers on the impacts of the tour operators' power in Eastern Mediterranean. *Tourism Management* 25, 151–170.

Baumard, P. (1999) *Tacit Knowledge in Organizations.* Sage, London.

BBC (2004) Call to boycott research scrutiny. Available at: http://news.bbc.co.uk/ 1/hi/education/1977479.stm# (accessed 10 October, 2004).

BC Ministry of Forests (2004a) Definitions of adaptive management. Forest Practices Branch, Victoria. Available at: www.for.gov.bc.ca/hfp/amhome/amdefs.htm (accessed 28 September, 2004).

BC Ministry of Forests (2004b) *Adaptive Management: Learning From Our Forests.* Ministry of Forests, Victoria.

Belisle, F and Hoy, D. (1980) The perceived impact of tourism on residents: a case study in Santa Marta, Columbia. *Annals of Tourism Research* 7, 83–101.

Bell, S. and Morse, S. (1999) *Sustainability Indicators: Measuring the Immeasurable?* Earthscan Publications, London.

Berkes, F. and Folke, C. (1998) Linking social and ecological systems for resilience and sustainability. In: Berkes, F., Folke, C. and Golding, J. (eds) *Linking Social and Ecological Systems: Management Practices and Social Mechanisms for Building Resilience.* Cambridge University Press, Cambridge, pp. 1–25.

BITC (Business in the Community) (2003) *The Business Case for Corporate Responsibility.* BITC, London.

Blake, A. (2000) The economic effects of tourism in Spain. *TTRI Discussion Paper,* 2000/2.

Blue Flag (2004) Blue Flag Campaign. Available at: www.blueflag.org (accessed 11 May, 2004).

Boo, E. (1990) *Ecotourism: the Potentials and Pitfalls.* WWF, Washington, DC.

Borrini-Feyerabend, G., Farvar, M.T., Nguinguiri, J.C. and Ndangang, V.A. (2000) *Co-management of Natural Resources: Organising, Negotiating and Learning-by-doing.* Deutsche Gesellschaft Fuer Technische Zusammenarbeit (GTZ) and IUCN, Kasparek Verlag, Heidelberg.

Bowie, N. (1990) Morality, money and motor cars. In: Hoffman, M., Frederick, R. and Petry, E. (eds) *Business, Ethics and the Environment.* Quorum Books, New York, pp. 440–446.

Bowie, N. (2002) It seems right in theory, but does it work in practice? In: Hartman, L. (ed.) *Perspectives in Business Ethics.* McGraw-Hill, New York, pp. 83–86.

BP (British Petroleum) (2004) *Defining Our Path: Sustainability Report 2003.* BP, Surrey, UK.

Bramwell, B. and Lane, B. (1993) Sustainable tourism: an evolving global approach. *Journal of Sustainable Tourism* 1, 1–5.

Bramwell, B. and Sharman, A. (1999) Collaboration in local tourism policymaking. *Annals of Tourism Research* 26, 393–415.

Brandt, W. (1980) *North–South: A Programme for Survival, Commission on International Development Issues.* Pan Books, London.

Brandt, W. (1983) *Common Crisis North–South.* Pan Books, London.

Briguglio, L. (2004) Vulnerability Index. Available at: www.home.um.edu.mt/islands/research.html (accessed 12 July, 2004).

Briguglio, L., Archer, B., Jafari, J. and Wall, G. (ed.) (1996) *Sustainable Tourism in Islands and Small States: Issues and Policies.* Pinter, London.

Britton, S. (1982) The political economy of tourism in the Third World. *Annals of Tourism Research* 9, 331–358.

Britton, S.G. (1983) *Tourism and Underdevelopment in Fiji.* Development Studies Centre, Australian National University.

Britton, S.G. (1987) Tourism in Pacific-Island States: constraints and opportunities. In: Britton, S.G. and Clarke, W.C. (eds) *Ambiguous Alternative: Tourism in Small Developing Countries.* University of the South Pacific, Suva.

Brohman, J. (1996) New directions in tourism for Third World development. *Annals of Tourism Research* 23, 48–70.

Bryden, J. (1973) *Tourism and Development: A Case Study of the Commonwealth Caribbean.* Cambridge University Press, London.

Budiansky, S. (1995) *Nature's Keepers: the New Science of Nature Management.* Weidenfeld and Nicholson, London.

Budowski, G. (1976) Tourism and conservation: conflict, coexistence or symbiosis? *Environmental Conservation* 3, 27–31.

Burns, P. (1999) Tourism NGOs. *Tourism Recreation Research* 24, 3–6.

Burns, P. and Holden, A. (1995) *Tourism: A New Perspective.* Prentice Hall, London.

Busch, D.E. and Trexler, J.C. (2003) (eds) *Monitoring Ecosystems: Interdisciplinary Approaches for Evaluating Eco-Regional Initiatives.* Island Press, Washington, DC.

Butler, R. (1974) Social implications of tourist development. *Annals of Tourism Research* 2, 100–111.

Butler, R. (1980) The concept of a tourist area cycle of evolution: implications for the management of resources. *Canadian Geographer* 24, 5–12.

Butler, R. (1990) Alternative tourism – pious hope or Trojan horse? *Journal of Travel Research* 28, 40–45.

Butler, R. (1991) Tourism, environment and sustainable development. *Environmental Conservation* 18, 201–209.

Butler, R. (1993a) Tourism – an evolutionary perspective. In: Butler, R.W., Nelson, J.G. and Wall, G. (eds) *Tourism and Sustainable Development: Monitoring, Planning, Managing.* Department of Geography Publication 37, University of Waterloo, Waterloo, pp. 27–43.

Butler, R. (1993b) Tourism development in small islands: past influences and future directions. In: Lockhart, D.G., Drakakis-Smith, D. and Schembri, J. (eds) *The Development Process in Small Island States.* Routledge, London, pp. 71–91.

Butler, R. (1995) Introduction. In: Butler, R.W. and Pearce, D. (eds) *Change in Tourism: People, Places, Processes.* Routledge, London, pp. 1–11.

Butler, R. (1998) Sustainable tourism – looking backwards in order to progress. In: Hall, M. and Lew, A. (eds) *Sustainable Tourism: A Geographical Perspective.* Longman, Harlow, UK, pp. 25–34.

Butler, R. (1999) Sustainable tourism – a state of the art review. *Tourism Geographies* 1, 7–25.

Cadbury Report (1992) *The Financial Aspects of Corporate Finance.* Gee Publishing, London.

Caffyn, A. and Jobbins, G. (2003) Governance capacity and stakeholder interactions in the development and management of coastal tourism: examples from Morocco and Tunisia. *Journal of Sustainable Tourism* 11, 224–245.

CAG Consultants (1999) Sustainable tourism indicators – candidate indicators. Unpublished report from the Second Workshop on Sustainable Tourism Indicators. Department of Culture Media and Sport, 3 June.

Calpers (California Pension Fund) (2004) About Calpers. Available at: www.calpers.ca.gov/index.jsp?bc=/about/home.xml (accessed 9 September, 2004).

Carey, S., Gountas, Y. and Gilbert, D. (1997) Tour operators and destination sustainability. *Tourism Management* 18, 425–432.

Carley, M. (1981) *Social Measurement and Social Indicators: Issues of Policy and Theory.* George Allen and Unwin, London.

Carmen, R. and Lubelski, M. (1997) Whose business is it anyway? In: Davies, P. (ed.) *Current Issues in Business Ethics.* Routledge, London, pp. 27–38.

Carnegie, A. (1889) *The Gospel of Wealth.* Applewood Books, Bedford, UK.

Carson, R. (1962) *Silent Spring.* Fawcett, Greenwich, UK.

Carter, R.W., Baxter, G.S. and Hockings, M. (2001) Resource management in tourism research: a new direction? *Journal of Sustainable Tourism* 9, 265–280.

Cater, E. (1993) Eco-tourism in the Third World: problems for sustainable tourism developments. *Tourism Management* 14, 85–90.

Cater, E. and Lowman, G. (1994) *Ecotourism; A Sustainable Option?* John Wiley & Sons, Chichester, UK.

Ceballos-Lascurain, H. (1991) Tourism, ecotourism and protected areas. In: Kusler, J.A. (ed.) *Ecotourism and Resource Conservation. Ecotourism and Resource Conservation Project.* Berne, New York, pp. 24–30.

Centre for Tourism and Hotel Management Research, Griffith University (1996) *Kangaroo Island Tourism Profile.* Tourism Kangaroo Island and South Australian Tourism Commission, Adelaide.

Ceron, J. and Dubois, G. (2003) Tourism and sustainable development indicators: the gap between theoretical demands and practical achievements. *Current Issues in Tourism* 6, 54–75.

Chambers, R. (1989) Us and them: finding a new paradigm for professionals in sustainable development. In: Warburton, D. (ed.) *Community and Sustainable Development.* Earthscan, London, pp. 117–147.

Cheong, S. and Miller, M. (2000) Power and tourism: a Foucauldian observation. *Annals of Tourism Research* 27, 371–390.

Christian Aid (2004) *Behind the Mask: the Real Face of Corporate Social Responsibility.* Christian Aid, London.

Chryssides, G. and Kaler, J. (1993) *An Introduction to Business Ethics.* Thomson Business Press, London.

Clark, M., Riley, M., Wilkie, E. and Wood, R.C. (1998) *Researching and Writing Dissertations in Hospitality and Tourism.* Thomson Business Press, London.

Clark, W.C. (2002) Adaptive management, heal thyself. *Environment* 44, no page numbers.

Clark, W.C. and Munn, R.E. (ed.) (1986) *Sustainable Development of the Biosphere.* Cambridge University Press, Cambridge.

Clarke, J. (1997) A framework of approaches to sustainable tourism. *Journal of Sustainable Tourism* 5, 224–233.

Clayoquot Sound Scientific Panel (1995) *Sustainable Ecosystem Management in Clayoquot Sound: Planning and Practices.* Clayoquot Sound Scientific Panel, Victoria.

Clements, F.E. (1916) Plant succession: an analysis of the development of vegetation. *Carnegie Institution of Washington* 242, 1–512.

Clifford, G. (2002) Indicators, risk and ecotourism – measurement as a planning tool. *Proceedings of the World Ecotourism Summit,* Quebec, May 2002.

Coccossis, H. (1996) Tourism and sustainability: perspectives and implications. In: Priestley, G.K., Edwards, J.A. and Coccossis, H. (eds) *Sustainable Tourism: European Experiences.* CAB International, Wallingford, UK, pp. 1–21.

Cohen, E. (1972) Towards a sociology of international tourism. *Social Research* 39, 164–182.

Cohen, E. (1978) The impact of tourism on the physical environment. *Annals of Tourism Research* 5, 215–237.

Cole, D.N. and McCool, S.F. (1997) Historical development of Limits of Acceptable Change: conceptual clarifications and possible extensions. *Proceedings of Limits of Acceptable Change and Related Planning Processes: Progress and Future Directions.* University of Montana, Lubrecht Experimental Forest, US Department of Agriculture, Forest Service, Inter-Mountain Research Station, General Technical Report, INT-GTR–371, 20–22 May, pp. 5–9.

Collins, A. (1996) The limits of tourism as an engine of sustainable development. *University of Portsmouth Discussion Papers,* October, no. 82.

Collins, A. (1999) Tourism development and natural capital. *Annals of Tourism Research* 26, 98–109.

Conca, K., Alberty, M. and Dabelko, G.D. (eds) (1995) *Green Planet Blues: Environmental Politics From Stockholm to Rio.* Westview Press, Oxford, UK.

Connolly, C. (1999) Research case study: tourism concern. *Tourism Recreation Research* 24, 109–114.

Conservation Ecology (2004) Ecology and society. Available at: www.consecol.org (accessed 13 May, 2004).

Consulting and Audit Canada (2003) Indicators of sustainable development for tourism. Unpublished background paper prepared for World Tourism Organization.

Conway, G.R. (1987) A review of sustainable development of the biosphere. *Environment* 29, 25–27.

Cowe, R. and Williams, S. (2001) *Who are the Ethical Consumers?* The Co-operative Bank, Manchester, UK.

Craik, J. (1995) Are there cultural limits to tourism? *Journal of Sustainable Tourism* 3, 87–98.

Crane, A. and Matten, D. (2004) *Business Ethics.* Oxford University Press, Oxford, UK.

Crocombe, R.G. (2001) *The South Pacific.* Institute of Pacific Studies, Suva.

Crompton, J. and Ap, J. (1994) *Development of A Tourism Impact Scale in the Host-Resident Context. Research Enhancement Program Final Report.* Department of Recreation, Parks & Tourism Sciences, Texas A&M University, College Station, Texas.

Crotts, J.C. and Holland, S.M. (1993) Objective indicators of the impact of rural tourism development in the State of Florida. *Journal of Sustainable Tourism* 1, 112–119.

Curtin, S. and Busby, G. (1999) Sustainable destination development: the tour operator perspective. *International Journal of Tourism Research* 1, 135–147.

Dahl, A.L. (1997b) From concept to indicator: dimensions expressed as vectors. In: Moldan, B. and Bilharz, S. (eds) *Sustainability Indicators: Report of the Project on Indicators of Sustainable Development.* John Wiley & Sons, Chichester, UK, pp. 125–127.

Dahl, A.L. (1997a) The big picture: comprehensive approaches. In: Moldan, B. and Bilharz, S. (eds) *Sustainability Indicators: Report of the Project on Indicators of Sustainable Development.* John Wiley & Sons, Chichester, UK, pp. 69–83.

Daly, H. (1973) *Towards A Steady State Economy.* Freeman, San Francisco, California.

Daly, H.E. and Cobb, J.R. (1990) *For the Common Good: Redirecting the Economy.* Freeman, San Francisco, California.

Dasmann, R.F. (1984) *Environmental Conservation.* John Wiley & Sons, Chichester, UK.

Dasmann, R.F., Milton, J.P. and Freeman, P.H. (1973) *Ecological Principles of Economic Development.* John Wiley & Sons, New York.

DCMS (Department for Culture, Media and Sport) (1999) *Tomorrow's Tourism.* HMSO, London.

De Araujo, L.M. and Bramwell, B. (1999) Stakeholder assessment and collaborative tourism planning: the case of Brazil's Costa Dourada Project. *Journal of Sustainable Tourism* 7, 356–378.

De Burlo, C. (1996) Cultural resistance and ethic tourism on South Pentecost, Vanuatu. In: Butler, R. and Hinch, T. (eds) *Tourism and Indigenous Peoples.* Thomson Business Press, London, pp. 254–274.

De George, R. (1978) Moral issues in business. In: De George, R. and Pilcher, J. (eds) *Ethics, Free Enterprise and Public Policy.* Oxford University Press, Oxford, UK, pp. 3–18.

De Kadt, E. (ed.) (1979) *Tourism – Passport to Development? Perspectives on the Social and Cultural Effects of Tourism in Developing Countries.* Oxford University Press, Oxford, UK.

DEFRA (Department for the Environment, Food and Rural Affairs) (2004) Indicators of Sustainable Development. Available at: www.sustainable-development.gov.uk/indicators/index.htm (accessed 1 September, 2004).

Denny, C. and Vidal, J. (1998) The real cost of living in Britain. *The Guardian*, 22 May.

Department of Lands, Surveys and the Environment and the South Pacific Regional Environment Programme (1997) Environmental impact assessment. Unpublished information booklet for the National EIA Training Workshop, Apia, 26–30 May.

DETR (Department for Environment, Transport and the Regions) (1999) *A Better Quality of Life: A Strategy for Sustainable Development in the United Kingdom. Department of Environment, Transport and the Regions.* HMSO, London.

DFID (Department for International Development) (1999a) *Tourism and Poverty Elimination: Untapped Potential.* DFID, London.

DFID (1999b) *Target 2015.* DFID, London.

Diaz-Benavides, D. (2001) *The Sustainability of International Tourism in Developing Countries.* OECD Seminar on Tourism Policy and Economic Growth, Berlin.

Dixey, L. (1998) An environmental assessment of tourism in St. Lucia. *UK CEED Bulletin*, Autumn, No. 54, pp. 22–23.

Dixey, L. (1999) Industry and NGOs: the UK CEED experience. *Tourism Recreation Research* 24, 83–87.

Dogan, H.Z. (1989) Forms of adjustment: socio-cultural impacts of tourism. *Annals of Tourism Research* 16, 216–235.

Donaldson, T. and Preston, L. (1995) The stakeholder theory of the corporation: concepts, evidence and implications. *Academy of Management Review* 20, 65–91.

Doorne, S. (2000) Caves, culture and crowds: carrying capacity meets consumer sovereignty. *Journal of Sustainable Tourism* 8, 116–130.

DJSI (Dow Jones Sustainability Indexes) (2004) Guide to the Dow Jones Sustainability World Indexes, Version 5.0. Available at: www.sustainability-index.com (accessed 25 June, 2004).

Doxey, G.V. (1976) When enough's enough: the natives are restless in old Niagara. *Heritage Canada* 2, 26–27.

Driskell, D., Bannerjee, K. and Chawla, L. (2001) Rhetoric, reality and resilience: overcoming obstacles to young people's participation. *Development, Environment and Urbanization* 3, 77–89.

Dumanski, J. and Pieri, C. (2000) Land quality indicators: research plan. *Agriculture, Ecosystems and Environment* 81, 93–102.

Dymond, S.J. (1997) Indicators of sustainable tourism in New Zealand: a local government perspective. *Journal of Sustainable Tourism* 5, 279–293.

EC (European Commission) (1992) *Towards Sustainability: 5th Environmental Action Programme.* EC, Brussels.

Ekins, P. (2002) *Sustainable Development and the Work of Policy Studies Institute's Environment Group.* Presentation given at University of Westminster, London, 4 December.

Engeldrum, D., Lindberg, K. and Epler-Wood, M. (1998) *Ecotourism; A Guide for Planners and Managers 2.* The International Ecotourism Society, Burlington, Vermont.

ESA (Ecological Society of America) (1995) The Report of the Ecological Society of America Committee on the Scientific Basis of Ecosystem Management. Available at: www.esapubs.org/archive/ (accessed 16 March, 2002).

Evan, W. and Freeman, R.E. (1993) A stakeholder theory of the modern corporation: Kantian capitalism. In: Hoffman, W.M. and Frederick, R.E. (eds) *Business Ethics: Readings and Cases in Corporate Morality.* McGraw-Hill, New York, pp. 145–154.

Fairbairn, T.I.J., Morrison, C.E., Baker, R.W. and Grove, S.A. (1991) *The Pacific Islands – Policies, Economics and International Relations.* East–West Centre International Relations Program, Honolulu, Hawaii.

Farrell, B.H. (1986) Cooperative tourism in the coastal zone. *Coastal Zone Management Journal* 14, 113–129.

Farrell, B.H. (1990) Sustainable development: whatever happened to Hana? *Cultural Survival Quarterly* 14, 25–29.

Farrell, B.H. and Runyan, D. (1991) Ecology and tourism. *Annals of Tourism Research* 18, 26–40.

Farrell, B.H. and Twining-Ward, L. (2004) Reconceptualizing tourism. *Annals of Tourism Research* 31, 274–295.

Farrell, B.H. and Twining-Ward, L. (2005) Seven steps towards sustainability: tourism in the context of new knowledge. *Journal of Sustainable Tourism* 13, 109–122.

Farrell, T.A. and Marion, J.L. (2002) The protected areas visitor impact management framework: a simplified process for making management decisions. *Journal of Sustainable Tourism* 10, 31–51.

Faulkner, B. (2001) Towards a framework for tourism disaster management. *Tourism Management* 22, 135–147.

Faulkner, B. and Russell, R. (1997) Chaos and complexity in tourism: in search of a new perspective. *Pacific Tourism Review* 1, 93–102.

Fernando, S. (1995) Theory and practice of participatory development at grassroots level: fact and fiction in Sri Lanka. In: Schneider, H. and Libercier, M.H. (eds) *Participatory Development: From Advocacy to Action.* OECD, Paris, pp. 171–183.

Filho, W.L. (1996) Putting principles in to practices: sustainable tourism in small island states. In: Briguglio, L., Archer, B., Jafari, J. and Wall, G. (eds) *Sustainable Tourism in Islands and Small States: Issues and Policies.* Pinter, London, pp. 61–68.

Folke, C., Carpenter, S., Elmqvist, T., Gunderson, L.H., Holling, C.S., Walker, B., Bengtsson, J., Berkes, F., Colding, J., Danell, K., Falkenmark, M., Gordon, L., Kasperson, R., Kautsky, N., Kinzig, A., Levin, S., Mäker, K.-G., Moberg, F., Ohlsson, L., Olsson, P., Ostrom, E., Reid, W., Rockström, J., Savenije, H. and Svedin, U. (2002) Resilience and sustainable development: building adaptive capacity in a world of transformations. Background Paper for WSSD, Johannesburg, Resilience Alliance for the Swedish Environmental Advisory Council and the International Council for Science (ICSU). ICSU, Series for Sustainable Development. Available at: www.resilliance.org/reports/resilience_and_sustainable_development.pdf (Accessed 28 September, 2004).

Fonda, D. (2004) Farming new words. *Time Magazine* (South Pacific Edition), 10 May.

Font, X. and Bendell, J. (2002) *Standards for Sustainable Tourism for the Purpose of Multilateral Trade Negotiations.* World Tourism Organization, Madrid.

Font, X. and Buckley, R. (2001) *Tourism Eco-labelling: Certification and Promotion of Sustainable Management.* CAB International, Wallingford, UK.

Font, X., Tapper, R. and Kornilaki, M. (2004) *Green Purchasers: Sustainable Supply Chain Management in Tourism. Tourism: State of the Art 2 Conference,* Glasgow, 27–30 June.

Fowler, F.J. (1993) *Survey Research Methods,* 2nd edn. *Applied Social Research Methods,* vol. 1. Sage Publications, London.

Frankel, C. (2001) Mixed messages. In: Starkey, R. and Welford, R. (eds) *The Earthscan Reader in Business and Sustainable Development.* Earthscan, London, pp. 267–281.

Fraser Basin Council (1997) *Charter for Sustainability. Fraser Basin Management Program,* Vancouver. Available at: www.fraserbasin.bc.ca/about_us/vision.html (accessed 14 July, 2004).

Fredline, E. and Faulkner, W. (2000) Host community reactions: a cluster analysis. *Annals of Tourism Research* 27, 763–784.

Friedman, M. (1970) The social responsibility of business is to increase its profits. *New York Times Magazine,* 13 September.

Furley, P., Hughes, C. and Thomas, D. (1996) *Threshold, Carrying Capacity and Sustainable Tourism: Monitoring Environmental Change in the Coastal Zone of Belize.* Department of Geography, University of Edinburgh.

Galbraith, J.K. (1972) *The New Industrial State.* Penguin, Harmondsworth, UK.

Gallopín, G., Hammond, A., Raskin, P. and Swart, P. (1998) *Branch Points: Global Scenarios and Human Choice.* Report No. 7, Global Scenarios Group, Stockholm Environment Institute, Polestar Series, Stockholm.

Gallopín, G.C. (1997) Indicators and their use: information for decision-making. In: Moldan, B. and Bilharz, S. (eds) *Sustainability Indicators: Report of the Project on Indicators of Sustainable Development.* John Wiley & Sons, Chichester, UK, pp. 13–27.

Garcia, S.M., Staples, D.J. and Chesson, J. (2000) The FAO guidelines for the development and use of indicators for sustainable development of marine capture fisheries and an Australian example of their application. *Ocean and Coastal Management* 43, 537–556.

Garrod, B. and Fyall, A. (1998) Beyond the rhetoric of sustainable tourism? *Tourism Management* 19, 199–212.

Gell-Mann, M. (1994) *The Quark and the Jaguar: Adventures in the Simple and the Complex.* Freeman, New York.

GEO-3D Inc. (2001) Technological breakthrough in the field of environmental monitoring, Electronic Press Release. Available at: www.geo-3d.com/ (accessed 16 March, 2002).

Getz, D. (1986) Models in tourism planning: towards integration of theory and practice. *Tourism Management* 1, 21–27.

Gleick, J. (1987) *Chaos: Making a New Science.* Penguin Books, New York.

Godfrey, K. (1998) Attitudes towards sustainable tourism in the UK: a view from local government. *Tourism Management* 19, 213–224.

Goodall, B. and Stabler, M.J. (1997) Principles influencing the determination of environmental standards for sustainable tourism. In: Stabler, M.J. (ed.) *Tourism and Sustainability: Principles to Practice.* CAB International, Wallingford, UK, pp. 279–304.

Goodpaster, M. and Mathews, J. (1982) Can a corporation have a conscience? *Harvard Business Review,* February–March, 34–43.

Gordon, G. (2001a) *Worlds Apart: A Call to Responsible Global Tourism.* Tearfund, London.

Gordon, G. (2001b) *Tourism: Putting Ethics Into Practice.* Tearfund, London.

Government of Samoa (2001) *Samoa Census of Population and Housing.* Department of Statistics, Apia.

Government of Samoa (2002) *Strategy for the Development of Samoa 2002–2004: Opportunities for All.* Department of Treasury, Division of Policy and Planning, Apia.

Government of Samoa and TCSP (Tourism Council of the South Pacific) (1992) *Western Samoa Tourism Development Plan, 1992–2001.* GWS and TCSP, Apia.

Government of Tonga and TCSP (1997) *Tourism Economic Impact Study. Kingdom of Tonga.* TCSP, Suva.

Green Globe (2004) History and Background. Available at: www.greenglobe21.com (accessed 10 May, 2004).

Greiner, R. and Walker, P.A. (1999) *Probing the Future: Systems Analysis for Nature-based Tourist Destinations. The 9th Annual Conference of the European Association of Environmental and Resource Economists,* EAEE, Oslo, 25–27 June.

GRI (Global Reporting Index) (2002) *Sustainability Reporting Guidelines.* Global Reporting Initiative, Boston, Massachusetts.

Gross, B.M. (1966) *The State of the Nation: Social Systems Accounting.* Tavistock Publications, London.

Gunderson, L.H. (2003) Foreword. In: Busch, D.E. and Trexler, J.C. (eds) *Monitoring Ecosystems: Interdisciplinary Approaches for Evaluating Eco-Regional Initiatives.* Centre for Resource Economics/Island Press, Washington, DC, pp. xi–xv.

Gunderson, L.H. and Holling, C.S. (eds) (2002) *Panarchy: Understanding Transformations in Human and Natural Systems.* Island Press, Washington, DC.

Gunderson, L.H., Holling, C.S. and Light, S.S. (ed.) (1995a) *Barriers and Bridges to the Renewal of Ecosystems and Institutions.* Columbia University Press, New York.

Gunderson, L.H., Holling, C.S. and Light, S.S. (1995b) Barriers broken and bridges built: a synthesis. In: Gunderson, L.H., Holling, C.S. and Light, S.S. (eds) *Barriers and Bridges to the Renewal of Ecosystems and Institutions.* Columbia University Press, New York, pp. 489–532.

Gunderson, L.H., Holling, C.S., Pritchard, L. and Peterson, G.D. (2002) Resilience of large-scale resource systems. In: Gunderson, L.H. and Pritchard, L. Jr (eds) *Resilience and the Behaviour of Large-scale Systems.* Scope 60. Island Press, Washington, DC, pp. 3–18.

Gunn, C.A. (1988) *Tourism Planning,* 2nd edn. Taylor and Francis, Washington, DC.

Haley, A., Snaith, T. and Miller, G. (2005) The social impacts of tourism in Bath. *Annals of Tourism Research* (in press).

Hall, C.M. (1994) *Tourism and Politics: Policy, Power and Place.* John Wiley & Sons, Chichester, UK.

Hall, C.M. (1995) *An Introduction to Tourism in Australia: Impacts, Planning and Development,* 2nd edn. Longman, Melbourne.

Hall, C.M. (1998) Historical antecedents of sustainable development and ecotourism: new labels on old bottles? In: Hall, C.M. and Lew, A. (ed.) *Sustainable Tourism: A Geographical Perspective.* Addison Wesley Longman, New York, pp. 13–24.

Hall, C.M. (2000) *Tourism Planning.* Prentice Hall, Harlow, UK.

Hall, C.M. and Butler, R. (1995) In search of common ground: reflections on sustainability, complexity and process in the tourism system – a discussion. *Journal of Sustainable Tourism* 3, 99–105.

Hall, C.M. and Lew, A. (1998a) The geography of sustainable tourism development: an introduction. In: Hall, C.M. and Lew, A. (eds) *Sustainable Tourism: A Geographical Perspective.* Addison Wesley Longman, New York, pp. 1–12.

Hall, C.M. and Lew, A. (1998b) *Sustainable Tourism: A Geographical Perspective.* Longman, Harlow, UK.

Hall, C.M. and Weiler, B. (1992) What's so special about special interest tourism? In: Weiler, B. and Hall, C.M. (eds) *Special Interest Tourism.* Halsted Press, New York, pp. 1–14.

Hammond, A., Adriaanse, A., Rodenburg, E., Bryant, D. and Woodward, R. (1995) *Environmental Indicators: A Systematic Approach to Measuring and Reporting on Environmental Policy Performance in the Context of Sustainable Development.* World Resources Institute, Washington, DC.

Haq, M.U. (1995) *Reflections on Human Development.* Oxford University Press, New York.

Hardi, P. (1997) Measurement and indicators program of the international institute for sustainable development. In: Moldan, B. and Bilharz, S. (eds) *Sustainability Indicators: Report of the Project on Indicators of Sustainable Development.* John Wiley & Sons, Chichester, UK, pp. 28–32.

Hardin, G. (1968) The tragedy of the commons. *Science* 162, 1243–1248.

Hardy, A., Beeton, R.J.S. and Pearson, L. (2002) Sustainable tourism: an overview of the concept and its position in relation to conceptualisations of tourism. *Journal of Sustainable Tourism* 10, 475–496.

Hardy, A.L. and Beeton, R.J.S. (2001) Sustainable tourism or maintainable tourism: managing resources for more than average outcomes. *Journal of Sustainable Tourism* 9, 168–192.

Harper, P. (1997) The importance of community involvement in sustainable development. In: Stabler, M.J. (ed.) *Tourism and Sustainability: Principles to Practice.* CAB International, Wallingford, UK, pp. 143–149.

Harrison, D. (1996) Sustainability and tourism: reflections from a muddy pool. In: Briguglio, L., Archer, B., Jafari, J. and Wall, G. (eds) *Sustainable Tourism in Islands and Small States: Issues and Policies.* Pinter, London, pp. 69–89.

Hart, M. (1999) *Guide to Sustainable Community Indicators*, 2nd edn. Hart Environmental Data, North Andover. Available at: www.sustainablemeasures.com (accessed 16 March, 2002).

Hart, S. (1997) Strategies for a sustainable world. *Harvard Business Review* January–February, pp. 67–76.

Hartman, L. (ed.) (2002) *Perspectives in Business Ethics.* McGraw-Hill, New York.

Hawkes, S. and Williams, P. (1992) *The Greening of Tourism; From Principles to Practice.* Centre for Tourism Policy and Research, Simon Fraser University, BC.

Hawkins, D.E. (2003) *Winds of Change: Sustaining Tourism in Times of Uncertainty.* Ulysses Lecture, World Tourism Organization, Madrid, 5 June.

Hein, W. (1997) Tourism and sustainable development: empirical analysis and concepts of sustainability – a systems approach. In: Hein, W. (ed.) *Tourism and Sustainable Development.* Schriften Des Deutschen Übersee-Instituts, No. 41, Hamburg, pp. 359–400.

Hertz, N. (2001) Better to shop than to vote? *Business Ethics: A European Review* 10, 190–193.

Hess, A.L. (1990) Overview: sustainable development and environmental management of small islands. In: Beller, W., d'Ayala, P. and Hein, P. (eds) *Sustainable Development and Environmental Management of Small Islands, Man and the Biosphere.* Series 5, UNESCO, Paris, pp. 3–14.

Hilton, S. and Gibbons, G. (2002) *Good Business. Your World Needs You.* Texere, London.

Hinsliff, G. (2003) Hospital A&E targets to be axed. *The Observer*, 7 September.

Hjalager, A. (1999) Consumerism and sustainable tourism. *Journal of Travel and Tourism Marketing* 8, 1–22.

Hoffman, M. (2002) Business and environmental ethics. In: Hartman, L. (ed.) *Perspectives in Business Ethics.* McGraw-Hill, New York, pp. 715–721.

Holland, J.H. (1995) *Hidden Order: How Adaptation Builds Complexity.* Addison-Wesley, Reading, Massachusetts.

Holling, C.S. (ed.) (1978) *Adaptive Environmental Assessment and Management.* John Wiley & Sons, New York.

Holling, C.S. (1986) The resilience of terrestrial ecosystems: local surprise and global change. In: Clark, W.C. and Munn, R.E. (eds) *Sustainable Development of the Biosphere, International Institute for Applied Systems Analysis.* Cambridge University Press, Cambridge, pp. 292–317.

Holling, C.S. (1993) Investing in research for sustainability. *Ecological Applications* 3, 552–555.

Holling, C.S. (1995) What barriers, what bridges? In: Gunderson, L.H., Holling, C.S. and Light, S.S. (eds) *Barriers and Bridges to the Renewal of Ecosystems and Institutions*. Columbia University Press, New York, pp. 3–34.

Holling, C.S. (2001) Understanding the complexity of economic, ecological, and social systems. *Ecosystems* 4, 390–405.

Holling, C.S. and Bocking, S. (1990) Surprise and opportunity: in evolution, in ecosystems, in society. In: Mungall, C. and McLaren, D.J. (ed.) *Planet Under Stress: the Challenge of Global Change*. Oxford University Press, Oxford, UK.

Holling, C.S. and Chambers, A.D. (1973) Resource science: the nurture of an infant. *Bioscience* 23, 13–20.

Holling, C.S. and Gunderson, L. (2002) Resilience and adaptive cycles. In: Gunderson, L.H. and Holling, C.S. (eds) (2002) *Panarchy: Understanding Transformations in Human and Natural Systems*. Island Press, Washington, DC, pp. 25–62.

Holling, C.S. and Sanderson, S. (1996) The dynamics of dis(harmony) in ecological and social systems. In: Hanna, S., Folke, C., Maler, K. and Jansson, A. (eds) *Rights of Nature: Ecological, Cultural and Political Principles of Institutions for the Environment*. Island Press, Washington, DC, pp. 57–86.

Horochowski, K. and Moisey, N. (1999) The role of environmental NGOs in sustainable tourism development: a case study in Northern Honduras. *Tourism Recreation Research* 24, 19–29.

Hudson, S. and Miller, G. (2004) Best practices in responsible marketing of tourism: the case of Canadian mountain holidays. *Tourism Management* (in press).

Hughes, G. (2002) Environmental indicators. *Annals of Tourism Research* 29, 457–477.

Hunter, C. (1995) On the need to re-conceptualise sustainable tourism development. *Journal of Sustainable Tourism* 3, 155–165.

Hunter, C. (1997) Sustainable tourism as an adaptive paradigm. *Annals of Tourism Research* 24, 850–867.

Hunter, C. (2002) Aspects of the sustainable tourism debate from a natural resources perspective. In: Harris, R., Griffin, T. and Williams, P. (2002) *Sustainable Tourism: A Global Perspective*. Butterworth-Heinemann, London, pp. 3–23.

IGBP (International Geosphere-Biosphere Programme) (2001) Global change and the Earth system: planet under pressure. IGBP Science No. 4, Stockholm. Available at: www.igbp.kva.se/cgi-bin/php/frameset.php (accessed 16 March, 2001).

IISD (International Institute for Sustainable Development) (1997) Measurements and indicators program. Available at: www.iisd1.iisd.ca/about/m&i.html (accessed 16 March, 2002).

IISD (2004a) The Bellagio Principles. Available at: www.iisd.org/measure/principles/1.htm (accessed 16 June, 2004).

IISD (2004b) The dashboard of sustainability. Available at: www.iisd.org/cgsdi/intro_dashboard.htm (accessed 12 July, 2004).

Inskeep, E. (1991) *Tourism Planning: an Integrated and Sustainable Development Approach*. Van Nostrand Reinhold, New York.

Inskeep, E.L. (1977) Physical planning for tourism development. In: Finney, B.R. and Watson, A. (eds) *A New Kind of Sugar: Tourism in the Pacific*. The East–West Centre, Honolulu, Hawaii, pp. 247–251.

IUCN (World Conservation Union) (1980) *World Conservation Strategy: Living Resource Conservation for Sustainable Development*. World Conservation Union, Gland, Switzerland.

IUCN, UNEP (United Nations Environment Programme) and WWF (World Wide Fund for Nature) (1991) *Caring for the Earth: a Strategy for Sustainable Living.* IUCN, Gland, Switzerland.

Jack, E. and Duka, T.J. (2004) Kangaroo Island Tourism Optimisation Management Model: it's easy for you you're an island. In: WTO (ed.) *WTO Signposts for Sustainable Tourism: Guidebook to the Development and Use of Indicators of Sustainable Development for Tourism Destinations.* WTO, Madrid, p. 399.

Jafari, J. (1989) An English language literature review. In: Bystranowski, J. (ed.) *Tourism as a Factor of Change: a Socio-cultural Study.* Centre for Research and Documentation in Social Sciences, Vienna.

Jamal, T. and Getz, D. (1995) Collaboration theory and community tourism planning. *Annals of Tourism Research* 22, 186–204.

Jamal, T. and Getz, D. (1999) Community roundtables for tourism-related conflicts: the dialectics of consensus and process structures. *Journal of Sustainable Tourism* 7, 290–313.

James, D. (2000) Local sustainable tourism indicators. *Proceedings of the 5th International Forum on Tourism Statistics,* Glasgow Caledonian University, 19–23 June.

Jennings, G. (2001) *Tourism Research.* John Wiley & Sons, Milton, Australia.

Joppe, M. (1996) Sustainable community tourism development revisited. *Tourism Management* 17, 475–479.

Kammerbauer, J., Cordoba, B., Escolan, R., Flores, S., Ramirez, V. and Zeledon, J. (2001) Identification of development indicators in tropical mountainous regions and some implications for natural resource policy designs: an integrated community case study. *Ecological Economics* 36, 45–60.

Kandelaars, P.P.A.A.H. (1997) *A Dynamic Simulation Model of Tourism and the Environment in the Yucatán Peninsula.* Interim Report IR97-18/April, International Institute for Applied Systems Analysis, Vienna.

Kangaroo Island Sustainable Development Committee (1995) *Kangaroo Island Sustainable Development Strategy.* Kangaroo Island Sustainable Development Committee, Kingscote

Kangaroo Island Tourism Policy Working Party (1991) *Kangaroo Island Tourism Policy.* Tourism South Australia, Adelaide.

Kates, R.W. and Clark, W.C. (1996) Environmental surprise: expecting the unexpected. *Environment* 38, 6–34.

Kates, R.W., Clark, W.C., Corell, R., Hall, J.M., Jaeger, C.C., Lowe, I., McCarthy, J.J., Schellnhuber, H.J., Bolin, B., Dickson, N.M., Faucheux, S., Gallopín, G.C., Grübler, A., Huntley, B., Jäger, J., Jodha, N.S., Kasperson, R.E., Mabogunje, A., Matson, P., Mooney, H., Moore, B., O'Riordan, T. and Svedin, U. (2001) Environment and development: sustainability science. *Science* 292, 641–642.

Kauffman, S. (1995) *At Home in the Universe: the Search for the Laws of Self-organization and Complexity.* Oxford University Press, Oxford.

Kay, J., Regier, H., Boyle, M. and Francis, G. (1999) An ecosystem approach for sustainability addressing the challenge of complexity. *Futures* 31, 721–742.

Kaynak, E. and Macauley, J.A. (1984) The Delphi technique in the measurement of tourism market potential: the case of Nova Scotia. *Tourism Management* 5, 87–101.

Kerr, A. (1997) The development of indicators of sustainability in Canada. In: Moldan, B. and Bilharz, S. (eds) *Sustainability Indicators: Report of the Project on Indicators of Sustainable Development.* John Wiley & Sons, Chichester, UK, pp. 302–309.

King, B. (1997) *Creating Island Resorts.* Routledge, London.

Klein, N. (1999) *No Logo.* Flamingo, London.

Klemm, M. and Parkinson, L. (2001) UK tour operator strategies: causes and consequences. *International Journal of Tourism Research* 3, 367–376.

Korten, D. (1987) Third generation NGO strategies: a key to people-centred development. *World Development* 15, 145–159.

Korten, D. (2001) The responsibility of business to the whole. In: Starkey, R. and Welford, R. (eds) *The Earthscan Reader in Business and Sustainable Development.* Earthscan, London, pp. 230–241.

Kousis, M. (2000) Tourism and the environment: a social movements perspective. *Annals of Tourism Research* 27, pp. 468–489.

Krause, D. (1997) Supplier development: current practices and outcomes. *International Journal of Purchasing and Materials Management* 33, 12–19.

Krause, D. (1999) The antecedents of buying firms' efforts to improve suppliers. *Journal of Operations Management* 17, 205–224.

Krause, D., Handfield, R. and Scannell, T. (1998) An empirical investigation of supplier development: reactive and strategic processes. *Journal of Operations Management* 17, 39–58.

Kreutzwiser, R. (1993) Desirable attributes of sustainable indicators for tourism development. In: Butler, R., Nelson, J.G. and Wall, G. (eds) *Tourism and Sustainable Development: Monitoring, Planning, Managing.* Department of Geography Publication Series, University of Waterloo, Ontario, pp. 243–247.

Krippendorf, J. (1982) Towards new tourism policies. *Tourism Management* 3, 135–148.

Ladkin, A. (2000) Sustainable tourism: eco-loving or marketing plot? *International Journal of Tourism Research* 2, 57–63.

Lanfant, M. and Graburn, N.H. (1992) International tourism reconsidered: the principle of the alternative. In: Smith, V.L. and Eadington, W.R. (eds) *Tourism Alternatives – Potential and Problems in the Development of Tourism.* International Academy for the Study of Tourism, University of Pennsylvania Press, Philadelphia, Pennsylvania, pp. 88–112.

Langaas, S. (1997) The spatial dimension of indicators of sustainable development. In: Moldan, B. and Bilharz, S. (eds) *Sustainability Indicators: Report of the Project on Indicators of Sustainable Development.* John Wiley & Sons, Chichester, UK, pp. 33–39.

Lankford, S.V. and Howard, D.R. (1994) Developing a tourism impact attitude scale. *Annals of Tourism Research* 21, 121–139.

Lawrence, J. (1998) Getting the future that you want: the role of sustainability indicators. In: Warburton, D. (ed.) *Community and Sustainable Development.* WWF, Godalming, pp. 68–80.

Laws, E., Faulkner, B. and Moscardo, G. (1998) Embracing and managing change in tourism. In: Laws, E., Faulkner, B. and Moscardo, G. (eds) *Embracing and Managing Change in Tourism: International Case Studies.* Routledge, New York, pp. 1–10.

Lee, K.N. (1993) *Compass and Gyroscope: Integrating Science with Politics for the Environment.* Island Press, Washington, DC.

Leiper, N. (1979) The framework of tourism. *Annals of Tourism Research* 6, 390–407.

Leiper, N. (1990) *Tourism Systems, Department of Management Systems.* Occasional Paper 2, Massey University, Auckland.

Lew, A. and Hall, C.M. (1998) The geography of sustainable tourism: lessons and prospects. In: Hall, C.M. and Lew, A. (eds) *Sustainable Tourism: a Geographical Perspective.* Addison Wesley Longman, New York, pp. 199–203.

Line, M., Hawley, H. and Krut, R. (2002) The development of global environmental and social reporting. *Corporate Environmental Strategy* 9, 69–78.

Lowe, I. (2001) Sustainability science. Transcript of interview with Robyn Williams, Broadcast Sunday 24 June, 2001. Available at: www.abc.net.au/rn/science/ockham/stories/s317194.htm (accessed 10 October, 2003).

Luck, M. (2002) Large-scale ecotourism – a contradiction in itself? *Global Ecotourism Policies and Case Studies* 5, pp. 361–370.

Ludwig, D., Hilborn, R. and Walters, C. (1993) Uncertainty, resource exploitation, and conservation: lessons from history. *Science* 260, 17–36.

MacCannell, D. (1976) *The Tourist: a New Theory of the Leisure Class.* Macmillan Press, London.

MacGillivray, A. (1997) Social development indicators. In: Moldan, B. and Bilharz, S. (eds) *Sustainability Indicators: Report of the Project on Indicators of Sustainable Development.* John Wiley & Sons, Chichester, UK, pp. 256–263.

MacGillivray, A. and Kayes, R. (1997) *Environmental Measures: Indicators for the UK Environment.* Environmental Challenge Group, London.

MacGillivray, A. and Zadek, S. (no date) *Signals of Success.* World Wildlife Fund and New Economics Foundation, London.

MacLellan, R. (1999) *Establishing Sustainable Tourism Indicators: From Theory to Practice.* Paper given at 1 Conferencia Portuguesa, o Ecoturismo e a Sustentabilidade, Universidade De Aveiro, Portugal, 28 May.

Madrigal, R. (1995) Residents' perceptions and the role of government. *Annals of Tourism Research* 22, 86–102.

Malanson, J.P. (1999) Considering complexity. *Annals of the Association of American Geographers* 89, 746–753.

Manidis Roberts Consultants (1997) *Developing a Tourism Optimisation Management Model.* Manidis Roberts Consultants, Surrey Hills, UK.

Manitoba Environment (1997) *Reporting on Progress on Sustainable Development for Manitoba's Prairie Ecozone, Focus Chapter from State of the Environment Report for Manitoba, 1997.* Indicators of Sustainable Development and Manitoba Environment, Manitoba.

Manning, E.W. (1998) *Governance for Tourism: Coping with Tourism in Impacted Destinations, Centre for a Sustainable Future.* Foundation for International Training, Toronto.

Manning, E.W. (1999) Indicators of tourism sustainability. *Tourism Management* 20, 179–181.

Marien, C. and Pizam, A. (1997) Implementing sustainable tourism development through citizen participation in the planning process. In: Wahab, S. and Pigram, J.J. (eds) *Tourism, Development and Growth: the Challenge of Sustainability.* Routledge, London, pp. 164–178.

Marion, J. (1991) *Developing a Natural Resource Inventory and Monitoring Program for Visitors Impacts on Recreation Sites: a Procedural Manual.* National Park Service, Natural Resources Report, NPS/NRVT/NRR-91/06, Denver.

Marten, G. (2001) *Human Ecology: Basic Concepts for Sustainable Development.* Earthscan Publications, London.

Mathieson, A. and Wall, G. (1982) *Tourism: Economic, Physical and Social Impacts.* Longman Scientific and Technical, Harlow, UK.

McArthur, S. (2000) Visitor management in action: an analysis of the development and implementation of visitor management models at Jenolan Caves and Kangaroo Island. PhD thesis, University of Canberra, Australia.

McCarthy, M. (1998) Quality of life index will test national happiness. *The Independent,* 24 November.

McElroy, J.L. and De Albuquerque, K. (1996) Sustainable alternatives to insular mass tourism: recent theory and practice. In: Briguglio, L., Archer, B., Jafari, J. and Wall, G. (eds) *Sustainable Tourism in Islands and Small States: Issues and Policies.* Pinter, London, pp. 47–60.

McIntyre, M. (2000) Review of Initiatives for the Development of State of Environment Reporting (SOE) and Environmental Statistics in the Pacific. Unpublished report, SPREP, Apia.

McKercher, B. (1993) The unrecognised threat to tourism. *Tourism Management* April, 131–136.

McKercher, B. (1999) A chaos approach to tourism. *Tourism Management* 20, 425–434.

McMahon, S. (2002) The development of quality of life indicators – a case study from the city of Bristol, UK. *Ecological Indicators* 2, 177–185.

MEA (Millennium Ecosystem Assessment) (2002) Millennium Ecosystem Assessment methods. Available at: www.millenniumassessment.org (accessed 18 July, 2004).

MEA (2003) Ecosystems and human well-being. Island Press, New York. Available at: www.millenniumassessment.org/en/products.aspx (accessed 18 July, 2004).

MEA (2004) What is integrated ecosystem assessment. Available at: www. millenniumassessment.org (accessed 10 July, 2004).

Meadows, D.H. (1998) *Indicators and Information Systems for Sustainable Development: a Report to the Balaton Group.* The Sustainability Institute, Hartland.

Meadows, D.H., Meadows, D.L., Randers, J. and Behrens, W.W. (1972) *Limits to Growth.* Potomac Associates, Washington, DC.

Meadows, D.H., Meadows, D.L. and Randers, J. (1992) *Beyond the Limits: Confronting Global Collapse, Envisioning a Sustainable Future.* Chelsea Green Publishing Co., Post Mills, Vermont.

Middleton, V.T.C. and Hawkins, R. (1998) *Sustainable Tourism: A Marketing Perspective.* Butterworth-Heinemann, Oxford.

Middleton, V.T.C. and Hawkins, R. (2000) A practical research framework for measuring local progress towards sustainable tourism on a Europe-wide basis. *Proceedings of the 5th International forum on Tourism Statistics,* Glasgow Caledonian University, 19–23 June.

Mill, R.C. and Morrison, A.M. (1985) *The Tourist System: an Introductory Text.* Prentice Hall, Englewood Cliffs, New Jersey.

Miller, G. (2001a) The development of indicators for sustainable tourism: results of a Delphi survey of tourism researchers. *Tourism Management* 22, 351–362.

Miller, G. (2001b) Corporate Responsibility in the UK Tourism Industry. *Tourism Management* 22, 500–512.

Miller, G. (2003) Consumerism in sustainable tourism: a survey of UK consumers. *Journal of Sustainable Tourism* 11, 17–39.

Miller, G. and Ritchie, B. (2003) A farming crisis or a tourism disaster? An analysis of the foot and mouth disease in the UK. *Current Issues in Tourism* 6, 150–171.

Miller, G. and Twining-Ward, L. (2003) *Indicators of Sustainable Tourism.* European Union and University of the South Pacific Public Lecture, Suva, Fiji, 27 August.

Milman, A. and Pizam, A. (1988) Social impacts of tourism on central Florida. *Annals of Tourism Research* 15, 191–204.

Milne, S. (1997) Tourism, dependency and South Pacific Microstates: beyond the vicious circle. In: Lockhart, D.G. and Drakakis-Smith, D. (eds) *Island Tourism: Trends and Prospects.* Pinter, London, pp. 281–300.

Moisey, R.N. and McCool, S.F. (2001) Sustainable tourism in the 21st century: lessons from the past: challenges to address. In: McCool, S.F. and Moisey, R.N. (eds) *Tourism Recreation and Sustainability.* CAB International, Wallingford, UK, pp. 343–352.

Moldan, B. (1997a) A tentative proposal for a comprehensive set of policy relevant indicators. In: Moldan, B. and Bilharz, S. (eds) *Sustainability Indicators: Report of the Project on Indicators of Sustainable Development.* John Wiley & Sons, Chichester, UK, pp. 164–169.

Moldan, B. (1997b) World Bank perspectives on sustainable development. In: Moldan, B. and Bilharz, S. (eds) *Sustainability Indicators: Report of the Project on Indicators of Sustainable Development.* John Wiley & Sons, Chichester, UK, pp. 138–141.

Moldan, B. and Bilharz, S. (1997) *Sustainability Indicators: Report of the Project on Indicators of Sustainable Development.* John Wiley & Sons, Chichester, UK.

Moore, B. III, Underdal, A., Lemke, P. and Loreau, M. (2001) The Amsterdam Declaration. *Proceedings of Global Change Open Science Conference: Challenges of A Changing Earth,* Amsterdam, 13 July.

Morhardt, J.E., Baird, S. and Freeman, K. (2002) Scoring corporate environmental and sustainability reports using GRI 2000, ISO14031 and other criteria. *Corporate Social Responsibility and Environmental Management* 9, 215–233.

Moser, W. and Petersen, J. (1981) Limits to Obergürgl's growth: Alpine experience in environmental management. *Ambio* 10, 68–72.

Mowforth, A. and Munt, I. (1998) *Tourism and Sustainability: New Tourism in the Third World.* Routledge, London

Muller, H. (1994) The thorny path to sustainable tourism development. *Journal of Sustainable Tourism* 2, 131–136.

Munro, D.A. (1995) Sustainability: rhetoric or reality? In: Trzyna, C. and Osborn, J.K. (eds) *A Sustainable World: Defining and Measuring Sustainable Development.* IUCN, California Institute of Public Affairs, Sacramento, California, pp. 27–35.

Murphy, P.E. (1985) *Tourism: A Community Approach.* Methuen, London.

Neil, J. and Wearing, S. (1999) *Ecotourism, Impacts, Potentials and Possibilities.* Butterworth-Heinemann, Oxford.

Nelson, J.G., Butler, R. and Wall, G. (eds) (1993) *Tourism and Sustainable Development: Monitoring, Planning, Managing.* Department of Geography, Publication Series Number 37, University of Waterloo.

Nettenkoven, L. (1979) Mechanisms of intercultural interaction. In: DeKadt, E. (ed.) *Tourism – Passport to Development?* Oxford University Press, Oxford, pp. 135–145.

NEF (New Economics Foundation) (2001) *Taking Flight: the Rapid Growth of Ethical Consumerism.* NEF, London.

NEF (2003) *Making Indicators Count.* New Economics Foundation, London.

Newman, P., Marion, J. and Cahill, K. (2001) Integrating resource, social, and managerial indicators of quality into carrying capacity decision-making. *The George Wright Forum* 18, 28–40.

Noon, B.R. (2003) Conceptual issues in monitoring ecological resources. In: Busch, D.E. and Trexler, J.C. (eds) *Monitoring Ecosystems: Interdisciplinary Approaches for Evaluating Ecoregional Initiatives.* Island Press, Washington, DC, pp. 27–72.

NORAD (Norwegian Agency for Development Corporation) (1997) *The Logical Framework Approach Handbook for Objectives-Oriented Planning,* 2nd edn. Norwegian Agency for Development Co-operation, Oslo.

NPF (Norwegian Petroleum Fund) (2004) The Norwegian Government Petroleum Fund. Available at: odin.dep.no/fin/engelsk/p10001617/006051-990060/dok-bn.html (accessed 9 September, 2004).

Nowicki, P. and Nowicki-Caupin, N. (1987) The state of the environment in the European Community. *European Environmental Review* 4, 42–46.

NRC (National Research Council) (1999) *Our Common Journey, a Transition Toward Sustainability.* National Academy Press, Washington, DC.

NRC (2001) *Climate Change Science: an Analysis of Some Key Questions.* National Academy Press, Washington, DC.

Nunez, T. (1989) Touristic studies in anthropological perspective. In: Smith, V.L. (ed.) *Hosts and Guests: the Anthropology of Tourism,* 2nd edn. University of Pennsylvania, Philadelphia, Pennsylvania.

Nyberg, B. (1999) *An Introductory Guide to Adaptive Management: for Project Leaders and Participants.* BC Forest Service, Victoria.

ODI (Overseas Development Institute) (2003) *The UK Outbound Tour Operating Industry and Implications for Pro-poor Tourism.* Pro-poor Tourism Working Paper No.17, ODI, London.

Odour-Noah, E., Asamba, I., Ford, R., Wichhart, L. and Lelo, F. (1992) *Implementing PRA: a Handbook to Facilitate Participatory Rural Appraisal, United States Agency for International Development.* Clark University, Worcester, Massachusetts.

Odum, H., Odum, E. and Brown, M. (1998) *Environment and Society in Florida.* Lewis Publishers, Boca Raton, Florida.

OECD (Organization for Economic and Cooperative Development) (1993) *Core Set of Indicators for Environmental Performance Reviews.* OECD, Paris.

OECD (1998) *Towards Sustainable Development: Environmental Indicators.* OECD, Paris.

OECD (2003) OECD environmental indicators: development, measurement and use. Available at: www.oecd.org/env/ (accessed 1 April, 2004).

Page, S.J. (1996) *The Pacific Islands.* Economist Intelligence Unit International Tourism Reports No. 1, EIU, London.

Palme Commission (1982) *Common Security: a Blueprint for Survival, Independent Commission on Disarmament and Security Issues.* Simon and Schuster, New York.

Parsons, E.A. and Clark, W.C. (1995) Sustainable development as social learning: theoretical perspectives and practical challenges for the design of a research program. In: Gunderson, L.H., Holling, C.S. and Light, S.S. (eds) *Barriers and Bridges to the Renewal of Ecosystems and Institutions.* Columbia University Press, New York, pp. 428–460.

PASTILLE (2002) *Local Sustainability Indicator Sets in their Context.* FP5, European Union.

Pearce, D.G. (1995) Planning for tourism in the 1990s: an integrated, dynamic, multi-scale approach. In: Butler, R.W. and Pearce, D. (eds) *Change in Tourism: People, Places, Processes*. Routledge, London, pp. 229–244.

Pearce, D.W., Turner, R.K., O'Riordan, T., Adger, N., Atkinson, G., Brisson, I., Brown, K., Dubourg, R., Frankhauser, S., Jordan, A., Maddison, D., Moran, D. and Powell, J. (1993) *Blueprint 3: Measuring Sustainable Development*. CSERGE, Earthscan Publications, London.

Pearlman, M. (2002) *Key Issues in the Implementation of the Kangaroo Island TOMM*. Victoria University, Wellington.

Pedelty, M. (2004) Being ethical pays dividends. *Sunday Times*, 14 March.

Peterson, G., Allen, C.R. and Holling, C.S. (1998) Ecological resilience, biodiversity, and scale. *Ecosystems* 1, 6–18.

Peterson, P.J. (1997) *Indicators of Sustainable Development in Industrializing Countries: the Roles of Indicators of Sustainable Development, Volume II, From Concepts to Action*. Lestari Monograph No 1, Universiti Kabangsaan Malaysia Press, Bangi.

Pheby, K. (1997) The psychological contract. In: Davies, P. (ed.) *Current Issues in Business Ethics*. Routledge, London, pp. 76–86.

Pigram, J. (1990) Sustainable tourism – policy considerations. *The Journal of Tourism Studies* 1, 2–9.

Plog, S. (1974) Why destinations areas rise and fall in popularity. *Cornell Hotel and Administration Quarterly* 14, 55–58.

Poon, A. (1993) *Tourism, Technology and Competitive Strategies*. CAB International, Wallingford, UK.

Potts, T.D. and Harril, R. (1998) Enhancing communities for sustainability: a travel ecology approach. *Tourism Analysis* 3, 133–142.

PPK Planning (1993) *Kangaroo Island Planning Strategy: Statement of Investigations for the District Council of Dudley and the District Council of Kingscote*. District Councils of Kangaroo Island Region, Adelaide.

Pratley, N. (2004) Sisters who stirred the conscience of Coca-Cola. *The Guardian*, 10 April.

Prescott-Allen, R. (1997) Barometer of sustainability. In: Moldan, B. and Bilharz, S. (eds) *Sustainability Indicators: Report of the Project on Indicators of Sustainable Development*. John Wiley & Sons, Chichester, UK, pp. 100–111.

Prestbo, J. (2000) Explaining the Dow Jones Sustainability Group. Speech Given to the WBCSD Liaison Delegates Meeting, Montreux, Switzerland, 29 March.

Pretty, J.N. (1995) The many interpretations of participation. *In Focus* 16, 4–5.

Pretty, J.N. (1998) Participatory learning for integrated farming. In: Dolberg, F. and Petersen, P.H. (eds) *Proceedings of Workshop on Integrated Farming in Human Development*, March 25–29, Tune Landboskole, Denmark, pp. 12–34.

Ranganathan, J. and Willis, A. (1999) *The Global Reporting Initiative: an Emerging Tool for Corporate Accountability*. World Resources Institute, Washington, DC.

Raskin, P., Gallopín, G., Gutman, P., Hammond, A. and Swart, P. (1998) *Bending the Curve Towards Sustainability*. Global Scenarios Group, Stockholm Environment Institute, Polestar Series, Report No. 8, Stockholm.

Reed, M. (1997) Power relations and community-based tourism planning. *Annals of Tourism Research* 24, 566–591.

Reed, M. (1999) Collaborative tourism planning as adaptive experiments in emergent tourism settings. *Journal of Sustainable Tourism* 7, 331–355.

Reidenbach, R.E. and Robin, D.P. (1990) Toward the development of a multi-dimensional scale for improving evaluations of business ethics. *Journal of Business Ethics* 9, 639–653.

Resilience Alliance (2004) Introduction. Available at: www.resalliance.org/ev_en.php (accessed 20 September, 2004).

Richter, L. (1987) The search for appropriate tourism. *Tourism Recreation Research,* 12, 5–7.

Rigby, R. (2004) Cornering the niche market in responsible behaviour. *The Observer,* 25 April.

Ritchie, J.R.B. (1985) The nominal group technique. *Tourism Management* 6, 82–94.

Ritchie, J.R.B., Hudson, S. and Timur, S. (2002) Public reactions to policy recommendations from the Banff-Bow Valley study: a longitudinal assessment. *Journal of Sustainable Tourism* 10, 295–308.

Robinson, M. (1999) Collaboration and cultural consent: refocusing sustainable tourism. *Journal of Sustainable Tourism* 7, 379–397.

Roddick, A. (2004) Fair play. *The Observer,* 22 May.

Rollins, R., Trotter, W. and Taylor, B. (1998) Adaptive management of recreation sites in the wildland–urban interface. *Journal of Applied Recreation Research* 23, 107–125.

Romeril, M. (1997) *Jersey in the New Millennium: a Sustainable Future. Summary of the Consultative Process.* States of Jersey, Jersey.

Rostow, W.W. (1960) *The Stages of Economic Growth: a Non-Communist Manifesto.* Cambridge University Press, Cambridge.

Russell, R. and Faulkner, B. (1999) Movers and shakers: chaos makers in tourism development. *Tourism Management* 20, 411–423.

Russell, R. and Faulkner, B. (2004) Entrepreneurship, chaos and the tourism area lifecycle. *Annals of Tourism Research* 31, 556–579.

Rutherford, I.D. (1997a) Pieces of a greater picture. In: Moldan, B. and Bilharz, S. (eds) *Sustainability Indicators: Report of the Project on Indicators of Sustainable Development.* John Wiley & Sons, Chichester, UK, pp. 133–156.

Rutherford, I.D. (1997b) Use of models to link indicators of sustainable development. In: Moldan, B. and Bilharz, S. (eds) *Sustainability Indicators: Report of the Project on Indicators of Sustainable Development.* John Wiley & Sons, Chichester, UK, pp. 54–58.

Ryan, C. (2002) Equity, management, power sharing and sustainability – issues of the 'new tourism'. *Tourism Management* 23, 17–26.

Sachs, I. (1974) Environment and styles of development. *African Environment* 1, 9–33.

Saglio, C. (1979) Tourism for discovery: a project in lower Casamance, Senegal. In: De Kadt, E. (ed.) *Tourism – Passport to Development? Perspectives on the Social and Cultural Effects of Tourism in Developing Countries.* Oxford University Press, New York, pp. 321–335.

SATC (South Australian Tourism Commission), DEH (Department for Environment and Heritage) (2003) *Responsible Nature-based Tourism Strategy 2004–2009.* South Australian Tourism Commission and Department for Environment and Heritage, Adelaide.

Sautter, E.T. and Leison, B. (1999) Managing stakeholders: a tourism planning model. *Annals of Tourism Research* 26, 312–328.

Scheffer, M., Westley, F., Brock, W.A. and Holmgren, M. (2002) Dynamic interaction of societies and ecosystems – linking theories from ecology, economy and sociology. In: Gunderson, L.H. and Holling, C.S. (eds) *Panarchy: Understanding Transformations in Human and Natural Systems*. Island Press, Washington, DC, 195–240.

Scheyvens, R. (2002) *Tourism for Development: Empowering Communities*. Prentice Hall, Harlow, UK.

Scheyvens, R. (2004) Growth and benefits of budget beach fale tourism. In: Storey, D., Overton, J. and Nowak, B. (eds) *Contesting Development: Pathways to Better Practice: Proceedings of the Third Biennial Conference of the Aotearoa*. International Development Studies Network Conference, New Zealand, 5–7 December, 2002, Massey University, Palmerston North, pp. 229–233.

Schumacher, E.F. (1973) *Small is Beautiful: a Study of Economics as if People Mattered*. Blond and Briggs, Tiptree, UK.

Sharpley, R. (2000) Tourism and sustainable development: exploring the theoretical divide. *Journal of Sustainable Tourism* 8, 1–19.

Simmons, D.G. (1994) Community participation in tourism planning. *Tourism Management* 15, 98–108.

Sirakaya, E. (1997) Assessment of factors affecting conformance behaviour of eco-tour operators with industry guidelines. *Tourism Analysis* 2, 17–36.

Sirakaya, E. and McLellan, R.W. (1998) Modelling tour operators' voluntary compliance with ecotourism principles: a behavioural approach. *Journal of Travel Research* 36, 42–55.

Sirakaya, E. and Uysal, M. (1997) Can sanctions and rewards explain conformance behaviour of tour operators with ecotourism guidelines? *Journal of Sustainable Tourism* 5, 322–332.

Sirakaya, E., Sasidharan, V. and Sonmez, S. (1999) Re-defining eco-tourism: the need for a supply side view. *Journal of Travel Research* 38, 168–172.

Sirakaya, E., Jamal, T.B. and Choi, H.S. (2001) Developing indicators for destination sustainability. In: Weaver, D.B. (ed.) *The Encyclopaedia of Ecotourism*. CAB International, Wallingford, UK, pp. 411–431.

Smith, N.C. (1990) *Morality and the Market: Consumer Pressure for Corporate Accountability*. Routledge, London.

Smith, V.L. (ed.) (1989) *Hosts and Guests: the Anthropology of Tourism*, 2nd edn. University of Pennsylvania Press, Philadelphia, Pennsylvania.

Smith, V.L. and Eadington, W.R. (1989) *Tourism Alternatives: Potentials and Problems in the Development of Tourism*. University of Pennsylvania Press, Philadelphia, Pennsylvania.

Sparrowhawk, J. and Holden, A. (1999) Human development: the role of tourism based NGOs in Nepal. *Tourism Recreation Research* 24, 37–43.

SPREP (South Pacific Regional Environmental Programme) (1992) *The Pacific Way: Pacific Islands Developing Countries Report to the United Nations Conference on Environment and Development*. SPREP, Apia.

STA (Samoan Tourism Authority) and Government Department of Statistics (2004) Unpublished visitors arrival statistics, Apia.

Stabler, M.J. (ed.) (1997) *Tourism and Sustainability: Principles to Practice*. CAB International, Wallingford, UK.

Stankey, G.H. (1999) The recreation opportunity spectrum and the Limits of Acceptable Change planning systems: a review of experiences and lessons. In: Aley, J., Burch, W.R., Conover, B. and Field, D. (eds) *Ecosystem Management:*

Adaptive Strategies for Natural Resource Organizations in the Twenty-first Century.
Taylor and Francis, Philadelphia, Pennsylvania, pp. 173–188.

Stankey, G.H., Cole, D.N., Lucas, R.C., Peterson, M.E. and Frissell, S.S. (1985) *The Limits of Acceptable Change System for Wilderness Planning.* General Technical Report INP–176, USDA Forest Service, Intermountain Forest and Range Experiment Station, Ogden, Utah.

Stankovic, S.M. (1979) A contribution to the knowledge of the protection of nature and tourism. *Tourist Review* 34, 24–26.

Steffen, W., Andreae, M.O., Bolin, B., Cox, P.M., Crutzen, P.M., Cubasch, U., Held, H., Nakicenovic, N., Scholes, R., Talaue-McManus, L. and Turner, B.L. II (2004) The Achilles heels of the Earth system. *Environment* 46, 8–20.

Steinbeck, J. (2000) *The Grapes of Wrath.* Penguin, London.

Stepp, J.R., Jones, E.C., Pavao-Zuckerman, M. and Casagrande, D. (2003) Remarkable properties of human ecosystems. *Conservation Ecology* 7, 11.

Sternberg, M. (1995) *Just Business.* Oxford University Press, Oxford.

Stiglitz, J. (2002) *Globalization and its Discontents.* Penguin, London.

Stonich, S. (1998) Political ecology of tourism. *Annals of Tourism Research* 25, 25–54.

Suresh, K., Babu, H. and Siva, S. (1999) Reflections on the role of NGOs in tourism with reference to India. *Tourism Recreation Research* 24, 88–91.

Sustainability and UNEP (2000) *The Global Reporters. Engaging Stakeholders.* Sustainability Ltd, London.

Sustainability Science Forum (2002) Forum on science and technology for sustainability. Available at: www.sustsci.harvard.edu/ (accessed 17 July, 2004).

Sustainable Seattle (1998) Indicators of sustainable community, 1998. Available at: www.scn.org/sustainable/indicators.html (accessed 16 March, 2002).

SVB (Samoan Visitors Bureau) (2000a) *Summary of Annual Tourist Arrivals by Source Market and Purpose of Visit. 1992–1999.* SVB, Apia.

SVB (2000b) *Samoa Sustainable Tourism Status Report 2000.* SVB and NZAID, Apia.

SVB (2000c) *Samoa Visitors Bureau Corporate Plan 2002.* SVB, Apia.

Swarbrooke, J. (1999) *Sustainable Tourism Management.* CAB International, Wallingford, UK.

Tainter, J.A. (1996) Complexity, problem-solving and sustainable societies. In: Constanza, R., Segura, O. and Martinez-Alier, J. (eds) *Getting Down to Earth: Practical Applications of Ecological Economics.* Island Press, Washington, DC.

Tapper, R. (2001) Tourism and socio-economic development: UK tour operators' business approaches in the context of the new international agenda. *International Journal of Tourism Research* 3, 351–366.

Taylor, G. (1995) The community approach: does it really work? *Tourism Management* 16, 487–489.

Tearfund (2002) *Worlds Apart: a Call to Responsible Global Tourism.* Tearfund, London.

Terrorism Act (2000) The Stationery Office Ltd, London.

The Economist (1999) Seeing green, 28 October.

The Economist (2000) What to do about global warming? 16 November.

The Economist (2002) The great race, 4 July.

The Economist (2003) Beyond shareholder value, 26 June.

Thomas, H. and Thomas, R. (1996) The implications for tourism of shifts in British local governance. *Progress in Tourism and Hospitality Research* 4, 295–306.

Todd, S.E. and Williams, P.W. (1996) From white to green: a proposed environmental management system framework for ski areas. *Journal of Sustainable Tourism* 4, 147–173.

TOMM (Tourism Optimization Management Model) (2003) Unpublished results from Kangaroo Island visitor exit survey. *Annual Report 2002–2003*. Kangaroo Island, Kingscote.

TOMM (2004) Tourism Optimization Management Model, Kangaroo Island. Available at: www.tomm.info (accessed 17 July, 2004).

Tosun, C. (2000) Limits to participation in the tourism development process in developing countries. *Tourism Management* 21, 613–633.

Tourism Canada (1990) *An Action Strategy for Sustainable Tourism Development: Globe '90*. Tourism Canada, Ottawa.

Tourism Concern (2004) Current campaigns. Available at: www.tourismconcern. org.uk (accessed 18 August, 2004).

Trexler, J.C. and Busch, D.E. (2003) Monitoring, assessment and eco-regional initiatives: a synthesis. In: Busch, D.E. and Trexler, J.C. (eds) *Monitoring Ecosystems: Interdisciplinary Approaches for Evaluating Eco-regional Initiatives*. Island Press, Washington, DC, pp. 405–424.

Turner, L. and Ash, J. (1975) *The Golden Hordes, International Tourism and the Pleasure Periphery*. Constable and Co., London.

Turner, R., Miller, G. and Gilbert, D. (2001) The role of UK charities and the tourism industry. *Tourism Management* 22, 463–472.

Twining-Ward, L. (2002) Monitoring sustainable tourism development: a comprehensive, stakeholder-driven, adaptive approach. PhD thesis. University of Surrey, Guildford.

Twining-Ward, L. (2003) *Indicator Handbook: Guide to the Development and Use of Samoa's Sustainable Tourism Indicators*. SPREP and NZODA, Apia.

Twining-Ward, L. and Butler, R. (2002) Implementing STD on a small island: development and use of sustainable tourism development indicators in Samoa. *Journal of Sustainable Tourism* 10, 363–387.

Twining-Ward, L. and Tuailemafua, T.S. (2004) Small island tourism: monitoring sustainable tourism development in Samoa. *The Journal of Pacific Studies* 26, 777–103.

Twining-Ward, L. and Twining-Ward, T. (1998) Tourism development in Samoa: context and constraints. *Pacific Tourism Review* 2, 261–172.

Twyford, K. (2001) Protected area management: principles and practices. In: Worboys, G., Lockwood, M. and De Lacy, T. (eds) *Protected Area Management: Principles and Practices. CD Compendium*. Oxford University Press, South Melbourne.

UK Roundtable on Sustainable Development (1997) *Round Table Report: Getting the Best out of Indicators*. Department of Environment, Transport and the Regions Publication, Wetherby.

UN (United Nations) (1948) *Universal Declaration of Human Rights*. UN, New York.

UN (1993) *Earth Summit Agenda 21: the United Nations Programme of Action From Rio*. UN Department of Public Information, New York.

UN (1996) *Indicators of Sustainable Development Framework and Methodologies*. UN Department of Public Information, New York.

UN (2000) Millennium Development Goals. Available at: www.developmentgoals.org (accessed 10 July, 2004).

UN (2004) International meeting for the 10-year review of the Barbados programme of action on small island developing states. Mauritius, August/September.

UNCSD (United Nations Commission for Sustainable Development) (1997) Outcome from the CSD Intercessional Working Group. CSD Update, 3, 5. Available at: www.un.org/esa/sustdev/publications/csd_update.htm (accessed 13 June, 1997).

UNCSD (2001a) From theory to practice: indicators of sustainable development, Secretariat of the UN Commission of Sustainable Development, New York.

UNCSD (2001b) Indicators of sustainable development and their use. CSD Update, 7, 3, 6. Available at: www.un.org/esa/sustdev/publications/csd_update.htm (accessed 16 March, 2002).

UNCSD (2002) Indicators of sustainable development: guidelines and methodologies. Available at: www.un.org/esa/sustdev/natlinfo/indicators/isdms2001/table_4.htm (accessed 1 April 2004).

UNDP (United Nations Development Programme) (1999) *Pacific Human Development Report 1999: Creating Opportunities*. UNDP, Suva.

UNDP, WTO (World Tourism Organization) and Government of Niue (1997) *Tourism and Private Sector Development Programme*. Niue, New York.

UNEP (1984) The Cocoyoc Declaration. In: Dasmann, R.F. (ed.) *Environmental Conservation*. John Wiley & Sons, Chichester, UK, pp. 453–462.

UNEP (1995) *Environmental Codes of Conduct for Tourism*. Technical Report #29, UNEP, Paris.

UNEP (1997) Recommendations for a core set of indicators of biological diversity. In: Liaison Group on Indicators of Biological Diversity (ed.) *Third Meeting of the Subsidiary Body on Scientific, Technical and Technological Advance*. UNEP/CBD/SBSTTS/3/Inf.13, 1–5 September, Montreal.

UNEP (1998) *Global Environmental Outlook: the Pacific Region*. SPREP, Apia.

Urry, J. (1990) *The Tourist Gaze*. Sage, London.

US Interagency Working Group on Sustainable Development Indicators (1998) *Sustainable Development in the US: an Experimental Set of Indicators*. US Interagency Working Group on Sustainable Development, Washington, DC.

van den Berghe, P. (1992) Tourism and the ethnic division of labour. *Annals of Tourism Research* 19, 234–249.

Van Esch, S. (1997) indicators for the environment programme in the Netherlands. In: Moldan, B. and Bilharz, S. (eds) *Sustainability Indicators: Report of the Project on Indicators of Sustainable Development*. John Wiley & Sons, Chichester, UK, pp. 310–317.

Velikova, M.P. (2001) How sustainable is sustainable tourism? *Annals of Tourism Research*, 28, 496–499.

Waddell, S. (2002) *The Global Reporting Initiative: Building a Corporate Reporting Strategy Globally*. The Global Action Network Net, Boston, Massachusetts.

Wadsworth, Y. (1998) *What is Participatory Action Research? Action Research International, Paper 2*. Institute of Work Place Research, Learning and Development, Southern Cross University Press, Alstonville.

Walker, B. (2004) Managing for resilience of coupled human-natural systems. Available at: www.resalliance.org/ev_en.php?ID=1010_201&ID2=DO_TOPIC (accessed 28 September, 2004).

Walker, P.A., Greiner, R., McDonald, D. and Lyne, V. (1999) The tourism futures simulator: a systems thinking approach. *Environmental Modelling and Software* 14, 59–67.

Wall, G. (1997) Sustainable tourism – unsustainable development. In: Wahab, S. and Pigram, J.J. (eds) *Tourism Development and Growth*. Routledge, London, pp. 33–49.

Walsh, C. and Morgan, O. (2004) UK firms face lawsuits as Watts quits ICC post. *The Observer*, 4 April.

Walters, C.J. (1986) *Adaptive Management of Renewable Resources*. Macmillan, New York.

Walters, C.J. and Hilborn, R. (1978) Ecological optimization and adaptive management. *Annual Review of Ecological Systems* 9, 157–188.

Ward, T., Kingstone, F. and Siwatibau, S. (1999) Indicators of success for the South Pacific Biodiversity Conservation Programme, Volume One: Technical report. Unpublished draft for discussion, SPREP, Apia.

WBCSD (World Business Council for Sustainable Development) (2001) *Sustainability Through the Market*. WBCSD, Geneva.

WBCSD (2002) The business case for sustainable development: making a difference towards the Earth Summit 2002 and beyond. *Corporate Environmental Strategy* 9, 226–235.

WCED (World Council for Economic Development) (1987) *Our Common Future, World Commission on the Environment and Development*. Oxford University Press, Oxford.

Weaver, D.B. (1998) Introduction to ecotourism. In: Weaver, D. (ed.) *Ecotourism in the Less Developed World*. CAB International, Wallingford, UK, pp. 1–33.

Weaver, D.B. and Lawton, L. (1999) *Sustainable Tourism: a Critical Analysis*. CRC Griffith University, Queensland.

Webster, K. (1998) Developing community LA21s. In: Warburton, D. (ed.) *Community and Sustainable Development*. Earthscan Publications, London, pp. 189–197.

Western, D. (2000) Conservation in a human dominated world. Issues in Science and Technology, Spring. Available at: www.nap.edu/issues/16.3/western.htm (accessed 16 March, 2002).

Westley, F. (1995) Governing design: the management of social systems and ecosystems management. In: Gunderson, L.H., Holling, C.S. and Light, S.S. (eds) *Barriers and Bridges to the Renewal of Ecosystems and Institutions*. Columbia University Press, New York, pp. 391–427.

WGBU (German Advisory Council on Global Change) (1996) *World in Transition: the Research Challenge*. WGBU Annual Report 1996, Springer-Verlag, Berlin.

Wheeller, B. (1991) Tourism's troubled times: responsible tourism is not the answer. *Tourism Management* 12, 91–96.

Wheeller, B. (1992) Alternative tourism – a deceptive ploy. *Progress in Tourism and Hospitality Research* 4, 140–145.

Wheeller, B. (1993) Sustaining the ego. *Journal of Sustainable Tourism* 12, 121–129.

Wheeller, B. (1994a) Ecotourism: a ruse by any other name. *Progress in Tourism and Hospitality Research* 6, 3–11.

Wheeller, B. (1994b) Ecotourism, sustainable tourism and the environment – a symbiotic, symbolic or shambolic relationship. In: Seaton, A.V. (ed.) *The State of the Art*. John Wiley & Sons, Chichester, UK, pp. 645–654.

Whitehouse, C. (2003) The ants and the cockroach: a challenge to the use of indicators. Unpublished UNDP discussion paper, Bhutan.

Wight, P.A. (1995) Environmentally responsible marketing of tourism. In: Cater, E. and Lowman, G. (eds) *Ecotourism: a Sustainable Option?* Royal Geographic Society in association with John Wiley & Sons, Chichester, UK, pp. 39–55.

Wight, P.A. (1998) Tools for sustainability analysis in planning and managing tourism and recreation in the destination. In: Hall, C.M. and Lew, A. (eds) *Sustainable Tourism: a Geographical Perspective.* Addison Wesley Longman, New York, pp. 75–91.

Wilcox, D. (1994) A guide to effective participation. Available at: www.partnerships.org.uk/guide/index.htm (accessed 16 March, 2002).

Wilkinson, P.F. (1989) Strategies for tourism in island microstates. *Annals of Tourism Research* 16, 153–177.

Willis, C.A.A. (2003) The role of the global reporting initiative's sustainability reporting guidelines in the social screening of investments. *Journal of Business Ethics* 43, 233–237.

Wilson, D. (2000) Corporate citizenship: the state of the business case. Available at: www.baa.co.uk (accessed 13 October, 2004).

Wilson, E.O. (2002) The bottleneck. *Scientific American* 286, 82–91.

Winderl, T. (2003) Response to Chris Whitehouse. Unpublished UNDP discussion paper, Bhutan.

World Conference on Sustainable Tourism (1995) The World Conference on Sustainable Tourism. Lanzarote, 24–29 April. *Insula*, 4, 4–7.

World Economic Forum (2001) 2001 Environmental Sustainability Index. Available at: www.ciesin.columbia.edu/indicators/ESI/ (accessed 13 October, 2002).

WRI (World Resources Insitute) (2000) World resources 2000–2001. People and ecosystems: the fraying web of life. Available at: www.wri.org/wr2000/ecosystems.html (accessed 17 July, 2004).

WTO (1985) *Development of a System of Statistical Indicators for Travel and Tourism.* WTO, Madrid.

WTO (1993) *Indicators for the Sustainable Management of Tourism.* International Institute for Sustainable Development, Winnipeg, Canada.

WTO (1996) *What Tourism Managers Need to Know: a Practical Guide to the Development and Use of Indicators of Sustainable Tourism.* WTO, Madrid.

WTO (1999) *Global Code of Ethics for Tourism.* WTO, Madrid.

WTO (2000) *Study on Indicators for the Sustainable Management of Tourism: Beruwala.* WTO, Madrid.

WTO (2001a) *Global Code of Ethics for Tourism: Preparing the New Millennium.* WTO Secretariat, Madrid.

WTO (2001b) *Workshop on Sustainable Tourism Indicators for the Islands of the Mediterranean,* Kukljica, Island of Ugljan, Croatia, 21–23 March, WTO, Madrid.

WTO (2004a) Global tourism to double in 15 years. Available at: www.world-tourism.org/facts/highlights/Highlights.pdf (accessed 17 May, 2004).

WTO (2004b) *Signposts for Sustainable Tourism: a Guidebook for the Development and Use of Indicators of Sustainable Development for Tourism Destinations.* Working Draft March 2004. WTO, Madrid.

WTO (2004c) *Field Manual for Indicator Development.* Working Draft March 2004. WTO, Madrid.

WTO (2004d) *Indicators of Sustainable Development for Tourism Destinations: a Guidebook.* WTO, Madrid.

WTTC (World Travel and Tourism Council) (2004) Competitiveness monitor. Available at: www.wttc.org (accessed 15 June, 2004).

WTTC, WTO and Earth Council (1997) *Agenda 21 for the Travel & Tourism Industry: Towards Environmentally Sustainable Development.* WTO, Madrid.

Zentilli, B. (1997) Criteria and indicators for sustainable management of forests. In: Moldan, B. and Bilharz, S. (eds) *Sustainability Indicators: Report of the Project on Indicators of Sustainable Development.* John Wiley & Sons, Chichester, UK, pp. 230–236.

Index

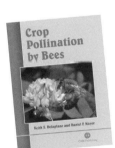
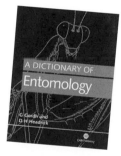
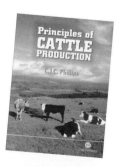